The Green Book of the Élus Coëns

The
GREEN BOOK
of the
ÉLUS COËNS

✠   *Translated & Annotated*   ✠
STEWART CLELLAND

Edited
JOSEF WÄGES

Designed
STEVE ADAMS

✠

VMXXI

First printing, 2021

ISBN: 978-0-85318-599-4

All rights reserved. No part of this book may be reproduced or transmitted in any form or by any means, electronic or mechanical, including photocopying, recording or by any information storage and retrieval system, without permission from the Publisher in writing

Copyright © 2021 Stewart Clelland, Josef Wäges, Steve Adams

Book Design & Illustrations Copyright © 2021 Steve Adams—EsotericEditions.com

EsotericEditions.com

Published by Lewis Masonic

An imprint of Ian Allan Publishing Ltd, Shepperton, Middx TW17 8AS.

Printed in England

Visit the Lewis Masonic website at www.lewismasonic.co.uk

Copyright

Illegal copying and selling of publications deprives authors, publishers and booksellers of income, without which there would be no investment in new publications. Unauthorised versions of publications are also likely to be inferior in quality and contain incorrect information. You can help by reporting copyright infringements and acts of piracy to the Publisher or the UK Copyright Service.

S.J.A. Clelland 1985–

Josef Wäges 1981–

Steve Adams 1972–

The Green Book of the Élus Coëns / Stewart Clelland, Josef Wäges, Steve Adams

Includes preface, introduction, translation, facsimile, and appendix

Contents

Contents...v

Acknowledgements...xi

Notes on the Translation..xiii

Preface..xv

Introduction..xvii

    Restoration..xix

    Reconciliation..xxiii

    Reintegration..xxvii

    Recollections: New Evidence......................................xxix

    Exile..xxxvi

Translation of: FM4 1282, BnF,
'Le Manuscrit d'Alger' (1772)..39

    Letter on the Relationship of Harmony with Numbers..................41

    Ceremonies of the four annual Banquets of the Order of the Coëns....51

        For the Feast of the Trinity.....................................51
        Renewal of Commitment..55
        After the Ceremony on the Day of the Trinity.....................58
        For the Feast of St. John the Baptist............................59
        For lunch see the Trinity..61
        For the Feast of St. John the Evangelist.........................61
        For Easter, the 3rd of the Three Feasts is celebrated............61
        Outline of a Speech of Instruction for the Feast of the Trinity..61
        In a Double Triangle...65
        In the Third Inner Circle..65
        In the Second Circle...66

In the First Outer Circle 66
Correspondances 66

Work on Adam 69

First Circle 69
Second Circle 69
Third Circle 70
Fourth Circle, Adam Alone 71
Correspondences 72
Vautours 72
Quarter Circles 73

Quarter circle on the Planets For testing a R✠ 75

Exconjuration Prayer on the Serpent at the South 79

Prayer of Invocation 81

Confession Made to the Centre after having lit the Candle 85

Extract Preparation and Precaution for Receiving R✠ 91

First Prayer to the Head in the North 93
Second Prayer to the Brains in the South 93
Third Prayer to the Tongue in the West 93
Prayer 94
Continuation of the Prayer 94

Secret Statutes of the R✠ 97

Consecration of the Eastern Angle 116

Reconciliation Operation for two Penitents R✠ and an Operating R✠ . . 119

Description of the Tracing 119
Conjuration against the Perverse 120
Sentence against the Perverse 122
Invocation 123
Conjuration on the Serpent 124
Prayer 125
Exorcism on a Penitent R✠ 127

Contents

    Oblation of Salt 127
    Manducation of Salt 128

Singular Dream 129

Quarter Angle for Commander of the East 131

    Prayer to God..131
    Prayer to Patrons..132
    Prayer to the Guardian 132
    Prayer to the Double Ray Spirits..133

Preventative Operation Against those who Labour in Evil 135

    Quarter Angle with Three Rays Plan 5 № 4........................137
    Quarter Angle of Body Purification with Three Rays..........138
    Exconjuration and Exorcism in the South..........................138

Extract from an Instruction of D[on] M[artinez] P[asqually] 141

Instruction on an Invocation of Reconciliation for
the use of Br[ethren] of the High Grades. (Inferior) 143

    Preparations...143
    Obligations of an Emulator of the High Grades 144
    Same Obligations with Some Differences..........................145
    Invocation called the Elu of the Above................................146
    Abjuration..148

Invocation of Master Coëns...151

    Conjuration..152
    Benediction of the Candles 155

Invocation of the G[reat] A[rchitect] 157

    Conjuration to the Guardian..159

Detached Pieces from The White Book...................................163

    Composition Perfume 164
    Prayer for the Incensing of Angles, Correspondences and Vautours..........165
    Abjuration of Metals 169

✠ vii

Fire Exorcism for Perfume 169
Benediction of Perfumes. 170
Blessing of the Circles. 170
Benediction of the Circle Candles. 170
Blessing of the Necessities for the Labour. 170
Benediction for the Chamber of Labour. 171
Prayer whilst Dressing. 172
Taking the White Cord. 172
Prayer to the Spirits of Labour. 172
In Presenting the Pentacle. 172
Return of the Spirits. 172
Prayer and Consecration at the East Corner.. 173
Benediction of Salt and Water. 173
Exconjuration of any Place. 173
Feu nouveau. [New Fire]. 173
Illumination of the Centre. 174
Exconjuration for the first of the days of Labour at the Four Angles. 174

Knowledge of Diseases. 177

Extract letters from D[on] M[artinez] P[asqually]. 179

April 3, 1770. 179
25 8bre [October], 1770. 179
August, 1768 № 3. 181
May 23, 1768 № 4. 183
4th September, 1767 № 5. 185
From September, 1766 № 6.. 187
From 8th January, 1772 № 7.. 188
20 7bre [September], 1766 № 8. 188
From 24 9bre [November], 1767 № 9. 189
From 23 7bre [September], 1769 № 10. 189

Reported from the Book of Parchment 191

The two kinds of human spirit 192
Incense. 192

Contents

Specifics of a Woman's Reception G 193
    For the second grade.. 194
    Things needed at the reception... 195
[The Prophecy of the Popes]... 197
    Masses... 202

T.4188 'Kabbalistic Names'.. 205

Transcription of: T.4188 'Kabbalistic Names'........................... 223

T.4188.1 Fonds Prunelle de Lière
'The Registry of 2,400 Names' 251

T.4188.8 The de Lière Serpent Drawings 349

Appendix: Catechisms of Coëns.. 393
    Catechism of the Philosophers Élus Coëns of the Universe (1770)........ 395
    Catechism of Master Coëns.. 413
    Grand Masters also called Grand Architects 427
    Grand Elect of Zerubabble also called Knights of the East 433

Colophon 439

Acknowledgements

This book would not have been possible without the help and assistance of a number of dear friends and mentors. I am especially indebted to Josef Wäges for his unflinching and never-ending generosity. I am eternally grateful to Robert Currie and Ian Robertson, as well as Shawn Eyer, Gabriel McCaughry, Piers Vaughan, Mathieu Ravignat, Sam Robinson, Lisa Kahler and Robert Herd, all of whom I have had the pleasure to work with. I am grateful to Steve Adams of Arcanum № 777 A.F.M. for his visionary work on the layout of the book and Martin Faulks for his patience and faith in the project. Thank you to Ivan. D. Ivanov for his wonderful author paintings. I would like to thank Graeme Nixon, David R. Smith, John Cassie, Peter Klieman, Beth Lord, Samantha Nisbet, and Jonathan Dale who have all been supportive of my career goals and who worked actively to provide me with the skills to pursue those goals. Barri Millar, Peter Taylor, Kenneth Jack, Mark Clifford, James Saunders and Michael Grewar have all provided me with extensive personal and professional guidance throughout the years by teaching me a great deal about both scholarly research and life in general. Thank you to Colin Beveridge, Robert Duncan, Scott Petrie, Kenneth Hepburn and Douglas Forbes for seeing promise in me. Alan Bennie, Gary Lumsden, Robert F. Sharp and Christopher Francis have all taught me more than I could ever give them credit for here. I would like to thank my parents and grandparents, whose love and guidance are with me in whatever I pursue. Most importantly, I wish to thank my loving and supportive wife, Lorraine, who provides me with unending inspiration - nobody has been more important to me in the pursuit of life.

Notes on the Translation

The significance of a word in translation is often the consequence of a considered and deliberate attempt to either metaphrase or paraphrase 'meaning' in any given text. An objective reader might suggest then, that any particular translation's individual fidelity to the original (whether formal in its equivalence or dynamic) will inevitably be, to a greater or lesser extent, an act of interpretation. If indeed every translation, even the most self-consciously and flat-footedly literal is an interpretation, surely there exists no such thing as a perfect translation in itself, but rather a transmission of sorts; a transmutation even of equivalence and meaning? The following book is in many ways a transmutation of equivalence and meaning, of both translator and text, with all the pain and change that one comes to expect with such a transformation. Throughout the change, I have tried, where possible, to retain much of the manuscript's original ambience, choosing to keep many of the French titles, names and offices, as clearly the actual words and exact phrasings held distinct magical and metaphysical properties for the original author, whereas their metaphrased English equivalence do not. My approach has been one that intended to allow the atmosphere and powers inherent in the source material to be invoked; to conjure something of the original experience, as it were. How far this has been achieved, I leave to the reader. I would, however, urge the reader to consider for themselves the extent to which our knowledge of the meaning in a text, indeed the text itself, particularly a sacred text such as this, is dependent on such interpretative and inherently transmutational acts? Are we to assume the meaning lies rather more in the way we read a text, rather than the text itself? The truth in the method? Or as Wittgenstein said, 'every sign by itself seems dead. What gives it life? – In use it is alive. Is life breathed into it there? – Or is the use its life?'

Stewart Clelland
Edinbourg
2020

Preface

Unceremoniously labelled FM4 1282, the manuscript better known as the '*Algiers Ms*' serves as the foundation on which this current volume is built. Referenced by some as the '*Green Paper*', or indeed, the '*Green Book of the Elus Coëns*', both titles refer to the physical condition of the actual manuscript and the colour of its original binding. The title '*Algiers Ms*' does not appear anywhere in the original document either. It comes rather from the fact it was found and bought on the market of Saint-Ouen by an antique dealer in Algiers during the Second World War. In an act of preservation, certain European Masonic bodies relocated their assets to Algiers in order to preserve their archives. French scholar Dominique Clairembault has written that the manuscript was sold to Marguerite Benama, friend of Robert Ambelain, in 1955. Benama then gave the entire acquisition to Robert Ambelain who, in turn, donated it in 1993 to the Bibliothèque nationale de France. We can assume the manuscript was written probably between 1770 to 1772 by André Pierre de Grainville (1728-1793). He was one of the officers of the Foix Regiment stationed in Saint Domingue from 1760 to 1765 and then returned to France. Pasqually personally initiated two officers from this regiment, Grainville and Champoléon, who later became his official collaborators and secretaries. It was through them that Louis-Claude de Saint-Martin, assigned to the Foix Regiment in the very month of its return to France, became acquainted with Pasqually. Grainville wrote to Jean Baptiste Willermoz in 1798 in Lyons: '*We had a temple in the Regiment; we have let the stones fall away imperceptibly... now we would hardly be able to find three stones joined together, of the more than twenty-five that once were there*'. The manuscript would appear something of a working manual for his Réau-Croix initiates, a *grimoire* of sorts - it has never appeared in English until now and is presented here solely for historical and personal reference.

In the broader context, it appears something of a tradition amongst Martinist circles to confuse the '*Algiers Ms*' with a selection of other documents from a larger manuscript known as the '*Prunelle fonds de Lière*', a document found in the public library of Grenoble, sections of which have also been reproduced here. Dominique Clairembault notes that Auguste Viatte, in 1928, and Alice Joly, in 1938, were the first to emphasise the *Prunelle* collection's importance. Since 1962, Robert Amadou had studied that collection, of which he published a very incomplete inventory. In 1969, the magazine '*l'Initiation*' announced a project to publish the '*Fonds Prunelle de Lière*' by Jacques Baradat, a collaborator of Robert Amadou. Strangely, this never happened and even more, considering that the original reproductions have been sold in the form of a CD-ROM since 1999. In an attempt to obscure the identification and location of the text, the public library of Grenoble stamps were removed on these copies. The publisher of the CD, *Les Gouttelettes de Rosée*, incorrectly attributed them as coming from the '*Algiers Ms*'. In the introductory text of this CD, Philippe Pissier and Matthieu Léon state that they obtained these documents during the second half of the 1980s, from Joël Duez, who had received them himself from Marcel Jirousek, Belgian disciple of Robert Ambelain. These documents were wrongly transmitted to them under the name of '*Algiers Ms*'. Presented here for the first time is the true '*Manuscript d'Alger*'.

The Coën cult instructed its initiates in the drawing of hieroglyphs on the floor of magical operations. The hieroglyphs found from among a list of 2,400 were provided by Martinès himself. A copy of the list is reproduced here in its entirety and in facsimile alongside some other important reference sources found within the Bibliothèque Municipale de Grenoble.

The '*Fonds Prunelle de Lière*', dossier T.4188 (*Alphabet hébreu, noms, nombres numériques et kabbalistiques* contains another title in a separate hand; *Notes, documents, dessins relatifs à l'étude de l'hébreu et de la cabale.*) This was written by Léonard-Joseph Prunelle de Lière (1741- 1824), a close friend of Louis Claude de St Martin, and contains a copy of Pasqually's list of the aforementioned, entitled '*Alphabetical Table of 2,400 Names*', or as it is more commonly known, '*The Registry of 2,400 Names*'. Understood as a kind of directory of the celestial world, angels and spirits are alphabetically classified and each are associated with two numbers. It is followed by a document of eighty-seven pages covered with hieroglyphic symbols from a variety of sources; Hebrew, Arabic, Egyptian and Phoenician. Pasqually saw in these *glyphs* signs that indicated to the theurgist, that a reconciliation was in progress. The *luminous glyphs* were believed to be the marks of divine favour on the road to 'reintegration'. For those in the English-speaking world that desire to do the same today, the current volume is dedicated to you and your efforts. Such is the text's luminosity that I myself have been blinded on occasion, and any subsequent shortcoming in the current volume are mine and mine alone.

Stewart Clelland
Edinbourg
2020

Introduction

As the high-degrees of *écossais* freemasonry swept across the landscape of eighteenth-century Europe, an obscure and occult order began to develop known as *l'Ordre des Chevaliers maçons Élus Coëns de l'Univers* or the Order of Knight-Masons Elect-Cohens of the Universe. Characterised by the practice of a gnostic infused form of Judeo-Christian theosophy with a Kabbalistic veneer, the Élus Coëns represented a high point in continental freemasonry's 'search for its own meaning'.[1] Requiring the utmost commitment and a decidedly monastic way of life, the Order prescribed everything from hairstyle to diet, and with it a very distinct theosophical mystic-millenarianism.[2] Indeed, far from the everyday festivities of mainstream freemasonry, the Élus Coëns saw themselves as knightly-priests engaged in a form of cosmic theurgical combat with angelic and demonic entities. Drawing its membership from the *bourgeois* and aristocratic, the rites of the Élus Coëns instructed its initiates, or rather 'emulators', in how best to enter into ecstatic relations with celestial and angelic 'spirits' sympathetic to Mankind's fallen state. The 'operating' Coën could, it was believed, thereby obtain providential favour on the path towards ultimate cosmic 'reintegration' with the Divine.[3] However, after the death of the Order's enigmatic founder, Martinès de Pasqually (1709 - 1774) in 1774, Port-au-Prince, Santo-Domingo (Haiti), the doctrine of the Élus Coëns may well have been lost to history had it not been for the efforts of a handful of particularly devoted disciples, perhaps none more so than Jean-Baptiste Willermoz (1730-1824). Such was Willermoz's enthusiasm for Pasqually's unique blend of masonic theosophy, that shortly after his initiation in 1767, he was made Master of the 'Grand Orient of Orients of Lyon, Grand Mother and Mother Lodge of France', and promptly promoted to the rank of 'Réau-Croix', the highest grade of the Order, in May 1768.[4] After Pasqually's death, Willermoz ensured the survival of the 'doctrine of reintegration' by preserving it within a secret class of degrees hidden in the wider overall masonic framework of the *Régime Ecossais Rectifié* (RER).[5] Known as

---

1 Edmond Mazet, "Freemasonry and Esotericism," in *Modern Esoteric Spirituality*, edited by Antoine Faivre and Jacob Needleman (London: SCM Press, 1993), p. 265.
2 The term 'millenarian' is used to describe a belief in a sudden, immanent and catastrophic Second Coming; in the context of the Élus Coëns, Pasqually clearly envisions a literal end - a spiritual restoration at the end of which period Christ would return, rather than any sort of internalised apocalypse of 'the self', as it were.
3 Michelle Nahon, 'Élus Coëns' in *Dictionary of Gnosis & Western Esotericism*, ed. Wouter J. Hanegraaff with Antoine Faivre, Roelof van den Broek and Jean-Pierre Brach (Leiden and Boston: Brill, 2005), p. 332.
4 Nicholas Goodrick-Clarke, *The Western Esoteric Traditions: A Historical Introduction* (New York: Oxford University Press, 2008), p. 139. Willermoz's Réau-Croix diploma is held in Bibliothèque nationale de France. Département des Manuscrits. FM5 (516), 'Diplômes. Supplément. Supplément' A. FM5 (516)
5 Edmond Mazet, 'Chevaliers Bienfaisants de la Cité Saint' in *Dictionary of Gnosis & Western Esotericism*, p. 256.

the *'Chevaliers Bienfaisants de la Cité Sainte'* (CBCS) and consisting of little more than long instructional discourses entitled the *Instruction secrète au Profès* (Secret Instruction to the Profès) and the *Instruction secrète aux Grands Profès* (Secret instruction to the Grands Profès), both written before 1778, this *Profès* class of Willermoz's served as a repository of sorts for Pasqually's complex doctrine, if not its actual practices.[6] Detailing a secret shadow history transmitted down through the ages, the doctrine of reintegration, as embodied by the *Profès*, recalls the existence of a 'primitive, essential and fundamental Order' to which freemasonry would be the final inheritor.[7] For Pasqually, this hidden primitive Order, or as he himself phrased it in his *Traité de la Réintégration (1773)*, this *'primitive cult'*, was a form of ecstatic devotional theurgy involving elaborate magical 'operations'.[8] The *Traité* details the complex mytho-theosophic framework underpinning this magical system as a divinely appointed form of cultic worship, explaining its roots stretch right back to Adamic and pre-Adamic Creation. The cult of the Élus Coëns is the *primitive cult* entrusted by God to Adam, and secretly transmitted down through the ages.[9] The Élus Coëns' *raison d'être* then is to perform this cult in its fullest sense as a form of *gnosis* for the betterment of all mankind and the eventual transformation of the entire universe. Adopting the title that the angel Gabriel gave to Daniel, Pasqually instructed his *hommes de désir* (men of desire) in a practice of personal 'reintegration' that acted as a prelude to this desired end time when the whole universe might be 'reintegrated' in divine Oneness.[10] Pasqually's 'reintegration', the major theme of the *Traité*, is by definition eschatological, millenarian and apocalyptic in nature. It would, therefore, not be unfair if we were to use Pasqually's own language in describing the Coëns as quite literally, an end-of-the-world cult in high french masonic garb. This clearly carries far too much of the pejorative however, so let us suffice in

---

6   Roger Dachez, 'Freemasonry' in *Dictionary of Gnosis & Western Esotericism*, p. 387. In 1926 the *Instructions secrètes aux Profès* (Secret Instructions for the Profès) were rediscovered and published by Paul Vuillaud; and in 1970, the *Instructions secrètes aux Grands Profès* (Secret Instructions for the Grands Profès) by Antoine Faivre.
7   Dachez, 'Freemasonry' in *Dictionary of Gnosis & Western Esotericism*, p. 387.
8   *Traité de la réintégration des êtres créés dans leurs primitives propriétés, vertus et puissances spirituelles divines* (Robert Amadou, ed.), Paris: Robert Dumas, 1974 (including the text of the first edition, Paris: Chacornac, 1899) *Traité sur la réintégration des êtres dans leur première propriété, vertu et puissance spirituelle divine* (Robert Amadou, ed.), Le Tremblay: Diffusion rosicrucienne, 1993 & 1995. The *Traité* was only ever intended to circulate in manuscript form, it was first published only in 1899; it was not until 1926 that the *Instructions secrètes aux Profès* (Secret Instructions for the Profès) were rediscovered and published by Paul Vuillaud; and in 1970, the *Instructions secrètes aux Grands Profès* (Secret Instructions for the Grands Profès) by Antoine Faivre. See, Jean-françois Var, 'Martinism: First Period' in *Dictionary of Gnosis & Western Esotericism*, p. 779.
9   Var, p. 776.
10 Daniel 9:23 (KJV) *'At the beginning of thy supplications the commandment came forth, and I am come to shew thee; for thou art greatly beloved: therefore understand the matter, and consider the vision.'*

saying only this - Pasqually's Élus Coëns represents the example *par excellence* of theurgical Christian millenarian masonic theosophy, and Pasqually himself - a masonic charismatic labouring intently to immanentise the eschaton.[11]

Restoration

'Today the Earth offers me nothing but sadness, horror and inconceivable torment!', Pasqually writes.[12] Indeed, in a letter from the 3rd April 1770, he elaborates on the details of his dissatisfaction with the transitory nature of the bodily and worldly;

> The true man of desire who fully trusts the Creator may well be in nature and thereby has the power to avoid the dangers that would threaten him with anticipating his reintegration of apparent bodily form, for the forms are only apparent.[13]

Those with trust in God, men of desire, can, Pasqually suggests, live within the confines of nature, and yet still avoid the dangers associated with the anticipation that it will be one's bodily form that will be reintegrated. The material is only apparent, indeed, it is a prison, and a nullified prison at that. Such a reintegration as Pasqually envisions, heralds a restoration of all humanity and nature to their pure original states. This reintegration requires the alchemical like disintegration of Man's physical body, so as to allow his original body of glory to reappear in all its splendour, as will the Earth reappear as a reintegrated Eden, a spiritual Temple to God, rather than a material Prison of Man. With its interdependent triangle of God, Man and Nature, and themes of Fall and reascension, the doctrine of reintegration, can fully be described a theosophy - a masonic theosophy informing a unique ceremonial *praxis* of theurgical worship. But the utility of the term 'theosophy' itself, is, however, still divergent and indistinct, and that is to say nothing of Pasqually's heterodox approach to freemasonry, or, indeed, Christianity. The ambiguity, multiplicity and antiquity of the term 'theosophy' does not help, as we see testified to by the work of James Santucci and Jean-Louis Siémons.[14] Surveying its use from late antiquity to the Middle Ages, Santucci's and Siémons' research highlights the Neoplatonic theurgist Porphyry (234-305)

---

11 Meaning the attempt to bring about the eschaton or the final, heaven-like stage of history in the immanent world.
12 Bibliothèque nationale de France, FM4. 1282.
13 Ibid.
14 Jean-Louis Siémons, *Théosophia. Aux sources néo-platoniciennes et chrétiennes (IIe-VIe siècles)*(Paris: Cariscript, 1998), p. 41. James A. Santucci, 'On Theosophia and Related Terms', in *Theosophical History*, vol. II, no. 3 (July 1987), pp. 107-110. James A. Santucci, *Theosophy and Theosophical Society* (London: Theosophical History Centre, 1985).

speaking of a *theosophos*: a perfected individual simultaneously the artist, philosopher and priest. Pasqually's Knight-Masons Elect-Priests of the Universe, and their mission to reintegrate Man into divine perfection, do embody this notion of the *theosophos* admirably, but in reality the Coën Order represents a matrix of many different heterodoxies, including the medieval *grimoire* tradition.[15] Historically then, Pasqually's '*primitive cult*' is perhaps best viewed as a reaction of sorts to the prevailing rationalism of the Enlightenment; as an attempt by Pasqually and his followers to 'allegorise' their own particular brand of *prisca theologia*.[16] In many ways, out of the chaos of 1760's French freemasonry, we see Pasqually attempting to re-enact his allegory in the form of a re-enchanted, or rather ecstatic style of *écossais* freemasonry, and indeed, for many, even today, this re-enchantment of Pasqually's brought with it a genuine spiritual goal to the Masonic Lodge.

In his *Theosophy, Imagination, Tradition: Studies in Western Esotericism* (2000) Antoine Faivre suggests that there exists no 'doctrinal unity' among theosophers such as Pasqually and his heirs.[17] Yet, he does suggest there exists some common traits in theosophical discourse; all of which are to be found within the doctrine of reintegration. These consist of: (a) *The God/Human/Nature Triangle*, with the points of the triangle being in a complex speculative relationship with one another as well as Scripture, (b) *The Primacy of the Myth*; a great emphasis placed on the creative imagination of the theosopher by Revelation (The Books of Genesis, Ezekiel, the Apocalypse etc.), and (c) *Direct Access to Superior World*; Man has the inherit potential to connect with divine and superior beings through the power of imagination. This process in itself also displays three distinct characteristics: (1) a continued exploration of all levels of reality, (2) a mutual co-operation between Man and the divine, and (3) to permit a 'second birth' as it were, in light.[18] Thus, while none of these traits are exclusive to theosophy, their simultaneous presence enables Faivre to characterise and present a certain commonality in a great many diverse and disparate figures of the seventeenth, eighteenth and even nineteenth centuries, therefore managing to clarify and specify a particularly historically ambiguous epitaph: 'theosophy'.[19] With Pasqually we

---

15 Most pronouncedly the '*Arbatel de magia veterum*', a book of white magic appearing around 1550 to 1560. Interestingly, Antoine Faivre suggests it is in this very text there starts to appear in the historical record something approaching a unified understanding of 'theosophy' as a recognisably consistent term which can be reasonably associated with specific examples of historical speculative discourses exhibiting sufficient evidence of the presence of his theosophical 'commonalities'. See, Antoine Faivre, *Access to Western Esotericism* (Albany, New York: State University of New York Press, 1994), p. 24.
16 *Prisca theologia* (ancient theology) is a doctrine that suggests that a single, true theology exists, which threads through all ages and religions, and which was anciently given by God to Man.
17 Antoine Faivre, *Theosophy, Imagination, Tradition: Studies in Western Esotericism* (Albany, New York: State University of New York Press, 2000), p. 7.
18 Faivre, p. 8.
19 Antoine Faivre, 'Christian Theosophy', in *Dictionary of Gnosis & Western Esotericism*, ed. Wouter J. Hanegraaff with Antoine Faivre, Roelof van den Broek and Jean-Pierre Brach (Leiden and Boston: Brill, 2005), p. 259.

shall do the same. Indeed, true to the masonic fashions of his day, Pasqually added to this already heavily laden theosophic romance, namely by his introduction of spiritual chivalry. Pasqually was almost certainly influenced in, at least, his chivalric aspirations, directly or indirectly, by the ideas of the Scottish quietist *Chevalier* Andrew Michael Ramsay (1686-1743), who's own 'traditional history' of freemasonry, erroneously but universally referred to as his *Oration* (1736), was probably originally delivered in France at St John's Lodge No. 1 on the 26th December 1736, although Mandleberg convincingly argues against this in his *Rose Croix Essays* (2005).[20]

Part of an influential Scottish circle of pietists, described by G.D. Henderson in 1934 as 'The Mystics of the North East', for whom the famous quietist Jacobite ideologue, Alexander, Lord Forbes of Pitsligo (1678-1762), had been the leading patron, *Chevalier* Ramsay's influential 'history' of the Craft is generally understood as to be distinctly ill at ease with that of James Anderson's (ca. 1679-1680 – 1739).[21] Anderson, a fellow Scot, also based in the North of Scotland near Aberdeen, gave an account of masonic apologetics that became Whiggish orthodoxy in the British Isles.[22] Whilst Ramsay's account reintroduced a particular emphasis on Christianity that Presbyterian minister Anderson (ca. 1679-1680 – 1739) in his *Constitutions* of 1723 clearly lacked. Nicholas Goodrick-Clarke (1953-2012), the eminent late historian of esotericism, was of the opinion that, 'Anderson's *Constitutions* had effectively de-Christianized the Craft in England, Ramsay's restored form of Christian Freemasonry was highly attractive in France'.[23] Clearly, Pasqually's system did not appear *ex-nihilo;* he was an adept in the marketplace of french masonic innovation, and the quietist infused influence of the Jacobite Ramsay should not be underestimated in this regard. For example, in his *Philosophical Principles of Natural and Revealed Religion* (1748-1749), Ramsay writes,

> God's primitive, positive, ultimate and absolute designs cannot be eternally frustrated [...]: therefore before the general re-establishment of lapsed beings, the earth and all its inhabitants are to be restored to their primitive, paradisiacal beauty.[24]

---

20 John Mandleberg, *Rose Croix Essays* (Surrey: Lewis Masonic, 2005), p.17.
21 G. D. Henderson, *The mystics of the North East* (Aberdeen: Third Spalding Society, 1934)
22 Mandleberg, p.17.
23 Goodrick-Clarke, *The Western Esoteric Traditions*, p. 133.
24 Andrew Michael Ramsay, *The Philosophical Principles of Natural and Revealed Religion Unfolded in a Geometrical Order,* 2 vols. (Glasgow: Foulis, 1748-1749) 1, p. 438.

Typical of wider quietist chiliastic beliefs surrounding a promised Stuart Restoration found within sections of the Continental Jacobite diaspora, Ramsay sets a clear masonic precedence for Pasqually's 'doctrine of reintegration'. It is Ramsay who first introduced the legendary chivalric origin to freemasonry, grafting the Crusaders and The Knights of St. John of Jerusalem onto Anderson's traditional Scottish connection; all of which Madelberg states, 'was well calculated to satisfy every Freemason in France'.[25] Such is Ramsay's influence, that the Scottish 'holy knight' motif becomes ubiquitous in European Freemasonry, manifesting as either Crusader, Templar or Jacobite. Shortly after 1730, it seems, the first masonic chivalric order, the *Ordre Sublime des Chevaliers Élus* is formed.[26] Clearly by the 1760's, Pasqually has a great deal to work with, and whilst it was still spiritually not enough for him, we can say with confidence that the *'primitive cult'* grew in already heavily fertilised soil. Goodrick-Clarke tells us in his *The Western Esoteric Traditions: A Historical Introduction (2008)*;

> This form of 'Scottish' or *Écossais* Freemasonry spread rapidly through French chivalric lodges – called chapters, directories, lodges of perfection- with activity in Bordeaux, Arras, Toulouse, Lille and Marseille by 1750... Ramsay's suggestion that there had been Mason-Knights led to the introduction in French Freemasonry of 'higher' degrees...they were assigned knightly titles involving references to Scotland... and their holders were possessed of esoteric knowledge.'[27]

By 1778 the Parisian lodge *Amis Réunis* worked twelve degrees.[28] Some of these degrees, such as *Le Chevalier de l'Orient* (the Knight of the East) are described as concerned with 'aristocratic affects', while others such as seventh degree of the Rose-Coix reflected what is described as 'fashionable mysticism'.[29] The first known archives tells us Pasqually had already incorporated such fashionability into his thinking during the beginning of his activities around 1760 in Toulouse.[30] His first experiment in high-grade Masonry was the *Chapître des Juges Ecossais* (Chapter of Scottish Judges) founded by him at Montpellier in 1754, before settling in Bordeaux in 1762 to begin formalising the Élus Coëns in his *Loge de la Perfection Élue Écossaise de Bordeaux*. We can see the influences in the masonic landscape around him, for instance, The Council of the Knight of the East, founded in

---

25 Mandleberg, p.17. These assertions, while useful, might well tell us rather more about author's views on the French and their perceived aristocratic sense of entitlement than Freemasonry.
26 Alain Bernheim, 'Avatars of the Knight Kadosh in France and in Charleston' in *Heredom* vol. 6. (Washington D.C. 1997), p. 156.
27 Goodrick-Clarke, pp. 133-134
28 Margaret C. Jacob, *Living the Enlightenment: Freemasonry and Politics in Eighteenth-Century Europe* (New York: Oxford University Press, 1991), p.146.
29 Jacob, p146.
30 Ibid, p146.

Introduction

1762, - 'The seventh and highest was that of the Chevalier Rose-Coix. For its part, the Grand Lodge of Lyon cultivated an eighth grade, that of the Chevalier de l'Epée et de Rose Croix'.[31] It would be naive to assume Pasqually's ignorance, and ridiculous to suggest the titles, grades and nomenclature of the Élus Coëns were anything other than clearly 'borrowed'. However, beyond this, the influence of the nascent 'Scottish' degrees of an emerging French Rite on Pasqually's magpie like system should not be overestimated. The content, meaning and motives have all been completely reengineered in Pasqually's ecstatic *écossais* re-enchantment. Such are his sacerdotal innovations, the various grades and degrees can no longer even be considered masonic 'initiations' as such, but rather 'ordinations'.[32]

In the broader context, the widespread proliferation of these high degrees indicate there was indeed a need for deeper spiritual 'truths' than the humble Craft could offer. Pasqually is part of this wider movement of freemasons who seem increasingly dissatisfied with masonry's growing alliance with the egalitarianism and secularising cosmopolitanism of the Enlightenment, as represented in the masonic sphere by the 1723 *Constitutions* of James Anderson. In response, many seem particularly attracted to the romantic allure surrounding the diaspora of spiritually inclined Jacobite Scottish nobles exiled throughout Europe prior even to the failure of the 1715 Uprising. Indeed, as the living embodiment of Ramsay's popular masonic spiritual knight motif, the exiled Scottish Jacobite becomes *en vogue* within the fashionable mysticism of the lodges. As Murray Pittock has noted, mystical-millenarianism lent itself to Royalist interpretations within the context of a Stuart ideology of Divine Right and 'manifest destiny'.[33] After the Glorious Revolution, such notions underpinned Jacobite hopes for political and spiritual 'restoration', with similar such hopes seemingly permeating both esoteric and masonic culture too, all of which it would appear makes its way into underpinning the emergent masonic theosophy of Martinès de Pasqually's Élus Coëns.

Reconciliation

Anderson's *Constitutions* claimed the revival of the 'Royal Art' of 'Masonry' in England was instigated by the Stuart Royal line, King James VI of Scotland (James I of Great Britain; b. 1566; reg. 1567-1625 in Scotland, and 1603-1625 in Great Britain), who 'being a

---

31 Roland Edighoffer, 'Rosicrucianism: From the Seventh to the Twentieth Century' in *Modern Esoteric Spirituality*, ed. Antoine Faivre and Jacob Needleman (London: SCM Press Ltd, 1993), p.207.
32 Var, 'Martinism: First Period' in *Dictionary of Gnosis & Western Esotericism*, p. 776.
33 Murray G. H. Pittock, *The invention of Scotland: the Stuart myth and the Scottish identity, 1638 to the present* (Lonon, 1991), pp. 30-31.

Mason King, reviv'd the English Lodges'.[34] The masonic fascination with Jacobite spiritual knights and Stuart ideology even reaches the German-speaking lands with one Baron Karl Gotthelf von Hund (1722-1776) and his Masonic Rite of the Strict Observance. Claiming to have been initiated into a Templar Degree in France in 1742 by the mysterious 'Knight of the Red Feather', a shadowy figure from the northern mountains of the Scottish Highlands, von Hund's system traced its origins back to the Knights Templar and implied that the unknown superior or *Superiores Incogniti* was the Grand Master of the Knights Templar, which continued to exist in hiding in, again, the mountains of the North of the Scotland, often referred to in masonic traditions as 'Heredom'. Supposedly accompanied by the soon to be Jacobite martyr, William Boyd, 4th Earl of Kilmarnock (1705-1746), this 'Unknown Superior', clearly intended to be Charles Edward Stuart (1720 - 1788), is said to have ruled through von Hund, with the members of his Rite expected to strictly observe the commands of this Superior. However, by the 1770s there were suspicions those Unknown Superiors were, in fact, a complete fabrication. Giving rise to reform, in 1781 Johann Joachim Christoph Bode (1731-1793), a counsellor at the ducal court in Weimar, printed his *Ordered Dutiful Considerations* (1781), for circulation within the lodges. As a direct result, from 16 July to 1 September 1782 representatives met in Wilhelmsbald to debate the wholesale reform of the Continent's Masonic Orders, eventually resulting in the birth of the Rectified Scottish Rite and the *l'Ordre de Chevaliers Bienfaisants de la Cité Sainte* - which in itself helped preserve Pasqually's doctrine in the agency of his devoted *protégé*, Willermoz.[35]

The grade structure of *l'Ordre des Chevaliers maçons Élus Coëns de l'Univers.*

Derived from B.M.G MS. 4123: *Extrait de ce qui et contenu dans les grades de l'Ordre des E* and *'manuscrit d'Alger'*, BnF FM4. 1282.

1. Apprentif
2. Compagnon

---

[34] James Anderson, *The Constitutions of the Freemasons (1723) and (1738)*, facs. ed. (Abingdon: Burgess, 1976). In recent years Anderson's 'traditional history' has seen an extravagant expansion within Marsha Keith Schuchard, *Restoring the Temple of Vision: Cabalistic Freemasonry and Stuart Culture* (Leiden & Boston: Brill, 2002). Schuchard's thesis presents as historical fact the presence of ancient Jewish Cabbalistic sources within the traditional Scottish and Stuart lineage of the *Écossais* lodges of the eighteenth-century century. Schuchard argues for the origin of Freemasonry in The Temple of Solomon as historical fact. Inevitably, this thesis has been heavily criticised. See, Andrew Prescott, 'Stuart Freemasonry: Restoring the Temple of Vision?' *Aries*, 4: 2 (2004).

[35] At this convention, the kabbalistic influence of one Samuel Jacob Falk (ca. 1710-1782), on various Illuminés was also discussed, arising once again at the Philalèthes conferences in Paris in 1783-1787. Falk was a Jewish Kabbalist known as the 'Baal Shem of London' (master of the divine names), and some Masons believed him to be the 'Old Man of the Mountain,' or an 'Unknown Superior' revealed. His most famous disciple was Joseph Balsamo (1743-1795), also known as Count Alessandro di Cagliostro who in 1776 helped Falk develop the Egyptian Rite, which Cagliostro carried to lodges in Holland, France, Germany, Poland, and Russia.

3. Maître

4. Maître Grand Elu (or Maître Parfait Elu)

5. Apprenti Coën, ou Fort marqué (strongly marked)

6. Compagnon Coën, ou Double fort marqué (Double strongly marked)

7. Maître Coën.

8. Grand Maître Coën (or Grand Architecte),

9. Chevalier d'Orient (or Grand Elu de Zorobabel),

10. Commandeur d'Orient (or Apprenti Réau-Croix).

11. Réau-Croix

The Élus Coëns Order was comprised of ten *écossais* grades, capped with an eleventh, the Réau-Croix, which uniquely involved direct theurgic operations, and can hardly be considered masonry at all. Spirits were summoned, and if successful, the candidate could be assured of celestial approval and possible 'reconciliation'. Before elevation to the Réau-Croix, candidates were required to prove they had achieved this state of 'reconciliation'. The theurgist Iamblichus (250-330) speaks of his '*theosophos* muse' helping achieve a similar state, while the Neoplatonist Proclus (412-485) uses *theosophia* to denote the 'doctrine' thereby used to achieve such a transcendent connection.[36] In the early Christian context we find first Clement of Alexandria (c.150-215) using the word *theosophos* to explain the effect of 'divine science'.[37] With Pasqually, the 'divine science' is his '*primitive cult*', which requires the 'reconciliation' of its candidates achievable only, it would seem, via the pageantry of a borrowed *écossais* style ceremonial. In the Coën *grimoire* known as the '*manuscrit d'Alger*' (FM4. 1282), Pasqually writes;

> I am giving you this as science, but only as one of the testimonies of science; and never forget that it does not consist of cold reasoning or ingenious observations, but in the virtuous desires of the soul and the use of all the forces of our being.[38]

He explains that this 'reconciliation', was an essential step in their advancement.[39] In order to work towards this, it instructs how a special prayer was employed known as the *Invocation de Réconciliation*. Its ultimate aim was to obtain a sign from the '*bon compagnon*', a spirit, or what we might understand as a 'guardian angel' - a *theosophos* muse, as Iamblichus would have it. This sign, which manifests itself most often in the form of a '*luminous*

---

36 Antoine Faivre, *Theosophy, Imagination, Tradition: Studies in Western Esotericism* (Albany, New York: State University of New York Press, 2000), p. 3.
37 Faivre, p. 3.
38 Bibliothèque nationale de France, FM4. 1282.
39 Ibid.

glyph', shows the candidate that he has henceforth been reconciled with his guardian angel, and has taken the first step on the path towards helping achieve the ultimate goal of cosmic reintegration. The *cult* instructed its initiates in the drawing of hieroglyphs before such magical operations. Any particular hieroglyph used, found from among a list of 2,400 hieroglyphs provided by Martinès himself, corresponded to a particular angel, and if the operation was successful, a further hieroglyph would appear in 'luminous form'. These *luminous glyphs* act as a signature of the spirits who have chosen to cooperate with the theurgist on his path to reconciliation with the Divine.[40] Understood as a kind of directory of the celestial world, angels and spirits are alphabetically classified and each associated with two numbers. It is followed by a document of eighty-seven pages covered with hieroglyphic symbols from a variety of sources; Hebrew, Arabic, Egyptian and Phoenician. Such a directory demonstrates Pasqually's masonic theosophy as one clearly based on a much earlier metaphysical doctrine of 'emanation', albeit infused within his own idiosyncratic syncretism. Rooted in the neoplatonism and gnosticism of the earliest forms of Christain theosophy, this doctrine of 'emanation' is one facilitated by the concept of the microcosm-macrocosm - an ancient basis of cosmological understanding, representing essentially a great hierarchy of being. God, for the Élus Coën, is the pinnacle of the hierarchy, disseminating down through the different orders of angels, elements and planets in various degrees of emanation to the plants, animals and minerals below; becoming symbolic in themselves, hence following the hermetic axiom 'As above, so below', albeit, again in Pasqually's own deeply idiosyncratic manner.[41] In a letter of instruction found within the *'manuscrit d'Alger'*, entitled *'Extract from an Instruction of D*[on]. *M*[artinez]. *P*[asqually]. *entrusted to the V*[énérable]. *M*[aître] *of ch. F.M. W. on the Temple'*, Pasqually demonstrates this doctrine in the teachings of Élus Coëns as he instructs in the spiritual construction of the Temple.

> The vault or hollow represents the place from which Adam's body of matter emerged; the virgin earth represents to us the separation of the material from the spiritual and reminds us what the creator says to Adam *'Look at this mountain which dominates over everything, it bears three names which announce the origin of your body, as well as the Law, the Precept and the Commandment that I gave you, and these names will multiply to infinity. This mountain was holy and*

---

40 A copy of the list is found at the Bibliothèque Municipale de Grenoble, under the title, 'Fonds Prunelle de Lière', T.4188 (*Alphabet hébreu, noms, nombres numériques et kabbalistiques* [under this title in another hand reads; *Notes, documents, dessins relatifs à l'étude de l'hébreu et de la cabale*]) Written by Léonard-Joseph Prunelle de Lière (1741- 1824), a close friend of Louis Claude de St Martin (1743-1803), it includes a copy of Pasqually's list, entitled *'Alphabetical Table of 2,400 Names',* or, as it is more commonly known, *'The Registry of 2,400 Names'.*
41 Goodrick-Clarke, *The Western Esoteric Traditions*, p. 38.

blessed by me before your creation, since it is on it that you were created. Respect her as your mother since she is holy! Whenever you lift your eyes upward or drop them on this earth, or fix the plants that it produces, you will praise and sanctify the living God who created you'.

Then, before leaving him, the Creator made known to Adam the various Masonic instruments, which he had used for the construction of his particular temple and his universal temple.' [42]

For the Élus Coëns, therefore, it is possible that Man might leave his prison and partake in a hermeneutical quest up through the higher light of each degree; working with and within his 'luminous' correspondences of the celestial hierarchy to achieve an initiation into greater levels of illumination in the light of an inner primitive Christian revelation. Pasqually's *primitive cult* is, in at least one sense, an allegorisation of this inner Christian revelation, which is itself described as a 'timeless Revelation within Christianity'.[43] Scholar Arthur Versluis describes this form of theosophy as an, 'authentic Gnostic tradition stretching from Pseudo-Dionysus the Areopagite ... to Jacob Boehme'.[44] Clearly more gnostic than hermetic, Pasqually's doctrine of Man's return to his original, natural state is indebted to earlier theosophical traditions and its historical gnostic elements.

Reintegration

The gnostics placed the origin of everything in a primary Principle. 'This first principle was a pure, perfect and supreme power and is eternal, infinite and absolute. This god is hidden, unknown and unknowable'.[45] Gnostic cosmology contrasted two worlds: the eternal world of God and the heavenly hierarchy of the Pleroma, or as Pasqually calls it the 'divine court', which includes angelic beings, cherubim, seraphim, omens, voices, virtues, guardians variously grouped into principalities, powers, thrones etc. Pasqually taught his Élus Coëns that God as celestial King emanated these 'emancipated' spiritual beings into existence within the 'divine immensity'. Emanated with free will, they where nevertheless instructed in a particular form of divinely appointed ritual worship.[46] These spiritual beings lived in the original state of reality and perfection - the noumenal world

---

42 BnF, FM4. 1282.
43 Goodrick-Clarke, p. 100
44 Ibid, p. 100.
45 Goodrick-Clarke, p. 20.
46 Nahon, 'Élus Coëns' in *Dictionary of Gnosis & Western Esotericism*, p. 333.

of things. But these beings desired to act as demiurges, to equal God, and create for themselves. God ordered the 'minor spirits' who had remained loyal to create and enclose these 'prevaricating spirits' in an encircled material space as punishment. Heavenly androgynous Man, the 'minor quaternary spiritual', was subsequently emanated, also with free will, in order to guard these spiritual beings and help guide them back to their original purity. However, this 'Man-God', Adam-Réau, permitted himself to be seduced by these capricious 'perverse' angels, and he too came to desire equality with God by creating spiritual beings. He fell, dragging the whole of corporeality with him - a process Pasqually calls the 'prevarication'.[47] For the Élus Coëns then, the Fall was a two step process.

For the gnostics, Man is trapped, separated from the real God by the demiurge. However, *gnosis* can restore man's inner spark. The gnostic believes that this universe we inhabit is produced not of this ineffable God but by an inferior being known as The Demiurge, identified with Jehovah of The Old Testament and the Demiurge of Plato's *Timaeus*.[48] For Pasqually and his Élus Coëns, however, it is Man himself that was persuaded to act as the Demiurge. Mankind has trapped himself - a prisoner in the very jail he was created to be warden of. Only *gnosis* gained in the practice of the *primitive cult* can reintegrate Mankind back to the true divinity. Exiled, the divine spark of *gnosis* enables the hermeneutical process to begin in Man and to aid him to ascend the multitude of spiritual plains; to spark an internal liturgical return through his practice in the nobility of the *primitive cult*. Willermoz encapsulates this beautifully in his own *Instruction secrète aux Grands Profès* - 'The king of the Universe is imprisoned in a dark abode, but there he maintains a striking image of his primal grandeur.' We might envision this in terms of Rousseau's 'noble savage', but on the cosmic scale; the Coën is a 'man of desire' aspiring to the primordial 'man of nature' - 'man is born free, but he is everywhere in chains'.[49]

The gnostic rejects the world, they portray man and the world in a miserable state; the Élus Coën labours tirelessly for the sake of Man to ensure his restoration back from existential exile to the glorious love of the 'divine court'. Pasqually is a man in exile. Alive at a time often characterised as the century of *lumière*, an age of reason, men like Pasqually were increasingly finding themselves in exile both from God, and their once 'divine' Royal court. A century characterised by individual liberty, freedom of expression and the eradi-

---

47 Ibid, p. 333.
48 For a useful account of Gnosticism see, Giovanni Filoramo, *A History of Gnosticism* (Oxford: Basil Blackwell 1990), pp. 1- 51. Details the ontological dualism and pessimistic characteristics of Gnosticism as opposed to the Neoplatonic and Hermetic systems as described by Antoine Faivre. Also contains a very useful list and analysis of the heresiological sources.
49 Jean-Jacques Rousseau, 'A Dissertation – On the Origin and Foundation of the Inequality of Mankind' (English Translation) in *The Social Contract and Discourses* (Middletown, RI: BN Publishing 2007), p. 1.

cation of religious authority, the *Aufklärung* (Geman: *Enlightenment*), with its rationalism and secularisation oversaw the preeminence of reason over religious dogma, giving rise to an *'anti-Aufklärung'* reaction constituting what has been called a 'Counter-Enlightenment', described by Goodrick-Clarke as 'nostalgic, traditionalist, even repressive'.[50] Like many Freemasons, Pasqually can be seen as part of this Counter-Enlightenment. Here was a deeply pious man, a royalist and conservative faced with the existential crisis of a new world of science and enfranchisement - both materialist and mechanistic. With their fanciful alternative histories and mythologised origins, the *écossais* and chivalric degrees may have been a way out of the perceived crisis between the mind and the soul prevalent at the time. In the age of Voltaire and Rousseau, Pasqually's is a man out of touch, both within and without the lodge. The Grand Lodge of France would in August 1766 exclude him from the lodges under its control, calling him a 'sectarian'.[51] Clearly alienated and exiled, he finds other increasingly marginalised acolytes in forms of freemasonry emphasising tradition and power, sovereignty, divine right and inherited wisdom.

Recollections: New Evidence

The rise and fall of the high degree systems of the eighteen century are distinguished by a common feature; dubious and spurious origins. The legends invented by various groups to explain their supposed authentic origins serve as the means of regularising a self-created system and are intertwined in the fabric of the legends of the degrees themselves. The Élus Coën are in this respect no different. Pasqually's masonic legitimacy has traditionally rested on the authenticity of an apocryphal patent from '1738', delivered by the 'Young Pretender', Charles Edward Stuart, to a certain Don Martinez Pasqualis who transmitted it to his son, Joachim Don Martinez-Pasqualis.[52]

> 'The four doors of the Temple being opened, by the power of the Grand Architect of the Universe and of Charles Stuard King of Scotland, Ireland and England, Grand Master of all Lodges spread over the face of the Earth, the Lodge of Stuard having right of jurisdiction over the French Province of Aix, the 20th May 1738, by virtue of Our Power and Authority, We, Grand Master of Scottish, Irish and English Masonry, have entrusted our right of power as Grand Master of the Lodge to our Respected Master, Don Martines Pasqualis,

---

50 Goodrick-Clarke, p. 137.
51 Var, 'Pasqually, Martines de' in *Dictionary of Gnosis & Western Esotericism*, p. 932.
52 Nahon, 'Élus Coëns' in *Dictionary of Gnosis & Western Esotericism,* p. 333.

ages sixty-seven, born in the Spanish city of Alicante, so that he may direct and build in peace on any point of the Earth, a Temple to the Grand Architect, having thus constituted it to this effect and constituting it by virtue of Our Power good and valid, Amen, Amen, Amen. We, Grand Master of the Lodge of Stuard, order our Deputy Grand-Master to direct our labors and those of his eldest son, the Powerful Master Joachim Don Martines de Pasqualis, aged 28, born in the French city of Grenoble, and this same Patent and Constitution will he remit to him in the usual way before his death or at his pleasure, so that he may, in turn, enjoy and exercise his rights and powers, having made Public this Constitution and Patent of Grand Master of the Lodge of Stuard, this 20th of May, in the Grand Lodge of the East and in 1738'.[53]

Fresh evidence would suggest, however, the '1738 Stuart' patent is nothing more than another rather elaborate fiction underpinning Pasqually's entire masonic system. A Coën diploma has recently been discovered in Minsk from the collection of famed collector Daniel Guéguen, awarded by Pasqually's *Loge de la Perfection Élue Écossaise de Bordeaux* on 22nd October, 1765 to Brother Izaac Piochau, aged 24, native of Ste Foÿ en Agenois, for the degree of '*Apprentif-Compagnon maçon*'. It is illustrated in black, red and green ink on vellum, signed and sealed with a red wax seal, affixed to blue, white, red and green ribbons, and framed in hand drawn triangles. It is almost identical to the well-known '1738 Stuart' patent, and, tellingly, it is written in the same hand, which appears to be that of the Abbé Bullet.[54] The 'Minsk' diploma originates from the Lodge founded by Pasqually in Bordeaux in 1762 until 1768. Later he enters the lodge *La Française* in Bordeaux and transforms it entirely in line with his own complex theosophic doctrine of masonic theurgy, renaming it *Perfection Élue et Écossaise*. It was recognised by the Grande Loge de France in 1765, the same year he went to Paris befriending Jean-Baptiste Willermoz. The 'Minsk' diploma spuriously claims that it too finds its masonic authority in 'Charles Stuard King of Scotland, Ireland and England', with the caveat - 'under the protection of William George today King of Great Britain'. Here Pasqually bears an interesting title.

> Dom Martines Pasqually G[rand] S[upre]me M[as]ter of the Order - Eminent of Freemasonry of the islands of Ireland and England, founder of the said Temple.

---

53 Translated by Nigel Jackson and shared widely and publicly on multiple different online digital platforms. It is suggested that the original is in the possession of an organisation known as the 'Friends of Martines de Pasqually'. It was returned into their keeping after the fall of the Berlin Wall. It had been taken by the Russians at the end of WWII and was rediscovered in Belarus among some other masonic items.
54 Michelle Nahon, *Bulletin de la Societe Martines de Pasqually*, 27 (2017)

Introduction

It would appear, based on this 'Minsk' diploma, that this 1760's prototype Coën system only had four high grades as late as 1765: *Maître Parfait Élu, Maître Écossais Grand Architecte, Chevalier Commandeur d'Orient, and Raoux Croix*. These are precisely the same high degrees in their correct progression being worked in the majority of French Lodges and officially codified later still by the *Grand Orient de France*. Here we observe an emerging system in its original state, anchored to tradition. More importantly, in comparison to the 'Minsk' diploma, drafted by the Abbé Bullet in 1765, the '1738 Stuart' patent is clearly identical in style, handwriting and form. This indicates that the apocryphal '1738 Stuart' patent, as it exists today, finds its true origins in the *Loge de la Perfection Élue Écossaise de Bordeaux* about 1765, and not some twenty-nine years earlier as a gift of the exiled Jacobite court. By this rational, the '1738 Stuart' patent appears to be nothing more than an attempt by the *Loge de la Perfection Élue Écossaise de Bordeaux* to 'self-charter' under factious Jacobite auspices, an abundantly prevalent practice within Continental lodges at the time.

A further discovery from the archives of the Grand Lodge of Ireland might also shed new light on the same question. Discovered by the author in the archives of respected Irish masonic scholar Dr Francis Clements Crossle, a transcript exists of a letter written by Pasqually dated 20th September 1765, barely a month before the issuing of the 'Minsk' diploma. A wonderful document, it reveals some rather profound details regarding Pasqually's, and ultimately the *Élus Coëns,* masonic origins. The letter is published here in its entirety for the first time. Whilst certainly rich in biographical details, Pasqually makes the fascinating claim to his unnamed British recipient (someone chosen for 'general leadership of our Orders') of a very literal Scottish origin to his particular brand of high degree *écossais* freemasonry.

> In the name of the Great Architect of the Universe, Joy, Prosperity and Salvation be given through Us, Grand Sovereign Master of the Orders of Freemasonry Spiritual, Temporal and Symbolic.
>
> Very High, Very Puissant and Very Respectable Master, having learnt by [an] indirect route that the G.A.O.T.U. had chosen you for the general leadership of Our Orders, for protecting and strengthening the seal, courage and devotion of the Folks who have voluntarily submitted to the Laws, Statutes, Regulations and discipline of Freemasonry, I have no doubt that all Our Brethren scattered over the surface of the two hemispheres are glorying in the choice and striving to further your desires for the Propagation of our orders, by imbibing from your enlightenment the learned teaching you will be good enough to give them on the knowledge of Our Mysteries.

Very High and Very Puissant Master, accept my homage: it derives its origin in the heart of my ancestors who ever since the Dispersion of the Coëns have laboured constantly with yours to preserve the purity of the Royal Art, and the sublime knowledge of spiritual Freemasonry. It is to them I owe its transmission; [a] favour that must for you be a certain warrant of my lively and sincere gratitude, and of my unshakeable devotion.

In 1721 your predecessors and many other Nobles came and spent some time at Aix en Provence. There my late father laboured with them in our sacred My[steries]. In 1733 I was fortunate enough to convince them of my zeal, courage and devotion to Our Respectable Orders, and to deserve their confidence. Thus it was your predecessors and the other Masters who comprise that respectable temple of true masonry, who enlightened me, and instructed me in the fixed and invariable Points of our spiritual Orders.

It was then that masonry appeared in France under the Puissance of the leaders of Scotland, Ireland and England, of whom you are still one of the chiefs Respectable in every respect and whom I recognise as such. My soul trembles with joy on learning that the G[reat] A[rchitect] on taking to Himself the truck has preserved in You its Sapling, so as to immortalise the memory of His among all Masonic brethren.

I cannot allow you to remain unaware that my attainment of the eminent place which I occupy about the Great Round Table of freemasonry was, after the Puissance of the G[reat] A[rchitect], due to the Kindness of Your predecessor Brother Master [the] Duke [of] Hamilton, who deposited in my bosom the illuminating instructions which direct us in Our M[ystic] Orders. I have before me the Constitutional Patents which they entrusted to my father with orders to transfer them to me before his Death, which he did; and which I shall have the pleasure of showing to you on the visit I propose shortly to make, to all my brother Masons existing at the Orient of Scotland, of Ireland, and of England, so as to inform them of all what is happening relative to the Good of the Order, [and] to give them knowledge of the temples I am erecting to the Glory of the G[reat] A[rchitect] in the instruction of which I am labouring, and which I shall fortify by an authentic constitution emanating from the tribunal of the Grand Sovereign Masters of the *l'Ordre de la franc maçonnerie des Coëns* estab-

Introduction

lished in the East, exercised in principle and method in the West, practised, followed and enjoyed in the South, and ignored in the North although it was in that region that most [of the] events of our Orders took place.

Freemasonry, Very High and Very Puissant Master, is Key to all knowledge of the things created by the Great Architect of the Universe, and men can learn nothing of what exists terrestrially and celestially without the perfect knowledge of spiritual freemasonry, or at least of the mystic numbers which brought knowledge of it to certain men chosen by the Great Architect, and this knowledge can only be acquired through exact Research, pure and sincere, in the presence of the Great Architect and of His Seven Elect, to whom He communicated that knowledge so as to perpetuate true masons over the surface of the earth and serve them as a flaming Star. The number of Masons is considerable in appearance, but very small in reality according to the Proverb of the Great Architect's Deputy who said: 'Many are called, but Few are Chosen'; Such are the Masons who only follow the Orders of Freemasonry in appearance; who, like the bark of the tree which bears many flowers and never produces fruit, are useless flowers and phantoms who practice illusion under the name of Masons. This parable, Very High and Very Puissant Master, should recall to us the sacred obligations which we undertook between the hands of of our former brethren in the name of the Great Architect. You are of the number of those who at present preside over the seven degrees of Glory of spiritual freemasonry: in consequence, convinced of the Necessity for observing them exactly, and sincerely persuaded that this sublime science brings before our eyes in their actuality present and future events, may the Great Architect of the Universe be pleased to have you always in His Holy Keeping, and perpetuate you for ever, from generation to generation, among the Number of His Elect for the maintenance of the Royal Art, and the guidance of true Proselytes summoned to the fixed point through freemasonry, for the glory of the Great Architect of the Universe: and you will obtain thereby Immortality and the Reward of Rewards in the Holy of Holies and for ever and ever. Amen. Amen. Amen.

Peace, Salvation [and] Health be with you and with your brethren through the mystic Numbers which characterise you, Very High, Very Puissant and Very Respectable Master.

Your very affectionate Brother∴

Bordeaux, 20 Sept. 1765.

Dom Martines Pasqually Ecuyer Gd. Sovn. Master of the Orders of Freemasonry of the 4 quarters and of the 3 Materials of Earth and World through the mystics Numbers hereafter∴

Whilst clearly showing that Charles Edward Stuart played no role in granting either Pasqually's or his father's masonic credentials, the letter gives us some startling new insights. In the first instance, it casts doubt on the belief that Pasqually was born in 1726/27 as has previously been suggested by information obtained from his death certificate. Our letter claims he was taken into the 'confidence' of these instructing 'Nobles' in 1733 - if Pasqually was born in 1726/27 he would have been five years old! The circa. 1709 date seems much more reasonable in this light, and also fits perfectly with the claim made in the '1738 Stuart' patent, that Pasqually was 28 in 1738. This is clearly an important piece of corroborating evidence in the historically scant picture of Pasqually's biography. However, from 1720 until 1722, the French region of Provence and parts of the Languedoc suffered an outbreak of plague which arrived from the Levant. Traditionally, this event has been known as the Great Plague of Marseille. Aix was under quarantine in 1721, so it is unlikely anybody was visiting. Perhaps then Pasqually is speaking allegorically here of the supposed first French lodge of English origin, *Amitié et Fraternité*, founded in 1721 in the north, at Dunkirk. In either case, the picture still remains typically unclear. Secondly, the letter is addressed to the general leader of the 'Orient of Scotland, of Ireland, and of England', with whom Pasqually is discussing his *'l'Ordre de la franc maçonnerie des Coëns'* as early as 1765, and from whom Pasqually's father, as early as 1721, was granted 'Constitutional Patents'. This may well be a reference to the *Royal Order of Heredom*, as no other masonic order at this time had jurisdiction over all the British nations. With its ritual demanding a chair be kept empty in anticipation of the messianic return of the heralded 'King of Scots', the *heredom* tradition went on to be hugely influential in France. However, it is also possible, and perhaps more likely, that it is merely some vague allusion to the mythical 'Lodge of Stuard' on Pasqually's part, as similarly presented in the 'Stuart' patent. Again, it is unclear. However, importantly the letter clearly states that it was British 'Nobles' that came to Aix en Provence in 1721. Presumably we can say with confidence here then that Pasqually's father did indeed become involved with philosophically inclined Jacobite exiles, as was the masonic vogue of the time. The incidental details regarding a British contingent arriving in Aix en Provence and Pasqually's father's meeting with them, does indeed match the details retold in the May '1738 Stuart' patent. Revealingly, and this is the third major point, in the September 1765 letter, Pasqually mentions only 'Nobles'. There is no reference to a

Introduction

Prince, nor to a King, nor even Charles Edward Stuart. Less than one month later in the 'Minsk' diploma of 22nd October 1765, these 'Nobles' seemed to have transformed into 'Charles Stuard King of Scotland, Ireland and England' himself. Even in his private correspondences, Pasqually mixes the symbolic and the actual.

The letter continues by stating that it was in 1733 that Pasqually was taken into the 'Nobles' confidence' and 'enlightened... and instructed... in the fixed and invariable Points of our spiritual Orders'. Once again, this contradicts the dates of '1738 Stuart' patent which states the event happened in 20th May 1738, some five years later. Pasqually goes on to describe in his letter 'the temples I am erecting to the Glory of the G[reat] A[rchitect]', which he will 'fortify by an authentic constitution emanating from the tribunal of the Grand Sovereign Masters of the *l'Ordre de la franc maçonnerie des Coëns*'. Is this 'authentic constitution' Pasqually speaks of the document we know today as the '1738 Stuart' patent? Pasqually states this 'authentic constitution' emanates from his 'tribunal of the Grand Sovereign Masters'; again, is this the same 'tribunal of the Grand Sovereign Masters' sitting in *Loge de la Perfection Élue Écossaise de Bordeaux* issuing diplomas, such as the 'Minsk' diploma? Which are virtually identical in style and handwriting to the '1738 Stuart' patent? It would appear so.

Perhaps the most fascinating revelation in the letter is the mention of the Duke of Hamilton, 'who deposited in my bosom the illuminating instructions which direct us in Our M[ystic] Orders.' Here Pasqually is saying that it is Hamilton, alongside the Jacobite 'Noble Masters who comprise that respectable temple of true masonry' ... [who] enlightened me, and instructed me in the fixed and invariable Points of our spiritual Orders'. Likely, James, 5th Duke of Hamilton. (1703- 1743), who was secretly made a Knight of the Garter and a Knight of the Thistle by the Jacobite 'Old Pretender' in 1723. One can only imagine the excitement such *bona fide* clandestine knightly investitures had amongst the continental masonic aristocracy. In 1737 Pasqually's uncle commanded a company of the regiment of Edinburgh Dragoons in the service of Philip V of Spain. Indeed, the very motto of the Coën order was 'Loyalty to the God and King!' Duty, peerage, tradition, Royalty and Divine Right, are the watchwords of Pasqually's elite military circle. Importantly then, Pasqually's family clearly has links with Scottish Nobility.

When the Grand Lodge of France was dissolved by royal edict on February 21, 1767, less than a year after his exile from the Craft, it must have been bittersweet. Pasqually was a pious catholic of noble descent, as were his Élus Coëns - their universe was not one that could be catalogued neatly in the pages of Diderot's (1713-1784) *Encyclopédie* (1751-1772). The complex hierarchical structure of the Coën system, earthly and spiritual, pays a great deal to its theosophical heritage, and as a reaction to Cartesian mechanics, but it may also be read as a reaction against egalitarian Enlightenment values prevalent in the french lodges of the time. Such a re-enchantment as Pasqually's, offers a real spiritual goal for disillusioned aristocratic masons faced with the first faint stirring of secularism and the Republic. Pasqually represents a way of life increasingly alienated from the world he knows. For many like him who entered the lodges, it was a struggle to reconcile themselves with the spirit of this new age; Pasqually's system offered reconciliation with a spirit rather more literally.

Exile

The Kabbalistic aspects of Pasqually's doctrine are often overstated. Strangely, being a Spanish Jewish covert to Catholicism, his notoriously clumsy handling of Hebrew, and indeed French, serves as evidence of his lack of acquaintance with the primary sources. However, certain Kabbalistic notions are evident in the *primitive cult*. The notions in question originate with Rabbi Yitzchak Luria ben Shlomo Ashkenazi (1534-1572).

Known as the 'Ari' or 'Lion of Safed' and taught by the influential Rabbi Moses ben Jacob Cordovero (1522-1570), Luria instigated a new school of Kabbalistic thinking known as Lurianic Kabbalah in Palestine. Luria himself writes very little, his work becomes known through its reference in the writings of his pupil Hassyim Vital (1543 -1620) and by their later translations into Western languages. He is credited with several specific Kabbalistic innovations that simultaneously clarify and yet complicate earlier Kabbalistic doctrines. Luria develops the earlier idea of *tzimtzum* (contraction). This is the contraction of *Ein-Sof*; God retracting into himself in order to make room, a void for creation to exist.[55] Introducing this sense of exile to the heart of Jewish mysticism, Luria envisages the eschatological beginning and end. Next is the process of *shevirat hakeilim* (the shattering of the vessels). He continues with the introduction of the concept of *partzufim* (faces) and elaborated on the idea of the *tikkun* (rectification or restoration).[56] While a certain amount of elaboration would be required to understand these complex ideas, it will suffice here to say that the redemptive qualities inherent in the restoration of the *tikkun* are at play within

---

55 Z'ev ben Shimon Halevi, *Kabbalah: Tradition of Hidden Knowledge* (London: Thames and Hudson, 1979), p. 5.
56 Anne Conway, *The Principles of the Most Ancient and Modern Philosophy*, trans. and ed. by Allison P. Coudert and Taylor Corse (Cambridge: Cambridge University Press, 1996), pp. xix- xx.

the doctrine of the Élus Coëns. Pasqually's 'reintergration' has a genuine Hebrew heritage, but as with most masons, Pasqually used it a means of vindicating Christianity as the true religion based on an esoteric interpretation of Hebrew mystical lore.[57]

The doctrine of *tikkun* places exile at the centre of a processional stage in a universal process of ultimate renewal, perfection and redemption. Moshe Idel disagreed with Gershom Scholem and his assertion that this was a reaction to traumatic historical Jewish expulsions, stating rather that it was a natural progression of pre-existing Kabbalistic principles.[58] Eventually matter would return to it spiritual state, although the progression would be long and difficult. Exile was therefore a necessary, though transitory, stage in a process which would end in universal salvation. Pain and suffering were inevitable, but as a result of human actions in the form of *tikkunim* (positive redemptive acts) every individual would eventually be purged.[59] Pasqually was an exile from the Grand Lodge of France, and from the Enlightenment; a masons who's dubious masonic legitimacy is founded in the authority of an exiled King. Wandering France, Pasqually taught a doctrine of exile from the lore of an exiled people. Such is the existential cry of the Coëns at the Western Wall of the Temple. *Eli Eli, lama sabachthani?*

What can we say of the Order of the Élus Coëns then? We can say that the Élus Coëns system should be understood a theosophical system designed around a liturgical understanding that is intended to facilitate an initiatic form of 'contemporaneity' with an authentic gnostic and primordial Christian soteriology. Encompassing prophetic pansophic notions of unity and rebirth prevalent in certain Illuminist groups of the time, its grades were revelatory, practiced for an inward second birth in the light of a primordial Christ, the presence of which Pasqually called *'la chose'* (the Thing). Theurgy, meaning 'work of God', is the defining feature of Coëns, but its theosophical underpinnings are fundamental. Pasqually's system represents the direct hermeneutical application of the 'correspondences' found within Nature that can effect the practitioner and the whole of nature itself. By exploiting these correspondences between the signs and text of the universe through the correct ontological hermeneutics (the 'operations', '*luminous glyphs*' etc.) the Coën can emancipate themselves and reach transcendence with the divinity. It is a sad footnote therefore, that the Élus Coën lineage effectively died when Pasqually left France for Santo-Domingo (Haiti) in 1772 in order to collect an inheritance. Saint-Domingue

---

57 Goodrick-Clarke, p. 51.
58 Gershom Scholem, *Major Trends in Jewish Mysticism* (New York: Schocken Books 1954), p. 419. See also, Moshe Idel, *Kabbalah: New Perspectives* (New Haven: Yale University Press, 1988), p. 265.
59 Conway, *The Principles of the Most Ancient and Modern Philosophy*, p. xix.

accounted for a third of the entire Atlantic slave trade. Always troubled by financial problems, it is a painful hypocrisy that a lifetime of debt accrued in the fight against spiritual evil, should be settled by the revenue of a very earthy evil.

In the following pages we can for the first time return to the 'true foundations of the allegories' as Willermoz would have it, and read for ourselves the secrets of a genuine masonic theosophy.

Translation of:

FM4 1282, BnF,
'Le Manuscrit d'Alger' (1772)

Letter on the Relationship of Harmony with Numbers

You absolutely want monsieur, to see in writing my relationship between harmony and numbers. Here they are: All I ask of you is not to believe that I am giving you this as science, but only as one of the testimonies of science; and never forget that it does not consist of cold reasoning or ingenious observations, but in the virtuous desires of the soul and the use of all the forces of our being. Only then, on this condition, will I write.

You know monsieur, that a sound is not heard without carrying with it, while ascending, three other sounds of which it is the generator. Here already is the unity of the quaternary; here in one form is the central point and the three angles of the triangle; here finally, is one of the traces of the law which directs any particular and universal production. I leave it for you to think whether this law could be observed as regularly, as universally in created things, if it was not the same in the uncreated order, especially since it is acknowledged that what is sensible does not only exist by what is not. Let us try to raise ourselves to the insensible quaternary, and we will have the principle of all things; a principle that will enlighten us about ourselves and will make us wise causing us to look for ourselves if we conform to our origin.

The three sounds that relate to the principal sound, do so by a relationship which has been well evaluated by the musicians; the first, under the name of the twelfth or the octave of the fifth; the second of the seventeenth major or double octave of the third; and the third under the name of the octave which is the repetition of the principal sound. Such are the relations given by Nature; such is the distance that she has established between the four corresponding sounds. But the twelfth and the seventeenth major are only octaves of sounds that are closer in relation with the bass sound; thus, the seventeenth major relates to the major third above the bass sound, and the twelfth relates to a sound that is two-thirds above the same bass sound. It is from there that the perfect harmony is formed, according to the received notion of the phonic; the third, the fifth and the octave. I know that the octave is only a repetition of the bass sound, and I could remove it like the other sounds out of the octave, but I cannot dispense with it, because without it, the scale would not be complete, and that it is the proof of unity. I will not go into detail about the other harmonic sounds that masters of the art claim to have discovered in the resonances of the body of sound.

Indeed, since these sounds are almost insensible and, moreover, given that they are only new octaves of the four primitive sounds stated, I will stick to these and will consider the numerical relations that I find between them in the perfect harmony they compose.

Firstly, the perfect chord carries the number 1, in that it is the one and only that it is entirely self-fulfilling and unalterable in its intrinsic value of unity, for I do not count the sixth or sixth quarter, which is only a transposition of the same sounds of the chord, and therefore, does not change the essence.

Secondly, this chord is composed of four sounds that contain between them three intervals. You have seen unity produce its three corresponding sounds and enslave them. You currently see the quaternary contain and somehow bind that same ternary number, which already shows us a quaternary relationship to unity. Let us consider for a moment this ternary and quaternary moment both in their rank and in their particular activity.

The first interval of the perfect chord is a third, the second is another third, and the third, a fourth: why should we not recognise there, the number and inferiority of the single and double triangle, as well as the true quaternary formed above one and on the other, to preside there and direct all action? As soon as we saw that it contained the All, why would we not also admit that it governs everything? Especially since we see it dominates by its natural rank on this double triangle, and that it is always this quaternary and superior note that determines the nature of the perfect chord, which one might call the Universal Chord. It seems to me that Nature itself establishes here the difference between the ternary in the quaternary of the period or the triangle at its centre. We see in one the terminal and the dependence, and in the other we see the Omnipotence. We see in the first two-thirds of the perfect chord the double triangle, or the senary; the factor of all inferior things, whereas the quaternary is raised above them and rests there as in its seat. One is composed of two different thirds and represents to us, the perishable nature of all the elementary things; the other, formed by a single quaternary interval, is a new image of the first principle, and by its number as by its rank it represents simplicity, grandeur, and immutability. It is not just that this harmonic fourth is more permanent than all other created things; as soon as it is sensible it must pass, but that does not prevent, even in its transient action, that it does not clip the intelligence, the essence and stability of its source. It is therefore within the assembly of the intervals of the perfect chord, which is passive and all that is active, that is to say, all that Man can conceive, that we see this relationship I have established between the quaternary and the unity from which everything comes.

Translation of 'Le Manuscrit d'Alger' (1772)

But to better perceive this relation, let us examine by what means this quaternary contains all things: it is because from its beginning to the end, there is really only 10, as you may already have noticed. Indeed, from the unity or the bass sound to the sound that ends the first interval of the perfect chord, there is a third; from the end of this first interval to the end of the second, there is yet another third, which is the sixth. Finally, since this last interval until the end of the third, there is a fourth: as 6 and 4 are 10, all is complete. Can you have a more sensitive proof of the Deity's power and Divinity? Is it not through him that the quaternary has all his virtue? Finally, it is the unity which, joined to its three correspondences, forms the quaternary and all that it contains. But, as this quaternary and all that it contains cannot do anything without the unity from whence it comes, it approaches it and at the same time brings it back to all things by means of a goddess who is the similarity and the most perfect image of this unity. You see by this, that it is by its correspondence with unity, that the quaternary acts; and in truth, it is always the unity of the quaternary which contains and limits the ternary, both in principle and in its divisions and subdivisions; that is to say, in all the productions, actions and qualities of which the ternary is susceptible. It is also what makes the perfect chord that contains the three intervals with all divisions and subdivisions that can be made, which produces all the tones of the scale, and from which come all the principles and all possible effects of harmony.

However, it is only in a manner concealed from materiality that this goddess seems to us to contain all things; we only discover it by our intelligence; instead, it manifests this truth to our very senses by means of the eighth which is its first action. So we only have eight sounds in our scale, in which the last and the first are the same, or if you like, Alpha and Omega; which tells us of the universal power of the eighth in Creation. I do not need to tell you, as you know as I do, who bears this number eight; the present observation confirms that which is taught to us, that it is He who has made everything appear, and that it is He who will sustain everything for the duration.

We know this eight better under the name of the double power; the order of the notes of the scale tells us still under this denomination, since this scale is divided into two equal tetrachords, as for the number of notes contained therein and for their intervals which are absolutely established according to the same ratio in the two tetrachords.

Examine the natural intervals of the first four notes beginning with Ut,[1] and those of the last four, and see if they are not alike? Do not they each contain two full tones and one half-tone and that in the same order? I do not stop to examine whether these full tones are major or minor; I know that none of them should look alike since nothing is alike, but compared to the limits of my material bounds, being reduced to being able to only feel their difference, I dare not take it upon myself to estimate it, and I find that Men have been very bold to fix the reports by the numbers of vibrations of 8 to 9, 9 to 10, etc.

After all, on which *A-mi-la*[2] did they take the tone? They have none of them, they are obliged to make one. Now, as this *A-mi-la* is not fixed, it follows that the relations that can be drawn from it are not so and that when Men give us the numbers they have admitted, they can also be under other numbers, according to whether the *A-mi-la* will be more or less. This knowledge, if it were deepened, could well give me some instruction like others, but having not weighed it up enough to find certainty, I limit myself to the present observation on the two tetrachords, and which is within reach of ears less trained; I limit myself to what my thoughts and eyes tell me, just as it is the eighth that has manifested the whole creature, so it is He who operates it and maintains it; and, as we have seen this creature was the assemblage of the passive and the active, it required a power for the one and a power for the other; and that is what forms this double power that one can read like me in two equal and quaternary parts, and whose harmonic scale is composed. For you monsieur, you will be able to read the power of what is to be called the Church, and the material proof that out of it there is no salvation, remembering what I said at the beginning, that the sensible only survives by what is not, and therefore is only the material expression of the laws of an immaterial principle hidden from the eyes of the body.

---

1   Possible reference to 'Ut queant laxis', a Latin hymn in honour of John the Baptist. It is famous for its part in the history of musical notation, in particular solmization. In Catholic worship, the hymn is sung in the Divine Office on 24th June, the Feast of the Nativity of John the Baptist. The full hymn is divided into three parts, with 'Ut queant laxis' sung at Vespers, 'Antra deserti' sung at Matins, 'O nimis felix' sung at Lauds, and doxologies added after the first two parts. The chant is useful for teaching singing because of the way it uses successive notes of the scale: the first six musical phrases of each stanza begin on a successively higher notes of the hexachord, giving ut-re-mi-fa-so-la; though 'ut' is replaced by 'do' in modern solfège. The naming of the notes of the hexachord by the first syllable of each hemistich (half line of verse) of the first verse is usually attributed to Guido of Arezzo. Guido, who was active in the eleventh century, is regarded as the father of modern musical notation. He made use of clefs (C & F clefs) and invented the ut-re-mi-fa-sol-la-si notation. The hymn does not help with the seventh tone as the last line, Sancte Iohannes, breaks the ascending pattern. The syllable 'si', for the seventh tone, was added in the 18th century. The first stanza reads: 'Ut queant laxis, resonare fibris, Mira gestorum, famuli tuorum, Solve polluti, labii reatum, Sancte Iohannes'. It may be translated as: 'So that your servants may, with loosened voices, resound the wonders of your deeds, clean the guilt from our stained lips, O' Saint John'.

2   Another Reference to Solfège, the musical education method used to teach pitch. Syllables are assigned to the notes of the scale and enable the musician to audiate, or mentally hear, the pitches of a piece of music which he or she is seeing for the first time and then to sing them aloud. Most English speakers distinguish musical pitches as C, D, E, F, G, A, etc. Most Spanish speakers still call these pitches; do, re, mi, fa, sol, la, si, do, etc.

Translation of 'Le Manuscrit d'Alger' (1772)

Although we have recognised that the scale was composed of eight sounds, the last being only a repetition of the first, there are in fact only seven sounds different from each other; and if the ear is not at rest on the seventh of these sounds, but only when it reaches the eighth, it is to me, a new confirmation that all things must return to their principle, and that has sprung up in unity, they are at peace and in their place only when they have returned to this unity. Nothing is clearer than this truth, since we see that the notes of the scale do not finish only in the eighth, which, as we have seen above, is only the sensible action of the goddess, which is the goddess of the first spiritual action of the unity. The seven notes probably seem to you monsieur, to have a great deal of relation, and it is true that the closer we come to what is created and temporal, the more analogies we easily find since we live in the land of time. So I think that without being imaginary, we can recognise the septenary principal agents of the universal creature whose corporal names you know, as well all the products, virtues, divisions, signs, and properties that belong to these septenary agents, also all that Men use every day to represent them without knowing either the principle or the effects. Finally, you will find evidence of this natural septenary in all that composes and contains the creature in his temporal action, because it divides and occupies it all from the surface to the centre.

Nevertheless, everything indicates that this septenary is only a temporal or operational agent and not a holy agent like the eighth who immediately touches the duenna[3] and who rests on the septenary like the Lamb on the seven seals. Observe that you cannot reach this eighth without having gone through the lower seven degrees and educating yourself... Recognise our staircase and make it different from the room where it leads; that it does not stop us from making it the greater case, and to regard it as our most dearest amongst things created, for finally we have but one way out of the land of Egypt, and I see nothing that prevents me from believing that it is this one. The Red Sea was the first step of the ladder, the forty-two camps were the six others, and all of them had to be climbed to reach the Promised Land.

I will not say more about the septenary, I leave the field open to your own reflections and I do not doubt that deep down inside, you have convinced yourself of the many of the things that I have just addressed. Let us move on to other observations.

So far monsieur, we have considered the scale only relative to what it is in itself and to the fundamental principles that compose it; we have not penetrated into the game and the particular march that all sounds in harmony can hold. Thus, in examining only their natu-

---

3   An elderly woman who serves as a governess for younger ladies in a Spanish or Portuguese family.

ral order, we have discovered only the constitution of all things established by the Creator. Let us now seek if another point of view will discover those which are not by Him; then we will feel if there is another power than His, if there is any other truth, other law, other perfection than that which is due to its incommutable essence; finally, it is possible that there is more than one unity? For this purpose, let us remember, I pray you, what is the nature of the three intervals which we have recognised should be included in the perfect chord? It is the repeated third and the fourth which measures them. Their sum gave us ten. Ten begot eight, and eight supposes seven, so that we have already the six agents who put into effect the six eternal thoughts that become sensible in temporal Creation. I say these six eternal thoughts, not in relation to the Creation whose cause and birth have had a beginning, and therefore will have an end, only in relation to the uncreated nature whose order has been and will be eternally the type of the visible nature. These six agents are 1, 3, 4, 7, 8 and 10. You know that 6 is only 3. You also know that as long as we are in our bodily form, the 3 will be all we can know; since His centre will be forever hidden from the created things and that the darkness cannot understand the light, so that no man has ever seen God.

What I am mainly trying to point out here monsieur, is that in all the numbers that we have just found and which contain the two universes, the liabilities and the assets, we have not seen any trace of the other three numbers that are contained in the *denary,* namely, the *binary,* the *quinary* and the *nonary;* well, do you want it to be your own ear that tells you where they come from? It is a witness of which you will not be defiant, and who must confirm to you the certainty of the things of intelligence.

You readily judge that if the perfect chord had always remained in its nature, order and a just harmony would have subsisted perpetually; but this monotony seemed boring, and those who were trained to hear it, were disgusted and determined to compose. And what progress did they follow for that? They altered the perfect chord by removing His octave and substituting it for the previous note, from which comes what is known as the seventh chord; this is the source of all musical productions, which is for me an image of the production universal, and where my mind discovers the principle as He discovered the constitution above. Let us examine then the nature of this seventh, and we shall touch on it and on Him the causes and results of the confusion which engendered the creature and perpetuates it.

The intention of creating another order of things than those contained in the perfect chord, placing another unity next to the first unity, coming only from a disordered thought, could produce only disordered effects, and therefore were in combat with the true essence of being, which can never be distorted. It was an opposed principle against principle, power against power, what we call walking by the number two. So this seventh chord is absolutely repugnant to any ear that is not disturbed, it keeps us in pain and worry until we save it inside ourselves by bringing it back to the perfect chord which is our principle. But why is this seventh so shocking to our ears? Is it not because the first and the last note of the chord are immediately adjacent to each other, and therefore bear the famous *binary* number, from which we form what we call a second? We cannot, therefore deny, that this number two is the cause of the disorder and that wherever it occurs, there is dissonance, according to the language of the musicians.

We find a new proof of the irregularity of this number in the ratio of all the notes of the scale within this grave sound, in which relations, we find evidence of the accuracy and perfection of our *quaternary*. Indeed, I considered the seventh as a second in relation to the bass note or, if you like, to its octave, which is the same thing; but this seventh is not at all the only dissonance; every diatonic connection is condemned by Nature; thus, wherever I find two neighbouring notes ringing together, I will hurt. Now, as in the scale there is only the second and seventh that can be found in relation to this grave sound, it makes us see that the creation is formed of two dissonances, just as we have seen that this could only be a dissonance, or the number two, which would have made him give birth. On the contrary, we find that there are only four notes and that there are only these four notes which accord perfectly with the bass sound or octave, namely the third, the fourth, the fifth, and the sixth. Is not this a new and clear proof of the relationship of our quaternary with unity? Is it not in another form our four universal correspondences and a new effect of the immutability of the principle? See, then, the difference between good and evil: eternity, the impossibility of the one; youth and instability of the other. Recognise these consonances, either by their quaternary number or by their effects, announces order and perfection everywhere; and that, on the contrary, dissonances, equally considered in their number and in their effects, produce directly opposite results. I will come back to this point to offer you a small image of yourself that can make you open your eyes. Continue.

It is on the dominant that the seventh chord is made, as the most sensible of all and the most opposed to the natural tone, since it cannot subsist for a moment without the latter taking over. This dominance in the intellectual order is raised from two thirds above the bass sound and carries the number six, as you have seen: but, in the sensible order of the eight tones of the scale, it really bears the number five. As long as this dominant remains attached to the bass sound which is its natural link, the consonance is perfect; but when it has separated from it and wants to walk alone, which it is supposed to be able to do without the generating principle and to put itself in its place, you have seen the seventh has resulted. You see then, that the *quinary* number could not appear alone without making a dissonance with unity, and therefore, without having an intimate connection with the number two. You could, I know, object to my words and tell me that what I take for the fifth in the sensible scale of eight notes is really the sixth in the base intellectual who composes the perfect chord, as I have just established it myself. But, just as the eighth scale is divisible into two tetrachords, so the scale is divisible into two, and in either of these two scales if you take the dominant, it will always be the first note and as the source of the division. If it is in the eighth, it will carry five by rank, and by joining the number four which is from this fifth to the octave, you will have the ninth that will remind you of the meeting of the animal part with the chief of the abomination. (I will speak later of this *nonary* number and will show you clearly that it makes the subdivision of matter). If you take your dominant in the bass, it will carry six by its rank, but doing the division as in the eighth, there will be five from this dominant to the bass, which will make eleven; so, from whatever side we look at it, as soon as you divide the scale either a denary or an eighth, you will always recognise that it is the quinary that brought the disorder and confusion everywhere. In the eighth scale, it is below; in the *denary* scale it is above, that is the difference.

What I have to tell you about the nonary is discovered perfectly in the seventh; is this seventh not composed of three thirds? I will let you do it for yourself on these three tiers, both together and separately, applying all you know about three, six, and nine. I leave you to meditate on the origin and constitution of bodies, either in the universal or in the particular, and draw for yourself the consequences of their incompatibility with what existed before them. Then considering this nonary in the sensible scale where it actually bears the number seven, you will see if this created nature can be supported otherwise than through the action and the reaction from which comes the fight and the violence that you see there; by assembling the consonances and dissonances that constitute all musical productions, the mixture of regularity and disorder of harmony faithfully represents us.

I have promised you monsieur, concerning dissonances and consonances, a little image of your being here below; we must give it to you.

You remember that I pointed out to you that in the scale there are four notes, namely the third, the fourth, the right fifth and the sixth, which agree with the root note, and that there are two, namely the second and the seventh, which do not agree at all. I only ask you to observe what place these consonances and dissonances occupy in the scale, both in relation to themselves and in relation to this root note. Do not the four consonances occupy the centre? Are they not limited by the two dissonances? And these by the bass note and its octave? So read with me the quaternary, or the Man in his dark form, who separates Him from his principle; read the road you have to take to get there; read the horrible division that matter put in all spiritual nature; finally, read both your own misery and your preparation.

There were wise men once who put a veil on what I am discovering here; they announced the man under the name of the red colour, in the black colour, and in the white colour: a physical image which is confirmed in this experience of the light impressed with the three elementary colours. The harmonic order also represents to us, in a natural aspect, their allegory, and I am quite convinced that, if we bothered to look, there is not a being who does not offer us so substantially in Nature.

I have only one article left to treat monsieur, it is that of the minor tone. I am sorry, but obliged, to tell you that it is not of Nature; the sound body does not give it, it is an invention of Man who created it in imitation of the major tone. He carried below the tonic two ropes mounted so that one responds to the fifth or dominant, and the other to the minor third above, and, as the vibration of the tonic has made them resound, Man has adopted his work and placed it in the rank of natural productions. It was all the less repugnant to him when he found this minor tone to be about the same harmony as the major tone. It also carries the bass or the perfect chord, making no difference except in the order of thirds; it extends accordingly and embraces like all the other notes of the scale; the sensible chord is the same for both, and finally, like the major tone, it has advantages which are peculiar to it, but which are infinitely more limited and less outgoing. Would it be an abuse to the right of comparison if we were to find in this the repetition of all that we know about prevarication[4] already?

I put the case entirely to your judgment, but I ask you to review the relations. You see the minor tone has double power like the minor tone since it is composed like Him of two tetrachords; with this difference, it is true, that the two tetrachords of the minor tone do not each have an equal order in their intervals because of the sixth which is minor. You see that the note that forms the first third of the minor perfect chord, is only a semitone of the second or the dissonance, and this slight observation may mean something; you see the sensible note of this minor tone engenders a diminished seventh chord, from which this tone draws its greatest beauty, an agreement which does not carry a single note of the perfect chord, and which on the contrary bears the only four notes which are in prescribed agreement, finally, which carries nine, being composed of three thirds like all the sevenths,

---

4   The fall of man from the Garden of Eden, which Pasqually calls 'prevarication'.

but whose relationship is the tightest of all relationships known in the harmony, since these three thirds are minor. Thus, everything announces the weakness and the infirmity of works formed by the hand of Man.

Here monsieur, are all the relations that I have thought I have seen so far between the laws of harmony and the laws of numbers. I do not doubt that there would be infinitely more to discover if one wanted to consider in detail the structure of all dissonant chords, the qualities and properties assigned to different modes and different tones, the sequence of modulations by means of correlative tones to the principal tone, the order that reigns in that which the composers call the seventh sequel, and finally all those laws which the ear and genius of Man have discovered in the science of sounds, and that Nature approves since its progress is the same. For I strictly forbid myself any research on the assumptions that have been admitted and admitted to every day in music. The ear, like all our senses, is susceptible to habit. I am very sure that there were some inventors who could be deceived in good faith and who made us laws of random things that time alone had made seem regular. But even leaving aside all these forced productions, an intelligent eye would surely discover in all the rest a multitude of things that have escaped me and that I will not bother to look for since there is better work to do. It is enough for me to have glimpsed the connection of the fundamental principles; if the others come to me afterwards, I will receive them, and that is all that I can and need to do.

Thus, I am far from believing that I have clarified all your ideas on these matters, of which the point of view that I present to you is surely brand new. Moreover, as a man I am subject to being deceived by my imagination, and I will not flatter myself in believing that I have been entirely safe from this danger; I urge you therefore, to challenge even the little that I advance and adopt nothing you have not weighed [up for yourself]. I urge you much more monsieur, not to regard as solid food, those kinds of research in which the mind sometimes shows as much of its laziness and mistrust as its penetration, and to always have before your eyes, that the most beautiful discoveries of this kind are not worth the least affections of the heart.

Fin

Translation of 'Le Manuscrit d'Alger' (1772)

Ceremonies of the four annual Banquets of the Order of the Coëns.

✠

The first banquet is that of the Trinity.
The second is that of St John the Baptist.
The third is St John the Evangelist.
The fourth is Easter [held] *at the 3rd feast.*

For the Feast of the Trinity

All the brethren of each establishment will attend Mass which will begin at half-past nine to be finished at ten-thirty; and will come back to the forecourt of the Temple.

All the dignitaries will go up to the Temple, all the lights will be lit, then the chief Conducteurs will bring in all the brethren in general to ordinary use.

The M[ost] R[espectable] M[aster] of the East[5] tells the Master of Ceremonies[6] to have placed in the circle, which surrounds the centre of the Blazing Star, the twelve eldest brethren of the most advanced grade without however, including any dignitary officers.

We attach to the floor, perpendicularly to the Star in the centre, an interior banner of which will hang a cluster of 12 flame-coloured ribbons, long enough for the 12 brethren positioned as said to hold in one hand each of these little ribbons. This banner will be white, bordered with a black favour on the side that looks to the South, with a blue favour on the side that looks to the North. The in-between will be lined with a red favour. The Wardens of the Porch[7] are placed within the Temple in front of the Wardens du Temple[8] below the circles, hence forming between them a perfect square as is figured in a great temple by the four stars placed in a similar manner. The M[ost] W[orshipful] M[aster] of the West[9] stands between the two Wardens; the M[ost] R[espectable] M[aste]r of the East is likewise between two of his own; the Master of Ceremonies of the Temple is on the right

---

5 French: T[rès] R[espectable] M[aitre] d'Orient. Substituted throughout the text as M[ost] R[espectable] M[aster] of the East.
6 French: Master des Cérémonies. Substituted throughout the text as Master of Ceremonies.
7 French: Surveillants du Porche. Substituted throughout the text as Wardens of the Porch.
8 French: Surveillants du Temple. Substituted throughout the text as Wardens of the Temple.
9 French: T[rès] R[espectable] M[aitre] d'Occident. Substituted throughout the text as M[ost] R[espectable] M[aster] of the West.

✠ 51

of the M[ost] R[espectable] M[aster] of the East; the Master of Ceremonies of the Porch is on the right of the M[ost] W[orshipful] M[aste]r of the West. The other dignitaries will stand in columns behind their respective chief Conductor. Other dignitary officers will be placed in columns behind their respective chief Conductor.

Whilst placing the 12 brethren, the Master of Ceremonies will make sure to leave a free passage to the East and West so that the two Masters of these feasts can enter the centre and leave without causing any disturbance.

On this day, there is no candle lit porch, everything remains in darkness, due to the 3 principal lights represented by the M[ost] W[orshipful] M[aste]r of the West and his two Wardens not being there. The brethren of the Porch will be placed in their class for ordinary purposes, they will stand facing the Throne of the East.

The Master of Ceremonies will make sure the six brethren who are placed on the South side keep the banner's tuft of small ribbons in their left hand, whilst the six who are on the North side keep it in their right hands.

If in a Temple there will be other additional brethren present, the Master of Ceremonies will place them outside the circle where the first 12 and those behind them are, therefore they can each hold the end of the cord *of the Elect*[10] from one of these first 12 on one or more of the circles.

The 12 celebrant brethren will be dressed in a jacket, breeches, stockings and white shoes; they will not have any metal on them, not even a pin. All other brethren on this day will have if possible a black coat, jacket, breeches, and shoes of the same; both will have no curls.

All the brethren will be bareheaded throughout the ceremony, except for the two Masters of the East and West, the other dignitaries will each have the hairstyle which is prescribed to them by the general statutes.

All the brethren in general will dress with only the cord *of the Elect* and the blue cord. Those who also have the white cord will also wear it according to their rank.

Everything being thus arranged, the two chief Conducteurs enter the centre of the circles without a sword in hand, one after the other, having the Star at the centre between them; they both take the prescribed posture. The M[ost] W[orshipful] M[aste]r of the East says to the M[ost] W[orshipful] M[aste]r of the West:

---

10   French: d'Elu. Substituted throughout the text as of the Elect.

'Blessed is he who comes to me in this place in the name of Jehovah ô + 10.'

The M[ost] W[orshipful] M[aste]r of the West answers:

'Praise be to him who speaks to me in the name of Jehovah.'

and utters the same word. All this is said softly. The M[ost] W[orshipful] M[aste]r of the East then says in the same way,

'I have watched over you Man, since your origin, so watch over me also, you who are my image and likeness.'

The M[ost] W[orshipful] M[aste]r of the West responds *'Amen'* after which they mark each other's brow between the two eyes, a little above the eyebrows, with red cinnabar[11] that they hold about themselves in a small box put in their belt. Only the middle finger of both will be elongated, the other fingers of the hand will be closed and contained by the thumb. Having the finger an inch from the forehead of the W[orshipful] M[aster], the M[ost] W[orshipful] M[aste]r of the East begins:

'Be marked by me, Man-God, image and divine likeness of the formidable and invincible seal that directs and leads the whole Universe in its race and all minors that adorn it by their presence and decorate it with their virtue and divine spiritual power; and that by virtue of this mark that I apply to your forehead, (he presses his finger on the forehead of the W[orshipful] M[aster] until the end) *your soul is joined with the Holy Spirit who is responsible for His conduct, His thought, His memory and His actions whatsoever; and purified by Him, he can read more particularly the Divine and Spiritual Book of Universal Science, as our predecessors had obtained by the help of one who has been marked by me in His name* (the same ô + 10).'

The M[ost] R[espectable] M[aste]r of the East kisses the forehead of M[ost] W[orshipful] M[aste]r of the West reciprocally resting both hands on the shoulders, then they bow one to the other with both hands each crossed on the chest, fingertips close to the muscles of the shoulder. They leave this position to resume that of both hands on the shoulders of each other. Then the M[ost] W[orshipful] M[aste]r of the West enacts the same ceremony on the M[ost] R[espectable] M[aste]r of the East and when the time comes for the fingertip to near the forehead of the M[ost] R[espectable] M[aste]r of the East he says,

---

11 Cinnabar is a bright scarlet form of mercury sulfide that is the most common source ore for refining elemental mercury, and is the historic source for the brilliant red or scarlet pigment known as vermilion.

'I give thanks to your infinite mercy, O' Most High and W[orshipful] M[aster], for the minors whom it pleased you to have marked with your formidable and invincible seal, for whose protection it has been and has become unto thee in all your works, virtues, words, thoughts and spiritual power and by this terrible word (pronounces the same word ô + 10) I persist in my immutable intention of being steeped in yourself as you are in me. Amen.'

He kisses the forehead of the M[ost] R[espectable] M[aste]r of the East, they both bow, their arms crossed as above and each return to their place.

The two Conductors sit in a chair placed at the feet of their Thrones and always between their Wardens. The M[ost] R[espectable] M[aste]r of the East will have on his right a stool on which will be the Bible, on the left another stool, on which will be the book of the statutes and the ceremonial order; he will hold in his lap a terracotta plate on which there will be the little box where is the colour red.

The M[ost] R[espectable] M[aste]r of the East asks the M[ost] W[orshipful] M[aste]r of the West to advance before him the eldest of the brethren that hold the ribbons of the banner to renew their obligation to the G[reat] A[rchitect] of the U[niverse], and to the Order. The M[ost] W[orshipful] M[aste]r of the West will take the eldest of these brethren, lead him with his right hand to the East, and put his right knee on the ground between the two stools which are a little in front of the M[ost] R[espectable] M[aste]r of the East, and puts his hands in the form of right angles on the two books above the stools.

When the eldest of the twelve brethren is so placed, the M[ost] W[orshipful] M[aste]r of the West returns to sit on his chair; after which the M[ost] R[espectable] M[aste]r of the East asks the Brother:

1º 'What is the manner in which to speak about the Order he has voluntarily embraced?'

2º 'What advantage he thinks he can gain from his entry into the Order?'

3º 'What purpose he imagines the Order may have?'

The M[ost] R[espectable] M[aste]r of the East then makes a small speech as a result of his answers to these three questions. Then he makes him renew his commitments as follows:

Translation of 'Le Manuscrit d'Alger' (1772)

Renewal of Commitment

'I, (NN family and baptismal [name]) *promise the G[reat] A[rchitect] of the Universe to be inviolably attached to His Holy Law, His precepts, His commandments, my religion, my King, my country and my brethren.*'

'*I promise to be a faithful observer of the laws, regulations and ceremonies of the Order of Coëns which I willingly embraced and in which I continue to persevere voluntarily. I promise on my word of honour not to evade in any way from these commitments, to obediently obey the chiefs of the Order, and of this temple in particular, in all that they will order me concerning the good of the Order and its members. I take all my brethren here present to witness the renewal of my commitments that I make in the presence of the chief Conducteurs and the dignitary officers of this temple. Thus God be my help and hold me for Time Immemorial in his Holy keeping. Amen.*'

Then the M[ost] R[espectable] M[aste]r of the East marks the forehead of the brother with the red colour, and with his finger on the forehead says:

'*Be marked, Man of the Holy and Most Holy Sign, fearful and invincible, whom the Lord hath given through the Holy Spirit virtue, strength and power as to his faithful servant Abraham; and by the same sign you are for your whole life the real emblem of Him who marks both you and I in virtue, in strength and in power. Amen.*'

As we mark the brother's forehead, the M[ost] W[orshipful] M[aste]r of the West leaves his place, comes behind him and when the M[ost] R[espectable] M[aste]r of the East has stopped speaking he takes the brother by the right hand and leads him to the free place where he was taken. He now takes the second brother, leads him to the East, makes him take the same position and returns to his chair. He does the same for the ten other celebrant brethren. The twelve celebrant brethren will continue being marked, in the same place and position in the circle as before until the end of the ceremony of the Renewal of Commitments.

If the other brethren around them are too numerous, so as not to lengthen the ceremony, the M[ost] W[orshipful] M[aste]r of the West will make two bands, the oldest of each band or the highest in rank will be at the head. He alone will take the position of the first 12 before the M[ost] R[espectable] M[aste]r of the East, he will answer for himself and his rank to the three questions and will do so for the Renewal of Commitments in his name and for all the brethren of his rank; all these brethren will have behind him their right knee on the ground, the left hand square and at a right angle to the ground, the arm lying along the body and the right hand equally square to the ground, the arm extended forward to its natural height. They will remain in this position until the brother who is at the head gets up, which they will also do to regain all their places.

After all the brethren and assistants have renewed their commitments, they have to receive the seal, given only to twelve of the celebrants. The M[ost] W[orshipful] M[aste]r of the West, if he is not a R✠, the R[espectable] M[aster], and the Inspecteur du Temple will divide the remaining dignitary officers into two bands; if there be too many brethren, he has them placed as has been said; they place themselves at the head of each band and successively lend their renewal of commitments as above.

This ceremony being finished all the dignitaries and all the other brethren resume their ordinary place of open labour, except the two Conducteurs d'Orient and d'Occident and the twelve brother celebrants. The M[ost] R[espectable] M[aste]r of the East instructs the M[ost] W[orshipful] M[aste]r of the West to have two brethren approach him from within the twelve celebrant brethern. The M[ost] W[orshipful] M[aste]r of the West takes each by the hand, one by one, and with three steps, leads them to the East and remains behind them. These two brethren and the M[ost] R[espectable] M[aste]r of the East together form a circle by reciprocally pressing their hands on each other's shoulders. Being so, the M[ost] R[espectable] M[aster] says to them in a low voice:

> 'My brethren, let him remember that the blood of the righteous cryeth vengeance again in heaven, and that in this memory you are forbidden by Jehovah to dip your hands in the blood of your Brethren, and defile your hands by any impurity, and do not be hungry for blood, nor eat it, because it is forbidden to you, because in it lieth life.'

After that, the M[ost] R[espectable] M[aste]r of the East has these two brethren placed, one on his right, the other on his left; during this time the M[ost] W[orshipful] M[aste]r of the West will fetch two other brother celebrants, which he will lead and place alike and thereafter stand behind. When the M[ost] R[espectable] M[aste]r of the East is done with them and told them the same thing as the first two, he has them placed on the right and on the left. This is used successively for these twelve brethren, so that in the end they are placed six on the right and six on the left of the M[ost] R[espectable] M[aste]r of the East; the M[ost] W[orshipful] M[aste]r of the West then takes his place.

Translation of 'Le Manuscrit d'Alger' (1772)

Note. All this ceremony has been held until now only for the dignitaries and brethren of the Temple and the Sanctuary.

After it is finished, the M[ost] W[orshipful] M[aste]r of the West enters the porch in his usual manner but without his two Wardens from the Temple where they remain. The Master of Ceremonies of the Porch then follows him by having two of the Guards bear the books that were on the two stools to the East; they will be placed in the same way to the West and will be guarded by the two brethren Guards, swords in hand and to order. The M[ost] W[orshipful] M[aste]r of the West tells the Master Inspector of the Porch to have all the Apprentices, Fellows and Masters of this class put in pairs, and thus leads them in front of him in a column, or two only if they are too numerous - the two oldest Masters will be at the head and the leader of each band will practice all that has been prescribed for the Temple.

Then all the dignitary Porch Officers will do the same.

After the M[ost] W[orshipful] M[aste]r of the West has finished his ceremony in the Porch, we will place the books back to where they were in the Temple. Then the Wardens of the Porch resume their regular seats in open labour.

This ceremony will be celebrated in the regularly assembled Temple with the four gates of the Temple open only. The three gates of the Porch do not open because there is none on this day. The battery for the opening of the Temple is that of the *Elect*[12] , four times four, which will, however, be repeated by the M[ost] W[orshipful] M[aste]r of the West and his two Wardens who are in the Temple. This battery with its addition indicates the spiritual number.

Whilst the Wardens of the Porch are returning to occupy their usual places, the Master of Ceremonies of this class goes step by step with a candle in hand asking for the Temple Light from the Master of Ceremonies of the Temple; he takes this candle and goes to light it on one of those burning on the Altar of the East; this is, in order, lit by the M[ost] R[espectable] M[aste]r of the East pronouncing in the centre [the word] ô + 10, returning it to the Master of Ceremonies of the Porch, both being in order. The latter, always in order, goes to the Throne of the West, presents the candle to the M[ost] W[orshipful] Master, who pronounces on it the same word, lights his candlestick, and then returns it to him; from there he will light the candles of the two Wardens of his class and then give this candle to the first brother guard of the Porch to light all those of other dignitaries whilst

---

12 Reference to the battery to open a lodge of Elus des Neuf; Elect of the Nine. 9 knocks; 8 together and one separate. ♪♪♪♪♪♪♪♪,♪.

another brother Guard, having lit another candle, will illuminate all those placed in the Porch according to the general ceremonial of the Order. After the lighting of the Porch is made, the M[ost] R[espectable] M[aste]r of the East or the M[ost] W[orshipful] M[aste]r of the West, or the Master Orator will make an informative speech about the ceremony of the day. We will find a specific one after this ceremony.

The instructional discourse being finished, the M[ost] R[espectable] M[aste]r of the East will close the four gates of the Temple and the three of the Porch, although the latter will not have been opened, and there would have been no word, instructions, sign, or battery given in this class. The Wardens, however, and M[ost] W[orshipful] M[aste]r of the West will usually return the signs and battery.

This closing of the Porch Class is made by ordinary usages and in accordance with those of the Temple, it alludes to the filial union of the idolatrous foreigners on leaving Egypt with the children of Israel, submitting themselves to follow the Divine and Spiritual Law that God had given by through the voice of Moses. This has been renewed ever since by the affiliation of the Gentiles to the Law of Christ, after all his spiritual operations contained in this Law were completely finished by him.

All the brethren, both of the Temple and the Porch, and the visitors who will have attended this ceremony, may afterwards make a very frugal meal together, where there will be no ceremony of the Order. The Chief will only recommend respect and decency after such a solemnity, and will see to it that there is no talk of religion, politics, or worldly things. The Chief Conductor will make a short prayer at the beginning and at the end of the meal.

After the Ceremony on the Day of the Trinity

After lighting a new flame and lighting the candle for the centre with the prescribed ceremonies, the M[ost] R[espectable] M[aste]r of the East, holding it with the left hand, draws the word of 10, then, after all that is prescribed for this ceremony, the candle is placed. After that, remaining on the right knee with only the left hand to order, the Master of Ceremonies gives him a sword. The M[ost] R[espectable] M[aste]r of the East, having taken it with his right hand, leans on it a moment during which he makes a prayer for his purification. Then he makes on himself the three signs of the sword and the fourth on the ground, which he repeats three times, ending by throwing the sword out of the circle, every time he makes a blow on the ground, he says *abrenuntio*.[13]

---

13 Latin: To renounce strongly.

Remaining in the same position, but advancing the right hand square in the field of the centre of the candle, he pronounces, at the sign of Moses, the word drawn there and says aloud:

> 'O' Lord our God, we give you the sacrifice of our spirits, of our souls and of our bodies, so that our thoughts, wills and actions will be pleasant to you in the solemnity in which we will celebrate in the honour of your Majesty and of your unitary essence: give each one of us the sincere desire and the strength to fulfil your Holy Law, so that we may all enjoy in you and by you the promises that you have deigned to make to us by thy pure mercy. Blessed be thy Holy Name ô + 10. Amen.'

Whereupon the Master of Ceremonies presents to the M[ost] R[espectable] M[aste]r of the East a candle lit by the candle of the centre, thus restored, he rises and then places it back for ordinary use. The Master of Ceremonies turns and lights all the candles, answering the words.

For the Feast of St. John the Baptist

After the return from the Mass and all the brethren having returned to the forecourt of the Temple, and the dignitaries have entered the Temple, the M[ost] R[espectable] M[aste]r of the East orders the route, which is on this day only a quarter angle to the East, ending in a double ray in the centre of which, on flat ground, is the head of a roe deer[14] placed beside the name of St John of 8, with his candle. The Master of Ceremonies then places seven swords in a circle in the centre of the room. The M[ost] R[espectable] M[aste]r of the East having lit the flame again, lights the quarter angle candle and places it with the ceremonies prescribed on the name of St John. After which he orders the entry of all the brethren into the Temple. The Master of Ceremonies places them all indistinctly with the dignitaries in a single line from the North to the West and even to the South if the brethren are too numerous, and if they were still more he would arrange them in two lines, then put himself within them. They will be placed by rank and seniority.

All the brethren being thus placed, the M[ost] R[espectable] M[aste]r of the East, will take one of the seven swords in the centre, and return to the West, whence he begins the ballet march of the right foot; At the first step, he throws his sword with his right hand around to the North saying *abrenuncio*,[15] on the second step, he does the same towards the North;

14　The original French states 'chevreuil' which means specifically a roe deer.
15　Spanish: To renounce strongly.

at the third step, towards North, and thus successively until he has arrived at the angle of the East. Having arrived there, he enters it by three steps, and drops his right knee to the ground; during this he must have his left hand to order; he makes on himself the three signs of the sword and the fourth on the deer's head by saying *abrenuncio*, which is repeated three times. He finally leaves the sword immersed in the deer's head, then remaining in the same position, he puts his right hand square on the candle, the left remains in order, pronounces three times, without any sign, the name of 8, which is below and says aloud:

> 'I exconjure thee, O' Spirit of IONAN, through you and those who are with you, to join with my spirit, my soul and my body and to present them to the Lord so that he may give me the grace that I can participate worthily in the holy operation that you have done for His greatest glory on this surface. Amen.'

The M[ost] R[espectable] M[aste]r of the East is then raised and remains standing next to the angle, after which he successively calls six other brethren of the Temple of the most advanced in ranks and age, beginning with the W[orshipful] M[aster] d'Occident who comes to do entirely the same thing, meanwhile holding on to the head of the one who makes his square. With the exception of these seven brethren, all the others are assistants.

The ceremony being finished, the M[ost] R[espectable] M[aste]r of the East will draw a circle in the centre of the room, in which he will trace the words, characters and hieroglyphs he has judged with their candles. That being done, and each having resumed his ordinary place, he opens the works to the ordinary. He makes an informative speech on the ceremony of the day and then proceeds to the appointment of the dignitaries or the confirmation of the elders; to the verification of the labours, and to the brethren for their advancement in rank and the inspection of the Temple records. After which he closes the labours for ordinary use and has the line erased.

This day is intended to give the Sovereign access to all of the operations which were made in the Temple during the year.

For lunch see the Trinity.
For the Feast of St. John the Evangelist

All the ceremonial is the same as the preceding ones with the exception of a goat's head with the name of the St John the Evangelist of 8 in the quartered angle. If there is some dignitary replacements to be done, the M[ost] R[espectable] M[aste]r of the East makes it a day acting without ceremony.

For Easter, the 3rd of the Three Feasts is celebrated

Good to copy, not to follow.

On returning from the Mass and all the brethren having returned to the court, the M[ost] R[espectable] M[aste]r of the East roasts a whole lamb after having removed all that was appropriate; all the brethren are decorated with their rank at the banquet served at the usual hour. We open the labour as the two previous holidays without order or instructions. Then the M[ost] R[espectable] M[aste]r of the East] makes an exorcism on the lamb placed before him and blesses it. Afterwards, he cuts out two fillets of the lamb in all their length being careful not to saw; he divides them into as many small portions as there are brethren at the table and presents them one to each at the end of a fork; a single bite is enough; he also gives each of them at the same time a mouthful of bread. The brethren remain standing throughout this ceremony without leaving their place; the M[ost] R[espectable] M[aste]r of the East does the rounds by making the relevant prayers in a low voice.

What will remain of the Lamb shall be given to the poor.

This ceremony alludes to the spiritual food that C[hrist] gave to his disciples through his death.

The lamb being eaten as mentioned, the brethren sit down and eat their meal as usual. See previous festivals.

Outline of a Speech of Instruction for the Feast of the Trinity

The M[ost] R[espectable] M[aste]r of the East is in the centre of a circle surrounded by twelve brethren each holding a ribbon of the banner, this alludes to the second operation in which the Lord manifested to Moses to give him the power and the strength to deliver his chosen people from the slavery of Egypt. The twelve ribbons allude to the twelve divine spiritual gifts which Moses received there, and which made him so strong, so learned, and so superior in all his spiritual operations good and evil. He himself became the 'second type'[16] of manifestation of the Living God's glory as Noah had been the first when the Lord chose him to be a spectator of his justice against the Earth and its inhabitants whom he reduced to corpses with the exception of the small number kept in the Ark to bear witness to this scourge of which God has punished the Earth and its inhabitants and of his righteousness that he exercised against those who march against his Law, Precepts and Commandments. Noah is, therefore, a 'first type'[17] by his testimony and by the reconciliation he made for the rest of the mortals with God as he learned to know by a mysterious sign, the rainbow, that God had given life to the Earth and reconciled the rest of the mortals with it. Noah reconciled all with the Lord. It was from this early period that Noah's labour was known as a powerful operation on the virtue of the waters which are the second principle of universal Creation. And Jehovah manifested his second divine operation in the presence of Moses in the wilderness of Horeb, where he had called him to receive his Orders of Power.[18] The forest of this wilderness was considerable; Moses, being in the centre of this forest, heard a terrible voice, and immediately saw around him twelve streaks of fire which surrounded him so promptly that he feared he would be consumed; his confusion was so great that he could not bear the position he had taken to receive the commandments of God, he completed his prostration by pressing his face into the ground, his material and physical sight could no longer bear the great spiritual fire which surrounded him. In this new position he finally received the orders of the Lord and was marked with the *quadruple* seal of God, two of which were visibly imprinted on his forehead beside each eye in the form of two rays of spiritual fire that made his face dazzling to everyone's eyes when he made use of his *quadruple* divine power. These are the two rays that are commonly taken for two horns on the forehead of Moses. It was this spiritual fire that surrounded the forest of Horeb to remove any layman just as God had appeared to Moses in a burning bush. The circle formed by twelve brethren is the figure of this mysterious circumference. The M[ost] R[espectable] M[aste]r of the East at the centre of this circle represents the Lord in the desert Horeb; the entry of the M[ost] W[orshipful] M[aste]r of the West into the circle alludes to that of Moses in the mysterious circumference. The secret communication

---

16 According to Pasqually, Hely, or the Christ, manifested through the line of prophets, the guides of humanity, and those called the Elect. Among these, he cites Abel, Enoch, Noah, Melchizedek, Joseph, Moses, David, Solomon, Zerubbabel, and Jesus Christ, who were all channels or 'types' for the manifestation of Hely. However, he considers that Hely manifested his greatest glory or 'type' in Jesus Christ.
17 Another reference to the 'types' or the Elect; the lineage of manifestations or embodiments of the Christ.
18 Deuteronomy 4:10, KJV. Specially the day that thou stoodest before the Lord thy God in Horeb, when the Lord said unto me, Gather me the people together, and I will make them hear my words, that they may learn to fear me all the days that they shall live upon the earth, and that they may teach their children.

that the two conductors of the Temple are heard saying in the centre of the circle allude to the conversation Moses had with God secretly in the presence of his spiritual court to bring his people out of slavery, to direct him and lead him into strength and power at his destination.

The twelve brethren holding flame-coloured ribbons allude to the twelve chief leaders of Israel on whom Moses made his twelve spiritual gifts reversible without diminishing his power for the special conduct of the people of God who were expressly subject to Moses.

The lights that shine in this Temple each have their mysterious name, their virtues and powers, and allude to the various holy spirits who witnessed the operation that the Lord made for Moses and his beloved people. The mark put on the forehead of the twelve brethren by the M[ost] R[espectable] M[aste]r of the East is the figure of the one whom Moses put on the forehead of the twelve chief leaders of Israel to whom he communicated by means of the Blood Sign of the Holocaust of Pacification, the virtue, the power and the spiritual authority of Divine correspondence.

The oath that the twelve celebrant brethren make in the hands of the M[ost] R[espectable] M[aste]r of the East refers to the ceremonial acceptance of divine worship which the leaders made in the hands of Moses to serve as a ceremonial rule for putting into practice the virtues and powers which had been transmitted to them by divine authority before the Law was given.

The obligation renewed by all present brethren of the Temple alludes to the acceptance that the Israelites made to God's Law that Moses gave them after having descended from the top of the mysterious mountain called Sinai.[19]

The Renewal of Commitment that all the brethren of the Order make in the hands of the M[ost] W[orshipful] Master of the West after the great ceremony, allude to the oath of fidelity, submission and affiliation which the idolatrous foreigners made to adopt the Divine Law that Moses had given to the Children of Israel.

(Closing: Exhortations to follow the Laws of the Order are made since they are the emblem of both the spiritual ceremonies)

---

19   The celestial realm is symbolised by Mount Sinai.

Personal Instruction
Work in the Presence of the Sovereign Alone for any Day of the Week Whatsoever

In a Double Triangle

A radiant circle in the centre of which W.36. [blank], West V.92. [vakem], North V.67. [vabam], South V.27. [vakiel].

At the angles of the double triangle, the East S.3. [sephas], to the Northeast I.8. [ïaaïm], to the Northwest Andreas, to the West M.18. [mael], to the Southwest I.9. [ïoanan], to the Southeast V.3. [vael].

In the Third Inner Circle

East	the character and hieroglyph of Sephas, in the middle T.16. [thuzraï]. on the right the sign of the angel of Saturn with his name v.r. P.22. [pielzal] on the left the sign of the angel of the Sun with his name M.14. [mikael].
North West	the character and hieroglyph of Andreas, in the middle T.25. [taphta] on the right, the sign of the angel of Mercury with his name N.1. [nuriel] on the left the sign of the angel of Mars with his name v.r. K.2. [kados].
West	on the right the sign of the angel of Venus with her name H.100. [blank] in the middle the sign ïaa. on the left the sign of the angel of the Moon with his name G.7. [gabbriel].
South West	the character and hieroglyph of ïoanan, in the middle K.83. [korieli]. on the right the sign of the angel of the Earth with his name v.r. R.18. [reziel]. on the left the sign of the angel of Jupiter with his name v.r. Z.3. [zebul].

In the Second Circle

East	the character and good intelligence of Saturn, in the middle S.22. [samabeï].
North-East	character and good intelligence, in the middle S.59. [sariepel]. *of the Sun*
North	the character, the hieroglyph and the good intelligence of Mercury in the middle M.2. [markiel].
North-West	the character and good intelligence of March in the middle M.66. [maba].
West	the character, the hieroglyph and the good intelligence of Venus in the middle V.1. [vaïel].
South-West	the character, the hieroglyph and the good intelligence of the Moon in the middle L.2. [lamaha].
South	all evil intelligences
South East	the character and good intelligence of Jupiter in the middle I.30. [ïadin].

In the First Outer Circle

All the characters, hieroglyphs and letters I have received, supported to the Northeast by A.13. [amaïel]. to the Northwest by C.6. [curaniel], to the Southwest by B.1. [bagnakin] and to the Southeast by D.2. [dabriel].

Correspondances

In the plan I have put the letters a b c d in the correspondences

East	A.58. [agrathum]. *in the centre and* E.3.5.10. [eraïn, eliazak, elim]. *in triangle*
West	B.74. [baïamas] *in the centre and* F.33.24.79. [femaraï, fermaoz, felimar] *in triangle*
North	C.41. [capherma] *in the centre and* G.10.16.19. [gaha, gradeban, grimar] *in triangle*
South	D.27. [danaïel] *in the centre and* H.23.12.17. [hoblïn, heloïn, hasmadaï]. *in triangle*

Translation of 'Le Manuscrit d'Alger' (1772)

A candle on each word and name, as well as that of the Sovereign.

This work will only be completed in order to ask for the repetition of the characters, hieroglyphs, hieroglyphic characters, names, letters and numbers that the operative has already received during the course of his labours; [e.g] to ask from whom each of these things is held, what they mean each in particular, and to what use they should be employed.

The operative will especially and strongly address his Patrons and his Guardian [by name]. If he knows not the latter, he will replace it by such a name of 7 as he wills, but from then on he will only adopt it until he is better informed.

If the operative often has the same character in front of his eyes, whether by day or by night, it appears that it is his Guardian's; he will therefore place it next to his real or adoptive name and will also ask for its confirmation, either in this very work, or in a dream or a vision.

The operative may specifically request the repetition and confirmation of such characters, names and letters that have affected him most in time. I would advise an operative that for this work of personal instruction he should call only the Sovereign into his circles, but moreover he should be alone at his operations, unless another well-connected R✠ agrees to solely serve during the operation, in revenge for another time and to avoid the confusion and uncertainty of not knowing which of the two the passes and appearances are intended.

The operative will make invocations, instructions and conjurations similar to this work.

This work can be done indifferently each day of the week, one day only or three days in a row; I would recommend the latter course because one can obtain during the second or the third day what one might not have obtained in a single day; moreover, the operative is better disposed the second and third day that the first.

One must have the intention of naming the Spirit of the Planet of the Day whenever one names his Patrons or his Guardian. Furthermore, it will be necessary to make sure and observe the preparations, precautions and ceremonies used for all the regular works in order to avoid the confusion that too large a quantity of requests can bring.

faith, hope, charity
Amen

Work on Adam, on All the Planets, with Junctions, 4 Circles, 4 Vautours[20] 4 Correspondences and 4 Quarter Circles.

First Circle

A triangle at its centre A.38. [algaïa], the angles in the East V.25.[viha] Southwest V.71. [verpiel] V.67. [vabam] Northwest; a candle on every word ....4.

Second Circle

East	the sign of the angel of Saturn, its planetary character, its character and its good intelligence, with the names Betsaléël and shannelé.
Northeast	the sign of the angel of Venus, its planetary character 1; his character, his hieroglyph, and his good intelligence, with the names Caleb and hei.
North	the sign of the angel of Mars, its planetary character 5; his character and good intelligence, with the names Ooliab, and Karina.
North West	the sign of the angel of the Earth, with the names Josuë and Rafaël.
West	the sign of the angel of the Moon, its planetary character 5; his character, his hieroglyph and his good intelligence, with the names Aaron and Gabbriël.
South West	the sign of the angel of Jupiter, his planetary character 6, his character and good intelligence, with the names heïbli, and Zaihab.
South	the sign of the angel of the Sun, its planetary character, its character, and its good intelligence, with the names Mozë and Mikaël.
South East	the sign of the angel of Mercury, its planetary character, its character, its hieroglyph, and its good intelligence, with the names Ur[iël] and Nuriël.

---

20 Vautours are the secondary circles figured on the operational cloth or tracings.

Third Circle

East...	Rab boni	R.48 [requel]
East North East...	Habukuc	O.33 [osamaz]
North East...	Jean	I.9 [iziael]
North North East...	Aaron	P.38 [pizimo]
North...	Cephas	S.3 [sephas]
North North West...	Abraham	K.63 [kierphaz]
North West...	Andreas	Andreas
West North West...	Ur	P.23 [porkatol]
West...	Henoc	K.74 [keph]
West South West...	Josuë	I.40 [ïabina]
South West...	Louis 9	S.59 [sariepel]
South South West...	Moïsées	H.31 [habad]
South...	Ozée	M.21 [misraïn]
South South East...	Betsahël	L.96 [learma]
South East...	Job	L.23 [liephim]
East South East...	Caleb	K.7 [kanema]
a Candle on each name...	16	

R.48 [requel]

O.33 [osamaz]

I.9 [ïoanan]

P.38 [pizimo]

S.3 [sephas]

K.63 [kierphim]

Translation of 'Le Manuscrit d'Alger' (1772)

P.23 [porkatot]

K.74 [keph]

I.40 [ïabina]

S.59 [sariepel]

H.31 [habad]

M.21 [misraïn]

L.96 [learma]

L.23 [liephim]

K.7 [kanena]

Fourth Circle, Adam Alone

East	West South West the character 53 and the hieroglyph 51 of Adam and between two O.52. [oliam].
North East	Character and hieroglyph 57 and between two S.56. [selseph].
North	Character and hieroglyph 55 and between two M.59. [milifin].
North West	Character 52 and hieroglyph 54 and between two L.60. [lazarab].
West	Character 54 and hieroglyph 52 and between two V.56. [vakaz].
South West	Character and hieroglyph 58 and between two M.54. [marzamon].
South	Character and hieroglyph 56 and between two T.6. [tauaha].
South East	Character 51.hieroglyph 53 and between two I.53. [ïepharez].
East North East	Character and hieroglyph 59 and between two D.26. [danaïel].

S.56 [selseph]

M.59 [milifin]

L.60 [lazarab]

V.56 [vakaz]

M.54 [marzamon]

T.6 [tauaha]

I.53 [ïerpharez]

D.26 [dabeba]

C.41 [capherma]

Correspondences

East... *S.29* [serpier]

West... *V.10* [vaïa]

North... *M.35* [meram]

South... *D.21* [darkaoz]

a candle on each name... 4

Vautours

North East... *E.4; C.48* [elia; crebiaman]

South West... *A.63; C.80* [avariel; carmaphal]

South East... *F.38; C.95* [fizamak; cebamaz]

North West... *T.27; C.65* [timial; cazueli]

a candle on each name... 8

Quarter Circles

East...at the centre in Hebrew the Great Word that one should never pronounce.[21] *It is supplemented by that of the centre of the Circles: in triangle around him, A.90* [atramaï]; *B.100* [babad]; *C.8* [cassiel].= *N.2.* [neran] *in the double ray; O.31* [orkiel].

North...the same word in the centre and same in the Triangle D.2 [dabriel]; *E.27* [eriepa]; *F.28.* [fizamak] = *P.41* [piar]; *Q.8.* [qarbier].

West...the same word, same in a triangle G.79 [gerpiam]; *H.66.* [heframnel]; *I.24* [ïumael] = *R.9* [rabazar]; *S.6* [sahen].

South...the same word, same in a triangle K.29 [kermiel]; *L.31.* [larzael]; *M.16* [maraï]. = *T.91.* [tau]; *U.93.* [urdaz].

A candle on each name...24

The Sun on the ray of the 3rd circle to the East;

The Moon on the ray of the 4th circle to the West;

The Serpent outside, with the word of the centre in a triangle and three candles each angle point on the word...3.

---

21 Tetragrammaton.

Quarter circle on the Planets For testing a R✠

--- ✠ ---

A large quarter circle will be drawn, the upper corner of which will be in the East corner of the room, if possible.

East	the sign of the angel of Saturn, its planetic character, its character and its good intelligence, with the names Betsaléël and shannelé.
Northeast	the sign of the angel of Venus, its planetic character 1; his character, his hieroglyph, and his good intelligence, with the names Caleb and hei.
North	the sign of the angel of Mars, its planetic character 5; his character and good intelligence, with the names Ooliab, and Karina.
North West	the sign of the angel of the Earth, with the names Josuë and Rafaël.
West	the sign of the angel of the Moon, its planetic character 5; his character, his hieroglyph and his good intelligence, with the names Aaron and Gabbriël.
South West	the sign of the angel of Jupiter, his planetic character 6, his character and good intelligence, with the names heïbli, and Zaihab.
South	the sign of the angel of the Sun, its planetic character, its character, and its good intelligence, with the names Mozë and Mikaël.
South East	the sign of the angel of Mercury, its planetic character, its character, its hieroglyph, and its good intelligence, with the names Ur[iël] and Nuriël.

At the top of the angle of the work, we will draw a dominant word of 10 between three candles that we will enclose within a single ray.

Below this ray are all the baptismal names and signs of the assistants with a candle placed on each name. If the operative is alone, or if it is considered appropriate, one can put other names such as those of the Apostles, Prophets, Patriarchs, etc.

These names will be enclosed by a double ray, and at each end a name of 7 with its candle will be placed, the rest will be filled by the names and signs of absent R✠, as well as those of the Sovereign in the centre of it all with their candles. Further down at a proportionate distance, a double circle in the centre of which a word of 10 and its candle, between the

✠ 75

two rays the sign and baptismal name of the operative but without a candle because it will be placed in a square with three of the upper triangles; outside this double circle, the character, the hieroglyph and the good intelligence of the planet of the day of labour will be drawn without candles.

Below, three spokes closing the quarter circle; at each end of the central rays a name of 8 with its candle.

In the inner intervals of these three rays, a planetary character of each of the seven planets, with as many names out of 7 as possible taken to their letters and to each a candle.

In the outer intervals of the three rays, the signs and names of the Angels of the four other planets and the Earth; as well as the characters, hieroglyphs and good intelligences of the four other planets with four names taken from 7 to their letters, and a candle to each of these nine names.

Below these three rays and at a proportionate distance, a double circle similar to that of the quarter circle, in the centre a word out of 10 with a candle, between the two rays in the East is the name of the Angel of the day, to the Southeast is the name of the Angel of the morrow, and to the Southwest the name of the Angel of the day before; outside and around this double circle the signs of the Angels of the three employed planets, placed next to their names. The Seven Psalms and litanies will be said and contemplation will be done in this outer circle.

Directly above the Eastern corner and at a suitable height, we will draw on the wall a Star enclosed in a circle and enclosing it a Sun in which we will put a word of 10.

At each corner of the Star will be placed one word out of 7, one out of 4, one out of 3, one out of 6 and one out of 9.

Between the Star and the floor, the character, the hieroglyph and the good intelligence of tomorrow's planet.

To the West, at the same height, the same Star and circle will be traced on the wall with a Moon in the centre and the same word as in the Sun on the East wall, the angles of the Star will contain as many names falling on the same numbers, both taken from the three employed planets.

Along the ray of the East to the South and about a foot or a foot and a half from this ray will be traced a large Serpent's head to the East from which it will release an arrow.

Between the Serpent and the ray, a triangle containing the word of the East between three candles, outside this triangle a name out of 5 of three syllables shared by the three faces: the rest of the intervals are filled by the evil intelligences of the seven planets and other evil hieroglyphs.

The triangle and the word which it encloses is in white chalk; the Serpent, his name, and the evil intelligences in charcoal.

This work will be done on the fourth day of the Crescent Moon as far as possible; at the will of the operative it could consist of one or three days preparations and as many days in thanksgiving.

One can turn at will the top of the angle of the quarter circle to the most favourable side which always becomes the East.

Work is begun by an exconjuration on the Serpent at the South after the blessing of the outline and all things customary in the work, and having been provided with the talisman and the dagger.

The following morning after all labours are complete, the Lord will be thanked by prayers at will.

If during the exconjuration, the operative or his assistants perceive some bad attractions, the operative will begin apostrophising the perverse:

> 'May your iniquity, your malice, and your action [be gone] spirits that I curse away from our presence and this place by the virtue of that formidable name that I invoke against you all and by which I command you ô + 10.'

The word dominating the work is pronounced.

If, on the contrary, we perceive something good, the operative will say, when addressing the good spirits:

> 'Blessed are those who come in the name of the Lord, by whom I call upon you ô + 10.'

The same dominant word is pronounced and we invite them to make themselves known more distinctly.

Translation of 'Le Manuscrit d'Alger' (1772)

Exconjuration Prayer on the Serpent at the South

'I conjure and exorcise you, cursed Serpent and all the demons subject to Lucifer, by the virtue and power of the terrible God ô + 10 that I adore; in a moment you will all leave my presence and flee from my operation here traced, as long as I am here, I will be present. Obey my command, get out of our presence and out of this room without causing scandal, noise or fright. I curse you all, Infernal Spirits by the power that the Creator has given me over you, He forbid you to ever dare try to induce me in any way whatsoever; I particularly curse you because of (this or that vice) to which you caused me and from which I release myself, there is naught between you and I any more, and I rely on this by the mercy of God ô +10.'

'It is by this name, before which all bends, that I conjure you and command you, so that His omnipotent power may work on you, according to my desire, in the earthly region and in this room in particular, as well as in your cursed region. See, perverse Spirits, whom I command as your Master, superior and inferior demons, then recognise my commandment which is founded and supported by these four words of the quadruple divine power ô + 10. ô + 8. ô + 7. ô + 4.'

One should then place the left foot on the head of the Serpent, extending the left hand forward over it with a talisman held between the fingers in the form of a globe and say:

'By the power of these four names, let the exterminating Angel of the Vengeful and Remunerating God put you all on the run and throw you into your hellish abyss as quickly as this straw breaks and this dust is scattered.'

One breaks a straw and blows on the dust, beats three shots of the left foot on the head of the Serpent, then places it back and continues:

'And thou, Infernal Serpent, because you dared to tempt the Man-God your judge, I curse you and bind you by the formidable name ô + 10, so that you may never take from me in the spiritual, nor the temporal, nor in the material *realm. I curse you, condemn and bind you, you and all demonic spirits of the Southern region, renouncing all my faculties and powers to your thoughts, your wills and your works and those of all your followers.'*

The Serpent's head is trampled with the foot, then it is stabbed on the head, once more in the middle of the body and one more on the tail; the dagger is then thrown into the southernmost angle. Then the labour begins.

Translation of 'Le Manuscrit d'Alger' (1772)

Prayer of Invocation[22]

'I exconjure you, powerful and pure Spirits who rule the Spiritual armies and who are constantly before the Throne of the Lord, I exconjure you, Spirits, who are sent in time for the manifestation of the Glory and Justice of the Creator; I exconjure you, Spirits, who are in charge of the formation, the maintenance, and the succession of all celestial and terrestrial forms; I conjure you and summon you all, by the formidable power of that sacred name ô + 10 of the God who alone has been, is, and will be; who alone is the principle, the life and the end of all things; who alone is strong, Holy, and High; who alone has founded the Ages, the World, the Sky, the Earth, and the Sea, and who alone will destroy them; who alone has been able to separate the day from the night, the Light from the Darkness, the pure from the unclean; and who alone has been able to seal the immutable works of his thought, his will, and his action by his name and by revealing two great luminaries; I exconjure you all, O' Spirits as infinite in number, as different in names and virtues, so that the invincible force of the name I invoke before thee, ô +10 and with you, you deign to be favourable in all occasions where I have recourse to you by this name for my spiritual and temporal needs. Help me according to the virtues and faculties that are distributed to you by the tenderness and the mercy of the Lord for the benefit of Man. Hear the requests that I make in this work, contribute by your intercession and by your care to their fulfilment according to my desire, and as much as in all or in part they be in conformity with the will of the Creator, our God. Substitute by your intelligence all that my uncertain will had contrary to this unalterable will. Purify now and forever my body, my heart and my soul by your purity, by your inspirations, by your charity for Man, for this creature so precious to the Lord, so majestic in its origin, so weak and so degraded today by his own fault, but still so worthy of your care and your help since the promise of his Redemption. O' Spirits emanated, as I do, from the fruitful bosom of the Eternal Father, you know that his glory of which you are so jealous is not complete so long as Man remains subject to his Justice; It is to shorten the course of this justice, the effect of which is necessary, however, you are commanded to watch over us

---

22 Manuscript note states; 'standing in the centre after confession'.

and to guide us when we call you sincerely to lead us to the foot of the Divine Repairer who has redeemed us by the greatest mystery of charity and by the loving comforter by whom this mystery is constantly accomplished.'

'*I particularly address you, O' Blessed Spirits, who are charged by the LORD, to watch over the complete reconciliation of my spiritual being; I conjure you by the powerful name of God, merciful and compassionate, ô + 10., to come to the help of my soul whenever it is in danger of succumbing to evil; whenever it calls you by its desires, its sighs, and its meditations; whenever it is hungry and thirsty for intelligence, instruction and advice. I ask it more particularly to you O'* (one names his known or adopted Guardian Angel) *to which I am expressly entrusted by the Eternal; and I implore you to help me to obtain the protection and assistance of the Spirits I have invoked and the submission of those who remain to in voke me.'*

'*I am also particularly speaking to you, Spirits who are charged by the Eternal to watch over the formation, the maintenance and the succession of the parts which constitute my material body; I conjure you by the same powerful name of the Creator God, and the first cause of all that appears, ô + 10, to come to the aid of my material bodily form whenever it is in danger of premature dissolution; Whenever any of its parts lose its equilibrium and the order established for its duration thus fixed by the Lord; and whenever I call you to restore and repair the disturbance of my health; I submit to you and the spirit powers superior to yours, which is my established guide and my Guardian ô +* (one names it) *and I order it even more particularly to you ô + L.64. [lakïeli] for the constitution of my form and to you ô + L.69 [levuit] for the work and maintenance of my form, and to you ô + L.76. [labaïel] for the repair and succession of the parts of my form until the moment becomes fixed for its complete destruction; Unite all three to fulfil my request and tell me clearly what I must do or avoid for the preservation of my health in general.'*

'*I am also addressing you particularly, namely, you spirits, freed from the bonds of matter, who now enjoy the fruit of your virtues and whose names I have the good fortune to wear, O'* (we call our real and adoptive patrons). *I exconjure you, by the name you have so faithfully and invoked fervently ô + 10 to contribute to my eternal salvation by your prayers and your intercession with the Father of Mercies, with the Son Redeemer and with the*

Translation of 'Le Manuscrit d'Alger' (1772)

Comforter Spirit. Get for me the graces, the help and the clemency of the Godhead who will reward you today in the battles that you have delivered in this stay of which I am bitter; make me come out triumphant as you assist me with your Light.'

'Finally, I address directly to you, the powerful Spirits who direct the planets by overseeing those who govern them, O' (we call the eight Angels of the planets) *I conjure you by this name which is your law ô + 10 to make known each one according to your load all that I need to know concerning your Stars, their inhabitants, their destinations and their actions and influences on each other, particularly on the Earth. I ask it more especially to you O'* (we call the Angel of the day) *to let me know everything about your planet and its direct relationship with the land that I live, with particular forms and with all reasonable and unreasonable beings therein enclosed.'*

'In the name of God Almighty ô +10 I conjure you all, Spirits that I have invoked in my image and divine likeness, by virtue of your relationships and your mission in the temporal because the only Man whose guides and whose companions you are established with, I implore you by the infinite power of the names of the Lord ô +10 that you hear favourably the requests and prayers that I make to the Lord through your channel, that you carry them to the foot of his Throne, purified by you, and that your ardent and efficacious vows will bring me to fulfilment in this Labour and throughout the course of my temporal life. O' Spirits who come closer to the Majesty of the One Who Is, carry also my prayers for all the works of the Creator, for all his creatures, for all Nature! Join me in obtaining from his infinite clemency a softening to the privation where are condemned those who have not yet satisfied his justice since their separation from matter; join me to obtain from his mercy the propagation of the light of his name, his worship, and his will among our fellows; join me finally to obtain from his immutability a means to shorten the time when everything must return to the loving Unity from which everything thus emanated. Amen.'

Specific demands will be made without confusion, by addressing Spirits similar to each request. If the planet in action is that of the day and offers a cross, it is a sign of success.

Translation of 'Le Manuscrit d'Alger' (1772)

Confession Made to the Centre after having lit the Candle

'O' Lord, Holy and Ineffable, Father of All Things, ô BAB, ô + 10, you whose fearsome eyes see and know all and whose essence embraces everything; you whose reign is Eternal and Majesty incomprehensible; you whose fertile flame is maintained by its own splendour, and which from your essence streams inexhaustible Light. Your infinite Spirit produces this inexhaustible source of virtue and power which will not be lacking in the generation of which your goodness constantly fills and whose nature you fill with Eternity ô BAB, ô AVA, you have created very holy beings who are standing near your Throne and who compose your divine court, beings who are admirably similar to your eternal Spirit and loving essence and have established themselves as superior to the Angels who announce your will to the world; O' Merciful Father, O' Most tender of Mothers, O' Son, O' Form of all Forms, O' Spirit Core; Harmony and Number of All Things, O' Holy, Holy, Holy (ô + 10) be forever praised, blessed, and adored. Amen, Amen, Amen.'

'O' my God, O' God of Power, Righteousness and Goodness, take a look (ô + 10) on your creature (NN) prostrate and humbled before you. All unworthy hear now my voice, hear it again, and hear my cry, O' thou who is more excellent than all that Man can know! I have sinned against you through my own fault, I have transgressed thy Law, I misjudged your power, I violated your Glory. I am at once a perjurer, an ingrate, a rebel; but, O' my Father, O' my Creator, I admit my crime and my error and I dare even to hope for your mercy and that you can forgive me. I love your invincible power that delivered me a criminal to the rigours of thy righteousness, I love your immutable Justice that is exerted on me only to wash my iniquity and I love your ineffable goodness that absolves me and gives me back innocence under your satisfied power. Finally, I adore you, (ô + 10), vengeful and remunerative God of Heaven, Earth and Hell, I praise you and bless you for all that you have done and will do for or against me since the beginning of time until its destruction. Amen, Amen, Amen.'

'It is through your Wisdom, ô + 10, that the Ruler has had all power in Heaven, on Earth, and on all the works that thou hast done to govern them in righteousness and holiness; it is through her that Enoch brought men from their errors, which Noah commanded the Spirits scattered in the elements; it is through thy Wisdom that Abraham, Isaac, Jacob were the objects of your Covenant, blessing and promises; it is through her that Moses saved your chosen people from the land of Egypt, built you a Holy Ark, and proclaimed thy Law, that Joshua brought this beloved people into the promised land and established it there according to your will; it is by your Wisdom that Solomon raised you a beautiful Temple in this Holy Land and placed there the Ark of your Covenant and that Zerubabble was another saviour of your people and another builder of a less perfect Temple, it is true, since he could not bring back your Ark; it is at last your Wisdom itself which in the time marked by your decrees has come down among us in the loving person of your Christ, to reconcile all things, to restore and renew. But, not yet satisfied with so many benefits spread over men of all ages your inexhaustible goodness also wants all these actions, all these gifts, all these powers to be united on the righteous man who fulfils your Law, who follows thy Precepts and observes your Commandments! By that, you make Man if not your equal, ô + 10, who alone is, at least your most perfect image and your most beautiful likeness and it is your wisdom that knows how to bring the creature closer to its Creator! O' Depth, O' Abyss of Charity! You give us blessings, ô +10, only to make us more and more worthy of all your love, and your glory does not seem satisfied if the least of your creatures has not yet returned to you; it is there, no doubt, O' Source of Mercy, the cause of the Divine Repairer whom you have deigned to grant us! O' who can ever understand this mystery of salvation, this work of your wisdom that reconciles the impure with the Saint, the Earth with the Sky, the Darkness even with the Light. But above all, O' my God, who will dare to ask you for this wisdom, this ineffable price which is given to the righteous man on Earth and which perhaps refuses in the heavens the purest Spirit?'

'Is it I who am so criminal in so many respects, I who is soiled from the womb; I who is perjured, ungrateful, and rebellious and every day more and more guilty? ...ô + 10, you are the terrible God of Vengeance, it is true...but a contrite and humble heart stands before you! a repentant soul giving way to your *just wrath...my God, are you also pleased to say to you the Father of Infinite Mercies while trembling over the wrath that I deserve, yes my God, it will be me, a poor sinner who dares to ask, me to you, I will dare to implore the mercy which you deign to continuously offer me so freely; I will dare to ask you for your wisdom with the confidence that I will be answered by you; For O' God, Great, All-Powerful, where are you? Where shall you find a righteous man on Earth if your grace does not go first to a sinner who, like me, is only worthy of your wrath? It is therefore you who justifies the sinner to be filled then with your blessings by the gift of your wisdom; it is you whose immutable kindness and justice absolutely desires that sooner or later Man, your beloved Labour, be happy in Thee by Thy wisdom; it is you, finally, who, to give us this salutary wisdom, have deigned to make it known to us in the midst of our errors, and our darkness, so that we may desire it and seek it in preference to all others. As like Solomon, who was found worthy to build you a Temple, to place there the eternal Ark of your Covenant, and deserved to hear your oracles there.'*

'*I therefore throw myself with confidence, ô + 10, into your merciful bosom; I carry the overwhelming burden of my iniquities, my defilements, and my horrible degradation. Receive your humiliated creature and allow yourself to yield by the confession of my crimes, by my repentance and by your hope in your mercy; Remember, ô + 10, the merits of your powerful Son, your Redeemer, whose powerful sacrifice is always between you and I. Take away from me all my iniquities. Erase all the stains with which I have stained your image; Break forever the criminal ties that subjected me to my enemy; Purify my whole being; thy Consoling Spirit be felt by my soul; thy mercy soften the rigours of your righteousness, ô +10, come and visit your creature; May I experience those delicious tears, those impulses, those sensations which are the forerunners of your Wisdom; pour out on me the salutary remedy of your grace and make me taste, O' God of Peace, ô + 10, these vehicles of a holy joy reserved for the soul converted. May my vows and my prayer extend, ô + 10, over all my fellows; May all of them enjoy the felicity of throwing themselves with confidence into the bosom of a God, of a Father who constantly holds out his arms and who calls us at every moment of life. Be praised, worshiped and blessed forever. Be propitious, ô + 10, ô + 10. Amen, Amen, Amen.'*

'O' Supreme Majesty, ô + 10, who deigns to watch over the fate of your creatures, hear your man (NN) whom you have loved from the birth of centuries, admit me to the number of thy elect to whom you grant your Wisdom; I exconjure you by the power you have given me and by the immutable promise that you made me, that you would answer me whenever I sincerely invoke you. Give me your Wisdom, that which goes before you, who knows your works, who applauds and without which your man has no knowledge, no virtue, no power. Hear my voice, ô + 10, hear my prayer and give it the strength it lacks by my indignity. Hear my prayer as you have answered that of your elected ones at all times, give me, like them, your Wisdom whom has taught them to know thy Will, thy Glory and thy Works. Shine on me a ray of your Wisdom, just to make me worthy of your eyes, O' God of Love and Mercy, then O' God of Love and Mercy, my thought, my will and my actions will be assured; then I will be wise in spiritual, temporal and material knowledge; then I will truly become your image and likeness on Earth; I know better how to love you, to lead you better at using all that you put in my power. When your wisdom will be with me; I protest you, ô + 10, to use it only for the benefit of the Earth and its inhabitants and to acquire the knowledge of what will be most pleasing to you: for it is your wisdom that will make me know all things, which will lead me in all my spiritual and temporal operations that will preserve me from all present and future danger and which will inspire me to lead men and to govern them with justice. It is your wisdom that will make me walk steadfastly in thy ways and faithfully observe thy Law, thy Precepts and thy Commandments; it will give me the intelligence of your judgments, of your law, of your worship and of your name, and by that I will one day return to the Glory that you had for me, all according to your Holy Will and for your Greater Glory ô + 10. Amen, Amen, Amen.'

'ô + 10, Almighty God, worshiped by your Celestial Spirits blessing thy Holy Name; by virtue of that ineffable name before which all things bow, in Heaven, on Earth, in Hell, after having forgiven me all my iniquities and erased them from before you, put the height to your mercy, give me thy Wisdom that will give me some correspondence with spirits to whom your kindness has deigned to put in intimate connection with all my present existence; I desire this spiritual correspondence only to acquire what will be useful to me to glorify your Holy Name more worthily and to obtain a more

Translation of 'Le Manuscrit d'Alger' (1772)

perfect knowledge and understanding of the worship you require from Man; I desire it to better fulfil your will by a greater certainty of myself both in my past and future state than in my present state! Finally, O' Soul Immutable, give me a spiritual correspondence, receive my prayer so that I can, at last fulfilling my destination, be an active and useful minister of your glory, your justice and your mercy to all other beings. Be conducive to me, ô + 10 and let my cries rise to you. Amen, Amen, Amen.'

Translation of 'Le Manuscrit d'Alger' (1772)

Extract Preparation and Precaution for Receiving R✠

The R✠ only enjoy in their quality as men, images and divine resemblances two things that are really in their power, it is the various ceremonial acts for their operations which are four in number; at each operation they are given a single power which makes four powers, which with the four ceremonies or consecrations complete the number eight. To all these things are accurately given hours, days, weeks, moons, months, and years: so by following exactly and scrupulously what is prescribed to us by God himself, we must expect a happy success.

The accuracy of the ceremony alone is not enough. Great accuracy and holiness of conduct are still required from the leader who conducts the circles of spiritual adoptions and from the one who aspires to adoption; they need to make spiritual preparation by prayer, retreat, fasting and meditation according to what is prescribed. (1). It is necessary for this ceremony to make a layout according to the Plan. (2). If the operation is done in the proper time, we will attack the East angle directly; but if forced by circumstances which cannot be avoided to do the operation outside the prescribed time, we will attack the angle of the West as the chief angle; the same perfumes and prayers indicated for the plan will be used. (3).

For the Holocaust of Atonement, the head of a male roe deer taken indifferently from the market, still with his skin and his hair, will be offered; we will prepare it as we prepare the deer before slaughtering it. (4).

Then three new fires will be erected, one in the mantelpiece of the room which will represent the North, the other two in two large stoves which will be in the South and the West in accordance with ancient practice whereby grill boxes were carried for the making of burnt offerings. The tongue and brain will be burned in these stoves: the head in the fire from the mantelpiece or from the North, and the brains in the Southern stove, the tongue in the West. Only these two parts should be removed from the head. When the whole thing burns, the candidate will throw three large grains of salt in each fire; then he will then pass his hands thrice over the flame of each fire as a sign of purification; he will have for this purpose the right knee on the ground and will say the ineffable words indicated below for each fire. If one cannot have a deer's head, one will take that of a lamb also covered with its skin and wool; it is absolutely necessary that the skin be black otherwise the Holocaust would be one of Grace and not Atonement.

The candidate will perform the deer or lamb head ceremony before any other ceremony. The circles and the room where the operation is carried out will be fully prepared as the Plan (5) indicates, as well as the Water. The operation will take three days. We will begin with the usual invocations and conjurations between which we will add those of the Commander of the East.[23]

After the three days of operation, the ashes of the three fires will be carefully collected and added to those from the previous operations. We will form the scapular of the new R✠ according to the prescribed model (6) and we will make him a talisman similar to that of other R✠ also according to the model (7).[24]

If there are several R✠ together, the three operations will be made by two of them and by the MP for this adoption which will be the last.

It will be seen to that the candidate says the prayer that were a result of the words that first passed over open hands on the flames of the Holocaust.

He who receives an R✠, especially in times out of the ordinary must try to prevent all R✠ absences, by giving enough notice and time in advance so that they can join him at his side and also so that they can recognise the legitimacy of the reception.

After the reception, the Chalice (8) will be made available to drink to the new R✠ with the usual ceremonies (9) and the same will be made to eat the mystic or cementic bread (10).

---

23 French. Commandeur d'Orient. Substituted throughout the text as Commander of the East.
24 The scapular is a Christian garment suspended from the shoulders. Devotional scapulars typically consist of two rectangular pieces of cloth, wool or other fabric that are connected by bands. One rectangle hangs over the chest of the wearer, while the other rests on the back, with the bands running over the shoulders.

Translation of 'Le Manuscrit d'Alger' (1772)

First Prayer to the Head in the North

WA GLA. 8.

Second Prayer to the Brains in the South

WA BN. 4.

Third Prayer to the Tongue in the West

TWAK EM. 10.

The candidate will repeat the prayer at the three fires, beginning with the one in the North where the head is and where are traced, as above, the word with its two characters above and below and two hieroglyphs on both sides.

The words, characters and hieroglyphs will be traced in front of the fire with white chalk prepared in the usual way; they are here marked with their numbers and measures.

The word will be changed at each light only, and it will be pronounced at the indicated places as many times as it is marked for the first fire in prayer.

Prayer

'ô + 10, you are Holy, O' Father of All Things, whose will is fulfilled by your own power, you are Holy and you want to be known to every man of intellectual sense, having established all things for him; you are Holy and greater than all praise, you whose image is in all Nature; receive my verbal sacrifices by the Holocaust which burns before you, which is purified by this flame and which I present to you with all my heart and with all my soul.'

The candidate speaks three times, his hands open square on the flame of the fire where he makes his prayer, by pronouncing the word that is traced there; and then he continues the prayer.

Continuation of the Prayer

'ô + 10, O' God Inseparable, Indivisible and Infinite, you who can be pronounced only by silence, give me strength, power and help so that I do not fall back into ignorance of the knowledge that is according to my essence. ô +... strengthens and enlightens the regenerating leaders who make me commune to the rank which you grant by your pure mercy to your true Elect; Examine their vows and prayers so that I may be marked by them with the seal of reconciliation and receive accordingly the intelligence and power attached to them. Enlighten the men of this generation, your children who are still locked in darkness by ignorance when they are of your divine knowledge that you make me communicate today by your Faithful Elect. I will bear witness to all human beings as much as you will allow it, for the truth and holiness of the knowledge I have acquired in this grade for your greater glory and greater satisfaction. Give me the gift of coming back to you ô + 10; who are and who loves your creature. ô + 10, your man who by your infinite mercy has just been blessed in your name, on whom your name has been imposed and who has had the felicity to gather your holy name, your man desires to be sanctified and in union with you ô + 10. As you have given him the power, grant me never to use the virtues, faculties and powers that I receive for this purpose. Amen. Amen. Amen. Amen.'

While the candidate is praying, the operative will be at his right side and will tell him at each fire:

Translation of 'Le Manuscrit d'Alger' (1772)

'May it be granted to you by Jehovah ô + 10, what you have asked him, what you ask of him and what you will ask him according to his will. Amen.'

Then the deputy ℛ✠ for the reception will take receipt of the ashes of the fire in front of the candidate to the North and put a pinch at the top of the forehead at the hairline. He will then make the same oratory wish and the same ceremony of ashes to the candidate to the South above the right eye, he will do the same to the West above the left eye so that the candidate is marked at the front by a triangular figure of the ashes of his Holocaust; he will keep this sign until the end of the first operation. The candidate will also be marked by the seal (11).

We will go to the operating room on the first day at six o'clock in the afternoon to draw the circles. The planets will be drawn on the two angles of East and West and not elsewhere: (12) At nine o'clock the new fires will be lit with wood and charcoal prepared.

Then he will open the head with the ceremonial knife (13), in circumference removing the brains, removing also the tongue: it will be necessary to put the detached bone back into the head to be able to remove the brains so that it burns with the rest of the head. The other ceremonies that follow this operation will be performed, as it is said (14).

At midnight we enter the circle of retreat for invocations and incantations to get finished in accordance with the usage at one o'clock.

We will make the four prostrations at the four angles where we have placed each name out of 7 more than usual.

Here are some names for this effect. They are taken from the big alphabet (15) of 7. 9. 5. 4. These names relate to each day of the week, so they should not be served for two days in a row, which would be against their destination. They are marked by celestial algebraic letters (16); these names are selected, by the figures that we see of their rank, their number, their power and their product and junction (17).

It is necessary to use a prescribed perfume (18).

A 93 [adornaïk]	Sunday	adornaïk	Sun	7.3
B 13 [betsaléel]	Monday	brammati	Moon	7.3
C 34 [cimarmora]	Tuesday	cimarmora	Mars	7.3
D 62 [dazalmun]	Wednesday	dazalmum	Mercury	7.3
E.86. [ednemor]	Thursday	éduenor	Jupiter	7.3
F 55 [ferphiel]	Friday	serphiel	Venus	7.3
G 94 [gezmoriak]	Saturday	gezmoria	Saturn	7.3

Secret Statutes of the R✠

Specific instructions that R✠ must adhere to during the special daily invocations throughout the seven days of the Equinoctial operations, or three-day operation. The R✠ will follow with precision the ceremonial of preparation to work these operations as it is prescribed in the present statutes. *Know.*

Article Premier (copied)

R✠ who are married will observe not to use their wife for three days before opening their operations; they will also deprive themselves during the seven days that their circles remain open, otherwise they will be deemed unclean and will operate solely in demonic confusion; they will be unable to use their wife until twenty-four hours after their seventh operation, this delay is consecrated for the thanksgiving that the R✠ must render unto the Lord in favour of the fruits which they have drawn from their operations.

Article 2

The R✠ will begin to recite the seven Psalms of Penance during the first three days of their wife's abstinence; they will say them aloud two hours before midnight according to the prescribed use and they will continue until the last day of thanksgiving.

Article 3

If the R✠ operates within the circles of a G[ran]d S[overeig]n, or one of their Substitutes, and have been expressly ordered to receive one or more Apprentice R✠ in the course of their Equinox operations, they will take care to collect the subject [celebrant] assigned to them during the three days of preparation and to instruct them on the grade they will receive. They will begin to ordain them for the small Office of the Holy Spirit that they must say during the course of their temporal life as soon as they are raised. They will also instruct them that they must recite one of the seven Psalms of Penance every night before going to bed; said prayers will be made facing eastward for a time immemorial.

Article 4

The R⳨ will only have one meal a day during the seven days of their operations; this meal will be confined to dinner only and nothing further will be eaten for twenty-four hours, which makes the perfect fast they are obliged to observe under penalty of prevarication and prohibition of said operations.

Article 5

However, if some R⳨ cannot sustain the rigour of this fast he will be allowed to drink water in the course of the day and make a small snack after the operation, which will end at quarter of a pound of bread, a piece of cheese, or something else dry. All meat is forbidden to him, but he can eat a fish fried or roasted on the grill, but he will eat it only cold and its size will be only the weight of four ounces, under no pretext at all should this snack weight more than eight ounces.

If it happens that any Apprentice R⳨ or M[aster]s R⳨ themselves cannot absolutely support the fast, one will not expose himself to any work in these circles or make any invocations; the main operatives will content themselves with having eyewitnesses instead to their operations, his place will be alone in the retreat angle which is towards the North, but more often than not he will be put behind the Vautour circle which is to the South as that is their ordinary place; he will, however, be held to the same spiritual exercises and the same discipline as the R⳨ who operates.

Article 6

The R⳨ will do their Equinox operations on the first day of the March moon revival and will finish them on the seventh at one o'clock after midnight. + They will observe to make an exact diary of all that they have done during the course of their operations in order to use them at the Equinoxes in the following September. They will trace the characters and hieroglyphics that they will have received from their work, for from their future circles of operation will emerge as many figures as they have received from the G[ran]d. S[overeig]ns; from the centre of their circles they will eventually place those [characters and hieroglyphics] given to them by *la chose*.[25]

---

25 'La chose' translates as 'The Thing'. The active and beneficent divine reality which thus epiphanies itself was mysteriously known by Martinez, and after him by his disciples, as La Chose (the Thing). According to Amadou, 'the Thing is not the person of Jesus Christ…, the Thing is not Jesus Christ, it is the presence of Jesus Christ, as the Shekinah was the presence of God in the Holy of Holies'.

It is for this reason that the R✠ may be able to show the disciples their true labours and to instruct them in this regard as they deem appropriate.

Article 7

The characteristic or hieroglyphic plans and tracings that G[ran]d. S[overeig]ns, or their Substitutes, have given to M[aster]s and Apprentices R✠ to perfect them in *la chose* should be considered by said R✠ only as a means by which to help with the advent of other further figures regardless of how different they ultimately are from those they may have received from their patrons; whilst not the same, they may in fact have been given by the same subjects [spirits], such as the septenary, octonary, denary or others, which may well have been used in the first operations that the chiefs of *la chose* entrusted to them.[26]

Article 8 (copied)

The chief operatives will see to the washing of their hands and feet in a small quantity of lukewarm or cold water into which half a handful of salt has been thrown. This ceremony will be performed by all M[aster]s and Ap[p]r[entices] R✠ who must attend their operations. This ceremony will take place three hours before midnight on the day when the first operation is to begin and will continue during the seven days of operation in a room of the premises where the Great Work is to be done; we will no longer put shoes on our feet and we will only wear slippers intended solely for this use during the course of operations, and we will lock them away carefully to serve this purpose and no other.

Article 9 (copy)

The chief operatives will observe that the M[aster]s and Ap[prentices] R✠, who will assist him in this work, are dressed with their four regional colours; blue, black, red and water-green (The colour white, which they must also have on, is not confounded amongst these four colours because it is the upper colour designating the spiritual part of God, the other colours only designate the four temporal spiritual majors as follows: the blue, the

---

26 Categories of spirits within Pasqually's system e.g. octonarys or octenaires spirits. This class, second in the angelic hierarchy, neither dwells within the divine immensity, nor is trapped in a certain region.

Celestial East, the black, the Terrestrial North, the red, The Central Axis of [Uncreated] Fire and the water-green, the Aerial Lower Beings (said chief operatives will as well as their assistants be stripped of all kinds of metals before the start of labour).[27]

Article 10 (copy)

For a three-day operation, the chief operatives will observe and observe for their assistants the same abstinence from women as prescribed for the labour of seven days (during the same interval they will also do thanksgiving after the third operation as is mentioned in the closing of the Great Work. The ceremonial of this last labour is the same as that of the first).

Article 11

The chief operatives will ensure to locate an adequate room, as stated below, to perform their labours; the room shall be twenty feet square or at least twenty feet long and eighteen wide; it is better that it be rather spacious than constricted to avoid the confusion of subjects [spirits] which one commands in the course of the operations. If it is smaller, it could be very detrimental to the chief operatives and their assistants; it would be even more convenient if the chamber in which the different plans of operations were to be drawn was a long square; one should follow the figure of the long square of Solomon's Temple.

Article 12

Said room will have no opening other than a window which will be placed on the Northwest side, it will be made of a small square, about two feet high by one foot wide; it will be seen to that there is a wall in the room which is situated in a straight line to the East without any other opening as mentioned. The door of the room will be placed, if it is possible, towards the West, southwest or northwest and not elsewhere. Without these precautions, it could result in confusion in the course of operations.

---

27 The Immensity of the Axis of Uncreated Fire. Part of Pasqually's 'Universal Table'. The axis gives the principle of life to any terrestrial body, activates and reactivates them.

Article 13

The chief operatives will consecrate said chamber with a small invocation, which will be given to them in particular. This ceremony will be done by them alone without any assistants. They will check that there are no animals in the place where they to do the work and that there are no neighbours too close to the house, as this would be a great hindrance to the operatives' voices; it would even be appropriate that this house be filled with walls or a good entourage.

Article 14 copy

The chief conductors of the circles of operations will ensure conformity in the layout of their different operations with the orders and plans they have previously received from their principal chiefs. They will begin their first operation on the Sabbath at three o'clock before midnight on the first day of the March moon revival for the first Equinox and on the first day of the September moon revival for the second Equinox. One will observe that all kinds of invocation are made at midnight precisely in order to have the prescribed hour of contemplation which is from midnight to one o'clock.

Article 15

Chief operatives will observe to put no other candle in their circles of operation or angles other than those which are marked in the different plans. The candles will be consecrated by them before being lit and put in place; everything being thus prepared, they will perfume the four angles of the chamber and the circles of their operations in the manner which will be explained below.

Drugs for perfumes[28]

For twenty French silver sols of each object

Church Incense	Cloves	Oriental saffron
Cinnamon	Black pepper grain	Sandaraque (gum)
Putty in tears (gum)	Sunflower seeds	Sulphur flowers
Henbane seeds	Black poppy seeds	White poppy seeds

Article 16

When the chief operatives have fulfilled all the prerequisites of the ceremonial of operations, they themselves will make an offering of perfume at the angles and circles which are traced in the chamber where they are to operate; they may, however, have this offering made by one of their assistants, if they think fit.

The offering will begin at the angle of the West, then the North, the South, and finally the East; after this ceremony the one who makes the offering comes down from the East angle and goes to the centre of the circles of operation after leaving his slippers at the first outer circle. From there, he incenses these circles with the terrine; the perfume is burned by making three turns in the circles from left to right and three other turns from right to left. After that, we will put the terrine in the East angle to let the perfume enter the fire.

Preparation of Perfumes

The R✝ chief operatives will crush all the drugs of the said perfumes together in a wooden mortar or any other; after they have been thus prepared, the operatives will take five or six good pinches of sulphur, which they will throw into the mortar where the crushed drugs are; they will amalgamate it all together and use it to make this offering.

---

28 The 'fleurs de soufre' or sulphur flower has for millennia been used as one of the best natural solutions in the fight against fungi and pests affecting plants. The odours emitted by sulphur vapours act as a powerful repellent for dogs and cats. Homeopathic practitioners often prescribe sulphur to treat skin conditions such as herpes or psoriasis, eczema, acne or scabies. 'Mastic en larmes' or Putty in Tears is a resin from a natural or induced exudation of the tree Pistacia Lentiscus. It is used in the manufacture of soft and glossy varnishes. The sandaraque or sandarac is a plant resin extracted from the Atlas Cypress (Tetraclinis reticulata) native to North Africa. It comes in the form of tears or grains. Known since Antiquity, it is used frequently in the composition of alcohol varnishes which ensures transparency. Henbane seeds or 'graines de jusquiame' is known to soothe toothache, it is also called St. Apolline's herb. In the past, henbane was considered a magical plant associated with black magic. Guy de Chauillac (c. 1300 – 25 July 1368), the famous 14th Century French physician and used fumigation based on henbane, onions and leeks to treat 'worms in the teeth' and fight plague.

Article 17

The chief operatives alone will see to the lighting of all the candles which have been placed in the circles and angles by their assistants before making the offering of perfumes. The assistants will not be able under any pretext whatsoever that it should be left to them to light the candles which are placed in the angles, nor those which are around the first inner circle; this illumination must made by the chief operative alone. The prerequisites of this last ceremonial being fulfilled, the chief operatives will begin by ordering one of their assistants to begin the invocations; they will choose for the beginning one which they have the most confidence in for gaining the favour of *la chose;* they will position the other assistants during the course of said invocations, one in the circles of correspondence which are in front of the three angles of the chamber which are that of West, North and South, and the other assistants, if the number is more considerable, will be placed each in Vautours circles that are in Northeast, Northwest and Southwest.

The chief operatives cannot, under any pretext, receive any of these assistants into the circle of correspondence of the East angle, nor in the Vautours circle of the Southeast, this place being consecrated only for the passes of the subjects [spirits] that have been claimed by him, and that may even appear in the place when the chief operatives makes the consecration of said angles most often.

The assistants thus placed will all look towards the wall which is in the Eastern part, they will also observe all the walls of the room which they should be able to see without turning their eyes to the rear; with the white chalk on a hard wooden pallet they will mark down exactly all the figures that they have been able to see before them and then give them to the chief operatives who, after all the labour is finished, will interpret them, if they deem appropriate.

Article 18

The chief operatives will begin the invocations, the Master Coëns and then of the Grand Architect; during this time they will make the consecration of the angles and then they will make by themselves the special invocation in a high or low voice as they deem it appropriate, which together will form all three invocations for a day of operation. We continue to do the first two aforementioned invocations during the seven days Equinox of operation, but the special invocation will change each day along with the entire operation plan, relative to the seven tables that direct the seven days of labour.

Article 19

The chief operatives as well as the Masters and Apprentices ℞☩ will ensure to take six convention characters, three for and three against that will work towards success in the things one wishes to know from the spirits which one claims, as they are marked in said plans. One may allow for the convention characters which one has taken from one's instructions throughout the course of the Great Work.

Article 20

The chief operatives will ask the Masters and Apprentices ℞☩ to see the convention characters they have taken from their instruction, and before making any other invocations, they will observe if any of the assistants have taken the same character as one another, and if they have, they will have another, or others, taken from the ℞☩, who will judge as to whether the characters are to be changed: by this means all sorts of confusion will be avoided in the conventions established by one and the other; the characters can be taken arbitrarily.

Article 21

If the chief operatives allowed the duplication of convention characters to subsist in an operation, it would certainly happen that one of the two subjects, who would be of the same character, would receive nothing at all from *la chose,* the subjects [spirits] who are claimed are not able to serve two beings at once, it is not in the law of their spiritual nature; so if the conventions were the same, there would be only one person who could derive some fruit from the operation.

Ceremony for the Consecration of Angles

The chief operatives will begin to devote the West angles, they will present themselves at a distance of three paces, holding the two arms extended in front of the said angle, and the two hands open at right angles, as if they wished to repel something that would come towards us; they will then advance in the angle by taking three steps forward and three steps backwards. The steps backward will be less open than the three steps forward so that the operative may be able to their make prostration in said angle and they can have the upper half of the body above the quarter circle which marks the space that said triangle is situated. (This space is closed only to provide the facility to trace divine words and spiritual names, as well as to contain half the body of the chief operative. This quarter circle will be at least three feet away from the angle above) The chief operative kneeling on the edge of the quarter circle, will raise his two open hands square to the sky, he will then reverse his face prostrate against the ground in said angle and in this position he will make the consecration.

Article 22

If it happens that the operation is delayed in receiving some fruit from the labour, at the mercy of the operative, it will be possible to repeat once or twice the special invocation of the day during the time of the contemplation in order to help dispel with all the inconveniences which contribute to the delay of the appearances of the things which one demands. The repetition of the special invocation can only be made by the chief operative in a high or low voice.

Article 23 (copied)

The chief operatives will perform the same ceremony to consecrate the other three angles, they will observe not to give two commands to the subjects [spirits] they claim, nor to give them two requests at once under pain of confusion. Also during the daily operations of Equinox, we cannot put into action for two days in a row the subjects [spirits] that were once asked under the same punishment and deprivation of a good operation, because in such a case we would rather have a bad one.

Article 24

First Daily Invocation to the Superior Solar Agents in Junction with the Superior Agents of Sabataïr called Saturn

'O' thou, S.15. [sarcamahau], (to the East) O' thou A.8. [abin] (to the West), O' A.9. [achila] (to the North) etc…I claim and invoke you as the higher power of the temporal interior where all the powerful daily and spiritual temporal operations are contained; it is upon you that the Eternal has manifested the law of order, of the action of every being created in virtue and power like you. This event took place only by the Deity for the benefit and greater glory of the Divine Man of the Earth: it is for this august title and in my capacity as a powerful Man-God that I command you to be submissive and obedient to my command. Obey without delay my dreadful and pow-

erful word, as it is conceived by my intention before you, and put into action by my operation Yes! I conjure you and submit you to my power superior to yours! I subjugate you to me by my wonderful word, I consecrate you by the ineffable name ô + 10 A.28. [alim] and by Him whom out of respect and fear I dare not name here and who is the major agent of my operation. I consecrate such to you by the authority I have received from the God of the Living Gods and by all that is most sacred to me and by the same ineffable name of the God of the Sabbath ô + 10 A.28. [alim] I enclose the power of the main regional leaders of the planetary sphere of Sabataïr to yours. Yes! I invoke it and claim to be in union with you at the centre of my operation, O' S.16. [sarcabin], O' S.5. [sisim], O' S.15. [sarcamahau] Listen to the voice of the one who speaks to you on behalf of the Eternal God of Israel!'

'Obey without delay the force of the word of the Man-God of the Earth, who makes you conspire and commands you to be in ternary conjunction with the general terrestrial body! Reveal to my sight and understanding all the things I desire to know about Him, of you, and of those with whom you join, according to the strong power of my invocation and convention! Let him remember for a time immemorial the awesome command given to you by Joshua when he suspended your temporal spiritual reaction and stopped the course of your daily operation on the valley of Gabaon, where you have satisfied the intention and to the word of Joshua in his capacity as Man-God of the Earth.

Yes! I am that Joshua, who, however, like him in virtue and divine spiritual power, command you to obey promptly my word of immutable power, all together by the formidable name of Jehovah ô + 10 A.28 [alim]. Terror and trembling are given to you by him and by him who invokes you, O' S.15. [sarcamahau], O' A.8. [abin], O' A.9. [achila], O' S.16. [sarcabin], O' S.5. [sisim] and I subjugate you by the true word which Joshua used when he commanded you to work with him to the defeat of the enemies of the worship of the Eternal and his own who opposed all his divine spiritual operations. Be wholly devoted to the one who claims you to cooperate together in our temporal spiritual power for the greater glory and justice of the Creator and his creature! Be it as it is yours. Amen. Amen. Amen. Amen.'

Article 25

Second Daily Invocation to the Superior Agents of Meraï called Mercury, for the Spiritual Monday and not for the Temporal Monday

'Ô you M. 10. [meliael], Ô M.93. [mubim], Ô M.21. [misraïn], *I call upon you and invoke you by the triple and the quadruple strong power which the Eternal Creator has put by force of his on his minor creatures[29] that are, however, greater than the major temporal ones! I am that mighty creature that the Lord has consecrated to be the most perfect agent to the temporal spiritual ones. Your power is limited in its faculty of action and operation, and that of the Man-God of the Earth was not before its transgression. Let him remember the truth of what I am saying before you! I repeat to you the first commandment made to you by the First Man who subjected your power to his by the power of his word! I am this First Man who comes before you all, clothed with his first virtue and spiritual power. Warning, terror and trembling are given to you by the triple and quadruple power of the word which commands you and orders you to obey without delay the content of my invocation drawn before you by the tracings of my operation. I exconjure you by all that I hold sacred, by all that is most holy and by the formidable power of ô M.52 [marckimouz] and of ô M.47 [mibiath] who presides over all of you from the East and West angles to your visual region, I conjure you again by the most holy name of the action of the Lord ô M.68 [matazab], who still presides over you from the angle of the North to your region, so that the most powerful intelligence that is innate to you will join my spiritual and temporal being. I command you by all the powers superior to yours that you join with him who commands you from the Lord, by his action and by his operation, to be in all the circumstances of this temporal life intimately bound and subject to the one who claims you. Yes, ô M.10. [meliael], ô M.93 [mubim], ô M.21. [misraïn], I subjugate you, and consign you to me only as you did by order of the Creator to the Man-God of the Earth after his spiritual reconciliation. By this eternal superior order you become the subjects of that First Man in whose favour all the powers of action and of operations that were given to you for his greatest temporal spiritual glory. ô M.10. [meliael], ô M.93. [mubim], ô M.21. [misraïn] Yes, I speak to each one of you in particular, I subjugate*

---

29 Mankind.

your spiritual and temporal virtue, I command you accordingly and I summon you to follow scrupulously the temporal spiritual direction that I am going to give to each one of you in particular. Go, walk, and spiritually operate your power in the three regions of the Earth where I record you for such limited time as is fixed at will, report to me faithfully all the temporal things that you know to be the most necessary and the most urgent for my spiritual wellbeing and for the temporal one. I give you the same command and give you the same instruction in favour of my fellows and especially for those who claim to me and for whom I am forced to invoke you. (We name the people we want to promote in the operation). *I am pointing you to the centre of the said regions so that you may show your power against those of the ordinary men of the Earth; their powers are more conventional than spiritual; it is, therefore, that I have attached to the higher beings temporal material conventions so that you may determine their actions and their operations according to my desires; also determined by their thoughts similar to mine, arranged their intention in my favour and for those to whom I am interested; obtain from these worldly beings and from the creator all the indispensable things which are attached to the temporal and spiritual life which I greatly need. I exconjure you all that I am and by all that you are in the immensity of your planetary region so that you remain firm and unwavering in the instruction I have just given you for the time limited by the Man-God of Earth; that your retirement be made only after any operation or any success of convention has taken place according to the intention and the operation of the one who can more than you report exactly, promptly and effectively to the one in favour of which you must operate, and of all the things for which he puts you in action and as he has marked them in his circles of operation! Go by the dreadful word ô M.52* [marckimouz], *return by the formidable word of his double power ô M.72* [magiel] *and bring back with the wonderful word of his Triple Essence ô M.3* [maumor], *to the Man-God of the Earth which is the conclusion of the quadruple divine essence. Amen. Amen. Amen. Amen.'*

Article 26

Third Day Summoning Superior Agents
Maïr dubbed March for Spiritual Tuesday and not for Temporal Tuesday

'Ô PR.24, ô PR.25, ô PR.26! I claim you and invoke you as the highest power of the immensity of your planetary region! It is upon you that the Creator has established by immutable laws the powerful daily operations, of action, of reaction, and of corporeal, temporal, and spiritual vegetation, in favour of the general terrestrial body and all the particular celestial bodies. It is by virtue of these same laws and powers that I claim and invoke you by the power superior to yours that the Almighty God Creator has put innate in me; it is by this same power that I command you to be always ready in all the circumstances of my temporal and spiritual life to obey the command of the Man-God of the Earth; all power has been given to you only in favour of the spiritual and temporal creature, that same power is subject to the force of that which the Creator has put innate in me, ô, ô, ô (the same). Hear my invocation and answer my operation! I command you to submit your power to mine so that they are intimately bound together in all the works and operations that I will be doing in this world for the benefit of my temporal and spiritual being and those for whom I am interested as to make them worthy of the fruit of my operations. Obey my word and his divine spiritual power! Yes! I conjure you by the dreadful word ô M.6 [mor], by the ineffable word ô M.68. [matazab], and by the omnipotent almighty word ô M.76.[megum], that you may vegetate in my spiritual being and in the temporal one that I live for a limited time, the various principles of divine operations that could dissipate in my spiritual being. I conjure you again, ô, ô, ô (the same spirits), to relate to me faithfully all the different things you know to be necessary for the various operations of divine worship for which the Man-God was emancipated from the divine immensity; I am also ordering you, in favour of those for whom I am obliged to recall, for the same subject. I command you to manifest your divine and temporal spiritual vegetative power in the centre of the tracing I have well-placed before you, and where the various figures for your attention are drawn, so that I may no longer wander in my spiritual and temporal *conduct, in the product of my operation and my various invocations; these are the things that I expect and claim from the strength of your power and that of my operation for a time immemorial. Amen. Amen. Amen. Amen.'*

Article 32[30]

Only Substitute W[orshipful] M[aster]s R✠ have the authority, the right, and the power to operate their great Equinox work in eight circles or in seven if they deem it appropriate, which is not in the power of M[aster]s R✠. and Ap[prentices] R✠ who do not have the eminent rank of Substitution. The latter cannot, under any pretext, arrogate to themselves the same virtue and authority as that given by the G[ran]d. S[overeig]ns to the M[aster]s R✠ on pain of prevarication, divorce and confusion in all their temporal and spiritual operations and unlimited suspension of virtual circles of operation.

Article 33

Only the Substitute W[orshipful] M[aster]s R✠ have in themselves the virtue and the power to work their great labour in eight circles because they have acquired a double power, namely that which they have by right and by the force of their work, by the eminent rank of R✠ and the one that the G[ran]d S[overeig]n gives them, when he orders them, as Sovereign Substitutes; they thus have this double power so that they can represent the G[ran]d S[overeig]n in everything and everywhere; this means all that they do is authentically marked by the temporal and spiritual seal for time immemorial.

Article 34

The R✠ will not admit Sunday in the course of their spiritual operations; beginning on Saturday for their Equinox work, Sunday will be counted for the Monday of the Spiritual Operation Week and viewed as such by all R✠ Élus Coëns.

---

30   Articles 27 through 31 are missing in the original Ms.

Article 35

The ℞⳨ will observe that although the days of the week recall the conventional names of the planets; the planets follow in no way the same order of arrangement as the days of the ordinary week, as explained below. This arrangement cannot agree in any way with the fixed and immutable order of the planets which fix the seven days of operation for the ℞⳨.

Article 36

We will see clearly the true arrangement of each of the planets according to its rank of operation, as will be explained, and that they can be operated only in accordance to their true places of daily spiritual and temporal operation. Saturday is given for the operation of the Sun in conjunction with Saturn and in conjunction with the general terrestrial body. The conventional Sunday that sets the Sabbath for Christians is the second day for the ℞⳨ for their spiritual operations; this Sunday is the true Monday day given to Mercury.

Conventional Tuesday is the day given to Mars. The conventional Wednesday is the day given to Jupiter. The conventional Thursday is the day given to Venus. Conventional Friday is the day given to the Moon; and on the Saturday when all kinds of spiritual operations are finished is given to Saturn.

These are the true days of the temporal and spiritual week of the ℞⳨, as it is of all the nations of the earth, except for the few Christians who have the day Sunday to refer to the resurrection of Christ and to evade the true days and weeks of time that set the real operations of divine worship in all different nations.

Article 38[31]

The ℞⳨ must know the real names of the different planetary bodies to operate on the various subjects [spirits] that are contained among them, as well as the names of their different inhabitants; there is no doubt that they each have their spiritual name which distinguishes their daily operations. It is only in this way that one can know their characters, their hieroglyphs, and their spiritual operations, good and bad. Here are therefore the true names of planetary bodies as the first Man-God of the Earth knew them (named them) and transmitted them to his posterity.

---

31 Article 37 is missing in the original Ms.

The Sun has the immutable name Solaïn, which means elementary spiritual reaction. Mercury has the immutable name Meraï which means divine spiritual response in favour of the Man-God of the Earth. Mars has the immutable name Maïr which means the vegetative reaction of the temporal spirituous essences of earthly and elemental material bodies. Jupiter's immutable name Iova which means temporal putrefaction and spiritual corruption. Venus has the immutable name Vaour which means temporal corporal reproduction and spiritual corruption. The Moon has the immutable name Ouva which means light of darkness. Saturn's name is immutable Sabataïr which means rest and divine spiritual reconciliation. These are the real names of the planetary bodies which one must pronounce in the different operations that one makes towards the inhabitants of said bodies.

Article 39

Ceremony to Recite the Psalms of Penitence [32]

The R✠, as well as the brethren of the Order who were given the power to recite the psalm by virtue of their ordination and according to the power of their rank, which begins at the rank of G[rand] A[rchitect], will say the seven psalms in full each day of their operation as follows. The R✠ will begin to bow from the West to East angle; they will turn their face to the West angle and also bow; this bow will be with the right hand at a right angle on that part of the heart and the left hand will be angled towards the ground. They then begin by saying in front of said angle psalm *'Domine ne infurore'*[33] at the end of which they will say,

'Glory be given to the thought, to the action, and to the operation of the God of the Eternal Gods of Israel.'

They will do the same after the greeting bow to said angle.

We will recite the second psalm *'Beati quo rum'*[34] at the angle of the North, which has the same ceremony as at the angle of the West. We will do the same to the other two angles saying to the South the third psalm 'Domine infurore' and to that of the fifth psalm

---

[32] The Penitential Psalms or Psalms of Confession, are named as the Psalms 6, 31, 37, 50, 101, 129, and 142 (6, 32, 38, 51, 102, 130, and 143 in the Hebrew numbering) which are specially expressive of sorrow for sin. The name belonged originally to the fiftieth Psalm, which was recited at the close of daily morning service in the primitive Church.
[33] Latin. 'O Lord have mercy upon me'. Psalm 37. Domine ne in furore tuo arguas me. (in rememorationem de sabbato). (O' Lord, rebuke me not in thy indignation. (For a remembrance of the Sabbath.)
[34] Latin. 'Blessed are'. Psalm 31. Beati quorum remissae sunt iniquitates. (Blessed are they whose iniquities are forgiven.)

*'Domine, Exaudie'.*³⁵ The fourth psalm *'Miserere'*³⁶ is said prostrate in the centre of the circles, face pressed to the ground, one will say it immediately and in the same way the sixth psalm *'De profundis'*³⁷ before reciting these last two psalms we will make the salutation of the angles of East and West as we did the first time, then we will bow our head facing the East angle. After this ceremony we will say the seventh Psalm *'Domine Exaudi* [meaum] *auribus*³⁸ to the northwest, the face turned towards the East angle.

It is up to the *Master* and *Apprentice* R⳨ alone to recite the seven psalms in a row on the days of labour or once all the revivals of the Moon are done, as they alone are obliged to and forced to by their ordination. The Gr[and] Arch[itectes] and the Chevaliers d'Orient can recite only one psalm of the seven aforementioned days, they will observe the same ceremony as the Master R⳨ to recite the seven psalms.

Article 46 ³⁹

Consecration of the Angles and the Seven Circles of Operation or the Three Days of Equinox First Consecration made to the Circles as follows

The chief operative having made the suitable illuminations for the operations will leave his slippers at the edge of the first outer circle and go to the centre of the first inner circle; he will have the candle burning in the centre of the circle between his legs, his face turned towards East angle, he will bow respectfully having both arms cross over the chest and both hands open at right angles. After this he turns to the West angle where he makes the same gesture. He then salutes the same angle and the North and South. After this ceremony, and remaining standing, he consecrates the circles of his operation as follows.

> *'I conjure thee a curse, I curse you, you and your elected for a time immemorial E.24* [emacaï], *and all your demonic court, all your unclean and illusory spirits, in the quadruple name of the eternal essence, ô A.28* [alim] *of these elementary spiritual lights which represents the covenant that the*

---

35   Latin. 'Hear, O' Lord'. Psalm 101. Domine, exaudi orationem meam, et clamor meus ad te veniat. (O Lord, hear my prayer, and let my cry come unto thee.)
36   Latin. 'Mercy'. Psalm 50. Miserere mei, Deus, secundum magnam misericordiam tuam. (Have mercy on me, O God, according to thy great mercy.)
37   Latin. 'From the depths'. Psalm 129. De profundis clamavi ad te, Domine. (Out of the depths I have cried to thee, O' Lord.)
38   Latin; 'Hear, O Lord, = listen'. Psalm 142. Domine, exaudi orationem meam: auribus percipe obsecrationem meam in veritate tua. (Hear, O Lord, my prayer: give thy ear to my supplication in thy truth.)
39   Article 40 to 45 missing in the original Ms.

celestial and super-celestial regional leaders make with me and with those whom I claim and invoke to contribute in favour of my divine spiritual operations for the greater glory and justice of the Creator and his creature. Yes. I conjure you and defend you eternally by the ineffable name of the vivifying God to penetrate within my virtuous circles in which as a Man-God I will operate the divine worship. I consecrate the circles here before me and before thee to be the fixed abode of the Spirit of Divine Communication and to be that of the Spiritual beings that I invoke and claim to hold you and yours for an eternity in your place of worship, subjection, iniquitous and demonic privation. By all the virtues superior to yours and by mine invincible, these circles are hallowed and in all purity of virtue and power by the Spirit of the Creator, his action and his operation for a time immemorial. Amen. Amen. Amen. Amen.'

Article 47

After the ceremony, the chief operative repeats the same bows at the said angles as he did before the consecration of the circles. After bowing he will consecrate the West angle; then that of the North, that of the South and after that of the East. The operative will be very careful to extinguish all the candles of the said angles as and when he has consecrated them, the subjects [spirits] who must appear in the said angles do not need elementary lights to show themselves with brilliancy, having at their disposal the true spiritual light with which they constitute and illuminate their apparent bodily forms.

Article 48

After the chief operatives has returned to the West corner with the same ceremonies mentioned in Article 21, he will pronounce the consecration of the said angle as follows.

'I bless you and consecrate you to the name of Jehovah and by his dreadful ineffable word, A.28 [alim], whose immutable creator served to set and limit the stable abode of the place where every spiritual being, created in virtue and in the power of the spiritual temporal operation, must operate the divine worship each according to the order and the faculty of action and operation which it received from the Creator to be put by him in practice in the different parts of the created Universe. Yes. I consecrate you, temporal Western region,

Translation of 'Le Manuscrit d'Alger' (1772)

by the strong and formidable virtue of the double power, A.13 [amaïel], *and by the invincible word of my word of divine spiritual power A.5* [abaca], *so that you may be kept in holiness and without defilement during all the time that I prescribed for the consignment of* (we name the spiritual subject that we take to be in this angle) *so that it remains at home during the course of my daily operation I conjure you O'* (the name of the spirit of the angle) *who are in this West corner that I have just consecrated to be the proper place for the manifestation of your virtue and power of action and spiritual operation divine in favour of the one who invokes and conjures you to operate all things to his advantage and to the benefit of his assistants. I consecrate you, elementary light, which illuminates temporally the angle of the West region; I bless you in the name of the Eternal God of Israel and conspire against you so that your temporal material virtue may be during the course of my spiritual operations the true type of the radiant divine light which the Lord manifested in favour of operations of the God and Divine Man of this Universe. O you + 7* (we pronounce the name of the spirit of the angle)*! I invoke you and command you to obey the triple essence of my word! Teach me and give me the Knowledge of all things that are in the Western region that you know to be the most urgent and most necessary for my education and for the benefit of my temporal and spiritual welfare, as well as for the benefit of the subjects whom the Divine Mercy has entrusted to my conduct and my elementary spiritual and temporal instructions. I am summoning you, your name, your character, your hieroglyph in the East angle, and generally all the product of the action you must perform under my command in this region of the West. I am still assigned to appear in the region of the East clothed with virtue and divine power so that you can operate with me an indissoluble bond in favour of all my elementary spiritual, temporal and material operations and that you answer without confusion and without illusion to all the characters of convention which I have attached to my circles of operation for the greater glory and justice of the quadruple divine essence. Amen. Amen. Amen. Amen.'*

After the consecration is made, the chief operative erases with his right hand all the words and names that are inscribed in the said angle, extinguishes the lights and will make the consecration of the angle of the North as he did that of the angle of the West.

Article 49

The chief operative will make the same consecration to the angle of the North as it has been done for the West, except that he will appoint the *septenary* name of the spirit that is placed in the angle of the North.

The upper dedicatory word of consecration is always the one who presides in the East angle for each operation of the daily Equinox works. The chief operatives will also make the consecration of the angle of the South, as he did that of the North and West, by naming the two *septenary* spirits which he placed at the said angles to be the contraction of the demonic part.[40] The chief operative may ask anything they wish over the course of their consecrations, the demands being arbitrary.

Article 50

Consecration of the Eastern Angle

'*I consecrate to you, an angle that is temporal and material by the incomparable name, A.28* [alim]*, that you may become the Holy of Holies of every divine spiritual being and that you may also be the interior and receptacle of every virtue, power, action and operation of every heavenly and temporal elementary spiritual being. Yes! I consecrate all your temporal material immensity to be the particular place of assignment of all the spiritual beings that I have recorded in the three terrestrial regions, West, North and South; I summon them and conjure them to appear in this place dedicated to their operation and mine. Yes! I exconjure you O'* (we name all the septenary spirits who have been placed in the other three angles) *by all that is most formidable, most holy and most sacred in immensity and super-celestial temporal heaven and the quadruple strong word of Almighty everlasting and immutable God, which is without beginning and without end, ô A.28* [alim]*, I command you and constrain you by the word doubly strong, ô A.13* [amaïel]*; may you manifest your power of action and divine operation together with mine, all the things that I claim in all the extent of the four heavenly regions and in the three lands, as I have designed by my thoughts, my word and by my operation, and which I have contracted with you all by my convention of charac-*

---

40 Superior septenary spirits; Guardians of the divine Law.

ters. *Pass my convention for and against together with yours in the Eastern Region which I have consecrated to be the perfect place for any spiritual, divine, spiritual temporal, and material appearance for a time immemorial. Amen, Amen, Amen, Amen.*'

Article 51

The chief operative will make the same consecration at the East as for all the other operations as he did for the first, with the exception of the change of words and spiritual names which he will name according to where he has placed them, as well as the various plans of operations that have it marked. He will observe again to extinguish a third of the lights of the circles at the end of each daily invocation. He himself will extinguish the lights of the first inner circle; he will raise all the lights of the Centre and place them in the Western angle, where he will hide it so that it can gives a dim light in the apartment and without it reflecting on the wall where we must contemplate the passes that will be made. The operative may, if he thinks fit, burn said light for a quarter of an hour in the centre of the inner circle to see its effect and then transport it to said angle.

Article 52

The chief operatives will observe to make a register of all the characters, hieroglyphs, words and names that they will receive from *la chose* during the course of their operations. They will also take all that their assistants have received from *la chose* so that they can make a general spiritual register to help serve the interpretation of the fruit gained from their work in temporal spiritual operations. This register can be used for the same objective with ap. ℞☦ and for any brethren that *la chose* favours with its natural spiritual gifts that are likely to be advanced in the Order without waiting for the time prescribed by the general statutes. It is necessary that the S[overeig]n's Substitutes or those who represent them are perfectly convinced of the grace that *la chose* gives to the said subject [celebrant]. For this purpose they will make a single daily labour of Meraï also known as Mercury, with four circles in which they will inscribe all the baptismal and family names of the subject [celebrant] that one believes is favoured by *la chose,* to have a physical knowledge of all the subject [celebrant] will have said in this respect, and to know further whether the subject [celebrant] is not deluded or whether what he receives comes from the right or the wrong part. The S[overeig]n Substitute will, for this purpose, conform to the particular chart which will be given to them to trace the Operations of the Ballot, as well as the special invocation of Meraï, which will also be given to them by the G[ran]d S[overeig]ns of their nation. These polls will be particularly for and against subjects [celebrants] who ask to enter the first degree of the Order. The said Substitute shall act in favour of the subject [celebrant] whom they have thus examined with regards to the reception of the characters, for or against, which they have received from *la chose,* for the admission or refusal of the subject [celebrant].

Translation of 'Le Manuscrit d'Alger' (1772)

Reconciliation Operation for two Penitents R✝ and an Operating R✝

--- ✠ ---

Description of the Tracing

A large circle composed of two rays; between these two rays, from West to North, the good intelligences of the seven planets, from West to South, their evil intelligences; outside and close to the circle, to the South: a Serpent.

An equilateral triangle filling the inside of the circle, with an angle to the West, one to the North and one to the South.

One word out of 10 and his candle in the centre of the triangle.

If there were six penitent R✝, we would make a double triangle whose operative would occupy the centre.

There will be no other sign or character drawn in this work.

Each operating and penitent R✝ will have next to him his candle lit that he will carry wherever he goes during the operation.

If all R✝ present are or believe themselves equally guilty, they will draw lots to decide who should start to operate on others.

A small piece of black ribbon, a penknife, an oat straw, a little sand, and a few grains of salt should be placed on the operator's side.

The operative having blessed the room and tracings and having made the new fire as it is prescribed, proceeds to the consecration of the centre. Immediately afterwards, he and the penitent R✝ will light their candles and go outside the circle, namely the operative in the West of the apartment, a penitent in the North and the other in the South, all facing the centre.

They will say together or separately the seven Psalms of Penitence and the litanies of the saints; each in particular make their confession and other special prayers and as each one has finished, he will rise up and go out to order until all have finished.

When all the R✠ are thus standing, operating alone in the centre in accordance with the prescribed uses, he will take up new powers, at his discretion, then rising, he will instruct the penitent R✠ to enter the angle which is opposite them, which they also do in accordance with prescribed usages, remaining at order with one hand whilst the other holds the pentacle. The operator at the centre makes the following conjuration:

Conjuration against the Perverse

> 'In the name, ô + 10, [W] let alertness, terror and trembling be given to the chief of perverse spirits and a curse on them by Jehovah and by me in my capacity as Man-God in his image and likeness. Hasten yourself, you unjust spirit, to obey my commandment according to all the power given to me by the awesome name of the Jehovah (the same) ô + 10 (which is proclaimed three times to the Serpent).'

> 'Come, hasten to my orders, (both names on 5) [fadal and viam]. Get out of your Southern region! Appear in front of this invincible circle, which is the mighty seat from which emanates the sacred decrees that the avenging and rewarding Lord has cast upon your iniquities and by which he has subjected you for an eternity to the lowest power of the Earth. Come to shame, execrable as you are, submitting your demonic power to my feet, and then to my animal and spiritual power, re-enchained in your deepest abysses!'

> 'Yes, this terrible power I have over you is my good desire and according to will of him that is alone formidable, O' [W], O' [W], O' [W].'

> Note ...the word of the centre is pronounced three times towards the angle of the South, each time extending to that part the pentacle which one holds with one's right hand to moderate the hasty arrival of the perverse spirits, and to have time to fix them, curse and conjure. They appear fadal and uvam.

> 'I exconjure you (the same two names out of 5), by the Triple Essence of God and by these three words of eternal power that I hold you by, ô A + 10 [atvamaï], ô B + 8 [zaglaïm], ô C + 7 [lezphar], so that from now on your four main chiefs of the demonic regions Lucifer, Barau, Belzebu, and Leviathan no longer have any authority, virtue, or power over our souls and those of our

brethren and sisters in a thousand circumstances of our temporal, animal and Spiritual life, which is fixed by the ineffable Creator in weight, count and measure, as he desired and did.

By the power that I hold from the mercy of the God of our fathers, from Abraham, from Isaac, and from Jacob, ô + 10 (the same), I conjure you and constrain you (both names out of 5) Lucifer, Barau, Belzebu, Leviathan, and all perverse Spirits, so that your desires, thoughts, will, words, and all that you will generally want to do to make us fall into prevarication and dissension become like the dust that the wind drives out and dissipates. May the Angel of the Lord Almighty God, ô + 7...'

The blue book states here ô atvamaï for the father, ô zaglaïm for the son, ô lezphar for the Holy Spirit.

They are the deputies of Leviathan, Belzebu, Barau and Lucifer.

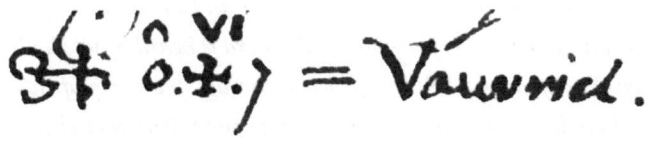

'...principal chief guard of the North, break you into as many parts as the sand in the sea! May your dark and infernal chasms be an embarrassment and an eternal chain! And that in this horrible situation you serve as an immemorial example to all the demons and to all mortals. Amen.'

> Note. Operative and penitent R✠ gather standing in the North corner of the triangle facing the South; there, they present their pentacles towards this part, remaining at order with their candles beside them: in this position the operative pronounces against the perverse Spirits the following sentence that the R✠ penitents follow with attention and joining his intention to his.

Sentence against the Perverse

'In the formidable name, ô + 10, of the very strong God of Heaven, Earth, Sea and Air, and all their inhabitants; of the mighty God of the armies of Heaven and Earth; from the just God of vengeances and rewards; and by virtue of our power, action, and authority over you all, unclean, dissentient, and accursed spirits, we command you that by obeying henceforth our commands and wills, you no longer seek to induce us into prevarication, error, dissension, and into no act contrary to the holy will of the infinitely good God in whose name, ô + 10, and by which we confidently exercise our omnipotence over all of you, accursed spirits.'

'By all the virtues and powers of God, heavenly and earthly, and by all the divine spirits, we conjure you to be relegated, bound, and subjugated by the invincible and indissoluble bonds which the Lord gave you in punishment of all your attacks against his divine majesty and against ours, his image and his likeness. By all these powers united to ours and to the name, ô + 10, we command you to obey us as promptly as the word is heard by us all directly or indirectly; We defend you (NNN) who are, through the mercy of God, in this worshipful circle, to enter the future in any of our spiritual circles, temporal and earthly for any pretext whatsoever, in inspiration, insinuation, revelation, seduction or any other way whatsoever to misguide and distract us from all that we owe to God our creator and yours, to the holy spirits that he has given us as conductors and to men our brothers and our fellow men.'

'We will bind you for an eternity, you and your lying, dissentient, seductive, disruptive powers and all other fatalities for us and for all our other brothers the faithful chosen of the Most High.'

'We are especially grateful to you at this moment, spirits accursed with disorder, confusion, and troubles, by the helping name of the God of Peace, ô + 10, by the mighty virtue of all the holy spirits attached to the seven planets and all those who we are given as guides and by all the secret characters that are in these pentacles, which force you to submit to us and to recognise us as your superiors and your masters in the circles of divine sciences spiritual, animal and terrestrial, we bind you and make sure that you all go to the destiny that our sentence pronounces against you, and that, covered with shame *and rage, you receive with the fatal poison of prevarication and dissension which you have subtly made slip among us who are all brethren and equals and friends, who in this circle and in preference to the one who searches the hearts, ô + 10, we swear and promise to love each other, to forgive ourselves to help us spiritually and temporally, by all the holy operations of our fathers, patriarchs, prophets, apostles and above all by that of Christ for whom and in whom we want to live and die. Amen.'*

Note. The operating ℞ and penitents take their places in the West, North and South; they will put their knees on the ground at the angle of the triangle, their heads bowed, their arms crossed on their chests; the operative will make the next invocation, their candles in front of them on the ground and they all face the centre.

If there is no division among the ℞ we will say any such other prayer as we want, that of Manasseh[41] or another.

Invocation

'ô + 10, O' LORD God Almighty, O' God Creator, Avenger and Rewarder; I am prostrate before you in the midst of your infinite power, covered with shame, overwhelmed with remorse and penetrated with repentance for having outraged the one who has deigned to regenerate humanity in you, in him and in your Divine Spirit; all the spirits which he has submitted to our authority by the correspondence of intelligence which he has given us with all the holy spirits of your divine, heavenly and spiritual court; we beg you, by the formidable name, ô A + 8, which gave Heli,[42] thy elected faithful this same name I invoke, ô + 8, we redouble our virtue and power from you to obtain the general forgiveness of all our faults, (NNN), who are here present

---

41 The Manasseh Prayer' is a short text of 15 verses in the Old Testament. It is a penance prayer of Manasseh, king of Judah captive in Babylon, who was, according to the Bible (II Kings, XXI, 1-18), among the most idolatrous. However, after being taken prisoner by the Assyrians, he prayed for his pardon (II Chronicles, XXXIII, 10-17) and turned away from his idolatry. It is part of some editions of the Septuagint, as an appendix in the Vulgate, but is considered apocryphal by the Roman Catholic Church, Jews and Protestants. The Orthodox regard it as deuterocanonical.

42 Pasqually uses the word Hely for the Christ, meaning 'the force of God'. According to Pasqually, Hely, or the Christ, manifested through the line of prophets, the guides of humanity, and those called the Elect. Among these, he cites Abel, Enoch, Noah, Melchizedek, Joseph, Moses, David, Solomon, Zerubbabel, and Jesus Christ, who were all channels for the manifestation of Hely. However, he considers that Hely manifested his greatest glory in Jesus Christ.

and those of all our brothers ℞☩ absent; We pray to you also, O' God of Peace and Mercy, ô + 10, to disperse from us forever all influences of trouble, of discord and of dissension, so that our supplications, our prayers and our praises to your adorable majesty, can emanate only from pure and peaceful hearts! If there still remains in our heart some vestiges of dissension such light and under such shadow that it is, deign to dispel it and erase it, O' thou who alone can give us peace, at this moment where in your holy presence as we give ourselves the sign and the assurance. Amen.'

Note. Operative and penitential ℞☩ come together for prescribed purposes in the centre, their candles in a triangle around that of the word, form the chain, all together say in ordinary voices the Pater Noster give themselves the Kiss of Peace by saying *sicut et nos dimitti me*[43] and taking their candles, return to their places. The operative will then make the following conjuration on the Serpent.

Conjuration on the Serpent

'In the name of the terrible God, ô + 10! Cursed Serpent, who sought to corrupt and make the Man-God succumb in your unholy thought, remember your sentence and shudder! I command you to obey me now! Appear and remain in my presence in the vicinity of this circle without making any noise capable of frightening us here present, nor the other inhabitants of this house and without causing any disorder! Put on your accursed soul with an honest and graceful body! Be docile and answer me, in French without mental reservation, fraud, or subterfuge, to all my questions, I command you by the name of the God of all Domination, ô + 10.'

Note. The operative asks his questions as if he has saw the perverse spirit, who is indeed present, who sees and hears all that happens even if he does not see or hear; then he continues the conjuration.

---

43 Latin: sicut et nos dimitti me (As we forgive'). Kiss of Peace; in Catholicism, the term now used is not 'the kiss of peace', but 'the sign of peace' or 'the rite of peace'. It was the widespread custom in the ancient Eastern Mediterranean for men to greet each other with a kiss. That was also the custom in ancient Judea and practiced also by Christians. It is placed after the Pater Noster and before the Fractio Panis.

Translation of 'Le Manuscrit d'Alger' (1772)

'I constrain you, subtle and Cursed Serpent, so that you remain aggravated, molested and degraded by me from the centre of this circle without whisper; receive from me your judgment Serpent that I curse by the ineffable name of God, ô + 10, by whose will you must come and go everywhere and it pleases him who has power over you; Go for an eternity with all your legions in your abysses so that there is never more question of you and all your henchmen being among us. And all you perverse Spirits, in the name of our God and yours, ô + 10, leave our presence and that of our circle; obey, depart from before us without noise, and without fear for anyone! May my omnipotence on you in the name, ô + 10, operate according to our desires in our image and likeness of him who created us! Hear my word to the depths of the abyss.'

Note: when you say the following, the operative knots a small piece of black ribbon nine times, cuts a piece of oat straw with a penknife in several pieces, throws a handful of sand with his arms towards South and ends giving three kicks on the serpent's head.

'Be all bound by me N. and N. N. here present and by the exterminating Spirit of the Almighty Living God ô W. 4; be so quickly broken up and scattered in your hellish abyss that the straw is broken and the sand is scattered; and be always molested as I molest you.'

'Note: the operative enters the circle, places himself in the centre and calls the penitent R✠; they stand up in a triangle with their faces in the centre, their arms crossed over their chests, their candles also circling that of the word; in this position the operative pronounces the next prayer.'

Prayer

'ô + 10, merciful God; God of Peace, Mercy, and Love, O' Father of the Living, cast a ray of grace upon your afflicted servants N.N.N. whom thou hast deigned to call to the mighty labours of thy divine knowledge, and which thou hast brought into the path of faith in thy holy name; do, O' my God, that by this same faith our guilty hearts may be healed of the evils which were heartbroken; Preserve us from all sorts of spiritual and temporal misfortunes and attacks from our enemy; give us the strength to resist all his Spirits, to fight him and to conquer him for your greater Glory and Justice.

ô + 10, break the deceptive links that could still retain our souls in matter; open to us the door of your love, your fear and your wisdom, according to the promise you made to our Fathers, so that being marked...'

> Note: The operative and penitent ℞✠ [draw on] each other a triangle on the forehead with the first three fingers of the right hand, the thumb on the right, the index in the middle of the forehead and the finger from the middle on the left he then they resume their position of crossed arms.

'...from the seal of intellectual reconciliation, we are free from corruption, prevarication, error, fornication, dissension, and the habits of yielding to the attacks of the perverse spirit which we have just expelled in your name; and so that, being now filled with the virtue of your mighty blessings, we now observe with joy, peace, and holiness, the laws, precepts, and commandments which it pleased you to have made us unworthy in the bosom of circumferences of your wisdom.'

'Hold us, O' Lord, and make us as firm and steadfast in your circles of power as the Earth is in the centre of its Aquatic Circumference; Do also, O' Divine Father of all Created Being, that by advancing day by day in the worship which you have made known to us, that by redoubling our joys and our desires to tend to perfection, we are found worthy by you of your eternal reward and a salutary remedy for all our faults, so that we may fearlessly and without troubling recourse to you and invoke you in all our operations and in all our spiritual and temporal needs by your holy and ineffable name, ô + 10 ; May this admiral name protect us, strengthen us, console us and guide us against all the perverse powers that are prevalent in our Earth and Air region; May the strength and virtue of your name bring us into contact with the holy spirits who surround us and to whom you entrusted our guard.'

'O' God of Clemency and Mercy, ô + 10, be conducive to your elected faithful gathered here for confession and repentance of their sins against you, grant us forgiveness of all our sins, and cleanse us of all our filth; Make us men new before you. Remember that thou adopted us in the invincible circumferences mysterious by your divine science, to know it and practice it as you please and in your time. Take pity on us N.N.N. Most Holy God give power to the

Spirit that sustained me, to strengthen my soul because of your glory so that the word that I will speak in your name is neither trembling nor uncertain to those who will hear ô + 10, that your name is blessed. Amen.'

Note: During the following exorcism, the operating R✠ holds his right hand at right angles to the penitent R✠ kneeling. In the places indicated he takes the grains of salt, holding the oblation in the right hand which it then spreads on the centre, he puts a grain of salt in the mouth of each penitent and one in his own.

Exorcism on a Penitent R✠

'I exorcise thee, creature N, I exorcise thee, creature N, in the name ô + 10, of God the Father Almighty, ô + 8 of God the all-powerful Saviour Son, ô + 7 of God the Holy Spirit and all-powerful engine; in the name ô + 10, of one God whom I adore, who created you, who preserved you from eternal death and who keeps you for the fulfilment of his immutable decrees; I am exorcised by all the powerful virtues which he has given to his holy spirits to be the support, the guides, and the companions of his faithful servants, and to bless, sanctify, and give power to all who are men of true desire in God. Amen. Amen. Amen.'

Oblation of Salt [44]

'ô + 10, O' God of Incomprehensible Power, I exconjure you by your quadruple essence to sanctify this creature of salt by your blessing as I consecrate it by your holy name ô + 10, so that it is a perfect remedy for those who receive it.'

---

44 Oblation, the offering of bread and wine at the Eucharist.

Manducation of Salt [45]

'*May this Salt abide in your bowels, N (baptismal) N that you may henceforth be free from all dreadful falls, and overflowing dissension, and all other defilements during the whole of your passing life.*'

'*We exconjure you, ô +10, hear us in the name of him who is to judge the Living and the Dead; Hear us by the help of the God of our fathers, from the God who took the children of Israel from the land of Egypt by giving them a holy Spirit to protect them, to enlighten them and to lead them by day and by night in the desert. We rely with confidence on your infinite mercy and all that it pleases you to make us be in Thought, Will, Action and Power; we exconjure thee, ô + 10, for all our Spiritual faculties and time it may please thee grant the prayer we humbly do you N.N.N. who are here present in the expectation of your mercy, give command to the liberator, defender and custodian Spirits to come out of their circles of power whenever we call on them and call on our Spiritual and temporal help by your holy and ineffable names, so that through them we can regain the powerful word that you deign to give, in your mercy, to Man, your beloved creature, and now strong and invincible by it, we can fight and destroy it with our enemies and those of your Holy Law for the fulfilment of your glory and righteousness. Amen, ô + 10. Hear us, Almighty God, Amen, Amen, Amen.*'

The R✠ will together say the *Te Deum Laudamus*.[46]

Then each R✠ prostrating himself in front of the word in the centre and at the top of the triangle's centre, will make any particular prayer that he wills, then hiding the candle from the centre, he will be able to contemplate for a while. This work can be done at any time. We will raise the words to ordinary uses.

If without any reason for dissension, a R✠ simply wishes to be reconciled with *la chose*, the operative will make the appropriate changes in this operation.

---

45   Manducation is the act of eating. Used in Catholicism to describe the belief that eating the bread of Eucharist is eating the actual flesh of Jesus.
46   Latin: 'Thee, O God, we praise'. Likely reference to the Te Deum (also known as Ambrosian Hymn or A Song of the Church) an early Christian hymn of praise

Translation of 'Le Manuscrit d'Alger' (1772)

Singular Dream

I was, for a few days, in that most lonely place of Trifaven wood, meditating on the causes of our degradation, when suddenly my eyelids grew heavy. I was forced to sit at the foot of a tree and yield to this soporific condition, during which my heated imagination led me to this singular dream that you will hear and which all my life I have never forgotten.

It seemed to me that I was in an exceedingly dark forest, planted with cypresses, pines, yews, and other funereal trees, to which I saw no way out. The land was covered with hippomane, hemlock, mint, aconite, wormwood, brambles, thistles, nettles, and all the most offensive, venomous and bitter plants we know. This place of sadness was lit only by lightning strikes. A bituminous, sulphurous, thick, and foul vapour was rising from a damp and corrupt soil, which the rays of the Sun had never touched. The bat, the owl and the raven, were the only birds to be heard. The most fearsome monsters, the most ferocious animals, the most dangerous reptiles and the most troublesome insects seemed to be gathered from all the world over. I walked slowly, wanting to leave this horrible place. Fright froze me. I was without pulse, without strength and breathless. I dragged myself up a mound from the top of which I hoped to penetrate more easily the darkness which surrounded me. I had scarcely reached the summit when I heard these words spoken by someone whom I did not see: 'look, listen, and take courage'; then the forest seemed to me all on fire, and I saw that it was inhabited by an abominable people composed of all the nations of the earth divided under different signs, offering to my eyes all the crimes that make Nature groan since Man blinded by pride abandoned truth for the prestige of his imagination. This spectacle tore my soul apart. I covered my face to give some respite to my spirit overwhelmed by so many horrors; but the same voice was heard again, and said to me, 'look and comfort yourself'. These words restored me to my first virtue; I looked with confidence and there was the most enchanting figure of which I was witness.

I found myself in the middle of an alabaster building of majesty, grandeur, of unspeakable magnificence. I saw that this edifice had four gates which looked East, West, North, and South, which were reached by so many columns of divine architecture, each of which was more than a hundred fathoms in length; the greatest whiteness and unmistakable polish, without gilding, without mosaics, without paint, all seemingly carved from the same block.

In the midst of this august temple was a platform of three steps, serving as the base of a tomb, on which appeared an exact cube supporting a sepulchral urn of triangular form, from whence issued a continuous, bright and pure fire. In the four angles of this superb mausoleum were four statues of exquisite workmanship carried on pedestals no less worthy of admiration. With faces covered with tears and arms stretched out to the sky, the figures could be seen in the open, because there was no vault, dome, or ceiling in this place. The first of these statues had a flame on its head, second a radiant sun upon the breast, the third held a level in his right hand, and the last had a serpent around its waist.

The Protecting Genius, who had already spoken to me twice, manifested himself again, and I had this mystical proclamation, to which I could understand nothing.

> 'The ages have elapsed - The temple of profanation is destroyed. The principle of darkness returned to the bosom of Light - weakness returns to strength. It will not be exposed - It will no longer be discovered - It is imperturbable, invulnerable, and unalterable in its particular unity, like Nature in its plastic unity.'

So the fire issued forth from the urn, rose, spread, and formed a glory whose brilliance made the Sun disappear, as the Sun makes the stars of the night disappear. Little by little, light and brilliant vapours gathered at the centre where they composed a creature so beautiful, so perfect, that I would have taken for the very divinity, if I had not witnessed its creation. She was naked. I noticed that she had no sex; that she united to a sovereign degree of perfection all the beauties, all the graces, all the charms of a young virgin shaped by love, to all male beauties of a man accomplished. She was sitting at the base of two broken columns. I dared to gaze at the immortal and I saw in their eyes the character of a compassion so touching that mine filled with tears. I could not bear the excess of my rapture anymore, my heart was too full. The shadows of the dead gathered around me. I lost consciousness. I fell, not in a dream, but truly, which awoke me.

Translation of 'Le Manuscrit d'Alger' (1772)

Quarter Angle for Commander of the East [Apprenti Réaux+Croix] Plan 5 № 1

At the top of the corner a word out of 10.

Below, or, in a triangle around this word, the three baptismal names of the emulator.

At each end of the double ray of the quarter angle one name out of 7, and one if one wants in the centre on 8.

The foremost circle contains one name out of 7 and preferably that of its known or adopted keeper on whatever number.

A candle on each word and name.

The candle of the emulator outside the double ray and towards the centre.

After all the preliminaries of the garment, the new fire, etc..., the emulator, having done well, collected and willing, will begin his prayer this way;

He will take three steps of an Apprentices while advancing and three whilst receding, at the third he will fall to his knees on the ground, then the body half raised, both hands resting on the ground, he breathes three times on the flame of the candle which is on the word 10 from the top of the angle and then pronounces on it rendering his breath saying the word three times with the exclamation 'O' every time, adding likewise:

'in quâcumque die invocavero te velociter Exaudi me.'[47]

Then remaining in the same position, the emulator will do this prayer.

Prayer to God

'O' LORD, ineffable and sacred Father of All Things; you who see and embrace everything, hear the prayer of your servant prostrate before you; grant me the recollection, the fervour, and the sincerity for the feelings I am

---

47 Latin. 'In whatever day, I shall call upon thee, hear me speedily'. Psalm 101. Non avertas faciem tuam a me in quacumque die tribulor inclina ad me aurem tuam in quacumque die invocavero te velociter exaudi me (Turn not away thy face from me: in the day when I am in trouble, incline thy ear to me. In what day soever I shall call upon thee, hear me speedily)

about to present to you; be conducive to me, O (the word out of 10) and to all those for whom I invoke you (we name them) and in general for all my brethren in order, for all my parents, my friends, my enemies, for all the living and the dead and for all your creatures. Hear me, O (the same word), give me the gift of praying to you effectively. I abandon myself to your holy guard, take pity on me and your will be done. Amen.'

The emulator will invoke the three names of his patrons, remaining in the same position and their will do this prayer:

Prayer to Patrons

'O' Spirits released from the bonds of matter, which now enjoy the fruit of your virtues, and whose names I am happy to bear; I exconjure you by this name that you have invoked with so much confidence and success O (the word out of 10) to contribute to my eternal salvation, through your intercession and your protection with the Father of mercies, with the redeeming Son and with the custodian Spirit. Get for me (invoking the three Patrons) the graces, the help and the clemency of the deity who today rewards you for the fights you have given in this stay where I am still; make by your help that I live and die like you in peace and in the joy of holiness. Amen. Pray for me and with me, at this time especially for the Lord to have mercy on me. Amen. O' (we invoke the three Patrons) intercede for me! Amen.'

The emulator standing upright will go with the same steps to the leading edge of the circle where he will invoke in the same position as above the spirit of his known or adopted Guardian, and will make this prayer:

Prayer to the Guardian

'O' pure Spirit, who are charged by the Lord to watch over me for the reconciliation of my whole spiritual being, I exconjure you by the name of the God of Mercy, O (the word out of 10) come to the rescue of my soul every time it be in danger of succumbing to evil; whenever it calls you by its desires, its sighs, and its meditations, and whenever it is hungry and thirsty for advice, instruction, and intelligence. Help me (the Guardian spirit) to also obtain the

protection and assistance of O' (we call the Patrons) *that I have invoked and the submission of O'* (we call the two Spirits of the double ray) *that I remain to invoke. Help me, help me in my poverty, in my nakedness and in all my needs, O'* (Guardian). *Amen.'*

The emulator standing upright will go with the same steps to the double ray where he will invoke separately in the same position the Spirits he will have placed there, making them the following prayer in common:

Prayer to the Double Ray Spirits

'*I exconjure you that by the strength of Jehovah's mighty name, O* (the word out of 10), *you deign to be in favour of me on all occasions when I will have recourse to you for my spiritual and temporal needs and for those of my kind. Help me according to the virtues and faculties which are distributed to you by divine mercy for the sole advantage of Man. Contribute by all that is in you to the purity of my soul and my body, to the accomplishment of my desires as much as they will be in conformity with the will of my God.'*

'*Join for this with* (we name the Patrons and the Guardian) *whom I invoked as I call you O* (the names of the Spirits of the double ray). *Amen.'*

The emulator on his knees in the corner facing East, his candle on the floor in front of him, will call the word on 10 from the top of the corner and say in a low voice (if there is no 'indiscretion') the first five verses of the *Miserere* after which he will invoke the word on 10 in the same position of Moses adding immediately '*in quâcumque die...*'[48] etc.

During the *Miserere,* the emulator holds his pentacle with his right hand, making it pass from time to time to his left from his right.

Remaining in the same place and in the same position, the emulator invokes the same Spirit of the South and says the following five verses of the said psalm.

He does the same for the Spirit of the North by continuing the next five verses.

Finally, the emulator completes the *Miserere* in the foremost circle with the same attentions.

---

48 Latin. 'In whatever day'. Psalm 101.

Then the emulator will prostrate the whole body, his head towards the top of the angle resting on the back of his hands on the ground, his pentacle before him; in this position he invokes his three patrons with *quâcumque die...*[49] etc and says all along the *'De Profundis,'*[50] after which he repeats the same invocation of the Patrons.

The emulator is free to do at this moment such another prayer that he will dedicate to God or to his Saints or his Spirits.

The prayers finished, the emulator observes a moment of meditation, then resuming his pentacle, he stands up entirely; go through the steps prescribed to the foremost circle, dismisses the Spirit with the word out of 10, draw the candle three times, extinguish it, knocks it over and erase the name.

> Note: you must always delete the words and names as you extinguish the candles on them. The emulator does the same thing to the North and South of the double ray, then to his patrons whom he thanks and dismisses. Then he gives thanks to Jehovah (by such prayer as he wills), being prostrate all his length before the word on 10 from the top of the angle; and rising from the upper half of the body, he inhales the candle that covers him three times by pronouncing the said word and repeating every time *'in quâcumque die...'*[51] etc, extinguishes it, going backwards erasing the word.

---

49 Latin. 'In whatever day'. Psalm 101.
50 Latin. 'From the depths'. Psalm 129.
51 Latin. 'In whatever day'. Psalm 101.

Translation of 'Le Manuscrit d'Alger' (1772)

Preventative Operation Against those who Labour in Evil

In general, to retain the power that God has kindly communicate to Man, his image and likeness, one must have great faith in God, in his power, and in the different names that are accordingly given; Moses had great faith in these names when he used them so effectively to deprive the wise men of Egypt of the power they abused.

The sign of the Christian is an emblematic figure of the universal receptacle on which the Man-God and God completed all their natural operations, as has already been represented by the wise in the early days. By this figure he contained, fixed, and bounded all things created in the course of their temporal actions.

In order to oppose the evil of which we have suspicion or certainty, we must do our utmost to know the baptismal and family names of those who want to harm or labour in evil [against us], and write them with red chalk in the South part of the receptacle, one foot away from the circle formed in the centre of said receptacle. We will draw with a white chalk a Serpent in the bottom of the receptacle in the West, from his mouth will come four arrows to which we will attach as many terrestrial words of 3.

In the Southern corner at a great distance from the receptacle; another Serpent will be drawn with black chalk, having a large gaping mouth, his head will look to the names of those whom one wishes to thwart.

In the circle of the centre of the receptacle, one name out of four will be placed in the South, which will represent the names of those who wish to do evil; in the West a name of double power which will do the same service to the four terrestrial names placed before the four darts of the white Serpent; in the North one name out of 7 and in the East a divine word out of 10.

All these things will be enclosed in a large circle of white chalk.

The operative is placed in the inner circle of the receptacle having his sword in hand; he will take the proper precautions when beginning his operation, to trace on the top of the blade a name of 7 in whole with virgin wax to prevent it being poisoned; the wax not retaining any impression of evil.

If he can the operative will attend the Mass every day of the work and during the consecration he will make a prayer similar to what he wants to undertake and will pronounce at the elevation one word out of 10 that he will keep to make him dominate over all the names he will have to use for this work; it will be by virtue of this word that he will make his conjurations on the names that are in the centre of the receptacle, being careful not to confuse them or compromise with the other names used outside this centre.

The names and the word placed internally around the centre of the receptacle will be used for the exorcisms against the two Serpents, to avoid the surprise that the evil could do under the guise of truth. They will also serve each of the three conjurations that will be done on the Serpent.

At the end of the conjuration, the operative will give a [heavy] blow from the point of his sword to the head of the Serpent in the North and where the names of the perpetrators are; by removing the sword where the blow was dealt, he will sink into the hole a few drops the candle from the centre and press it with the thumb for a moment.

The second ceremony will then be made on the head of the white Serpent, as in the case of the black Serpent, thus alternately making the six conjurations from one Serpent to another, and giving at the end of each a blow from the point of the sword on the body of the snake, 1°, to the head as it has been said, 2°, in the middle of the body, 3°, towards the tail of each.

Exorcisms and conjurations will be found in the psalms, in Moses, and in the ritual; we will only change the names to that of those of the evildoers: and if we do not have their names, we curse the serpent by using this name and the evildoers under names numbered 9.

That being done, the operative will make a conjuration on the spirits at number 8 and number 7 of the centre of the receptacle to procure the strong and double strong exterminator Spirit against all men who seek to harm others or to give in the evil. He will conjure these spirits, by the word of the centre, to always be in his custody and help him to destroy all bad operations.

The operator will be careful to keep the same words and names that he has used in this work, to use them on the same occasions. We can extend this work for three days, observing to trace each day.

At the end of each operation, the operative will spread salt, well pounded, on the names of the evildoers, it will then erase these names by crushing with the foot this salt on these names.

Quarter Angle with Three Rays Plan 5 № 4

At the very top end is the Sun and 12 stars outside to the East.

Make a triangle proportionate to the room where you labour, with three circular ray circles, in front of which three circles of correspondence or vanguards in the West, North and South.

At the top of the triangle one BAB; below him three words out of 10 of the day in triangle, then three names of patriarchs; and three names of Angels forming two parallel lines, that of the angles along the first circle and within the quarter-angle N.1. [nuriel]; M.4 . [mozé]; I.26. [ïeremiel];

At the forefront of the West G.7. [gabbriel] with the hieroglyph of Jacob's strength, ahead of the Moon and one

South to the vanguard V.4. [vriel] with the hieroglyph of the Earth.

At the forefront of North PR.25. [pikim] with the hieroglyph of Christ.

In the first inner circle four numbers on 7 and 8 on guard.

In the second circle, the four Angels of the four parts of the world, arranged according to their parts.

In the third circle the four elements arranged according to their parts, with the name of the good intelligence of the planet of the day in the middle and the character of the intelligence, having on its right its character and on the left the hieroglyph.

Quarter Angle of Body Purification with Three Rays

At the top of the angle, a triangle in which a word out of 10 and below the three names of the patrons of the operative placed triangularly.

In the inner ray, the names of the Angels of the planets of the day, the day before and the next, with their hieroglyphic characters.

In the centre ray, the names of the same planets with their characters and hieroglyphs and good intelligences.

In the outer ray planetary characters of the same planets, dominated by the Angel of the earth in his hieroglyph, with three names including one in 3, one in 6 and one in 9.

On the wing of the South, a charcoal Serpent with its head toward the East.

A rear-guard circle to the West with a name of 7 or 8.

The convention characters outside the outer circle.

Everything being arranged according to the ordered preliminaries and the operative wanting to begin the operation, he will light three small candles on the Serpent in the South, and in this part the exconjuration and the exorcism which he will judge to be appropriate. Here is an idea:

Exconjuration and Exorcism in the South.

> 'I exonerate you and exorcise you, O' Cursed Serpent, O' Lucifer, as well as all the Spirits who are subjected to you, by the power of the terrible God O + 10 whom you blaspheme against in vain and whom I adore, so that you come out of my presence and you flee from my operation here traced.'

> 'Obey my command without causing any scandal, no fright, no noise. I call on Jehovah my God, O + 10, that His omnipotence may work on you according to my desire, both in this region and in my dwelling place, and in the depths of the abyss into which you are so precipitated.'

The operative puts his left foot on the Serpent's head and presenting the pentacle on him, he continues:

> 'Be put to flight and shut up in the infernal abysses, O' Cursed Serpent, by the exterminating Angel, O' W.4 of the vengeful and remunerating God! Be it as quickly as this straw breaks and this dust is scattered.'

(One breaks a straw and blows on the dust; one beats the left foot three times on the head of the Serpent).

> 'I curse you, perverse spirit, because you dared to tempt the Man-God your judge. I bind you by this formidable name O + 10 so that you never have any hold on me in the spiritual, in the temporal nor in the material; and in this particular labour which I offer to the Lord, your God and mine, for the particular purification of my corporal form, I bind you more strongly so that you can no longer attack or seduce my form bodily by any of your impure acts and I put it to be in the middle guard of +++ my patrons and + my Guardian and his intellect, giving up all my faculties to you and your adherents, to your pageants and your works.'

The operative thrusts at the head of the Serpent with blow a of the sword, one on the middle of the body and one on the tail and then throws the sword in the angle of the South: he extinguishes the small candles which are above with the foot.

This exconjuration being finished, the operative begins the labour similar to that of a Commander of the East [Apprentice Réaux+Croix]. The work being destined for the purification of the corporeal form, he will ask his Guardians and patrons for their help and their Guardianship over the spirits laden with his form; He will enjoin these spirits to conform to his desires and the orders and instructions of his Guardians and patrons. He will make the same prayer to the conducting Angels of the planets and to the spirits of the planets. etc.[52]

---

52 The original Ms. then instructs, 'See the work page 29'...'see page 77 of the Blue Book No. 878'.

Translation of 'Le Manuscrit d'Alger' (1772)

Extract from an Instruction of D[on] M[artinez] P[asqually] entrusted to the W[orshipful] M[aster] of ch[evalier] F[ranc] M[açon] W. on the Temple.[53]

A pillar of earth to the North, one of clouds to the South; and one of fire to the East.

The temple is divided into 3, 5, 7.

3 represents the three chief principles of Creation and the three heads of the temple at Jerusalem: Solomon at the North pillar, Hiram Abi at the South pillar, and Abhiram at the East pillar.

Ja, bin, ia are the three names of the three columns

Ja; Wisdom of Solomon; bin the strength of his crime; ia Beauty of the Temple. 3 on the North column, 5 on the South column, 7 on the East column.

There were seven temples raised on the Earth, each supported by seven columns; that of Adam, of Enoch, Melchizedek, Moses, Solomon, Zerubbabel and finally that of Christ that exists today. By these columns are meant the seven chiefs who are each endowed with a particular gift.

The mountain on which the Temple of Jerusalem was built was hollow and this void was surrounded by seven arches.

The Western Arch held various materials and precious stones.

The North Arch held iron, cast iron, tin, cedar, coral, gold, and silver.

The Eastern Arch contained many hieroglyphs by which Solomon knew that the temple was not built on a common ground, since it did not take its origin from the earth from below (which is proved by the hollowness and the arches), but that it was a virgin land descended or transported expressly for this construction of the Temple.

The Central Arch served to make known to Solomon the strength and power which his wisdom had acquired for him, as much over all nations as over all created things; he also learned to perpetuate himself in all the divine, spiritual, temporal, celestial, animal, and terrestrial knowledge which the Creator had made him communicate.

---

53   This section has direct quotes and from the 1770 Elus Coën catechism.

The Fifth Arch contained a quantity of characters and hieroglyphs which Solomon could neither read nor number; he learned from this that he was stripped of the power and the universal science which he had had in his state of wisdom.

He was then no more than an ordinary man, a simple mortal and even more guilty than the rest of the mortals, because the creator had forbidden that this arch be opened before the prescribed time under penalty of incurring his disgrace and to make his posterity wander among the nations, the opening of this arch is reserved for the one who had to manifest the divine glory in the centre of the Universe.

Solomon did not open the Sixth and Seventh Arch because they were the figure and likeness of the Creator, and so they could only be opened by him who alone is the beginning and the end of all things.

These Seven Arches are represented to us by the seven planets in each of which is a particular virtue.

The vault or hollow represents the place from which Adam's body of matter emerged; the virgin earth represents to us the separation of the material from the spiritual and reminds us what the creator says to Adam;

> *'Look at this mountain which dominates over everything, it bears three names which announce the origin of your body, as well as the Law, the Precept and the Commandment that I gave you, and these names will multiply to infinity. This mountain was holy and blessed by me before your creation, since it is on it that you were created. Respect her as your mother since she is Holy! Whenever you lift your eyes upward or drop them on this Earth, or fix the plants that it produces, you will praise and sanctify the living God who created you.'*

Then, before leaving him, the Creator made known to Adam the various Masonic instruments, which he had used for the construction of his particular temple and his universal temple.

Instruction on an Invocation of Reconciliation for the use of Br[ethren] of the High Grades. (Inferior)[54]

On Wednesday evenings before going to sleep we will say the following and on Saturdays too, this invocation is not specific to the other days of the week. These two days are consecrated to the two principal universal spirits, one of whom is under the sign of Mercury, who governs, directs, and actuates the Earth and all the bodily forms; the other is under the sign of Saturn, who governs, directs, and actuates souls, and who has more power over the animate creature than Mercury; which one can easily understand by the different distances of the terrestrial surface to which these planets are. Saturn is above the Sun and below the three heavens: Mercury is above the third terrestrial horizon presiding over the other two lower; these horizons are usually called the rational, visual, sensible circles.

This invocation will be begun on Wednesday evening in order to dispose our soul to receive and retain some impression of the spirit of Saturn through the spirit of Mercury who strips our soul of the grossest matter that envelopes it.

In order, there are seven main signs each designating a planet; it is absolutely necessary for an emulator to know perfectly the virtues and spiritual powers that are contained in these different planets, as well as their exact and reciprocal correspondences with Man and with his bodily form, since the spirits who direct each of them they are subject to the power of the man of desire.[55]

This invocation is given so that the emulators use it with respect, with discretion and with confidence and not deviating in any way from what is prescribed in order to be able to communicate with the spirits who are within the power of Man.

Preparations

It is necessary to have a private room where there are neither tapestries nor paintings, it does not matter if there are other pieces of furniture as long as the part of the wall facing East is particularly clear.

The days when you want to make this invocation, you will only [eat] a simple meal.

---

54 In the top left hand corner of the original Ms. it states 'transported here from the white notebook'.
55 Hommes de désir; Adopting the name that the angel Gabriel had given to Daniel (Dan. 9:23).

We will have yellow candles and if we are not sure that they are pure and without resin, we will take some white ones; the defect of purity in the candle would be contrary to la chose. Cut the excess wicks with scissors before blessing them. Then we will put all the candles together on the ground at the corner of the East, we will decorate them all in colours and we will bless the candles as it is said elsewhere.

(The hour of midnight to one o'clock is the most favourable to invocations of reconciliation, it is necessary to observe to do them only in the first or the second quarter of the moon and not in the last two quarters, because then its influences are bad and could harm the emulator.)

One will observe to always have the face turned towards the angle of the East when one will make the invocation without ever diverting it, only to look to the right and to the left after the divine words uttered in the invocation have been pronounced and are transferred immediately to the East.

If the angle of the room does not look positively East, it will always follow that it would be in the middle of the wall. The emulator will be standing in the middle of the room facing East, he will trace on the ground all he receives with white chalk. As the work began at midnight, he will wait an hour to finish his operations, and say:

'Blessed are those who came in the name of the Lord, may the peace of the Lord always be with us. Amen.'

He will extinguish his candle and will undress to another simply holy light. This invocation will be as often as one feels disposed to do it; if an emulator cannot do it in the first quarter of the moon, he will do it in the second, but never in both last quarters.[56]

Obligations of an Emulator of the High Grades

The emulators will observe very carefully not to eat the fat of the kidneys, nor the kidneys of any animal, nor the blood of the animal, nor any animal which would have been smothered in its own blood.

They will abstain twenty-four hours in advance from the commerce of women; if they are in the case of adultery, they will make an invocation only after absolutely renouncing it and being well reconciled.

---

56 The original Ms. then states 'Taken from the white notebook'.

The emulators will make their invocation every Friday at the ninth hour of the day, which returns at three o'clock in the afternoon, and if that is not possible at any other convenient hour of the evening.

They will have for this purpose a special room, out of any profane communication, where there will be no tapestry or paintings on the walls. There can be a chair and a table to write.

This invocation has the property of disposing the one who does it with faith and accuracy in order to receive all temporal and spiritual impressions that the mind must make temporally on his bodily form and spiritually on his spiritual soul in order to prepare him to see and hear the faculties of this spirit, which he calls to his aid, in whatever tribulation, and that he can conceive them perfectly without fear and without risk.

Whoever makes this invocation will only have a lighted candle in his hand to be able to read it; he will place himself in the centre of the room without making any circle; when he begins, he will have his face turned towards the side of the Rising Sun, and towards the middle of the invocation he will turn it towards the West.

The emulator, being in the centre of the chamber, will put both knees on the ground, and put the burning candle of the new fire standing on the ground beside him on the right; then he will bow his face to the ground, his head resting on both hands whose fists will be closed. In this position he will say the whole *De profundis;*[57] after which he will make his confession of faith to the Creator, then taking his candle with his right hand, he stands up. This candle is an allusion to the fire of the spirit which is called upon to help him to be inflamed, enlightened, sustained and led spiritually by him in all spiritual and temporal operations.

Same Obligations with Some Differences.

The emulator will make the following invocation on Friday at the ninth hour of the day; this invocation refers to the one Christ made at the same time on the same day when he was temporally put to death. This hour returns to that of nine o'clock in the morning, but if we absolutely could not make the invocation at the prescribed time, we can do it at nine o'clock in the evening.

---

57 Latin. 'From the depths'. Psalm 129.

The emulators who makes this invocation, and especially those who are married, will abstain at least twenty-four hours in advance from the commerce of women, otherwise the invocation would will bear no good spiritual fruit, it will become prejudicial and *la chose* would be indisposed against them for the future.

Anyone who commits adultery can in no way take part in any invocation except after a sincere repentance and after the perfect expiation of his crime is complete. He who repeats will be forbidden from all invocation for the whole course of his temporal life.

The face turned to the East by beginning the invocation alludes to [illegible] that Christ made for the first time to the Lord as a Man-God of the Earth in human form in favour ordinary men. The face turned towards the West at the end of the invocation alludes to the last operation that Christ did to the Lord according to the order that he had received from his Divine Father, and after having completed the required number of operations that he had to do in favour of the reconciliation of Men with God: he looked at the land and its inhabitants and finished [his operations] whilst saying this word *Consuminatum est*.[58] He then returned the four words of power which he had received from the Lord in order to perform all his divine temporal spiritual works in favour of the Universal Creature, which is represented by the four words *Eli, Lama, saba, tani*.[59]

The emulators have no other power higher in their invocation than that of a septenary being; being able to act consequently only on the quaternary faculty which constitutes the spiritual power of the soul of Man. This invocation will be worked especially on Good Friday.

Invocation called the Elu of the Above.

> *'O' LORD, which of us weak mortals will ever be able to claim, before your supreme majesty, the state of virtue, power and commandment that you had given to your first man? Who can ever invoke thy holy Name and sincerely call you to his aid, without obtaining the grace that, by your pure mercy, you always accord to contrite and humbled hearts? To think otherwise would be, O' righteous God, to incur your indignation and anger; it would be to disregard your clemency, your love for Man, your beloved creature; it would be to forget that it was in his favour that you created this chaos of temporal*

---

58 Lat. It is finished. John 19:30, KJV, When Jesus therefore had received the vinegar, he said, It is finished: and he bowed his head, and gave up the ghost.
59 Matthew 27:46, KJV, And about the ninth hour Jesus cried with a loud voice, saying, Eli, Eli, lama sabachthani? that is to say, My God, my God, why hast thou forsaken me?

Translation of 'Le Manuscrit d'Alger' (1772)

material darkness for the expiation of his crime and for the operation of his reconciliation. Thus, O' my Creator, the wonders of your justice and of your mercy exist for the sinner and the ungodly; your righteousness purifies to the least spot of sin, and your clemency is so great that its smallest act is enough to erase all the iniquities of the world and even those of hell. I do not doubt, O' my Creator, the effective nature of your kindness to Man!'

'It is for this reason that I come to claim your mercy and forgiveness, as you forgave your first man, our temporal Father, who sinned before you in the beginning. He deserved the temporal punishment to which you so justly condemned him, subjugating him to the fatigue of the body, to the pain of the soul, and to the labour of the Spirit.'

'I have the same origin as your First Man by my form. It is therefore right that I participate in his punishment; I have it also through thy Spiritual being: I must therefore finish what it still owes to thy justice: but, O' God of Goodness, you have reconciled the Man with you and the Earth with him! Why cannot I, being like him emanating from you, pretend to the same grace? Your name is so great and your mercy is so wide for those who have recourse to it that I dare to put all my hope in the state of misery in which I am immersed. Grant me, omnipotent, to invoke your holy name with dignity so that I may obtain the salutary help that I ask from the Spirits, holy ministers of our reconciliation with you, the means and the assistance they bestowed on your first man, whose death you dared stop.'

'It is with confidence, it is with desire, that I claim to you, O' merciful Father, by all your divine faculties, to remove from me the infamous stain that the prevarication of your First Man and my own iniquities have impressed! Removes this mark from me and my soul purified be whiter than the purest Spirit! Hear me, O' my Father and my God! Answer me not only so that I gain my temporal reconciliation spiritual with you, but for me to recover the powerful virtue of my first state, to manifest to the whole world your justice, your mercy, and your glory! Amen!'

The emulator now facing Westward continues:

'Listen, Spirits, who roam the Universe from the temporal East to the earthly West; by all that the creator has put most precious in his creature, listen to the powerful word that I have just received by my reconciliation; be all witnesses of what I will do, by a firm and immutable protest, for the greater glory and the greater justice of the Creator and his creature. Amen.'

Abjuration[60]

'I abjure and curse against the general and particular power of perverse Spirits, against their bait, their direct and indirect insinuations, their counsels, and their temporal and Spiritual operations; that never any impression, nor effect of their accursed wills can have any action on me nor on those who are friends of my heart and Spirit; May their thoughts, virtues, and powers be so swiftly dispelled from me as their leader was from the presence of the true Adam when he exercised all his power on Mount Thabor[61] to seduce this Divine Man and make him operate against the power of the Creator. For this purpose, I claim the power of the true Adam under the name of Messias.[62] I claim the dreadful word of him who put me under the names of Ja, Seth, abel. I claim the freedom of all my divine, Spiritual, temporal operations under the names of Neran 4, Maakin 4, Ribblas 10 as the chief leaders of the three terrestrial regions, conjuring their powers to join with my Spiritual power so that it can act and operate by virtue of their united virtue in favour of all material corporeal beings, so that the magnificent demon and all his adherents can no longer attack and defile my senses and those of my fellow men for a time immemorial. Amen.'

'O' my Guardian, be so promptly submitted to my request that my thought is made known to the Lord who has subjected you to the word and power of man! I invoke this same power to defend you and support me in the state of divine Spiritual virtue that I have just reconquered by the pure mercy of the Creator. Forewarning and fortifying me visibly or invisibly against all the adversities of this life of misery! Become from this moment for me a rampart

---

60 Abjuration is the solemn repudiation, abandonment, or renunciation by or upon oath, often the renunciation of citizenship or some other right or privilege. The term comes from the Latin abjurare, "to forswear".
61 Mount Tabor is believed by many Christians to be the site of the Transfiguration of Jesus. Mount Tabor is known as Itabyrium in the Graeco-Roman world, and the Mount of Transfiguration in some Christian contexts.
62 Portuguese. Messiah.

Translation of 'Le Manuscrit d'Alger' (1772)

of defence against all the pitfalls that the demons could try and train to corrupt my bodily and spiritual senses! May the Lord who gives us life in all our actions and operations ternary, quaternary and septenary, rejoice in our Labours in every place created and uncreated! May your voice and mine be heard from the highest degree of glory of the Lord to the bottom of the abysses of privation! May my thought and my power become yours, unite with those who have regenerated me and washed you of the defilement that had come back on you by the prevarication of the first man! That clothed with the sacred character of spiritual perfection, we may in the future perform acts pleasing to the one from whom we emanate in order to authentically fulfil the object of our emancipation. By virtue of my firm and serious protest made in the presence of the Lord and in yours, O' my Guardian, I declare to you that I have bound you and bind you forever with me, so that you may walk in my presence in all places, at all times and in all the spiritual, temporal and corporal circumstances in which I will need your help and without any delay, so that together with you, my body, my soul and my spirit will be eternally preserved in all purity and spiritual chastity in this temporal and impassive life. Amen.'

'To pray to you and to invoke you with dignity, Lord, I ask you to help yourself with your grace; you will not allow, O' God of life, that he who claims you thus to be never confused in the abysses of darkness.'

Translation of 'Le Manuscrit d'Alger' (1772)

Invocation of Master Coëns

'Who will grant me to be from now on as I had once been at the origin of my divine creation and to be restored to the virtues and spiritual powers that I had received for an eternity? Who will make me return to this happy and holy place where my Father and my Creator took special care of me where his kindness and His benefits were watching over my steps and all my needs! Where in the splendour of a single ray of his divine light, I walked safe in my vast domain. Today I am abandoned, left to myself and away my from my heavenly home; my power, my strength, and my will were unlimited as long as my thought was in accord with that of my Creator, and my faculties could not be without action, O' my God, my Creator and my Father, you know and see all my humiliation and my degradation, since, by an admirable excess of your love, you still deign to dwell among us; my God! What will become of you, I, your man, that you have established as the God of the Earth, if I am not supported by your help and that of the beneficent ministers of your power and your glory? I went out, through my own fault, of the glorious sphere in which you made me the first and most useful of the beings you had emanated; I have fallen, by the same fault, on this surface where I am no more than a binary being, subject to all your beings, subject to all the elements, a stranger, a slave and persecuted. I am so degraded and so unworthy that hardly a simple good intellect deigns to be heard by me! To me, O' terrible and just God, whom you had set above all your creatures, and what he says to me is impenetrable and unintelligible, if you do not give me your help.'

'It is in this state of misery in which I have reduced myself that I have recourse to you; O' God infinitely good, I write to you from the deepest abyss, to expose my tears and sorrows; see my repentance! Hear the sincere admission of my misguidance! How very guilty I am, in my own judgment, of being separated from you! I lay before you the remorse I feel; hear me, Lord! Lord, have mercy on me! Disgrace and confusion are the result of my ill behaviour towards you, for I am an ungrateful son, a treacherous friend, a rebellious subject; I too ignored your power and I have too much presumed of mine, which, however, I had nothing but your kindness, but I recognise today, O' God alone, all my error, and I feel that your power and your soul will surpasses all my faculties, and in punishment of my criminal pride you have limited my power and deprived me of the knowledge of your truth; so I am no longer surrounded by errors and darkness, any other being than myself shakes me; I know nothing more than with effort and with doubt and all superficially and I cannot do anything for myself if I do not get from your goodness the freedom to use my faculties.'

'O' LORD, it has pleased your mercy to establish very holy Spirits to watch over and operate in my favour; you have made them in strength, virtue and power on Earth and in Heaven on all the things you created for the fulfilment of your decrees! Permit me, O' my God, to lay down at the foot of their thrones my prayers and my needs, my evils and my hope.'

'O' Divine Son, O' doubly strong and powerful Spirit in all the Labours of the Creator! O' saviour and repairer of all Nature! I invoke you and claim you, so that you take me under your protection and that you are my mediator and my advocate during all my life and especially in this worship that I want to make pleasant to the Lord, God of the Living and the Dead.'

'O' Divine Spirit, eternal and infinite love, universal consoler, O' Septenary Action of the Ternary, let me adore you! Be my guide and my light in the choice of my thoughts, in the purity of my wishes and in the virtue of my actions! Give strength to my word and power to my command! I invoke and claim for this purpose for the whole course of my life and especially in this worship which cannot please the Lord if you do not animate your divine fire.'

Conjuration

'O' all ye Spirits emancipated in Creation, to make the powers and faculties, which the Lord hath distributed according to his will, and the need of his other creatures! O' zealous agents and ministers of the glory, justice and mercy of the God whom I have offended so often, but adore with you!'

Translation of 'Le Manuscrit d'Alger' (1772)

'O' pure Spirit! Come! Join me! Let us praise and bless together whoever has made us what we are! I bless you that you have remained faithful to the Creator when I had the misfortune to abandon him; bless me for recognising my fault and I beg your pardon!'

'O' pure Spirit! Come! Now recognise your brother; the Lord hath heard me, his mercy hath worked upon me, and I am purified: and I have been cleansed: my word is again as it was in my beginning, and it has returned to its state of virtue, power, and power: and Jehovah hath given me my first place of glory. Praise the Lord. Amen'

'O' all ye Spirits who live and travel the celestial and terrestrial areas, I you exconjure all ++++ by the Holy Name of the Lord to make you look at me, visibly or invisibly, in the angles of this work I have consecrated to be your abode and that of your intellects, so that you may be witnesses of my temporal and Spiritual labours which I operate at this moment. Come! Help me! I actively put myself under your care. I also commend all my brethren here present and all those who have joined us in heart and Spirit. Join me with the strength and power of my word and my command on you! Recognise in me the Man of the Creator and the purpose of all he created! Yes, it is for my use, for my utility and for my felicity that he has created all his labours! So be true and faithful to my invocation, by the power that I received on you! In the name the Living God, Spirits endowed with different faculties in favour of Man, I exconjure you all to bear your eyes, your care, your attention and your virtues on me, on each of my brethren here assembled in the name of the Lord and on all those who unite and join with us! I exconjure you in the name of Father + 10, in the name of the Son + 8 and in the name of the Spirit + 7. Amen.'

'By these same three names, I record + 7 at the angle of East; + 7 at the corner of West; + 7 at the corner of the North; and + 7 at the Southern corner; and I fix to myself + 7 my neighbour and my Guardian.'

'I exconjure Ye, O' Spirits, whom I have just attached to the four regions and the centre of this work, to see that I am not seduced by the perverse Spirit who always wants to disturb my labours by his own! By all my powers and my faculties, by all your virtues, and by the formidable name of the vengeful and remunerating God, I curse Satan and all perverse Spirits. I renounce all their *labours in kind and figure, whether in thought, will or action and everything which would be contrary to the purity of my body and my soul. By the same names +++ and with your help +++++, I stop the effect of all kinds of temporal and spiritual dangers that the perverse spirits could arouse in me either against my form, against my passive being, or against my spiritual being; I stop all communication between them and me so that they no longer have on me, on my brethren here present, and on all those for whom we pray, any action in this life or in the other. Amen.'*

'By the same names of the God who have given me power over every being created in this Universe, I summon you and conjure you all, the spirits that I have invoked, and more particularly ++++, you that I have attached to the angles and to the centre of my work, so that you have to mark by some characters, hieroglyph or other sign of fire, the convention which I have contracted with you, and especially with you, and my Guardian, as it is traced in these circles. Meet with my desires and my determination, which I, nevertheless, submit to the holy will of the Lord! I conjure you with the powerful names of the Creator o +++. Amen'

'O' ye, who is given to me and whom I prefer to be my guide and my Guardian, O +..., come to me without delay, surrender to my desire! Be clothed and endowed with all thy divine spiritual power, so that I may strengthen all my faculties, and may our combined virtues and powers work together in all my private and general labours, both civil and domestic, temporal and spiritual. I submit to you, O' pure spirit, despite the equality of our spiritual being, because of the flesh that envelops and offends me since the fall of the first man; but at the same time, by the power superior to yours which I have received from Jehovah, and in my image and divine likeness, I have united and attached you singularly and eternally to me, so that you are accurate and favourable to my demands in all the circumstances of my life. I exconjure you + 7 in the name of the Almighty Creator, to warn me with certainty of all the happy or unhappy events that will occur to me in all my temporal and spiritual endeavours. Suggest to me all the precautions that I must take, all the reflections I must make, both for my conservation and for my needs in the temporal as in the spiritual; inspire me in the different duties that I must fulfil towards all my fellow-men, equal and inferior; keep me in sight; keep me in sight; trust me for trust defends me from the pitfalls of the demons;

help me overcome; help me especially to overcome myself; always accompany my thought, my will, and my action; that by my union with you my temporal and spiritual enemies are all confounded and overwhelmed; their perverse virtues and powers never prevail over mine, which I desire by thy help to keep pure; their plans and ambushes be forewarned and destroyed by my dual power, by my will sanctified and by my increased faith in the Lord. Amen.'

Benediction of the Candles

'I purify you wax and bless you in the name of Jehovah, +, and by the virtues and powers that were given to me by Him. Be ordained and consecrated by my word and my will for the service to which I intend you, which is to help me retain an impression of the things which will be communicated to me here by the Spirits which I invoke according to my innate power within. Be fair and true to me, as were the lights that the privileged elect of the Creator used in their holy operations for the Spiritual regeneration of men, my fellow men.'

Then we will take one of the candles that will light a new flame and put it standing in the middle of the room.

Translation of 'Le Manuscrit d'Alger' (1772)

Invocation of the G[reat] A[rchitect]

> 'O' Jehovah, to whom I owe my spiritual and physical being, my thought, my will, my action and my word; help me by thy infinite goodness and firmly convince me that I live in you as I do myself; I am the image and true likeness of your virtues and powers; I am truly a chief leader of all your works, by these formidable names that I dare to pronounce only by trembling + 10, + 10, + 10.'

One pronounces these three words having the face inclined towards the ground with the eyes covered by both hands or by the pages of the invocation itself; one then looks for a moment on the walls and floor high and low, and if one perceives something one will mark it on the floor next to you with white chalk, to be picked it up after the work; we will do the same with each word uttered; and if it is collected, we resume the position and continue:

> 'I ask you, O' Almighty, + the virtue, the strength, and the power I need, that my spiritual soul may sustain and usefully receive the effect of the communication of your Divine Intellect; I ask you, O' my God, that my soul be forewarned and strengthened by your Spirit over all the events of its present and future acts which may tend to its bliss or eternal perdition. Erase all the defilements of my soul, relieve its temporal evils, and thereby make it worthy to receive and preserve all the salutary impressions that you like to give to the man of desire who invokes you with faith. O' righteous God +, I am only horror and darkness before you and before all your pure Spirits; the confession I make of it, my repentance and the evils which surround me are known to you, and you cannot be insensitive to it, for you describe yourself as Father of infinite mercies towards thy creatures. I am one of those creatures for whom you had so much complacency and in whom you deigned to put your trust. Do not rebuke me, O' terrible God, in the rigour of your Justice! Have mercy on the terrible evils that besiege my bodily being and my spiritual being! but, O' my God, thy will be done; I know that these evils remind me of my first principle, my first submission, and my first virtue, and make known to me all the justice of your judgments in the privation where you put me of my power and your presence, because of the lack of case and accuracy which I had in the execution of the laws which you had attached to

the felicity of my original state. O' living God +, put my repentant soul back into its first state of innocence and faithfulness to you; I am your image and your likeness, give me all the virtues and powers attached to this glorious title! Hear my cries and moans, dispel the dangers to which I am exposed and which I cannot avoid except by your divine help. + God vengeful and remunerative, do not lose sight of him for whom you did everything, do not let him fall without resources! Give back to your contrite and humiliated Man all that you have pleased to give him to strengthen him, to support him, and to lead him in all his temporal and spiritual labours which he was to perform for your greater glory. You made it to form a temple for yourself, but it did not work like anything that pleased you. Penetrated by the deepest pain of my ingratitude and my rebellion, I rise to you from the deepest abyss of my privation! Yes, I am guilty, O' my divine Father, but take pity on me, hear my prayer and I will become just again; purify my spiritual and bodily faculties and my word will be powerful. + Then I will build spiritual temples that will be pleasing to you and that will be eternal; their foundations will be like those of your firmament; you will delight in them as the wisdom of your Spirit is pleased in your works and powerful operations of Creation. O' clement and merciful God, I can now say to you your son, since I believe I am perfectly purified by you: yes, I am because I sincerely desired him and you have granted me according to your immutable promises and I testify the heavens and all their inhabitants to recognise me for such. O' my Father, O' my Creator, I am finally put back by your pure will in this first state of virtue and power from which I had been: flee away from me, foul and perverse spirits, persecutors and deceivers of the Man-God of the Earth; of that same Man to whom the Lord has given all virtues and powers against you all. I command that you all be dispelled from before me by my speech and my will as dust is by the most impetuous winds! Be eternally confounded by me and my equals, helpless as the smallest grain of salt would be in the deepest depths of the sea. By the Lord, so be it. Amen.'

We will say the following, until the conjuration, having the face inclined towards the ground, the right hand square on the heart. The word Earth indicates the body.

Translation of 'Le Manuscrit d'Alger' (1772)

'Lord God of All Nature + deign to bless this Earth once abandoned by the one who was in charge of its preservation, how it has pleased you to bless that of Adam and Eve, since I am bodily in one and the other sex; Bless so strongly this Earth that you have blessed Man. Amen.'

One will observe for a moment what may appear on the walls to trace it as it has been said; then with a firm look and a confident voice, we continue:

Conjuration to the Guardian

'O' You, +, Spirit whom I invoke, hear my voice, obey my command you are subject to it by the Lord who has submitted you to my thought, my will, my action and my word! The LORD has clothed me with my first virtues and powers over all created things; it is by virtue of his Holy Name, and of the authority he has given me even on Spirits who, like you, have remained faithful to him, that I invoke and claim you for my help. Yes, come, +, be my guide, my support and my counsel in all my temporal and Spiritual labours! Make haste to run to me in the name of the Lord! Imprint upon me, now entrusted to your care, the sacredness of your divine intellect, so that I can henceforth retain the impression of all your temporal and Spiritual instructions that I ask you by the purity of my will and the strength of my word. Amen.'

'I ask you to intimately join me temporally and Spiritually +; I exconjure thee to hear me without delay; make yourself known to me by all the means which are in your power and according to the faculties which you know to be in me! Come with thy illumination to me in my darkness; strip me of the ascendancy of my old habit of matter, and to make myself susceptible to that intellectual light that makes me read clearly with you in temporal and Spiritual things! Yes + my faithful Guardian, pour out on me a ray of your divine fire so that it constantly illuminates me on all that I need to know about my bodily being, my passive animal being and my active Spiritual being! Give me a clear understanding of the five senses of intellectual correspondence I have in my power with you and with the Creator! Always walk before me during my stay on this material surface! Give me some evidence of your assistance and instructions that I ask you and about everything you will need of me! Teach me to know you undoubtedly if you appear to me under your own spiritual form or in a human form or by characters, hieroglyphs or other figures of fire, or finally by my sign of convention established with you so that you answer me by making it, by your fire of different colours, to my desires and my demands. Make + that I receive without trouble, without embarrassment, and without uncertainties, the instructions, and the advice that I expect from you on all things of which I must be specifically instructed by you and by your intellect. On all things, +, I conjure you to give me a perfect knowledge of the divine being, the pure spiritual being and the human being; all for the greater glory of the Lord, for my temporal and spiritual felicity and for that of my brethren and kindred, and for the advancement, instruction and edification of those who are or will be entrusted to my care. I think before you, my Guide and my Council, which these three things that I have just asked you must give me the knowledge that I need for myself and for my fellow men of the correspondence that really exists between Man, Man and woman, Angel and God; and that by this knowledge not only will I become better with your help, but also that I may more worthily become the instrument of the mercy of the Creator towards his other creatures. Amen.'

'For this purpose I protest to the Living God of Abraham, Isaac, and Jacob and in your presence + my Guardian, whom I submit for ever and ever, my free will, my spiritual, temporal and material being, and generally all that I am and all that is in my power, to the care and the conduct of the almighty Creator and to the greater glory of my neighbour, so that the whole be promptly reintegrated into him who said; and everything has been done. Amen. O + 10! Hear us! Amen. Amen. Amen.'

'Pass my convention by the three dreadful words that I uttered at the first invocation +++ and that it be repeated by you + my Guardian. Amen.'

'Pass your name, your character, your hieroglyph, your sign and your colour, + my Guardian, by the three powerful words that I pronounced at the second invocation +++. Amen'

We look at the walls with firmness and attention.

'I conjure you, O' Lord, by yourself and by myself and by these holy and ineffable words +++ so that I can make a real spiritual connection with Him to whom I belong directly, before whom and in whom I am eternally and him in me.' [63]

'Come unite to your reconciled brother with our common Father; carry at the foot of His Throne the remorse, the repentance, and the burning regrets that I feel at my fault and the privation into which he has precipitated me. Unite with what you will find good in me, reject and make me reject everything that you will find bad!' [64]

'Assure yourself that my heart is a place worthy of receiving you.'

The crime of Man is to have taken (or wanted to take) the Throne of God by the strength and power that the Creator had put into him by emancipating him in his state of glory. This crime shook the whole Universe of temporal creatures: the heavenly spirits were defiled by the crime which he committed against God and against his divine order with the abominable power which he had received from perverse spirits.

---

63 In the original manuscript 'page 94' is written in the margin.
64 In the original manuscript, 'page 95' is written in the margin.

Translation of 'Le Manuscrit d'Alger' (1772)

Detached Pieces from The White Book

The raw material was in a principle state of indifference in the chaos. This matter was only one, but this unity was ternary as we will explain. It was only one and only one volume. In the envelope of this volume were contained three essences which were in appearance part of each other but did not spawn together; it is this which made this first matter received the name of indifference, but when it was operated or worked on by the central fire on which it was placed, an intimate connection was formed between them, and for that reason the matter was no longer indifferent, in that it lost its first nature by the cooking of the central fire and it took a consistency different from that which it had and by this means, it became susceptible to take different body shapes and to receive the impression that the LORD had intended for it.

We know that no bodily being can exist on this surface without having the three spirituous essences we call Salt, Sulphur, Mercury. Each of these essences are just like the elements; they cannot be one without the other. As each element cannot be alone and without being mixed, so these three essences cannot be enclosed in a body without having an exact match. In fact, the Mercury presides over the solid body of man, so we apply it to the action on the bony part; Sulphur presides over the fluid body, we apply it to the action on the blood; Salt presides over the surface of the body, we apply it to the action on the flesh or envelope.

'The sweat and perspiration of a man's body forms proof of this last fact'

The judgment pronounced by the Lord on the First Man was just and his prevarication was to be punished by the privation in which this judgment precipitated him. Today's Man having the same origin by his corporal form must participate in the corporal punishment of the same origin. How great must be the fault of our first temporal father that he may have degenerated from his state of glory to a body of matter that had not been made for him; until he understands all his posterity in his crime and his punishment; and here is the source of the original sin of which all men are wicked.

R✠ Fornication among free people, well hidden is more susceptible to forgiveness and grace than adultery, a sinning temporally against God and the other against the divine and human laws.

Man cannot ignore that his spiritual being is an emanation of the divine being. He has only to judge by the different faculties of his intelligence, and by the particular combinations which are innate in him. As a consequence of this emanation, Man must have a virtue and a property analogous to his origin of emanation and divine spiritual emancipation; he can therefore, if he so wishes, operate on things that relate to the very Creator from whom he is spiritually emanated and from which he has been temporally emancipated. If Man does not act thus, it is because he allows himself to be prevented by a material cause, much inferior to the spiritual cause which alone should direct him.

We find evidence of what the true man of desire could do in the Messie; that being who, being holiness and purity itself, came into this world to be clothed in a body of sensible matter and similar to that of the sinful man. The Messie has clearly proved in his state of ordinary man and by all his temporal spiritual operations the strength and divine spiritual power which is entirely at the disposal of the man of desire. The incorporation of the Messie into a human body form physically proves the prevarication of the first Adam. The corporal temporal death of Christ shows us the annihilation of Adam and his reconciliation after the penalty of privation. The resurrection of Christ in the form of a body of glory perfectly represents to us the first state of the first Man-God of the Earth, when he was clothed in a similar body pure and glorious, not subject to corruption.

It is therefore in the power of every man of desire to act in consequence of his origin or divine emanation; he can fear nothing on the side of the divinity to use the right, the virtue, and the power which he has received innate in him and which he can reacquire since his Fall by a thought, a will, a pleasant action to the Creator; as Christ has shown by Himself and confirmed by His Apostles, and confirmed by His disciples in all their temporal spiritual works and operations; and by the transmission that they made to their emulators gifts that had been reversible on themselves. According to this, how much should we not strive to reach the same state of favour with the Creator!

Composition Perfume [65]

Grind two or three salts of each drug. We mix everything well and we make two parts, one for each incense. We incense by turning three times round the terrine on the spot. Encens mâle, saffron, peppercorns, mastic en larmes, cinnamon, cloves, a pinch of salt.

---

65   Encens mâle or 'Male incense' is one of the oldest known incenses in Africa and the Middle East. It is considered the spiritual perfume par excellence and its properties are among the most powerful incenses. It comes from Eritrea and, originally, only men were allowed to burn it, hence its name 'male incense'. Mastic en larmes or 'Tear Putty' is a resin of plant origin from a natural or induced exudation of the tree Pistacia Lentiscus. It is used in the manufacture of soft and glossy varnishes.

Translation of 'Le Manuscrit d'Alger' (1772)

Prayer for the Incensing of Angles, Correspondences and Vautours.

'I purify you, from the East by those aromatic perfumes which I have consecrated, by my will and my word, to make the purification of your apparent matter; and for you to serve during my work to contain the one or those of the pure Spirits that will please the Creator to make me see and hear by his infinite goodness and according to my desire for his glory, for my reconciliation and for the sanctification of my fellowmen. I consecrate to you as Zerubabble consecrated the four Spiritual regions whose Spirits reconciled the rest of Israel with the Creator and brought them out of the slavery of the demons figured by the Babylonians.'

This will be repeated at the angles of the West, North and South by naming them as we did at the angle of East; then we will say the same and the same to the four circles of correspondence and Vautours.

The circles will then be perfumed by turning three times around from the North to the East and we will say:

In the first round

'O' Jehovah, +, may the perfume that I offer in these circles be a true image of the purity of my word and of my intention for your greater glory and justice. Amen.'

In the second round

'O' Jehovah, + may this perfume that I offer in purity of soul be as successful as that offered to you by Zerubabble in Babylon for the deliverance of the remnant of Israel. Deliver me from the servitude of the darkness that surrounds me and keep me from depriving you of your will and your science! Execute my prayer as much as my word and may my will be in accordance to your will. Amen.'

In the third round

'O' Jehovah +, may my prayer be the true perfume that I offer for an eternity! May this perfume be the emblem of the fervour with which I will invoke for my reconciliation, so that I may be sincerely united with the one to whom you have given the care of my conduct, by establishing my Guardian! I invoke him, this helpful Guardian, within these circles, though I do not see him, to be my counsel, my guide and my support in this world and in the other, for your greater glory and for my perfect sanctification. Amen.'

We will successively turn to the four angles, pronouncing the same four names of their spirits and saying:

'I conjure + + + +, who are here present visibly or invisibly to be witnesses of my protest in which I want to live and die and join them + my Guardian. Amen.'

When the incense is finished, we will make the prostrations to the same places in the same order by taking three steps of the Apprentice forward and backward.

Prayers of Prostrations to the East Angle.

'Prostrate at the feet of your supreme majesty, O' Jehovah + 10, I come to place in this angle of atonement the multitude of crimes that I have committed against you, against your Son and against your Spirit and against all the spirits that you have created. Covered with shame and penetrated with repentance, I come to groan in your presence and in theirs to implore your infinite mercy, this mercy, O' my God, that you grant with satisfaction to all those who sincerely claim to you. I write to you from the depths of the Abyss and offer you my body, my heart and my soul to satisfy your justice. Lord, hear my prayer, hear my prayer! Rectify the power of my soul, strengthen my heart, and purify my body, so that all that I am works of itself only for your greater glory, for my temporal and spiritual salvation and for the edification and felicity of my kind. For this purpose, O' my God, yes and it will be done, that I will be ordained and marked with the sympathetic seal with which you once marked your true elect by your servant Moses and as I see firmly that you design to destine me to your divine election. Permit me, Almighty, to be marked by the Spirit that marked John in the Jordan Desert; attach to your election in my favour the strength which you had attached to this worthy ser-

vant, and which was confirmed to him by the appearance of your Divine Son. I invoke, +++, my patrons and +, my Guardian so that they are together my guides, my advice and my supports in all my thoughts, my wills, my temporal and spiritual actions; May they be eternally united with me; and so be done as I am ordained by the Living God +, by the Living God +, and by the God of Life +. Amen. Amen. Amen.'

At the West Angle.

'Prostrate before you, O' Living God, action of the Father, universal Saviour, I dare to ask you for the confirmation of the election and ordination that I have just received for the three divine powers which the Creator granted to his servant Zerubabble for the entire deliverance from captivity, where the people of Israel were reduced by the force of their prevarication. At this example, O' God, powerful and merciful, I prostrate myself before you to offer all my being and submit it to your power, your justice, your clemency; may it please you, O' my God, to deliver my penitent soul from the slavery of the demons and the servitude of their intellects, so that under your holy guard and your protection I shall be robbed of all worldly passion and affection, and not be more clothed and penetrated than with spiritual feelings for the greater of the Father Creator +, of the Saviour Son +, of the custodian Spirit + and for that of your faithful servant and Elu (n n) who no longer wants to live, but only to act and die in God. Amen, Amen, Amen'

At the Angle of the North.

'Prostrate before you, O' Spirit, God of Life, Action of the Father and the Son and all created beings, universal custodian, receive the humble prayer that I address in the name of the Almighty Father who has forgiven me; hear it in the name of the Son by whom I am spiritually regenerated in all my virtues and powers. Sanctify me for yourself, who is cleansed from my defilements and made whiter than snow. Receive the sacrifice I make to you of my mind, of my soul, and of my body; Bless all my being so that henceforth he may be worthy of your purity, becoming your refuge and dwelling for a time immemorial; Bless me so that you can unite with me by the power of your divine intellects and keep it there, during my temporal and spiritual journey, in the path of virtue, strength and the constancy to which I have been restored by the mercy of Jehovah. Give me one of your divine intellects to be forever and inseparably my guide, my support, and my counsel as you did for the children of Israel under the guidance of Zerubabble. Correct the ordination and the election to which the Creator has pleased to call me and to admit me by the one who prays for me and supports me by his salutary instructions, for the greater glory of the Father + of the + Son and of the Holy Spirit + in whom and by whom I only want to operate in the future. Amen. Amen. Amen.'

At the Angle of the South.

'Prostrate before all of you, the spirits that surround the Throne of Jehovah, I come to invoke you to subdue my authority and spiritual virtue to yours, that they may be one; I conjure you by all that it pleased the Creator to make me be in his spiritual sanctuary, to answer my word and my intention; let your intellects join my spiritual soul and keep it elevated above the senses of matter, so that I may be eternally occupied with the spiritual understanding of your intellects, and thereby be spiritualised and circumcised by your pure fire. Amen. Amen. Amen.'

At the Centre of the Circles.

'Prostrate before you, O' ternary unity, I come to submit to your divine circle all the virtues and powers that you have enjoyed returning to me in favour of my reconciliation, my election, and my ordination, so that under all spirits of darkness, errors and abominations shudder at my word and feel all their horror at my command. Let there be no other communication between them and me other than to receive their condemnation and to see themselves by me driven back and precipitated in their frightful abysses for an eternity. May these monsters of privation and all their adherents distance themselves from me and my fellow men! I abjure them, their pageantry and all that belongs to them; let them be bound together and reincarnated for an eternity by virtue and the divine spiritual force which I have received from you, O' only Almighty God! Amen. Amen. Amen. Amen.'

'I invoke + + + my patrons and + my Guardian, so that they are for a time immemorial, my associates, my guides and my friends, that they are always attentive to my prayers to my requests, to my needs and that they answer my word and my intention. By you, O' LORD +! Amen, Amen, Amen.'

Second Incensing

After the prostrations are finished we do the second incensing, observing to say at each place the same things we said at the first incensing.

Abjuration of Metals

When all is over, we will record what has been reported and we will cast copper, lead and iron in the water, saying:

'May these three chief materials, which I rush into the abyss of water, be a sure proof of the abjuration I do, in the face of the Eternal, and of the one who sees and hears me by his order, material principles harmful to the man of desire. Amen.'

Fire Exorcism for Perfume

We stretch our right hand over the flame; stretched out at right angles we say:

'Exorciso te, Creatura Ignis, Per Illum per quem omnia facta sunt + 10, ut statim omne phantasma Ejicias âte, ut nocere ne quiat in aliquo. Amen.'[66]

'Benedic, Domine + 10, creaturam Istam ignis et sanctifica, ut benedicta sit in collaudationem nominis tui sancti, ut nullo nocumento sit gestantibus nec videntibus, Per Dominum nostrum Jesum Christum qui tecum vivit et regnat in Unitate Spiritus sancti, Deus. Amen.'[67]

---

66   Latin, 'Exorcismus, Creatures of fire, by him through whom all things are + 10, as the phantom drive at all, in order not to harm in any way. Amen.
67   Latin; Bless, Lord + 10, this creature of fire and sanctify it, so that by this blessing for the glory of your holy name, there will be no danger for me and for those who will carry it and see it. By our Lord Jesus Christ, who always lives and reigns in the unity of the Holy Spirit. Amen.

Benediction of Perfumes.

'Deus Abraham, Isaac and Jacob, + 10, benedic huc creaturas Specierum, ut vim and virtutem odorum suorum amplient do hostis ultimate phantasm in cis intrare possiut. Per Dominum, etc...'[68]

Blessing of the Circles.

'Benedic, Domine + Deus omnipotens, locum istum et hos circulos, ut sit in eis sanctas, castitas, victoria, virtus, humilitas, bonitas, manusactado, plenitudo legis, et gratiarum actio Deo Patri et filio et Spiritui Sancto: et hoc benedictio maneat super hos circulos et super habitantes in eis mene et semper. Amen.'[69]

Benediction of the Circle Candles.

'Benedic, Domine +, hos candelas sient benedicta suit illa quam 'angelus obtulit Moïsi in medio silva Bin et Oreb! In nomine Patris +10, In nomine filii +8, In nomine Spiritus Sancti +7, extinguatur in eis et in omnibus circulis hic presentibus, omnis vitus Diaboli per Impositionem manuum mearum et per Invocationem omnium angelorum et sanctorum Dei. Amen.[70] Veni Sancte Spiritus, Reple etc...'

Blessing of the Necessities for the Labour.

'Exorciso vos, creaturas omnium rerum que in meo conspectu sunt ad usum laboris mei, ut effugiat ex vobis omnis nequitia et virtus Diaboli et niehi, nec nobis, nec illis noare possint'

---

68 Latin: God of Abraham, Isaac and Jacob, + 10, bless this creature that is manifested, so that by its smell and its virtue it can contain and does not allow the demons of the imagination to be introduced here. By the Lord.
69 Latin: Bless, Lord, omnipotent God, this place and these circles, made here for your holiness, purity, victory, virtues, modesty, benevolence, traced by the hand, collected in fullness and giving thanks for the action of God, Father, Son, and Holy Spirit, and may the blessing be gained over these circles and above these people in your place and forever.
70 Latin; Bless, Lord, these candles, as they were blessed when the angel presented himself to Moses in the middle of the forest of Bin and Oreb! In the name of the father + 10, in the name of the son + 8, in the name of the Holy Spirit + 7 makes disappear in them and in all things and circles here in the presence, all diabolical virtues by the laying on of hands and the invocation of all the Angels and saints of God.

Translation of 'Le Manuscrit d'Alger' (1772)

'Benedic, Domine+, hos omnes creaturas hic adstantes et sanctifica ut ad meam utilitatem prosint sine imprevimento, et ad majoram gloriam nominis tui sancti. Amen.'

'âte, ut nocere ne quiat in aliquo. Amen.'

'Benedic, Domine + 10, creaturam Istam ignis et sanctifica, ut benedicta sit in collaudationem nominis tui sancti, ut nullo nocumento sit gestantibus nec videntibus, Per Dominum nostrum Jesum Christum qui tecum vivit et regnat in Unitate Spiritus sancti, Deus. Amen.' [71]

Benediction for the Chamber of Labour.

'Pax huic Domie and habitantibus omnibus in ea'

'Asperges me, Domine,' etc...

'Miserere mei, Deus,' etc...

'Gloria Patri' etc...

'Asparagus me' etc...

'Domine Exaudi orationem' etc...

'Exaudi nos, Domine + sicut domos habrerorum in Exitu of aegipto Agni blood linitas ab Angelo percutiente disting caste; ita mittere dignesis sanctum angelum of Coeli; which custodiat, forcat, protegat, visitu, at that deffendat omnes habitantis in hoc habitando.' [72]

---

71 Bless, Lord + 10, this creature of fire and sanctify it, so that by this blessing for the glory of your holy name, there will be no danger for me and for those who will carry it and see it. By our Lord Jesus Christ, who always lives and reigns in the unity of the Holy Spirit. Amen.
72 Peace to this house and to all the inhabitants who are there.
Bless me, lord
Take pity on me, God, etc...
Glory to the Father, etc...
Bless me, etc...
God, answer our prayers, etc...
Hear us, Lord, just as you have saved the houses marked with the blood of the lamb struck by the angel; lead us with dignity to the angelic sanctuary of Heaven; be kept, tested, protected, visited and defended all the inhabitants in this house.

Prayer whilst Dressing

'Per merita angelorum tuorum sanctorum, Domine+, induam vestimenta salutis, ut hoc quod, desidero possim perducere ad effectum; Per te, sanctissime + cujus regnum permanet in aeternum. Amen.' [73]

Taking the White Cord

On the left eye + 8, on the right eye + 7, on the forehead +10, on the left shoulder + 8, on the right shoulder + 7, on the mouth +10.

Prayer to the Spirits of Labour.

'ô vos angeli supra invocati in nomine Dei nostre +, estote mihi adjutores in omnibus rebus et petitionibus meis in codem nomine. Amen.' [74]

In Presenting the Pentacle.

'Per pentaculum quod ante vestram adduri presentiam et quod super vos potenter impevat per virtutem Dei + Venite Ergo, festinate et obedite praeceptori vestro, in nomine + (we will only name here the words of the Work).' [75]

Return of the Spirits

'In nomine Patris + 10, et filii+ 8, et Spiritus Sancti + 7, ite in pace ad loca vestra! Pax sit semper inter vos et nos, et parati sitis venire vocati in istes nominibus. Amen.' [76]

---

73 By the merits of your holy Angels lord, allow me to put on these salutary garments so that I may attain the effect of what I desire; by you most holy whose reign has always existed in eternity.
74 O great Angels whom I invoke in the name of Our God, come to my aid in all my desires and grant me in effect in my call.
75 By the pentacle that I brought in your presence that commands you and forces you by the power of God, come, hurry and obey your master, in the name of +
76 By the pentacle that I brought in your presence that commands you and forces you by the power of God, come, hurry and obey your master, in the name of +.

Prayer and Consecration at the East Corner.

'Deus abraham +, Deus Isaac +, Deus Jacob +, Deus qui Moïsi famula tuo in monte Sinaï apparuisti, et filius israël de terrâ aegipti eduxisti, deputens eis angelum pietatis tua qui custodivat nos die de noɛte, te quaesumus, Domine, ut mittere digneris sanɛtam angelum de coelis in hunc locum, qui similiter custodiat me famulum tuum (N, N) et omnes xxxx, et perducat nos ad vitam aeternam. Per Dominum noſtrum, etc...'

Benediɛtion of Salt and Water

We raise our eyes to the sky and wearing salt on both hands at right angles we say:

'Sanɛtify, O' Lord +, this creature of salt, purify it so that he may be a sovereign medicine to those who receive it. Spread from him any ghoſt that could harm me and to those who are with me and do that by its purity, I can use it happily in all circumſtances where I need it. By J.C. our etc.'

Exconjuration of any Place.

'Deus omnipotens +, adeſto propitiens invocationibus noſtris et virtutem tua benediɛtionis infunde, ut creatura tua (NN) miſteriis tuis servicus ad abijendos demones ex meridio sumnut effeɛtum, ut angulus iste, (ant ciruclus ant medium) careat ab omni Immunditur, nec illic resideat ſpiritus peſtilens, nec aura corrunpens, desiedant omnis insidia latentis inimici quem abjuro per tuum hoc inefabile nomen + 10. Amen.'

Feu nouveau. [New Fire]

'I conjure you, Spirit + 7, whom I invoke by my power and by all that is in your power and mine, so that your ſpiritual fire may ignite the matter that I consecrate within these circumferences; let the elemental flame that dwells there unite with yours by contributing to the ſpiritual light of men of desire and animating your fire of life.'

'For the greater glory of the eternal thought ....SAME+ 10'

'For that of the eternal will ....SEDM+ 8'

'And for that of eternal action ......SATE+ 7'

With each word it is necessary to strike a blow on the stone in the circumference. If the fire takes before the third word is pronounced, it must be extinguished and kept only for that which comes after the third word.

Illumination of the Centre.

'O' Pure Light, a symbol of the chief of my soul, to whom Jehovah has entrusted the care of my thought, my will, my action and my word, do as thy bright flame, my soul be purged and my lips be purified, that the word which I am about to speak may work for the greater glory of the eternal, for my instruction, and for the edification of my fellow men. Amen.'

The flame of the candle, which is held by hand, is then blown on three times by pronouncing the word traced in the centre, and immediately adding each time *'Inquacum die'* etc... then we put the candle on the word of the centre; you stay standing, you hold your hands on your face, your body and your head bent over the candle and say in a low voice:

'Come, Holy Spirit + 7 surround the fire which is consecrated to you to be your powerful and dominant Throne in all the regions of the universal world! Dominate by my thoughts about myself and my brethren present here! Remove from these circles all darkness, error and confusion, so that our souls may enjoy the fruits of the works which order gives to those who are worthy to be penetrated by you + 7, who live and reign with Father and son forever. Amen.'

Exconjuration for the first of the days of Labour at the Four Angles.

'I exconjure you Sathan, Belzébuth Barrau, Leviathan, all of you beings of iniquity, confusion, and abomination; be quick to my voice and my command! All of you, demons of the four universal regions, legions and subtle

Translation of 'Le Manuscrit d'Alger' (1772)

Spirits of confusion and horror, listen to my voice, shudder to hear it and be forced to conform to it, since I command you by the one you have misunderstood and who has pronounced the punishment of eternal death against you and your adherents, as you deceive my fellow-men.'

For East Sathan

For West Belzébuth

For the North Barrau

For South Leviathan

'To you directly (according to the angle) *I exconjure you I bind you and limit you in your accursed region, by the name of the highest + 10, that the Lord put back into the power of Man for he had authority over you and all yours. May you, by this same terrible name, remain eternally destroyed in your abysses of darkness and divine spiritual privation! May my thought operate on you, O'* (according to the angle), *by my omnipotence and that of the pure Spirits who surround me and whom the Creator has spiritually subjugated to be my supporters, my guides and my invincible defenders against you, and all your adherents, against whom and against you, abjure and curse for a time immemorial!'*

'I command you (according to the angle) *by the quadruple divine power, O'* [vabaham, vakiel, dianuel, ardï], *and by the power of the four divine spiritual regional leaders + 8* [diaphas], *+ 7* [darmaïn], *+ 4* [heli], *+ 3* [memaïaï], *that you are, by the Eternal, contained in the bounds I fix you; that you are forever devoid of all power and correspondence with me, that any action of operation on your part can never reach me except to be confounded and destroyed by me according to my power over you and all your fellows that I limit and bind with you, for your greatest confusion and theirs. Let it be done as I have conceived it, and let my power as a Man-God of the Earth have pronounced it with the help of Jehovah + 10. Amen.'*

Translation of 'Le Manuscrit d'Alger' (1772)

Knowledge of Diseases

To find out what kind of illness someone has, one will place one's baptismal and family names and the day of one's birth in order to attach the planet under which the person was born.

If the planet casts an abundance of tears of fire or is coloured red, it is the blood that is attacked.

If it launches only side by side, the disease is on the side designated by the blade of fire.

If it throws them pale, the dissolution is in the blood and there is no remedy; to make sure of the fact, the patient must have the tip of the tongue red with blood.

If the planet gives small whitish globules firing on the azure, the disease is between flesh and skin, it requires sudorific and fumigations.

If the planet produces circumferences the colour of red earth, all the remedies will fail, it is pulmonie.[77]

If below it gives tears of fire, it indicates the dropsy.

If it throws a multitude of hieroglyphs crossed with each other and varying colours, it announces too much fire in the blood, which causes delirium.

If the planet in action, the same as above, offers a cross, it indicates success in any enterprises with *la chose* in the work.

Eve, the mother of the living, was not criminal in the early days; her origin does not come from the spirit, the will, action or speech or the word of Jehovah: so it is not the power of Eve that the Lord has degraded first, neither his person whom he has smitten, and it is not upon him, that he has at first manifested the rigour of his justice, nor the glory of his glory; but on the person of the First Man whom he cursed with all the Earth; He then curses the works wrought by the speech and the thought of the Man-God of the Earth; it is not Eve that the Lord has reconciled with him, it is the First Man and not the work of his thought: in reconciling Man with him, the Lord reconciled the Earth with Man, and he crowned his justice and glory by blessing the first woman with divine wonders.

---

77 Lung disease, especially pulmonary tuberculosis.

Extract letters from D[on] M[artinez] P[asqually]

April 3, 1770.

The true man of desire that puts his trust entirely in the Creator can truly be a part of Nature, and thus he has the power to avoid the dangers that threaten to make him falsely anticipate his reintegration in an apparent corporeal form, because that form is only apparent. (God created all bodies as well as Man in his imagination; here is the image, and in the spiritual substance, here is the resemblance).

25 8bre [October], 1770.

The Creator's elect are His tributaries; He had the tribes elected to become the Hebrew people, to bring about a tribe of people through which He could choose men who were destined to become the manifestation of His Glory and Divine Justice. These chosen ones were the strongest tributaries to the Lord, because the tribute they paid to the Creator was wholly spiritual and without any combination of the material; to those Jehovah did not withdraw any portion of the spiritual and temporal goods which He had entrusted to them in the moment of their election, as he did to the elect who wanted to pay their tribute to the Creator materially and only in part spiritually. These are those who are now wandering and scattered, without divine spiritual distinction, poor in every way, with no other resource to be handed over to their first principle until after their perfect reconciliation which alone can bring them back to their reintegration; one can only obtain one and the other by paying a tribute pure and simple without any junction of matter.

La chose never abandons and never abandoned his [own], it is too just and equitable for this, it does not interrupt (or withdraw) its general correspondence with those whom it knows to be entirely devoted to it; otherwise *la chose* would be left wanting and unable to make a distinction between the just and the guilty; and what would become of the free will which the Creator has given to Man by creating him free in all his faculties of doing good and evil? For the reward or punishment announced to the spiritual creature is based on free will.

The number of *la chose's* elect are few, due to the time it expends in favour of those novices whom it brings into its circle of truth.

This is not the way of reproach, complaint or remonstration against those that are a mere depositary for the attributes of *la chose,* but on the contrary, it is a necessary path that the man of desire must follow leading him in peace and tranquility to the goal that *la chose* reserves for those who pursue it without reserve. Impatience and inconstancy prove that in truth we care very little, because we tend to only think and not act humanly and in a way completely opposed to *la chose,* which, we, as the first echelon ascended from it, often flatter ourselves in the thought that we are constantly attached to it; but, [given the fact that] this is being done differently by the effect of bad thought and temporal action contrary to that of the divine spiritual, it is not surprising if *la chose* withdraws entirely from such subjects, and if its interpreter withdraws into his circle only to come out again by force in favour of those who have patiently desired their reconciliation after the time prescribed for the new ordeal *la chose* imposes on those who have been unable to confidently persevere in what they had freely embraced by an inviolable oath.

It is not the chiefs of the Order that hold an oath, since they are only intermediaries of *la chose* who uses them in order to enact its will in favour of the man whom it wishes to share in its graces and whom it cannot refuse, as they deserve it.

The temporal chiefs of the Order are only witnesses to the oath that a subject [celebrant] makes to the Lord for his admission to the first degree of the Order, as *la chose* is witness to the good or bad of the subject [celebrant] who contracts it; thus the chiefs, as witnesses of the oath, are appointed only in order to be informed of the prevarications of the contractor [celebrant]. The proof of what has been said, that *la chose* works for or against the advantage of men and what leaders can operate to the same level, is found in Adam, Enoch, Noah, Abraham, Joseph, Moses, David, Solomon, Zerubbabel and Christ. It is enough to convince yourself of the validity and goodness of *la chose* and the constancy and fervour of the true disciples called to the circle of truth.

For receptions by correspondence, the recipient and the leader who receives each have, namely for the particular grade Apprentices, before them a single light; for the Fellow, two; for the Master, five; for the Elu nine; for the strong marked, one; the double strong, three; for the thrice strong, six; for the Gr. Arch, ten; for the Kn. of the East, thirteen; for the Com. of the East, seven; and for the ordination of a R^{+}, eight.

August, 1768 № 3.

The mysterious numbers we use in the Order represent;

1° The division of the whole Universe that the Sages made by divine inspiration to acquire the knowledge enclosed in him both in general and in particular.

2° The heavenly division in its four regions.

3° The terrestrial division in its whole form.

4° Knowledge of the three main elements and their compound.

5° The origin and existence of the three and five different material parts that make up the body of Man and the precision of each of these innate parts in the three different terrestrial angles.

6° The incorporation of the spiritual soul into the human body.

7° The strength, power, activity, function, or action of the spirit that operates in general and especially in concert with the spiritual soul.

8° The simple and double power given by God to Man in his image and divine likeness.

9° The Terrestrial division and subdivision in all its virtue and innate power of vegetation, conception, progression and reintegration.

10° The certainty, the knowledge and the immutable stability of the Creator in his universal temple and the sympathetic correspondence that there is between him and man.

11° The different spiritual, temporal, animal, fungous, aerial, aquatic and terrestrial revolutions.

12° The knowledge of the three blood parts that are innate in man.

13° The higher power that is given by God to Man over every creature in the Universe.

14° Demonic superior and inferior power over the material man.

15° The operation of Moses to deliver the chosen people from the land of Egypt.

16° The reconciliation operation that Noah made of the rest of the men with God.

17° The operation of Joshua to the manifestation of the double divine power which was transmitted to him for the defeat of the enemies of his law and his chosen elect.

18° The nine unpleasant epochs that have come to Earth since its creation and are still reversible to today's men.

19° Spiritual, animal and terrestrial line.

20° The law of ceremony to the Sages, either for their way of living among the laymen, or for their mysterious spiritual operations.

21° The ceremonial law of material operations.

22° The four principal chiefs who, since 2448, have succeeded the first Sages and whose memory we will revive, and then operations analogous to theirs, which they have transmitted to us to be faithfully observed by every man of desire.

Here is a small discourse on the mysterious numbers which we use in all the circumstances and the different operations of the Order; we must leave the rest to the will of the Lord. The number 3.3.3. in its totality gives 9, the original number of the place from which the body of Man is derived. In his division, the first 3 gives The Terrestrial Form Δ[78]; the second gives the knowledge of the three different material parts which make up the body of man, which we distinguish by bones, blood and flesh; we admit the bone part to the West as being the first inmate of the human body in its first terrestrial angle, the blood in the south as the vegetative part, and the warmest and the flesh in the North as the colder and more likely to influence as surface; what appears to us the terrestrial and corporeal totality; the surface, the centre and the abyss.

It is absolutely necessary to know and admit the earth in its true division, to be able to operate on the three different diseases of the human body and to be able to remedy our bodily ills. The third gives the age of the dignity of the body of the first man; that is to say, he was 30 years old when he was placed on earth to receive the spiritual being that God placed in him, giving him power and command to operate on all created things, according to his quality. Man God of the earth, and image and divine likeness. The same number 3.3.3. indicates the fixed time in which Christ began and ends all his general operations for the reconciliation of this Universe with the Creator. 1° he began to operate at the age of 30, which alludes to the age of the creation of Adam where he also began his operation of prevarication. 2° three years after the 30, he finishes his spiritual operation and Adam completes his reconciliation with the creator. 3° three days after these 3 years, Christ separated from the material men, so Adam was reintegrated in his first state of power on all created things and separated from the material part. The number 3.5.7 gives the perfect knowledge of the whole Universe, of the earth, of the rightness of the body of Man and the knowledge of the passive soul and the active soul. The total addition of these three figures gives 15 or 6 which is the animal number; The addition of 3 and 7 gives 10 which is the divine number; l addition of 3 and 5 gives 8 which is the number of double power; the addition of 5 and 7 gives 12 = 3 which is the terrestrial number in its three contents; number 3 gives the first three material parts which make up the body of man; the number 5 gives the correctness of the acquired body by the addition of the cartilaginous and nervous parts to the bony, sanguine and fleshy parts, which forms the material number; the number 7 indicates the power of the Spirit over the active soul of Man (or the power of the soul active on the passive soul of man) by junction. By this same junction we learn to know the seven spiritual powers which are designated to us by the seven planetary powers. We

---

[78] The Terrestrial Form, part of Pasqually's Universal Table who's Centre was inhabited by Noah.

cannot know too well these powers of the planets to succeed in our different operations, in imitation of wise men and prophets who knew them perfectly for having been able to act as they did and as we must do.

The *septenary* number is a compound and a convention number 763 to God for the benefit of man; one to God, two to the confusion of animal actions, three to the earth, four to the power of the active soul of man, five to material power, six to animal power (or passive soul) and seven to divine spiritual power or pure spirits. When we see the number 5.7.9. in the writings of some operative, one can believe that this one will operate on the knowledge of some demonic operation to oppose it: by the number 5 for its invocation to the demonic spirits, this number being their chief number; by the number 7 to contain the demonic brashness against the active soul; and by the number 9 to repress the three earthly and material powers.

May 23, 1768 № 4.

Moses could neither read nor write, nor even speak since he was a stutterer, and yet he was a great man, who was able to recall to his principle all the people whom God had entrusted to him. The choice of this man proves to us that the will and the science of Man are nothing if they do not emanate from the All-Powerful.

No matter how great the knowledge and power is of the one who been instructed to teach us, let us always beware of putting our faith entirely in him; the Divine Spirit has filled the earthly limits, it is up to Him alone to fill the voids of men. The wise man will feel more by himself, as the manifestation of the Almighty moves towards him than by the repeated experience of his various operations each day.

Do not lose the characters you will receive in the future, they are more essential than the hieroglyphs, that is to say that one leads to the other. When the characters are triple, they contain three names; the letter A is given to God as the Alpha is given to the Greek and Hebrew alphabet; A is the principle of a name of God; B is the principle of a name of a good spirit and D is the principle of a word of power given by God to the soul, as I am going to detail. A. R. I. is a four-letter word given to God as it relates to his denary number. When the letter A is in junction with the letter B, as AB BA they form a word of power of a good spirit; in that it bears on four letters against one another by junction, it gives by its number of power that of four; and the letter D when it is by ternary junction with the A, they form a word of double power which the soul must use to attract to it the knowledge of the Spirit which it wishes to know with regard to look for or against its advantage, as it is seen by this figure and its number CBA-8. In summing these three numbers together, one will find by the product of 22 - 4 the truth and the certainty of all spiritual things either in name or in virtue. The last letter B is pronounced as if there was a U at the end because of the Hebrew point that is next to it. All the characterised words of which I speak here are all strong words, pronouncing them as they are in your particular operations.

One must be wary of plotting any work on any other matter than on earth, stone or brick, because one would render the operation totally impotent and it would be entirely disturbed: the earth is the footstool of spiritual things. One could still fail to better draw on a floor.

The Earth is triangular and the triangle is the emblem of the real form of the Earth, as God Himself gave to Moses and Solomon to put on the frontispiece above the Holy Void, which they did by putting the Holy Name of God in four letters in a triangle.[79] This proves that the name of God dwells in the centre of the earth as the soul dwells in the centre of the three material parts which compose the body of man; so God dwells in the centre of the three terrestrial elements.

If in an interesting case or circumstance your intention is to act according to the will of God, it will enlighten you with a ray of its light by making you see clearly in your thought what you must do or wait. For that you will ask the LORD in a prayer similar to your desires, with the face turned to the East; you will pronounce the Holy Name of God, which Moses used to secure the lot of his people on leaving Egypt. By pronouncing this name four times, one to each part of the world East, West, North and South, you will say immediately each time *In quâcumque die invocavero te, velociter exaudi me.*[80] You will have your spiritual counsel in vision, either by sleeping, or by watching, and for that you will act accordingly.

W. V. V. the Second V stands by, or; or else, or, between the two V or V.

---

79 Martines assigns symbolically a "triangular form" to the earth, explaining that it 'has only three noteworthy horizons: north, South, and West'.
80 Latin. 'In whatever day, I shall call upon thee, hear me speedily'. Psalm 101. Non avertas faciem tuam a me in quacumque die tribulor inclina ad me aurem tuam in quacumque die invocavero te velociter exaudi me (Turn not away thy face from me: in the day when I am in trouble, incline thy ear to me. In what day soever I shall call upon thee, hear me speedily).

4th September, 1767 № 5.

The state of a true Elu Coën is a happy, sure, and advantageous state to those who follow Him with heart and without any desire other than to serve Him well, even in His apparent contradictions; for if we are not always satisfied according to our desires, if our wanting is often deceived, it is only to test our zeal and perseverance; and when He has thus treated us and is fully satisfied with our care, He rewards us with joy; He leaves us wanting nothing, He takes an exact care of us, either in our temporal needs or in spiritual ones.

Nothing that is done in the revolutions of this world can surprise or shake the tranquility of a real Coën; he will not be affected by the stripping of men because he knows that the only glory is in God alone; it will not be the loss of wealth, because he knows that he can really be rich only in the possession of God; he will not regret the favour of the great ones of the earth, because looking at it only as a chimera, he never wanted to lean on an arm of flesh; he will look upon his evils and infirmities only as the answer of his mortality; he will see in the death of his relatives and friends only a happiness which they enjoyed before him; finally he himself expects death as the end of his desires in the comforting hope of a spiritual homeland where he will find himself in his place. The true Cöen indeed must be well persuaded that all the enjoyments of which men feed themselves are as many outrages made to God himself who alone is right and who alone wants and can satisfy them.

An R☦ must be familiar with the following:

1° The alphabetical square that gives shape to what an operative desires.

2° The alphabetical square that counterbalances the spirits called.

3° The five alphabets used to verify the correctness of the spiritual and material names of good and perverse spirits.

4° The transposition of the planets that were used once and their hieroglyphics.

5° The divisions of the planets in the corners of the apartment, as well as the hieroglyphs which bind them.

6° The numbers of the circles in which the planets must be operated and the transpositions of the numbers of the circles taken in the 64-10 which direct the Universe.

7° The general alphabet of the names of divine, spiritual and demonic powers which are to be used for operations.

8° The division of a planet in all its content and the names of the different good and bad spirits that inhabit it.

9° The knowledge of the numbers of these spirits which must be used to call them, to contain them, and to reject them.

9b° The numbers of the names of the prophets, the apostles, and others, those of both good and bad spirits.

10° The names of single and double power which must be placed in each of the three names used in the circles and in the half and quarter circle divisions.

11° The different consecrations of angles and circles.

12° The way to raise a consecration and dismiss the names of the spirits that served.

13° The choice of the angle to leave a spirit of care from one evening to another during a whole work and the replacement of this spirit.

14° The names of the Cherubim and Seraphim, their place, their power, their hieroglyphics and their words of triple power which must be used by placing them in the centre of the circles and in the centre of the rear guard or retreat.

15° The composition of the circles with three colours, their receptacles, their correspondences, their Vautours, their hieroglyphics, their good and bad words, as well as the words of single and double power which direct them.

16° The ceremony of the various sacrifices and the hieroglyphics that must be thrown into every fire where the burnt offering of any nature is consumed.

17° The different areas where the Holocaust must be offered.

18° The different quarters of the moons where we must work, the composition of the perfumes, the way and the time to pick them.

19° The different ways to invoke, the invocations, conjurations and exconjurations.

20° The way to use the different rods that are cut at the Equinoxes for operations.

21° The ballot operation.

22° The solar operation.

23° The female operation.

24° The six operations in six hours.

25° The operation for or against those who operate.

26° Prayer divisions in parts of the work room.

27° The different blessings and excommunications.

28° The different rings; the different solar, lunar and planetary woods.

29° The different pentacles, their figures and sympathetic images.

30° The different salts.

31° Different ways to observe appearances and counterbalance them to learn what they want to say.

32° The different ways to reverse an operation from East to West, North or South.

33° The different ceremonies and prostrations that must be done while operating.

34° The various figures and sympathetic images that can go in circles and their different sections.

35° Circles chained by the four correspondences with their hieroglyphs.

36° The operation of contradiction to the four quarters of the Moon to demons and the solar the same, one by a receptacle with four quarters of the Moon and a full, the other at the four fires of the Sun and under the horizontal perpendicular.

37° The location of the four R✠ each in its outer circle of correspondence, the three main Vautours circles, the operating ones at the West, and the other two that of the North and the South.

38° 3.5.7.9. different operations that are done in the perverse part.

39° 4.5.6.7. different operations that are done in the spiritual part.

40° Different fasting and different prayers for operations; days, moons, months and sun.

41° How to transport an operation from one place to another in case of interruption.

42° The way to operate on the water and in an open field.

43° The way to operate on a single planet without any junction.

44° The way to operate on any Spirit without junction.

From September, 1766 N° 6.

It is necessary to follow the East of the day to trace a work without always necessarily going to that angle of the apartment; it is necessary to take the horizon of the current Sun as well as its meridian; otherwise, we only scratch at the circles that must fulfil the purpose of the work.

Let us have no weapons against our enemies but the word of truth, the square and the compass. There are no weapons in the world stronger than these; since the Lord has given us enough grace to entrust us with the same weapons which he used to remind the Israelites of their errors, let us work to bring back our brethren who deviate from the natural law and who make efforts only to deteriorate more and more spiritually and temporally, and even to deprive themselves of the glorious title of Man.

From 8th January, 1772 № 7.

The doctrine of the Order is too sublime, and its purpose too high for us to doubt that it has always subsisted, that it subsists and will subsist eternally either in this passive temporal life or in the spiritual life impassive. So why do we not put all our trust in Him rather than ordinary mortals like ourselves? If we are convinced that Man can only obtain happiness and certainty through Him, it is therefore to Him alone that we must resort to obtain His gifts and favours, by rendering ourselves worthy of them. In good faith what consideration, what case would we make of something like the one we are talking about if it is the only power of the Man who likes us can wander and make us wander? But if, on the contrary, far from being dependent on man, the man to whom he confides is only His agent or His organ, or the instrument which He uses to communicate with Himself or to manifest Himself to those whom He finds worthy of His benefits, this Man, instrument of grace and second agent can promise nothing, give nothing by itself, it is therefore to *la chose* alone that we must ask, if we deserve it, and then the instrument will act in our favour.

20 7bre [September], 1766 № 8.

Sometimes noises are heard, as if small stones are falling and rolling on the floor above us, they are the product of the different attractions that our prayers and vows are having on the spiritual region; these attractions descend into small globules of fire of various colours and end with a more or less violent explosion, and this is what we ordinarily hear. Those who are so forewarned must redouble their ardour and confidence to engage the spirit to become corporeal or to be imperceptibly perceived by magical figures, characters or others almost always white or some other beautiful fire. It should be noted that the spirits that are invoked most often or which one thinks of at the time of occurrence without being worked or those whose idea and name you come to with their appearance; they are those who are attached to you to protect you and guide you through the storms of this temporary transit life.

The characters that you will receive in this way are the opinions that spirits give you to warn you of the goodness of your prayer and to commit you to redouble zeal and perseverance in the true science and the good way. You must remember these characters to place them in your next operations. They will then represent themselves to you and so will confirm themselves. But do not be discouraged if it is not for you to conceive what you see or hear; we are too happy to see and hear such things. Let us fortify ourselves and do not risk, by too much curiosity and precipitation, to lose even what we have.

Translation of 'Le Manuscrit d'Alger' (1772)

From 24 9bre [November], 1767 N° 9.

If Man wants to put all his trust in God, to have faith and a true desire, he can do whatever he wants in this world, but one must not bring about self-love in oneself, it would lead to nothing more than the means of falling back into that greatest ignorance and cause the forgetfulness of even the little that one already knows; that will all happen even more quickly than when one first learned it, and it will happen without any hope of returing unfortunately.

From 23 7bre [September], 1769 N° 10.

Man is born good; his present nature is weak, and the perverse is subtle and cunning; but also Man has received from the Creator enough to fight his enemies and to molest them whenever he wishes, for all power is given to him, it is enough for him only to want to use it; then his will, helped by his thought and his word, will make him superior to his enemies and will put him above all their attacks.

We must expect everything from God and not from men who act otherwise than they think: It is, therefore, very difficult to convince them today of the truth; it is too simple and naive for a man brought up in the sophistry with which he cannot live. This man can come back from his error only by physical truths which bring them to pieces and confound them.

Nothing is produced by Nature and fashioned by art that isn't already existing; an animal is power in the seed from which it is generated; a statue is potentially in the block the artisan works; it exists also in the imagination of the craftsman: thus the world existed in the divine spirit before its creation, by which God put into practice his ideal.

Sign of the general covenant of God with men in general.

Secret convention between the chiefs of the Order to recognise each other.

Translation of 'Le Manuscrit d'Alger' (1772)

Reported from the Book of Parchment

Analogy of the colours blue, green and red in the cords.

We wear the blue ribbon in memory of the recommendation made to us by our first Father before separating from us, preserving innocence, chastity and peace.

The blue colour represents the stay that Adam made in the earthly paradise.

The colour green represents the fault he made in engaging in the forbidden work.

The colour red represents the dissensions that rose among his own.

Adam was the first R✠, who alone did his Operations, by the power of the Creator who gave him freedom and power in the terrestrial paradise between the three aforementioned colours, which are here emblematic.

The blue cord is in memory of what it was he offered to him as soon as he had his eyes open.

The green cord is in memory of his fault and the loss of his knowledge.

The red cord is in memory of his expulsion from the earthly paradise that was made by vengeful fire.

The seven primitive colours are: black, red, yellow or orange, blue, green, purple, white.

O' ye simple, mere men of good faith who seek the path that leads to Wisdom by which the just man acquires eternal spiritual wisdom, cause your soul to listen to your Spirit and your Spirit will intelligibly speak to you about sublime and effective things that give you the desire of your heart. All sages, even Solomon, had no more than yourself, and found the science by themselves without [the aid of] eternal wisdom.

J. h. V. h.; J unity, h chaos, V design or projection, h return

Branch of aloe and its flower; branch of perfume and its flower; branch of myrrh and its flower; branch of cinnamon and its flower; acacia branch with odour and its flower; olive branch, flowers and fruits.

The two kinds of human spirit

Of the bodily spirit

This spirit is a magnet destined and peculiar to the movement of the body and to the earthly conception, without which any terrestrial part remains motionless, unable to act directly or indirectly, without knowledge and without execution in Man as in the brute. The brute has that Spirit.

Spiritual mind

This spirit distinguishes the man from the brute, the rational animal from the irrational animal. The man holds the spirit of its creator, being created in his image and likeness: there cannot exist such a picture on Earth that it is endowed with a mind of spiritual conception which is the main motive of reasoning. The reasoning is the operation of our design, the design is the operation of our genius (of our understanding) and the genius (or intelligence) is the execution and the demonstration of the spiritual mind which is in the man.

Incense

- Sulphur
- Saffron
- Peppercorns
- Rosewood
- Putty in essence
- Salt of nitre
- White cinnamon, or acacia lignea
- Myrrh

Translation of 'Le Manuscrit d'Alger' (1772)

Specifics of a Woman's Reception G

'What are you doing among us, a treacherous serpent-like woman? Would you like for the fourth time to rush into some other innovative trap on your part? No, you demon, you will not succeed! I have discovered all your past plans and I know in you all those you can still commit; O' Eve, Eve, far from being now seduced by your false and vain appearances, you will be subject to me and my dependence. It is ill-advised that you come to these places to face dangers and hazards, rather fear the burning flames of the flanks of my ramparts which will fall on you and on all yours to reduce you to ashes and dust. By these same flames, I defend mine and annihilate yours. Tremble and quiver at this threat! Oh! What sad object is offered to my sight and astonishes my eyes? Lord, defend me, by your power, the enemy who besieges me and that he can never shake the slightest capitals of your columns. But, O' woman, you are trembling, you are rightly crying! I perceive on your forehead the horror of your crime! This deathly pallor that covers you will constantly remind you of the kind of horrible crime you have caused and still cause throughout the world.'

'Remember, woman, your training, your first home and your first crime. Your creation seemed to be my felicity! But no, it has served only to dispel my constancy and to open the deepest abyss. Far from me, fatal object, of which my soul was seized! I did not think then that you were the only instrument that could wear at my bliss. See the state of misery and evil which thou hast reduced me? Why did you not let me live my whole journey and have you made me susceptible to the horrors of death? I lived in peace in the delightful abode of the soul, where everything was subject to my voice and my will. The low branches of the trees rose before me so as not to hinder my passage; the birds of the air flew to me when I called them; animals of all kinds went to me when I wanted to; the flowers gave me all the smells, the fruits, all the tastes that I desired, the Earth carried my body with pleasure and my steps with joy. Today the Earth offers me nothing but sadness, horror and inconceivable torment! Consider my pain and misery in the shadow of this sad fig tree to pay for your crime and the one where you knew me to rush!'

At these words, she lies on the left of the tree, the man is on the right.

> 'Who induced you to the approach like that without terror to soften my heart? But you undertake it in vain and our Master is offended by it: we expect to soon bring our regrets, our groans in the deepest abysses. O' Eli, Eli, but, Lord, what do I see and hear? What terror seizes me? The Earth under my feet moves, a voice strikes me, my eyes are dimmed, all things abandon me.'

The recipient is sentenced to the penalties of the fire, of air, water and earth; then she says;

> 'People, I have caused your doom, yet I dare appear before you without trembling. I confess I am guilty of your chains and torments, but I will deliver you by treading my feet at the head of the Serpent.'

The Master tells her;

> 'At this confession, at this promise from you, and from your sincere repentance, come to me and make a commitment!'

A contract is made and the Master continues;

> 'See, penitent woman, this tower on your right and that flame on your left which threatens to consume you and to reduce you to powder, you can avoid it only by practising exactly all the regulations that I have prescribed.'

For the second grade.

> 'The darkness in which you find yourself makes you understand how hard and painful your life will be on this earth; by this, you will see from what good you have fallen, without any resource or pretension for the present. The cutting edge of these swords that rest on your body represents the little solidity of your life on this earth and certifies your crime. The chain that surrounds your head ensures your slavery, and your slavery warns us against all your future plans. The first work that was done by your indiscretion on this earth was cursed. The second was predicted and the third was voluntary. Today you will work by submission and you will take to this work by obedience; you will sow two kinds of wheat on this earth, and when you shall harvest their

product thou shalt observe which of the two will have brought the most and thereby you shall judge your failures. What do you have to answer to what I just told you? Do you want to see the product of your seed?'

She answers 'yes'. She is shown a skull.

'Here! This is the product of your vile works which cause all our troubles. Advances to me face to the ground, come and confess your repentance and contract your commitment.'

Zipporah	Moses' wife
Elisheba	Aaron's wife
Debora	Judge and G.6
Abigail	David's wife

feis, feas, muramon for Appr.

hedith, Belzebu, Bethabara for Comp.

Akirob password

Things needed at the reception.

- *Half alder of black ribbon*
- *Half alder of white ribbon*
- *Half alder of red ribbon*
- *Half alder of blue ribbon*
- *An alder and a half wide of white linen girdle*
- *fifteen candles*
- *a gold ring, a silver coin*
- *a black rug crossed with white*

The mind, the intellect and the spiritual soul form a triangle, where the mind occupies the top, the intellect the right, the soul the left and God is at the centre.

The mind is too pure to communicate directly with our spiritual soul which is defiled by the union of the body, it uses the intellect as the way and means; the body is too impure to communicate directly with the spiritual soul which is in relation with the spirit, it uses fire (or the passive soul) as the way and means.

The mouth is the organ of active power; the eyes are of the communicative power; ears are passive power. Through these three organs, the soul receives and gives the knowledge of ideas, it receives through the eyes and the ears; it gives by the eyes and the mouth; it communicates through the mouth and ears. Our other senses are more material organs that also relate to our soul. The soul is affected by the sensations of the body because of its connection with it.

The Word is not the proof of God, it is the expression of it as our word is of our thought. Thought is in us, but it is hidden there from all others, and it manifests itself only by coming out, so to speak, of us by speech. The thought is then clothed with a material body, which is all spiritual; but thought 1°, which is in us, will not produce the word alone, what happens in us from the thought is the 2° willingness to manifest ourselves externally by an act 3°; this act forms the word 4° which is the expression of the thought to communicate itself outside of itself.

The marrow represents the original silt of which the First Man was formed; it is the cement and the principle of the body machine.

The world has been made with Time and this Time began with the World by the will of God, without God changing his eternal counsel and his immutable Will: there would be no Time if there was no succession of created Creations, for what makes Time is the succession and movement of created things that are given place to each other. So the World and Time date from the same era; the movement of the World generates Time, which is the measure of movement and rest.

Translation of 'Le Manuscrit d'Alger' (1772)

[The Prophecy of the Popes][81]

A circle having on one side the Sun surrounded by twelve stars and this motto 'du travail du soleil' [The labour of the Sun] and on the other, the Moon surrounded by five stars with this motto 'du milieu de la Lune' [From the mean of the Moon].[82]

Twelve banners on each of which the four Hebrew letters which signify:

1°   The high column.[83]
2°   The lightweight bear.[84]
3°   The ravishing eagle.[85]
4°   The religious man.[86]
5°   The light in the sun.[87]
6°   The burning flame.[88]

---

81 Description for a tracing representing aspects of a prophetic tradition related to the Catholic Papacy. The Prophecy of the Popes is a series of 112 short, cryptic phrases in Latin which purport to predict the forthcoming Roman Catholic Popes. First published by a Benedictine monk, Arnold de Wyon (1554-1610) in Lignum vitae (1595), Wyon attributes the prophecies to St Malachy (1094 -1148), a 12th-century Archbishop of Armagh, Ireland. Each description identifies one outstanding trait for each future Pope. The list is believed to cover the period between the time of St. Malachy to the present, describing, among many others, Pope John Paul II, Benedict XVI, and finally, Pope Francis. The prophecies conclude with a Pope identified as 'Petrus Romanus', whose pontificate will allegedly precede the destruction of Rome and the Second Coming of Christ.
82 The first motto surrounded by twelve stars corresponds to the Latin motto: De labore solis; 'From the labour of the sun / Of the eclipse of the sun'; Proponents of the prophecies interpret this motto to represent Pope John Paul II (1978–2005) due to the occurrence of solar eclipses on the dates of John Paul II's birth (18 May 1920) and funeral (8 April 2005). The second motto surrounded by five stars corresponds to the Latin motto; De modicitate Lunæ; 'From the meanness of Luna'; Interpreted to represent Pope Nicholas V (1447–55). Nicholas V was born in the diocese of Luni, Italy, the ancient name of which was Luna.
83 Latin motto: Columna excelsa; 'Lofty column'. Linked to Pope Clement XII (1730–40) as an allusion to a statue erected in his memory or the use of two columns from the Pantheon of Agrippa in a chapel he built.
84 Latin motto: Vrsus uelox; 'Swift bear'. Proponents have struggled to provide a satisfactory explanation of this motto, but it is generally attributed it to Pope Clement XIV (1769–74). Some authors claim without evidence that the Ganganelli arms featured a running bear.
85 Latin motto; Aquila rapax; 'Rapacious eagle'; Linked to Pope Pius VII (1800–23) by suggesting it is a reference to the eagle on the arms of Napoleon, whose reign took place during Pius' pontificate.
86 Latin motto; Vir religiofus; 'Religious man'. Linked to Pope Pius VIII (1829–30) by suggesting it is a reference to his papal name, or the fact that he was not the first pope from his family.
87 Latin motto; Lumen in cœlo; 'Light in the sky'. Linked to Pope Leo XIII (1878–1903) by interpreting it as a reference to the star on his coat of arms.
88 Latin motto; Ignis ardens; 'Burning fire'. Linked to Pius X (1903–14) by interpreting it as a reference to his zeal.

7°   Intrepid faith.[89]
8°   The angelic pastor.[90]
9°   Depopulated religion.[91]
10° The dog and the snake.[92]
11° The pastor and the sea.[93]
12° The Flower of flowers.[94]

and on its own flag 'the glory of the olive'.[95]

Fire is the first principle created, Water the second; these two principles contributed to all the forms that the raw material contained within the womb which was formless, confused, indefinite. This universal matter was the corporeal principle intended for the general and particular Creation.[96] This womb brewed in the water, and the fire fomented the water because the matter did not yet have the active power that these two principles were to give it.

The bodily principle is subdivided into three, the sensory, the vegetative, and the passive, which are the first three principles susceptible of ternary corporatisation, like the birds, fish, and creepers which have form or number, weight, and measure.

The form or number is the real figure of the universal and particular body taken in its ternary proportion; this body contains sensory, vegetative and passive. Weight is the value of the ternary matter that makes up the body. This matter is subdivided into three salts,

---

89 Latin motto; Fides intrepida; 'Intrepid faith'. Linked to Pope Pius XI (1922–39) by interpreting it as a reference to his faith and actions during the reign of Benito Mussolini.
90 Latin motto: Pastor angelicus; 'Angelic shepherd'. Linked to Pope Pius XII (1939–58) by interpreting it as a reference to his role during the holocaust.
91 Latin motto: Religio depopulata. 'Religion destroyed'. Linked to Pope Benedict XV (1914–22) by interpreting it as a reference to World War I and the Russian Revolution, which occurred during his pontificate.
92 Latin motto: Canis & coluber; 'Dog and adder'. Linked to Pope Leo XII (1823–29) by suggesting the dog and snake are allusions to his qualities of vigilance and prudence.
93 Latin motto: Pastor & nauta; 'Shepherd and sailor'. Proponents have attempted to link the 'sailor' portion of this motto to Pope John XXIII (1958–63) by interpreting it as a reference to his title Patriarch of Venice, a maritime city.
94 Latin motto: Flos florum; 'Flower of flowers'. Linked to Pope Paul VI (1963–78) by interpreting it as a reference to the fleurs-de-lis on his arms.
95 Latin motto: Gloria oliuæ; 'Glory of the olive'; Proponents of the prophecies generally try to draw a connection between Benedict XVI (2005–13) and the Olivetan order to explain this motto: Benedict's choice of papal name is after Saint Benedict of Nursia, founder of the Benedictine Order, of which the Olivetans are one branch. Other explanations make reference to him as being a pope dedicated to peace and reconciliations of which the olive branch is the symbol.
96 The three other circles, those of Jupiter, Venus, and the Moon, or rather the spirits attached to them, serve to "substantiate" the 'general terrestrial body', also called 'general creation'. From the latter 'emanate all the nutriments needed to substantiate the particular', or 'particular creation', namely 'all the inhabitants of the celestial and terrestrial bodies'. Both the general and the particular creation are "triangular" or "ternary" in constitution.

Sulphur, and mercury. The measure is the intimate union of these three spirit parts united in a single envelope and forming any body whatever in different forms. The sensitive relates to the moon, the vegetative to the sun, and the passive to the earth.

The land is divided into three parts West, North and South. Its shape is triangular; the East, which is the middle, remains with God. The Sun, the Moon, and the Earth form a triangle, remaining in appearance from each other; the Sun to the South, the Moon to the North, the Earth to the West at the bottom of the triangle to receive the influences of the Sun and the Moon.

The Earth has three kinds of bodily forms designated by latitude, longitude, and surface. The bodily form designated by the surface is that of creeping thing; that designated by the longitude is that of the bipedal animal; one designated by the latitude the quadruped animal. The triangle traced by these three bodily forms designates the earth, temporary residence of all bodily beings. The parts that make up each of these shared bodies in so many different forms are the solid, the fluid and the envelope. Each carries in itself its principle and its origin, one of the Creation and the other of the raw material taken in its indifference.

The raw material from which all bodies and their forms come out is fluid and has no consistency in itself whatever it is intended by the Creator to have one to cooperate subsequently with the various operations of which it is responsible.

These main aspects that have contributed to the consistency of the raw material from which all bodies are taken are: 1° Venus, who on one side receives the influences of the planets superior to herself, and on the other communicates her influences to that matter, which is inferior to her, 2° Saturn which is the first aspect of Venus; 3° Jupiter put in affiliation of Venus; 4° Mercury put in affiliation of Saturn.

Although the Sun, the Moon and Mars were also in the philosophical womb, they were not, however, in aspect of the raw material, because they were intended for exhilaration, the vegetation and the conception of the different bodily beings that were to emanate from this matter. The Sun was to preside over the corporeal life, Mars vegetation, and the Moon over conception; what we see on Mars in the spring and on the Moon in the seed time that is poured upon the earth, which develops the germ of all things, but which cannot be produced in germ without sufficient influence of the Moon.

The triangular earth formed of all things spirituous and become solid and mixed is the first body that took the raw material; it contains the different principles of conception specific to all the bodily forms that it had to produce by hour, day, week, month, time and year: they are the creepers, the reptiles, the fishes, the birds, the quadrupeds, the bipeds or the body of the man. The mean expression of an hour, day, etc. One understands by the expression of time, day, etc. the six thoughts of the Creator for the universal Creation; and by the different bodily forms that the earth has conceived, the different actions of said thoughts which could not be without their effect.

It took place at the seventh thought of the creator, after which, by his agents, he had made form from that which was formless. The explosion was felt in Nature: 1° by a formidable action, 2° a general movement, 3° a terrible noise, 4° a great calm.

At the moment of the explosion the first elementary bodies that emerged from the Womb were Saturn, the Sun, the Moon; then Venus, Mercury, Mars, Jupiter (and two others, it is said somewhere, but which I do not know).

Saturn is a terrible fire that would consume all the works of the Creator if it were not mixed; it attracts with its ardour the quintessence of the elements and especially of the water from which the most subtle air is formed.

The Sun is below and in front of Saturn, from which it receives the influences already moderated by this subtle air. The effect of the sun is to separate the most subtle air from the air which is not so much because it is the medium which prevents one from descending and the other from ascending; as he receives the influences of Saturn, he also communicates his own, which is done by reciprocal attraction.

The Sun through the region of air that it has attracted communicates to Venus and Mercury its influences; Mars and Jupiter also receive from him but from further afield. These last four planets send each other their influences; they also communicate them to the Sun by a general and reciprocal attraction.

The Moon, which is the lowest of the planets, receives the influences of all the higher planets moderated by one another and communicates them to the earth, which also returns its own to the Moon to be communicated by it to the other planets.

Translation of 'Le Manuscrit d'Alger' (1772)

Saturn is applied to the air, the sun to fire, the moon to water

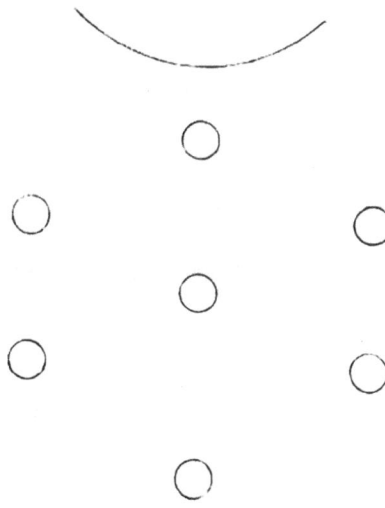

If Adam on one side and the Virgin on the other have each produced a being without the help of the other sex, what then should we think of Adam's physical crime?

Explanation of the Candlestick with Seven Branches referring to the Seven Angels before the Throne of God.

Moses	David	Mikaël	the Sun
Aaron	Solomon	Gabriël	the Moon
Joshua	Hiram son of the widow	Raphaël	the Earth
Ooliab	Hiram King of Tyre	Karina	Mars
Ur	Adonhiram	Muriël	Mercury
Bethsaleël	Abhiram	phannieli	Saturn
Caleb	Gabanon	heï	Venus
heibli		Zaïhab	Jupiter

Monday,	humbly and submissively	the Moon
Tuesday,	violently and abruptly	Mars
Wednesday	actively and strongly	Mercury
Thursday,	promptly, vivaciously and fiercely	Jupiter
Friday,	likely to dissension and contradiction	Venus
Saturday,	dedication, contemplation of all	Saturn
Sunday	rest, thanksgiving	the Sun

Masses

Thanksgiving to the Holy Spirit on Monday for the Sunday of 15 in 15 days at the first receptacle; To obtain the spiritual light, to the Holy Spirit on Saturday every 49 days at the second receptacle; To the Angels G[abriël] M[ikaël] R[aphaël] and Ur[iël] on Thursdays from 7 in 7 days or every 7th of the months to the third receptacle; to the Virgin on Wednesday or every 30th of the month to the fourth receptacle; For the dead every 21 days of the month at the attractions receptacles.

The eclipse of the Sun at the death of J[esus] C[hrist] was not found in the order of the normal course of the stars, Dionysius the Areopagite[97] cried out, *'for the world will end, or the God of Nature will be sulfur'.* The Sages of Athens, equally astonished and in the same persuasion, immediately erected an altar to the Unknown God.[98]

Being at Ephesus, St. John the Evangelist had himself buried alive in a Sepulchre in the presence of many people in the year of Grace 68 at the age of 99. Immediately a supernatural splendour surrounded and covered the tomb and hid it from the eyes of the spectators for a while; then it dissipated to reveal the empty Sepulchre and they no longer saw the Saint.

---

97 Dionysius the Areopagite, was converted by Paul and is considered the first bishop of Athens. From the ninth century, Parisians also identified him as their first bishop, Denis of Paris, who was martyred in the third century under the reign of Emperor Trajan Decius.
98 Reference to Paul's first Athenian convert described in Acts 17. 22-34.

Translation of 'Le Manuscrit d'Alger' (1772)

✠

The triangle is a just and perfect figure in all its points, representing to us nine and its real emanation from the Creator.

1°   The division of the Earth into three parts.

2°   Fire, Water, Air; the latter existed in the interval between the two other elements to make the soil act and grow.

3°   The Three Precepts God gave to Man to love God etc.

4°   The Three Mysterious Characters that God gave to Man to direct himself in all his operations

5°   The three sensible and substantial covenants that God made with Man

6°   The Three Gifts that God made to Man; Faith, Hope and Charity

7°   The three divine degrees of glory that God promises to Man in time

8°   The division of the three sons of Noah into the three parts of the Earth

9°   The three time elections of Enoch, Moses, Elie.

[*The Twenty-Eight Mansions of the Moon*]⁹⁹

The twenty-eight mansions of the Moon, or the different locations in which the image of the Moon must be placed in the 28 circles of operation for 28 days in a row, or in the four operations of the year at the Equinoxes and solstices of the seven days each.

1. alnath	8. alnaza	15. agrapha	22. Sadahc
2. allothaïm	9. alchaam	16. azabene	23. Sabadola
3. alchaomabone	10. Algelioche	17. alchil	24. Sadabath
4. aldebaram	11. arzobra	18. alchas	25. Sadalabra
5. alchataïa	12. auzarpha	19. allatha	26. alpharec
6. alhauna	13. alhaïre	20. abnaïa	27. alcharïa
7. aldimiach	14. achureth	21. abeda	28. albotham

Detail of an Operation
four circles, four angles and four correspondences

It is necessary to make a ligature at three junctions and to trace the Sun and the Moon which mark the beginning of the operation; these two Stars will each have on the right and on the left their hieroglyphics, one will also add Mars with its hieroglyphs. The name of the Apostle, the name of the Patriarch, the name of the Prophet, and the name of the chief rulers of the law from Moses, in each circle, shall be taken to be a ligament; three names of Angels shall be added to each Star, and to each division a word of power in the centre to dominate.

---

99 Copied directly from Heinrich Cornelius Agrippa von Nettesheim (1486-1535). See, *De occulta philosophia libri tres* (Three Books Concerning Occult Philosophy, Book 1 printed Paris 1531; Books 2-3 in Cologne 1533), Book II, Chapter 46.

T.4188 'Kabbalistic Names'

table alph. des 2400 n.

accompagné d'un tableau des
28 maisons de la lune

Transcription of 'The Registry of 2,400 Names'

#	A			#	A			#	B			#	B		
1.	aaron	25	7	51.	abal	15	6	1.	bagnakin	76	8	51.	belzamaka	29	3
2.	aran	24	6	52.	agiael	24	6	2.	belbara	42	6	52.	bataraïn	64	9
3.	abigaïa	25	7	53.	ananael	41	5	3.	beraï	29	11	53.	barabare	43	7
4.	abhielli	37	10	54.	afanuel	62	7	4.	bramaül	63	8	54.	bernagol	44	8
5.	abara	22	4	55.	abarid	42	6	5.	beroï	29	11	55.	binniada	27	9
6.	araï	28	10	56.	abaïam	26	8	6.	belbazan	29	3	56.	bisraï	32	6
7.	amema	30	3	57.	abifaii	31	4	7.	baniel	31	4	57.	bataram	61	7
8.	abin	16	7	58.	agrathum	73	10	8.	baraïel	42	6	58.	barnaïk	27	10
9.	achila	16	7	59.	abrathes	69	6	9.	betar	29	3	59.	balbaïun	64	5
10.	anena	33	6	60.	abriak	39	3	10.	berna	24	6	60.	binnan	43	7
11.	aglaï	23	5	61.	atariok	68	4	11.	belbaïa	34	7	61.	berzeroï	61	7
12.	agel	18	9	62.	aïabam	26	8	12.	baïk	14	5	62.	bianaï	34	7
13.	amaïel	35	8	63.	avariel	61	7	13.	betsaliel	51	6	63.	bathik	28	11
14.	abin	12	3	64.	aglatim	48	3	14.	belzebu	66	10	64.	bernael	76	9
15.	abahiel	26	8	65.	abelbah	33	6	15.	belphagar	62	7	65.	barakaïn	46	10
16.	abaï	13	4	66.	aphartu	71	8	16.	buteïn	48	3	66.	bededum	38	11
17.	abba		6	67.	aham	22	4	17.	bethabara	55	10	67.	beraman	46	10
18.	amabiel	36	9	68.	abematin	41	6	18.	barau	41	6	68.	biathok	54	9
19.	afafiel	60	6	69.	adiabani	33	6	19.	benaï	25	7	69.	baïnkaph	45	9
20.	ansel	27	9	70.	adaqum	36	9	20.	baraberam	62	7	70.	bethabaram	67	4
21.	armathaer	76	3	71.	abrumatha	65	11	21.	baïa	13	4	71.	bruuriael	68	4
22.	amoriak	40	4	72.	agranael	46	10	22.	balam	27	9	72.	balphagum	68	4
23.	abamati	47	11	73.	aquamel	60	5	23.	balaham	36	9	73.	benicau	29	7
24.	achiela	25	7	74.	agraïel	41	5	24.	babal	17	8	74.	baïamas	44	4
25.	athes	30	5	75.	adiozaï	23	10	25.	balzabac	22	4	75.	baïntar	42	6
26.	abra	20	2	76.	amiagrak	47	11	26.	bernaïn	29	3	76.	babraïn	29	5
27.	adiack	23	5	77.	agraphiel	57	3	27.	babb...	27	9	77.	barzaïbal	51	6
28.	alim	19	10	78.	asaphriel	74	11	28.				78.	bamora	23	5
29.	aba		4	79.	aryam	42	6	29.	bethrebel	67	4	79.	blaham	34	7
30.	abbel	16	7	80.	akaram	03	6	30.	biaoum	27	10	80.	bathiel	48	3
31.	aglaïa	24	6	81.	aniadim	34	7	31.	basaek	33	6	81.	batuael	27	10
32.	anenael	45	9	82.	aframoni	42	6	32.	balel	28	10	82.	borbundi	78	6
33.	abumati	62	8	83.	arkaïel	48	3	33.	bazarau	43	7	83.	brammali	64	10
34.	afidiof	54	9	84.	aryshamon	47	11	34.	braphiel	56	11	84.	braïnka	38	11
35.	agiae	17	8	85.	arkaul	47	3	35.	bressamel	75	3	85.	briamatho	79	7
36.	adouth	36	9	86.	adedaïon	27	9	36.	briuriael	60	6	86.	baraciel	27	9
37.	araïon	37	10	87.	adamon	23	5	37.	broyabahali	60	5	87.	biratoni	62	7
38.	algaïa	28	10	88.	alphu	38	11	38.	baïnamos	38	11	88.	braïnton	48	3
39.	afoaelo	28	10	89.	askuriel	64	10	39.	barbanara	57	3	89.	brenaïn	64	9
40.	amiega	26	8	90.	atramaï	46	10	40.	berdiarael	70	7	90.	braïam	41	5
41.	afiedil	27	9	91.	attamor	61	6	41.	bahakin	29	11	91.	baramati	64	10
42.	abaïlié	24	6	92.	alcowrun	60	6	42.	bebaraï	38	11	92.	biarmont	46	10
43.	amieïe	32	6	93.	adornaïk	37	10	43.	biratoï	61	6	93.	baïrmaï	37	10
44.	abiori	30	3	94.	acrotanier	66	3	44.	burnaüam	63	8	94.	batraïon	44	8
45.	arariel	41	5	95.	azmerodim	49	4	45.	bornaha	28	10	95.	barmaïoz	46	10
46.	aniel	31	4	96.	akiadvaraï	54	10	46.	benfaham	46	9	96.	burklael	48	3
47.	abrana	33	6	97.	abramiathum	81	9	47.	babaran	36	9	97.	balssabaton	65	10
48.	alyaï	27	9	98.	azmadiek	76	3	48.	balania	32	5	98.	bendiani	61	6
49.	atayna	36	9	99.	atharkamaï	81	9	49.	baïania	26	8	99.	biadkim	28	10
50.	anila	17	8	100.	arpagaust	55	10	50.	bolaem	33	6	100.	babad		10

✠ 207

C | C | D | D

#	Name	#	#	Name	#	#	Name	#	#	Name	#
1.	Casa	37...10	51.	Cripai	44.8	1.	dabehau	29.11	51.	diaphas	63.8
2.	charaüel	49...4	52.	Crasaüel	59.5	2.	dabriel	64.8	52.	dalphegar	54.9
3.	Cobaüel	50...5	53.	Cristanai	63.9	3.	darkiel	44.8	53.	dialphegor	64.9
4.	calzas	35.8	54.	Crasmiel	60.6	4.	damael	20.3	54.	diablatoni	36.11
5.	chorbiel	66.11	55.	Cresmaüel	84.3	5.	diamuel	66.10	55.	darmemor	48.3
6.	curariel	56.11	56.	Cebatiel	53.8	6.	dioi	22.4	56.	delbrakai	60.6
7.	Castiel	49.10	57.	Craplasim	72.9	7.	demon	19.10	57.	desmaüael	60.5
8.	cassiel	46.10	58.	Crepundi	72.9	8.	doriac	32.5	58.	derphamiam	60.6
9.	chadari	47.10	59.	Cridaüu	48.3	9.	dabaüel	29.11	59.	despharaim	67.3
10.	Colbaz	19.10	60.	Costael	35.8	10.	dazahor	26.8	60.	debaluzom	45.9
11.	Camüei	20.3	61.	Castamuel	69.6	11.	dardier	60.6	61.	demaraim	47.11
12.	Choremiel	63.9	62.	Castamanai	61.7	12.	din	15.6	62.	dazalmum	37.10
13.	Charina	42.6	63.	Capardiel	69.6	13.	dabu	26.8	63.	dearnim	39.3
14.	Caimoir	35.8	64.	Crabiel	41.5	14.	dazaim	21.3	64.	desphamam	58.4
15.	Casien	28.10	65.	Cazueli	34.7	15.	daianes	61.6	65.	dermioas	64.9
16.	Casiael	45.9	66.	Crazamiel	49.4	16.	dabraieli	48.3	66.	deüm	15.6
17.	chorbiebaz	68.4	67.	Crozamin	45.9	17.	dabas	26.8	67.	diael	23.5
18.	Calzaba	20.2	68.	Crusbamuel	87.6	18.	daphara	47.11	68.	dormamor	47.11
19.	Cazaram	36.9	69.	Crapiamin	63.9	19.	dataim	38.11	69.	dorphiel	44.8
20.	Corphanas	63.9	70.	Cirapael	57.3	20.	dardamin	68.4	70.	dermabaz	30.3
21.	chermamin	56.11	71.	Cracuzim	60.6	21.	darkaoz	46.10	71.	dormahar	30.3
22.	Cabaron	30.3	72.	Cepharmin	58.4	22.	darphaza	36.9	72.	Dormaüel	47.11
23.	Capshariel	66.3	73.	Cicim	28.10	23.	darmain	43.7	73.	doKaphael	37.3
24.	Ciurmain	46.10	74.	Cecem	20.2	24.	darazar	42.6	74.	doiolam	44.6
25.	Cordedamon	55.10	75.	Carpini	41.5	25.	dazaba	10	75.	doramaz	34.7
26.	Carmanari	68.5	76.	Cardamor	55.10	26.	dabeba	16.7	76.	Dormazim	49.4
27.	Cornaüi	35.8	77.	Ceraphain	58.4	27.	danaüel	40.4	77.	dorpaul	53.8
28.	Ceremiel	56.11	78.	Cepharama	57.3	28.	damonim	31.4	78.	Dormael	36.9
29.	Cememaram	61.7	79.	Cinciama	47.11	29.	daplataim	59.5	79.	dorphtakar	69.6
30.	Cimarmum	56.11	80.	Carmaphal	70.7	30.	darmakim	45.9	80.	dorbuzar	73.10
31.	Cinaün	29.11	81.	Carmeira	44.8	31.	dabazo	27.10	81.	dobaiam	41.6
32.	Cimiek	29.11	82.	Cicimzka	38.11	32.	dalbiat	54.9	82.	dobuzaphor	72.9
33.	Amaka	26.8	83.	Cadiphas	75.3	33.	delphagor	46.10	83.	dobiina	41.5
34.	Cimarmora	46.10	84.	Curphimas	61.7	34.	delphar	46.9	84.	dobraram	59.5
35.	Amakuz	37.10	85.	Cordaüaz	45.9	35.	dispain	38.11	85.	dolspiel	46.10
36.	Cikamiel	41.5	86.	Cermaz	27.9	36.	daüzarim	46.10	86.	dolferai	40.6
37.	Capharnill	67.4	87.	Carmazim	47.11	37.	darephaus	78.6	87.	donain	31.4
38.	Capardaum	81.9	88.	Carmamiel	66.11	38.	darKaphiel	68.5	88.	donii	27.9
39.	Calaram	46.10	89.	Carmiala	44.8	39.	dindarphali	69.6	89.	doniel	34.7
40.	Caphim	33.6	90.	Cervael	37.10	40.	dinsaos	34.7	90.	danarael	49.4
41.	Capherma	70.7	91.	Ceramiz	33.6	41.	Dirai	29.11	91.	danoçph	55.8
42.	Oribaüel	57.3	92.	Celussim	42.6	42.	Dirmaz	27.9	92.	dabaraham	47.11
43.	crablaniel	62.8	93.	Celaim	27.9	43.	Dimaüel	36.9	93.	dabelbaram	59.5
44.	crekaro	56.11	94.	Celiok	27.9	44.	dizurau	21.4	94.	diazaz	14.5
45.	Cremoriak	66.3	95.	Cebamaz	25.7	45.	dibzaham	41.6	95.	delbabim	38.11
46.	Craphimi	52.7	96.	Cebim	22.4	46.	dilazaram	66.10	96.	daielim	37.6
47.	Crapatel	76.4	97.	Cerbiam	56.11	47.	dilezmozam	66.11	97.	deboram	40.4
48.	Crebiaman	70.7	98.	Cediamas	46.10	48.	difaul	45.9	98.	deiazim	31.4
49.	Criblain	60.6	99.	Cimphis	38.11	49.	dismahor	42.6	99.	daKaraum	63.9
50.	Credalo	49.4	100.			50.	Dirzmazim	51.6	100.	diamha	28.10

Transcription of 'The Registry of 2,400 Names'

#	E		#	E		#	F		#	F	
1.	eli	15. 6.	51.	esathaüm	65. 11.	1.	fanael	33. 6.	51.	fadort	29. 11
2.	erua	23. 3.	52.	emriam	41. 5.	2.	famiel	37. 10.	52.	faglial	54. 7.
3.	eruaün	37. 10.	53.	embliak	48. 3.	3.	famiel	35. 8.	53.	fermum	45. 9.
4.	elia	16. 7.	54.	etain	35. 8.	4.	famiei	33. 6.	54.	ferphat	44. 8.
5.	eliazak	28. 10.	55.	ettaphim	61. 7.	5.	farmaes	60. 5.	55.	ferphiel	46. 10.
6.	enaïabam	40. 4.	56.	etimmar	55. 10.	6.	fursiael	60. 5.	56.	firdamot	55. 10.
7.	eshamaün	58. 4.	57.	etsiamaz	47. 11.	7.	fragne	42. 6.	57.	fragamaz	41. 5.
8.	eliael	28. 10.	58.	evim	23. 5.	8.	faluel	51. 6.	58.	flamaga	54. 7.
9.	eüblik	33. 6.	59.	enaphim	44. 8.	9.	faraïa	35. 8.	59.	flemlak	39. 3.
10.	elim	19. 10.	60.	enoïm	26. 8.	10.	faïel	28. 10	60.	flerdaüm	60. 6.
11.	ebaïol	29. 11.	61.	enemrac	41. 5.	11.	favriaï	62. 7.	61.	flarkam	61. 6.
12.	ofaraïn	40. 4.	62.	elka	15. 6.	12.	farmon	35. 8.	62.	flomar	27. 10.
13.	estaïn	36. 9.	63.	evaraï	60. 5.	13.	falahaï	37. 10.	63.	fekutar	45. 9.
14.	esbraïam	75. 3.	64.	esoara	49. 4.	14.	formaïul	47. 3.	64.	fumin	39. 3.
15.	eraï	28. 10.	65.	evionam	56. 11.	15.	fiathahar	69. 6.	65.	fuphial	49. 4.
16.	enoch	54. 7.	66.	eviaphas	78. 6.	16.	farmagaï	48. 3.	66.	fredanos	54. 9.
17.	eran	32. 5.	67.	evin	39. 3.	17.	farniel	46. 10.	67.	fradomiak	60. 6.
18.	egaüm	39. 3.	68.	evormiaz	46. 10.	18.	farmahor	50. 5.	68.	fraiamin	60. 5.
19.	elechiel	42. 6.	69.	evair	49. 4.	19.	farnaïel	51. 6.	69.	faröi	54. 7.
20.	elam	25. 7.	70.	edah	16. 7.	20.	fraïain	42. 6.	70.	farmacha	41. 5.
21.	emariel	62. 7.	71.	ediam	26. 8.	21.	furgaïab	49. 4.	71.	favirah	35. 8.
22.	ephratik	67. 4.	72.	ediemaz	28. 10.	22.	firmahum	56. 11.	72.	famam	32. 5.
23.	ebiam	30. 3.	73.	evin	17. 8.	23.	fusmaü	52. 7.	73.	famira	53. 6.
24.	emaraï	41. 5.	74.	ediaz	15. 6.	24.	fermaoz	45. 7.	74.	fazer	39. 3.
25.	eblaïa	30. 3.	75.	edimraz	28. 7.	25.	farnaïel	62. 7.	75.	faramiei	21. 6.
26.	eraza	21. 3.	76.	edomuar	48. 3.	26.	ferminael	49. 4.	76.	farvaraph	80. 8.
27.	eriepa	44. 8.	77.	edomiak	36. 9.	27.	firmortha	48. 3.	77.	feroar	43. 7.
28.	ermazara	45. 9.	78.	edozel	44. 8.	28.	fragnak	35. 8.	78.	fesbraïam	78. 6.
29.	ermozim	44. 8.	79.	edobram	60. 6.	29.	fimiaz	20. 2.	79.	felimar	40. 4.
30.	erbloi	64. 9.	80.	edomierk	51. 6.	30.	fiurak	17. 9.	80.	ferabam	27. 10.
31.	erpata	42. 6.	81.	edozaïm	35. 6.	31.	femphiel	42. 6.	81.	fiurek	45. 9.
32.	erzcaïn	61. 7.	82.	edargon	46. 10.	32.	famarik	48. 3.	82.	fiark	36. 9.
33.	erbas	63. 8.	83.	edophiel	42. 6.	33.	femaraï	44. 8.	83.	fiordaz	36. 9.
34.	erbim	46. 10.	84.	edimmaz	21. 3.	34.	felliak	31. 4.	84.	fresmaïa	62. 9.
35.	erbado	38. 11.	85.	edunaï	42. 6.	35.	fediam	29. 11.	85.	freymar	42. 6
36.	erbazar	54. 9.	86.	eduemor	55. 10.	36.	fiamin	32. 5.	86.	fismaïel	49. 4.
37.	erbumati	93. 3.	87.	ediuma	41. 5.	37.	fragma	33. 6.	87.	fraguiel	64. 10.
38.	errum	31. 4.	88.	eduem	48. 3.	38.	formidar	63. 8.	88.	fazam	21. 3.
39.	erphiel	43. 7.	89.	eduï	36. 9.	39.	forphia	33. 6.	89.	fragiel	41. 5.
40.	espat	43. 7.	90.	edar	25. 7.	40.	fordimak	54. 9.	90.	fizamo	27. 9.
41.	ezmiel	53. 6.	91.	edabba	13. 4.	41.	forkiel	41. 5.	91.	fordiel	61. 6.
42.	ezmaïel	59. 3.	92.	edabara	29. 11.	42.	forcatho	70. 10.	92.	fomara	27. 10.
43.	emmema	32. 5.	93.	ebratoü	52. 7.	43.	feleachim	58. 11.	93.	fortaüm	38. 11.
44.	enmork	30. 3.	94.	etaber	40. 4.	44.	fanelli	41. 5.	94.	fepamaz	27. 9.
45.	emarual	47. 11.	95.	etazim	40. 4.	45.	faraha	34. 7.	95.	frondia	41. 5.
46.	emaraïk	43. 7.	96.	etarphus	66. 11.	46.	faramos	45. 9.	96.	fiphark	61. 6.
47.	enaïam	37. 10.	97.	etiaüm	64. 9.	47.	fardam	31. 6.	97.	febem	24. 6.
48.	ezphaqor	42. 6.	98.	etaram	51. 6.	48.	farkac	36. 9.	98.	febiar	32. 5.
49.	elamaha	35. 8.	99.	ezamin	29. 11.	49.	farnam	42. 6.	99.	fuhai	44. 8.
50.	esabaha	32. 5.	100.	ebib	19. 10.	50.	fadamaz	26. 8.	100.	fedbadem	28. 10.

#	G.		#	G.		#	H.		#	H.	
1.	gamaliin	28. 11	51.	gaboim	33. 6.	1.	heirnuel	62. 8.	51.	haliaz	25. 7.
2.	gamiael	37. 10.	52.	gabarum	50. 5.	2.	helel	33. 6.	52.	hamaraz	41. 5.
3.	graphiel	66. 11.	53.	gabalim	29. 11.	3.	haht	46. 10.	53.	haueramaz	69. 5.
4.	gabahon	28. 10.	54.	gabaniak	40. 4.	4.	heli	22. 4.	54.	halimaki	40. 4.
5.	gabir	36. 9.	55.	gabiama	82. 5.	5.	hesmiiel	60. 5.	55.	halobiaz	47. 11.
6.	gasmaran	65. 11.	56.	gablim	27. 9.	6.	habaïel	33. 6.	56.	heziael	40. 4.
7.	gabbriel	49. 4.	57.	gadaphos	48. 3.	7.	heel	21. 3.	57.	herlin	29. 3.
8.	gerina	38. 11.	58.	gristaphabor	83. 11.	8.	helia	27. 9.	58.	heprin	47. 11.
9.	goames	60. 5.	59.	gremmaz	43. 7.	9.	hodäa	67. 10.	59.	hepizain	46. 10.
10.	gaha	17. 8.	60.	grabaim	36. 8.	10.	hauid	29. 3.	60.	heparzar	60. 6.
11.	grammena	30. 5.	61.	gradiabon	47. 11.	11.	hoba	29. 11.	61.	hapiar	48. 3.
12.	gazabaül	34. 7.	62.	giebaz	21. 3.	12.	heloin	24. 7.	62.	haprok	36. 9.
13.	graśaul	66. 11.	63.	gimmus	28. 10.	13.	hebef	22. 4.	63.	haplazel	66. 11.
14.	gramabin	47. 11.	64.	gimaram	45. 9.	14.	hiain	25. 7.	64.	haplimiel	42. 7.
15.	gramathon	72. 9.	65.	giermin	43. 7.	15.	hariael	48. 3.	65.	hafert	36. 9.
16.	gradeban	43. 7.	66.	gordam	46. 10.	16.	beïbli	38. 11.	66.	heframuel	71. 8.
17.	gramaïel	50. 8.	67.	gabebim	20. 3.	17.	hasmadai	49. 4.	67.	hestrmazor	48. 3.
18.	grazaieli	45. 9.	68.	gabernoz	36. 8.	18.	haraman	53. 8.	68.	hesfadim	29. 11.
19.	grimar	49. 4.	69.	gaharam	47. 11.	19.	haphan	50. 8.	69.	hafert	33. 6.
20.	graphael	66. 10.	70.	geha	15. 6.	20.	heda	15. 6.	70.	hafirim	41. 5.
21.	gospbai	47. 11.	71.	giho	16. 7.	21.	heia	18. 9.	71.	hadidoic	66. 10.
22.	geraim	37. 10.	72.	gimel	29. 11.	22.	hagieli	24. 7.	72.	hamafa	29. 11.
23.	gimaos	24. 7.	73.	goui	34. 7.	23.	hobloin	53. 8.	73.	hannark	30. 5.
24.	guimokar	66. 3.	74.	gathel	30. 5.	24.	hod	26. 8.	74.	hagrial	48. 3.
25.	guimphas	68. 5.	75.	garziame	61. 7.	25.	hagiel	21. 4.	75.	hagumark	65. 11.
26.	golga	25. 7.	76.	glaia	23. 5.	26.	hariel	36. 9.	76.	hagim	23. 5.
27.	galgatar	62. 8.	77.	glui	22. 4.	27.	huratapel	79. 7.	77.	hagarim	47. 11.
28.	gladimar	45. 9.	78.	glerbaz	50. 5.	28.	habamiah	37. 10.	78.	hogramm	30. 5.
29.	glazieli	43. 7.	79.	gerpiam	46. 10.	29.	habarin	43. 7.	79.	hagroton	66. 10.
30.	glenneir	60. 6.	80.	gatronni	42. 6.	30.	harael	29. 3.	80.	hayretim	70. 7.
31.	glimphas	50. 5.	81.	gasgatha	71. 8.	31.	habad	16. 7.	81.	hagloiaz	33. 6.
32.	graphaul	73. 10.	82.	garmiem	48. 3	32.	hair	27. 9.	82.	heglim	27. 9.
33.	guma	21. 4.	83.	gadalora	33. 6.	33.	hirmaz	27. 9.	83.	heguimor	62. 7.
34.	gumael	40. 7.	84.	gagamaz	30. 3.	34.	horspim	36. 9.	84.	hevaim	43. 7.
35.	gurphazi	62. 7.	85.	galgaim	29. 11.	35.	herkaz	36. 8.	85.	hevaraz	49. 4.
36.	guarpin	64. 9.	86.	gaguerat	78. 6.	36.	heurfaz	40. 4.	86.	huvael	36. 9.
37.	girgam	32. 5.	87.	gogiel	38. 11.	37.	hurph	36. 9.	87.	huva	24. 6.
38.	gismai	37. 10.	88.	gimiazam	33. 6.	38.	hairim	46. 10.	88.	hurvial	56. 10.
39.	gipshiel	29. 3.	89.	germebat	61. 7.	39.	herparin	49. 4.	89.	hurmiel	47. 11.
40.	gimari	20. 2.	90.	gerias	61. 6.	40.	hedimerk	53. 8.	90.	huidamiel	68. 5.
41.	gripaham	66. 11.	91.	girumiel	48. 3.	41.	hephial	45. 9.	91.	huzueb	45. 9.
42.	griphamiel	71. 8.	92.	girzaphim	61. 7.	42.	hepiatin	66. 3.	92.	himphas	45. 9.
43.	grodoni	61. 6.	93.	gliriel	45. 9.	43.	hindaraz	43. 7.	93.	hormatim	61. 7.
44.	grismazam	76. 4.	94.	gezmoriak	49. 4.	44.	harmaoz	48. 3.	94.	hordophor	65. 11.
45.	grimiar	62. 8.	95.	ginchupti	70. 10.	45.	harmazar	62. 7.	95.	hachaphul	66. 11.
46.	graphis	62. 8.	96.	germaraz	49. 4.	46.	hadifarz	69. 6.	96.	hakimak	36. 9.
47.	gabadon	29. 11.	97.	gueramon	68. 5.	47.	haruial	64. 9.	97.	haclaphin	52. 7.
48.	gabariel	49. 4.	98.	gewbaza	49. 4.	48.	harmier	54. 9.	98.	hagla	22. 4
49.	gabarna	34. 7.	99.	gaiara	76. 9.	49.	harphiari	66. 3.	99.	haelim	28. 10.
50.	gabew	22. 4.	100.	gadatel	28. 10.	50.	harimik	45. 9.	100.		

Transcription of 'The Registry of 2,400 Names'

#	I	#	I	#	K	#	K
1	iereskaë — 69. 6	51	iesem — 30. 5.	1	Kain — 25. 7.	61	Karia — 38. 11
2	iagiael — 33. 6.	52	ierzaph — 29. 2.	2	Kados — 31. 4.	62	Kazarba — 47. 11.
3	iariel — 48. 3.	53	ierpharez — 70. 7.	3	Kaphiel — 48. 3.	63	Kadamel — 43. 7.
4	iorad — 32. 8.	54	ierim — 40. 4.	4	Kauram — 48. 3.	64	Kiaz — 14. 5.
5	iabaim — 26. 8.	55	ierphim — 44. 8	5	Kasaïel — 51. 6.	65	Keiazim — 41. 5.
6	iniadin — 35. 8.	56	iardam — 54. 9.	6	Kabeba — 22. 4.	66	Karbaza — 47. 11.
7	iahanoda — 46. 10	57	iarmadin — 49. 4.	7	Kanena — 43. 7.	67	Karph — 39. 3.
8	iaain — 25. 7.	58	ioabin — 31. 4.	8	Kababer — 29. 3.	68	Kophim — 31. 4.
9	ioanan — 43. 7.	59	iaphim — 39. 3.	9	Kabahoïr — 44. 8.	69	Kubiel — 55. 10.
10	ianoda — 37. 10.	60	iaftaumor — 52. 8.	10	Kabahot — 35. 8.	60	Krabahot — 63. 7.
11	ia — 10.	61	iebinal — 42. 6.	11	Kaba — 14. 5.	61	Kisthom — 46. 10.
12	iudai — 48. 3.	62	iechal — 58. 2.	12	Kaaphon — 44. 8.	62	Kiesphot — 56. 11.
13	ioreps — 44. 8.	63	ieruim — 47. 11.	13	Kaphaniel — 65. 11.	63	Kierphaz — 43. 7.
14	ihab — 19. 10.	64	iesbaor — 64. 10.	14	Kiraham — 60. 5.	64	Kierphim — 47. 11.
15	iahe — 22. 4.	65	iesphas — 59. 4.	15	Kazhamaï — 60. 5.	65	Kierbas — 65. 11.
16	iabaham — 34. 7.	66	ierdimiaz — 57. 2.	16	Kalvel — 67. 3.	66	Kiork — 30. 2.
17	iaud — 47. 11.	67	iezbahar — 63. 9.	17	Kahel — 30. 3.	67	Keümaz — 27. 9.
18	iarel — 36. 9	68	iozdanor — 66. 10.	18	Kerina — 44. 8.	68	Kerbebaz — 55. 10.
19	izrael — 27. 10.	69	iozcaph — 60. 6.	19	Kasaek — 41. 5.	69	Kerial — 60. 5.
20	izariel — 49. 4.	70	iazkirim — 61. 7.	20	Kieman — 40. 4.	70	Kebrin — 60. 5.
21	iauiel — 40. 4.	71	iazphiel — 16. 10.	21	Kedemel — 43. 7.	71	Kabrozar — 62.
22	ialvel — 38. 11.	72	iendataz — 66. 10.	22	Kinael — 27. 9.	72	Kadedum — 45. 9.
23	ialiel — 36. 9.	73	ieim — 23. 5.	23	Kisiel — 44. 8.	73	Kinsk — 32. 5.
24	iumael — 43. 7.	74	iablina — 31. 4.	24	Kiphar — 45. 9.	74	Keph — 35. 2.
25	iabaïma — 27. 9.	75	iablaza — 25. 7.	25	Kiriel — 42. 6.	75	Kaleph — 48. 5.
26	iereniel — 64. 10.	76	iaftimak — 40. 4.	26	Kimazor — 31. 4.	76	Karsobuam — 65. 11.
27	iadai — 24. 6.	77	iaslinel — 60. 6.	27	Kaphier — 54. 9.	77	Kieku — 34. 7.
28	iakien — 36. 9.	78	iaraha — 37. 10.	28	Kandiel — 60. 6.	78	Kindar — 45. 9.
29	iabamiah — 58. 11.	79	iarbiel — 63. 9.	29	Kermiel — 61. 6.	79	Kophial — 29. 3.
30	iadin — 25. 7.	80	ierphimin — 63. 8.	30	Korziel — 46. 10.	80	Kara — 43. 4.
31	iophiel — 29. 3.	81	iarkier — 56. 10.	31	Karavial — 76. 2.	81	Kormai — 55. 8.
32	ülva — 24. 6.	82	iordiel — 51. 6.	32	Kadoïel — 71. 8.	82	Kordida — 46. 10.
33	iu — 14. 5.	83	iurman — 42. 7.	33	Karrim — 47. 11.	83	Korieli — 43. 7.
34	iaphé — 37. 10.	84	iruata — 45. 9.	34	Kurthiel — 64. 9.	84	Kairmorti — 56. 11.
35	idaumos — 52. 8.	85	irdaz — 34. 7.	35	Kefal — 30. 3.	85	Kelphizim — 67. 3
36	iorep — 43. 7.	86	irkariel — 72. 10.	36	Kerdiam — 55. 10.	86	Kalbaz — 55. 2.
37	iosuaim — 37. 10.	87	iramel — 60. 5.	37	Kedimaz — 53. 6.	87	Kriapts — 31. 6.
38	ioraki — 52. 5.	88	iverphaz — 66. 11.	38	Karmiau — 51. 6.	88	Kephaz — 37. 10.
39	iumiel — 46. 10.	89	ivramin — 67. 3.	39	Kistim — 29. 3.	89	Kierpsin — 45. 9.
40	iabina — 26. 8.	90	ivama — 36. 9	40	Kaik — 22. 4.	90	Kim — 16. 7.
41	iaphar — 51. 6.	91	iviar — 63. 8.	41	Kaez — 17. 8.	91	Kium — 23. 6.
42	ibimaz — 31. 4.	92	iviamam — 61. 7.	42	Karmel — 66. 10.	92	Kabrel — 49. 4.
43	ierabaz — 32. 5.	93	iviel — 29. 3.	43	Karim — 41. 5.	93	Kadrieli — 52. 8.
44	iamilkar — 46. 10	94	ivriel — 48. 2.	44	Kazamara — 44. 8.	94	Kazimari — 67. 2.
45	iazym — 23. 5.	95	ismat — 46. 10.	45	Karinel — 68. 4.	95	Karhai — 48. 3.
46	iazabor — 21. 4.	96	isphat — 49. 4.	46	Kaphzanar — 66. 3.	96	Keardim — 58. 4.
47	iabahimil — 23. 6.	97	isdim — 14. 8.	47	Kablim — 21. 4.	97	Kestokok — 52. 8.
48	iaxafel — 29. 11.	98	imnai — 26. 8.	48	Kahabar — 40. 4.	98	Kerfal — 66. 2.
49	iacoboz — 59. 5.	99	iopka — 26. 8.	49	Kakor — 30. 3.	99	Kofherim — 62. 7.
50	iacophal — 47. 11.	100	iakide — 28. 10.	50	Karmor — 41. 5.	100	Kanenac — 46. 10.

#	L		#	L		#	M		#	M	
1.	labetz	22. 4.	51.	l'berua	37. 10	1.	Marmarath	86. 5.	51.	macrapto	55. 10.
2.	lamaha	34. 7.	52.	libiemat	63. 9.	2.	martiel	52. 7.	52.	markimar	46. 10.
3.	labaïa	25. 7.	53.	lizimak	44. 8.	3.	maumor	29. 4.	53.	markien	54. 9.
4.	leel	27. 9.	54.	lermiok	42. 7.	4.	mozé	34. 4.	54.	marzamon	49. 4.
5.	larhama	60. 8.	55.	labarth	40. 4.	5.	maakin	31. 4.	55.	minphau	63. 8.
6.	labteka	34. 9.	56.	lakordi	41. 6.	6.	mor	19. 10.	56.	minifar	43. 7.
7.	lamatien	69. 6.	57.	lerramim	64. 10.	7.	mater	60. 6.	57.	mertazer	69. 6.
8.	labsaïa	42. 6.	58.	lorphi	44. 8.	8.	macha	22. 5.	58.	memahar	55. 10.
9.	labath	46. 10.	59.	lierbau	69. 6.	9.	machatam	55. 10.	59.	milifin	35. 8.
10.	laphaü	37. 3.	60.	lazarab	34. 7.	10.	meliael	43. 7.	60.	mialifas	54. 9.
11.	lamaz	26. 8.	61.	leazar	38. 11.	11.	michan	43. 7.	61.	morotas	48. 3.
12.	larim	42. 6.	62.	liepin	42. 6.	12.	maquth	48. 3.	62.	marfiel	68. 4.
13.	laraïe	44. 8.	63.	lakviel	69. 5.	13.	miael	29. 11.	63.	marai	40. 4.
14.	larphai	60. 5.	64.	latkiel	39. 3.	14.	mikael	31. 4.	64.	maphor	47. 11.
15.	larphau	61. 7.	65.	larim	60. 5.	15.	mihah	27. 9.	65.	mebar	42. 6.
16.	lavaïa	44. 8.	66.	liviatam	73. 10.	16.	maraï	40. 4.	66.	maba	16. 7.
17.	laviel	68. 4.	67.	leviazar	68. 5.	17.	malcha	40. 4.	67.	mablaïm	39. 3.
18.	lazim	71. 4.	68.	levimaz	54. 9.	18.	mael	25. 7.	68.	matarab	37. 10.
19.	labahor	34. 7.	69.	leduit	60. 6.	19.	mema	29. 11.	69.	matohar	63. 9.
20.	labum	42. 6.	70.	labieuf	58. 4.	20.	moriac	32. 5.	70.	malazor	29. 3.
21.	lamek	38. 11.	71.	larziek	64. 10.	21.	misraïn	43. 7.	71.	magum	43. 7.
22.	labaton	42. 6.	72.	larkiel	41. 6.	22.	misrael	41. 6.	72.	magiel	31. 4.
23.	liephim	44. 8.	73.	lazarzac	36. 9.	23.	maketo	60. 5.	73.	mugafor	42. 6.
24.	limph	70. 3.	74.	lamin	32. 6.	24.	mafafoi	61. 7.	74.	megeriel	60. 6.
25.	lamak	76. 8.	75.	labaï	24. 6.	25.	memaïai	48. 3.	75.	megim	70. 3.
26.	laibim	26. 8.	76.	labaïel	36. 9.	26.	matiieg	54. 9.	76.	megum	46. 10.
27.	lorphim	71. 4.	77.	lababam	36. 9.	27.	matomik	47. 11.	77.	mekel	54. 8.
28.	larfazel	68. 5.	78.	lafieli	37. 10.	28.	mauriel	68. 4.	78.	mahala	54. 7.
29.	lerraph	67. 3.	79.	lafamiel	47. 11.	29.	miliel	34. 7.	79.	miatroh	30. 5.
30.	laratiel	72. 9.	80.	lem	26. 8.	30.	matai	42. 6.	80.	mim	20. 2.
31.	larrael	43. 7.	81.	lemia	31. 4.	31.	mitraton	58. 4.	81.	maem	26. 8.
32.	laphiel	49. 4.	82.	lezim	77. 10.	32.	makael	36. 9.	82.	marchiel	66. 11.
33.	labiam	35. 8.	83.	letiaba	48. 3.	33.	mirma	32. 5.	83.	marmaon	52. 8.
34.	lervaz	38. 11.	84.	lambia	44. 8.	34.	miriak	25. 9.	84.	maratief	69. 5.
35.	limphiel	44. 8.	85.	lama	25. 7.	35.	meram	46. 10.	85.	maziel	40. 4.
36.	limeos	41. 5.	86.	linfiel	43. 7.	36.	mazero	49. 4.	86.	mafima	28. 10.
37.	larpiel	31. 6.	87.	liephaz	40. 4.	37.	matera	61. 7.	87.	marim	32. 5.
38.	ladiam	25. 8.	88.	liems	74. 7.	38.	matha	45. 9.	88.		
39.	ladamor	33. 6.	89.	limezar	45. 9.	39.	mataram	60. 3.	89.	murdiel	67. 3.
40.	labair	32. 6.	90.	limpiel	41. 5.	40.	marsaiel	54. 9.	90.	murgim	43. 7.
41.	laham	32. 6.	91.	lezjohar	52. 8.	41.	mortiphar	30. 6.	91.	murkad	38. 11.
42.	liabar	19. 10.	92.	lekaz	26. 8.	42.	mormier	47. 11	92.	mudina	60. 5.
43.	lierzim	51. 6.	93.	lekaham	46. 10.	43.	merkam	54. 9.	93.	mubim	52. 7.
44.	liah	23. 5.	94.	lerbas	66. 3.	44.	mimiar	42. 6.	94.	mabiadim	39. 3.
45.	limel	32. 6.	95.	lizarom	40. 4.	45.	mizraham	45. 9.	95.	mazmara	44. 8.
46.	limsiel	47. 11.	96.	learma	43. 7.	46.	miselel	61. 7.	96.	mazaur	39. 3.
47.	liaphos	30. 5.	97.	lorfauel	74. 3.	47.	mibiath	64. 10.	97.	mazaba	18. 9.
48.	ligtau	55. 10.	98.	ladabar	37. 10	48.	morphiel	44. 8.	98.	maduel	67. 3.
49.	loimaz	27. 9.	99.	liemim	36. 9.	49.	miam	29. 11	99.	madiam	36. 9.
50.	thauk	47. 11.	100.	lakife	28. 10.	50.	mizor	70. 3.	100.	maketoch	64. 10.

Transcription of 'The Registry of 2,400 Names'

N.	N.	O.	O.
1. nuriel 46. 10	51. neskaz 30. 3	1. orza 20. 2	51. olamon 45. 9
2. neran 29. 4	52. nakir 35. 8	2. orsaliel 47. 11	52. oliam 34. 7
3. nena 32. 5	53. nablai 36. 9	3. orka 27. 9	53. oliphaz 28. 11
4. neramah 57. 3	54.	4. opiel 36. 8	54. olial 33. 6
5. nerain 30. 3	55. namier 48. 3	5. odin 36. 3	55. orkok 36. 9
6. noriab 31. 4	56. namikal 24. 8	6. ofal 36. 8	56. obrassam 77. 5
7. neaketo 60. 6	57. namiam 45. 9	7. osmai 36. 9	57. ocak 27. 10
8. nazaiel 37. 10	58. napiel 48. 3	8. ormada 30. 3	58. omarab 28. 11
9. nehemah 47. 11	59. nathiel 29. 5	9. orcan 47. 11	59. ovrim 40. 4
10. naha 23. 5	60. natiaph 71. 8	10. orphia 32. 5	60. oviamas 67. 4
11. Noé 25. 7	61. nazidin 46. 10	11. orphieli 62. 8	61. overmos 66. 3
12. neum 47. 11	62. nadara 37. 10	12. oimar 42. 6	62. oquiak 45. 9
13. nehemias 61. 7	63. nezial 49. 4	13. odian 44. 8	63. oquin 39. 3
14. nain 28. 10	64. nimazer 54. 10	14. obiada 41. 5	64. oquimaz 40. 4
15. nerinas 60. 6	65. nia 19. 10	15. odaba 29. 11	65. osarmaz 49. 4
16. nerirun 50. 5	66. niparar 45. 9	16. odem 34. 8	66. osalim 28. 11
17. nerdabas 71. 8	67. nordaiar 45. 9	17. oean 45. 9	67. omisas 44. 8
18. nerphim 32. 7	68. norberph 61. 7	18. odazazar 47. 11	68. oror 26. 8
19. nerdai 59. 5	69. naba 17. 8	19. omim 25. 7	69. opheum 63. 8
20. nemro 40. 4	70. niopier 51. 6	20. omiar 39. 3	70. odiam 44. 4/8
21. Nermias 64. 10	71. nifari 49. 4	21. ophieil 29. 3	71. oclien 61. 6
22. nebin 39. 3	72. nelsiax 41. 5	22. ofiel 29. 3	72. ocliers 68. 6
23. naimaka 39. 3	73. nekil 44. 8	23. ocamos 47. 11	73. omdmiel 46. 10
24. norphiel 44. 8	74. nediel 42. 6	24. oliaba 25. 7	74. orkam 39. 3
25. narriel 34. 9	75. nacabos 38. 11	25. orapiel 63. 8	75. opatiel 69. 4
26. napus 38. 11	76. necam 38. 11	26. orphaz 31. 2	76. opel 34. 7
27. ninphas 62. 8	77. nekim 34. 7	27. oliel 33. 6	77. opreum 57. 3
28. nadamas 30. 5	78. necorim 54. 9	28. onuel 47. 11	78. oprim 62. 6
29. nerph 46. 10	79. neormin 51. 6	29. oparaz 36. 9	79. okiel 33. 6
30. nibim 34. 7	80. neodial 61. 7	30. obliak 51. 6	80. ozamel 40. 7
31. niaphim 48. 3	81. norizim 47. 11	31. ortiel 40. 4	81. ouriel 46. 10
32. neikaz 31. 4	82. noviat 66. 11	32. ozial 41. 5	82. opharim 66. 10
33. noimor 32. 5	83. novrier 66. 10	33. osamaz 34. 7	83. of
34. nabazar 36. 9	84. novrizav 66. 11	34. oraniel 49. 4	84. opleum 63. 8
35. nadimiel 44. 8	85. navior 58. 4	35. obima 40. 4	85. obigai 48. 3
36. nordinaph 68. 5	86. nivimar 30. 3	36. ochem 44. 8	86. oblias 58. 4
37. nephai 45. 9	87. niveron 67. 4	37. okathon 60. 6	87. olaphien 57. 3
38. nauph 48. 3	88. neron 41. 5	38. ochimias 61. 7	88. olimphur 54. 9
39. Namar 44. 8	89. norphor 67. 3	39. ouarem 56. 11	89. olarkiel 58. 4
40. nazieli 44. 8	90. nezzari 62. 9	40. ouael 30. 3	90. ouariem 66. 11
41. Nerdedum 79. 7	91. nisari 46. 10	41. odarzel 69. 6	91. oueman 47. 11
42. Nasal 44. 8	92. Hadermiz 44. 8	42. oiam 33. 6	92. oparpiel 56. 11
43. Nayor 33. 6	93. nobeun 40. 4	43. oviel 47. 11	93. ogliam 43. 7
44. nagimaz 30. 3	94. nargiel 67. 3	44. omariel 56. 11	94. ogum 45. 9
45. nariaz 41. 6	95. nerphial 60. 6	45. ouiraz 32. 5	95. ortatiel 64. 10
46. ninphur 48. 3	96. naridin 66. 11	46. obialim 64. 9	96. ogla 28. 10
47. Nierbaza 44. 10	97. nargael 66. 10	47. ocraphum 27. 6	97. oglazim 47. 11
48. niarscok 71. 8	98. nargol 34. 9	48. otraphim 57. 8	98. ogargaza 54. 9
49. Ninaii 32. 5	99. naigla 32. 5	49. otamazar 63. 8	99. oelim 78. 11
50. nestraz 47. 11	100. nada 19. 10	50. oquierk 60. 6	100. oieg 28. 10

✝ 213

#	P		#	P		#	Q. V.		#	Q. V.	
1.	Liel	1. 39. 3.	51.	Limia	31. 4.	1.	quaba	25. 7.	51.	qrediel	61. 6.
2.	Liexel	53. 8.	52.	Lizelph	61. 7.	2.	quael	44. 8.	52.	qravarel	79. 6.
3.	Liriel	62. 7.	53.	Lordas	54. 9.	3.	querbar	85. 4.	53.	qrakin	56. 9.
4.	Luzim	40. 4.	54.	Lrofor	27. 9.	4.	quophi	40. 4.	54.	qrazara	29. 3.
5.	Larsiel	57. 0.	55.	Lrisem	49. 6.	5.	quibazar	61. 7.	55.	qradramos	58. 4.
6.	Larmiel	44. 8.	56.	Lrunzel	46. 11.	6.	qaliers	54. 9.	56.	qrinzer	64. 10.
7.	Lazarim	48. 3.	57.	Lrakaz	31. 4.	7.	gauzarba	70. 10.	57.	qrimtazar	59. 5.
8.	Larbarar	69. 6.	58.	Lladiel	43. 7.	8.	qarbier	76. 4.	58.	qrapher	59. 5.
9.	Lermer	79. 6.	59.	Llaïm	34. 7.	9.	quirbem	70. 7.	59.	qrimar	41. 5.
10.	Lerdim	63. 9.	60.	Lluzari	48. 4.	10.	quiriat	71. 4.	60.	qazir	26. 9.
11.	Lermaz	47. 11.	61.	Lriphan	66. 10.	11.	qarziel	61. 7.	61.	qlazam	37. 10.
12.	Lotlier	44. 8.	62.	Lreziel	58. 4.	12.	querbim	78. 6.	62.	qlaum	52. 7.
13.	Loliamas	66. 11.	63.	Lresas	64. 10.	13.	quamazar	54. 9.	63.	qlaph	46. 10.
14.	perpazar	62. 8.	64.	Lrakari	44. 9.	14.	quorka	41. 5.	64.	qlandier	87. 6.
15.	Lroviaz	45. 9.	65.	Lrekim	43. 7.	15.	quorkin	47. 11.	65.	qlapas	57. 3.
16.	Lerbiam	76. 4.	66.	Lrakaim	42. 7.	16.	quazer	54. 9.	66.	qazaïm	52. 5.
17.	Lakaph	60. 5.	67.	Lrophaz	74. 7.	17.	qubiel	60. 6.	67.	qadaï	31. 4.
18.	Larkarath	91. 10.	68.	Lreblum	64. 10.	18.	quaciel	44. 8.	68.	qemuel	68. 5.
19.	Lisimas	66. 11.	69.	Lrokaliz	43. 7.	19.	quamiel	50. 5.	69.	qasfas	67. 4.
20.	Liuth	48. 0.	70.	Lraul	49. 4.	20.	quvriel	49. 4.	70.	qadumel	62. 8.
21.	Limandra	65. 11.	71.	Laul	46. 10.	21.	qorssiel	49. 4.	71.	qarkaz	44. 8.
22.	Lielzal	47. 11.	72.	Lauel	46. 5.	22.	quindiam	38. 4.	72.	qakai	27. 10.
23.	Lorkatot	61. 7.	73.	Lurkin	40. 4.	23.	qimkaz	00. 6.	73.	qaravael	69. 6.
24.	Larsaba	39. 3.	74.	Lauk	47. 11.	24.	quebrak	68. 5.	74.	qaziaïm	67. 3.
25.	Likim	70. 0.	75.	Larpak	47. 11.	25.	quephiel	70. 7.	75.	qiadamon	47. 11.
26.	Lissim	48. 3.	76.	Ligraph	60. 6.	26.	querful	87. 6.	76.	qizlim	67. 4.
27.	Lasath	64. 9.	77.	Lig	30. 3.	27.	qaba	20. 2.	77.	qkazz	43. 7.
28.	Lermel	60. 6.	78.	Laign	42. 6.	28.	quabaraz	44. 8.	78.	qrembas	69. 6.
29.	Larial	64. 9.	79.	Lagla	29. 11.	29.	qarak	45. 9.	79.	qranthas	70. 7.
30.	Ladaïn	35. 8.	80.	Layrazim	54. 9.	30.	quastork	66. 3.	80.	qeradas	65. 11.
31.	Laraet	64. 9.	81.	Loguel	62. 8.	31.	germaz	49. 4.	81.	qastiel	60. 6.
32.	Lanam	42. 6.	82.	Lolgiel	41. 5.	32.	querzer	82. 10.	82.	quariel	72. 10.
33.	Lerman	49. 5.	83.	Legreph	72. 9.	33.	qasamar	66. 3.	83.	qadamaz	26. 9.
34.	Lerzi	34. 9.	84.	Legim	56. 9.	34.	qaidaz	74. 7.	84.	qerpsum	74. 11.
35.	Lebokas	67. 4.	85.	Lebok	48. 0.	35.	quebaum	71. 8.	85.	qalater	77. 7.
36.	Ledabos	49. 4.	86.	Ladazar	42. 6.	36.	quimar	63. 9.	86.	qulmaïr	42. 7.
37.	Ledum	54. 9.	87.	Lataphel	70. 7.	37.	qulizeb	57. 2.	87.	quelzim	63. 9.
38.	Lizimo	44. 8.	88.	Litim	48. 3.	38.	quapiel	66. 11.	88.	qanemaz	49. 4.
39.	Lirma	78. 11.	89.	Liatar	60. 6.	39.	quekal	56. 10.	89.	qublar	68. 5.
40.	Lirdom	69. 5.	90.	Leisim	61. 7.	40.	queteph	86. 6.	90.	qambak	51. 6.
41.	Liar	40. 4.	91.	Lavar	39. 3.	41.	quaph	45. 9.	91.	qaorziel	62. 8.
42.	Lervazo	44. 10.	92.	Litariz	61. 7.	42.	quetak	63. 9.	92.	qaztaraf	62. 8.
43.	Leth	57. 10.	93.	Lateïram	77. 7.	43.	qatron	32. 5.	93.	qobiaram	66. 10.
44.	Baïlh	52. 5.	94.	Llimaz	29. 11.	44.	quekom	51. 6.	94.	qabliem	46. 4.
45.	Lindar	66. 10.	95.	Lerphazer	82. 11.	45.	qalak	29. 3.	95.	quaber	41. 5.
46.	Linzem	61. 7.	96.	Laramo	49. 4.	46.	qarief	50. 5.	96.	quapheraz	64. 10.
47.	Lephaz	47. 11.	97.	Lazabel	31. 4.	47.	qazkiel	63. 9.	97.	qelkar	55. 10.
48.	Ledari	55. 10.	98.	Lzerph	69. 6.	48.	qurkaniel	64. 10.	98.	qelbus	67. 10.
49.	Lekol	41. 5.	99.	Lethzebu	95. 6.	49.	qarasin	68. 5.	99.	qaïmer	61. 6.
50.	Lelph	46. 10.	100.	Laba	19. 10.	50.	qrestar	56. 10.	100.	qabeï	28. 10.

Transcription of 'The Registry of 2,400 Names'

#	R		#	R		#	S		#	S	
1	rahaba	30. 2.	51	riam	39. 3.	1	Sabaha	31. 4.	51	Seirph	67. 3.
2	raab	21. 3.	52	reümak	30. 5.	2	Samuel	63. 9.	52	Sem	40. 4.
3	raphiel	55. 10.	53	renaum	69. 6.	3	Sephas	70. 7.	53	Sablak	42. 6.
4	rachiel	41. 5.	54	rakozor	47. 11.	4	Soratha	60. 6.	54	Sabiau	60. 5.
5	rakie	35. 8.	55	radagor	42. 6.	5	Sisim	52. 7.	55	Sabraim	51. 6.
6	raphael	64. 9.	56	reüplier	68. 5.	6	Sahen	40. 4.	56	Selseph	80. 8.
7	renua	48. 3.	57	reim	79. 3.	7	Satel	60. 6.	57	Sacritas	76. 4.
8	rabaüa	31. 4.	58	raim	31. 4.	8	Seraphiel	83. 11.	58	Sratas	59. 5.
9	rabazar	40. 4.	59	raka	29. 11.	9	Sagum	49. 11.	59	Sariepel	79. 7.
10	rieph	60. 6.	60	rimpher	69. 5.	10	Samael	44. 8.	60	Sarph	47. 11.
11	radas	41. 5.	61	rimpolas	68. 4.	11	Samel	46. 10.	61	Seal	67. 11.
12	rem	38. 11.	62	remder	62. 8.	12	Sebenhakim	72. 9.	62	Seblar	64. 10.
13	rabas	39. 3.	63	rioph	42. 6.	13	Sackiel	42. 6.	63	Sebiam	57. 3.
14	rams	27. 10.	64	rimphalaz	66. 11.	14	Sabanai	44. 8.	64	Seloras	76. 4.
15	remara	57. 2.	65	radam	35. 8.	15	Saramahau	79. 7.	65	Sarphaŗal	61. 7.
16	raphim	47. 11.	66	rimtam	41. 6.	16	Sarabin	52. 7.	66	Sirus	44. 8.
17	ratamar	68. 5.	67	repim	52. 7.	17	Sariain	60. 6.	67	Sabdeba	31. 4.
18	reziel	67. 2.	68	relim	44. 8.	18	Subarmair	83. 11.	68	Sedim	44. 8.
19	raviel	64. 10.	69	ralarnos	49. 5.	19	Saba	22. 4.	69	Sedarph	63. 9.
20	raplaz	40. 4.	70	ralerk	57. 2.	20	Saiel	40. 4.	70	Sedre	61. 7.
21	ramiar	52. 7.	71	ramieph	58. 4.	21	Samiek	46. 10.	71	Seremiel	82. 10.
22	rakiel	42. 6.	72	reunial	56. 11.	22	Samabei	43. 7.	72	Saul	49. 4.
23	rakot	29. 3.	73	rutkiam	47. 11.	23	Sautauaeli	71. 8.	73	Surkiaz	37. 10.
24	radanuz	27. 10.	74	ruziart	57. 2.	24	Sucein	52. 7.	74	Sursian	56. 11.
25	rimphoth	67. 4.	75	rucidim	62. 8.	25	Saraha	46. 10.	75	Soltias	66. 3.
26	reniati	69. 6.	76	rabelar	68. 11.	26	Serphiaz	60. 6.	76	Sol	27. 9.
27	romor	31. 4.	77	ruchiem	60. 6.	27	Serthia	63. 9.	77	Soviadaram	69. 6.
28	reskiel	67. 4.	78	raskas	64. 10.	28	Serki	5. 10.	78	Savidas	78. 6.
29	riblas	63. 9.	79	ravael	52. 7.	29	Serpier	73. 10.	79	Satiel	61. 7.
30	ruzum	74. 7.	80	raviem	68. 11.	30	Sirphaz	39. 3.	80	Settinuadr	82. 10.
31	rus	24. 6.	81	rauph	52. 7.	31	SorKaph	59. 5.	81	Setim	62. 8.
32	raneau	52. 8.	82	rivar	57. 3.	32	Sotinas	63. 9.	82	Setraf	57. 3.
33	rabatar	42. 6.	83	rivopar	67. 4.	33	Sopliar	51. 6.	83	Semitra	59. 5.
34	rephalon	67. 4.	84	rizzium	63. 9.	34	Sokuel	62. 8.	84	Setraton	78. 6.
35	resimar	58. 4.	85	rescidi	82. 10.	35	Sorbas	62. 8.	85	Sethiaz	63. 9.
36	rimdar	57. 2.	86	reKamel	64. 10.	36	Sormiel	49. 4.	86	Sagigar	30. 5.
37	raKomm	30. 5.	87	reKemun	67. 4.	37	Sordiael	60. 6.	87	Sagaz	28. 10.
38	rezam	44. 8.	88	raio	32. 6.	38	Sordiel	68. 5.	88	Saciel	41. 5.
39	rapimas	64. 10.	89	reünziel	74. 11.	39	Sorkos	45. 9.	89	Soclial	59. 5.
40	rataqum	68. 5.	90	rodamiel	61. 7.	40	Sogomas	61. 7.	90	Socrapobas	93. 3.
41	ragraton	64. 10.	91	raphlaz	47. 11.	41	Soloif	41. 5.	91	Sasavar	77. 7.
42	rama	21. 4.	92	rabadaz	27. 9.	42	Solle	36. 9.	92	Sukapa	49. 4.
43	regoblam	77. 7.	93	raglai	40. 4.	43	Salper	59. 5.	93	Sukamadi	56. 11.
44	regual	59. 6.	94	ragamar	56. 11.	44	Sabamar	84. 9.	94	Surathiel	71. 8.
45	raquer	68. 5.	95	rorkar	51. 6.	45	Sodome	56. 5.	95	Spream	47. 11.
46	radinor	56. 9.	96	rophuel	67. 4.	46	Soko	38. 6.	96	Smarko	38. 11.
47	rafulm	67. 4.	97	roKaphial	64. 10.	47	Sunniel	50. 5.	97	Sosracar	69. 6.
48	requel	70. 7.	98	roboar	68. 11.	48	Sisobel	54. 9.	98	Sasparam	65. 11.
49	rosquiel	68. 4.	99	rasplas	64. 10.	49	Seraphim	76. 4.	99	Sobdabar	60. 6.
50	ramazer	63. 9.	100	rabels	28. 10.	50	Saregato	78. 6.	100	Sabefa	28. 10.

#	T	#	T	#	U	#	U
1.	thamael — 57. 3.	51.	tastha — 53. 8.	1.	uru — 28. 10.	51.	ureloz — 50. 5.
2.	tanié — 43. 7.	52.	trabliam — 51. 6.	2.	ustaek — 37. 10.	52.	urgabel — 49. 4.
3.	telnobech — 72. 9.	53.	trepieh — 62. 8.	3.	urataek — 56. 11.	53.	udamar — 68. 5.
4.	tetra — 53. 8.	54.	triimphos — 59. 5.	4.	uraüel — 46. 10.	54.	uglaï — 49. 4.
5.	tubiel — 60. 6.	55.	trigist — 49. 4.	5.	urmeiz — 44. 8.	55.	usizim — 52. 7.
6.	tawaha — 43. 7.	56.	trakiel — 47. 11.	6.	uael — 32. 6.	56.	
7.	tetramah — 74. 11.	57.	trephiel — 60. 6.	7.	urmaz — 32. 5.	57.	uynim — 46. 10.
8.	thahon — 49. 4.	58.	tugram — 69. 5.	8.	ursim — 44. 8.	58.	uquaras — 67. 4.
9.	thou — 40. 4.	59.	torphim — 46. 10.	9.	urkam — 45. 9.	59.	uraz — 26. 8.
10.	tubiela — 61. 7.	60.	tatuazor — 47. 11.	10.	udaz — 39. 3.	60.	utapiel — 67. 3.
11.	turiel — 46. 10.	61.	triakar — 60. 6.	11.	ubazar — 49. 5.	61.	uziab — 38. 11.
12.	tharapha — 74. 11.	62.	terzebul — 99. 9.	12.	uKaphiel — 69. 6.	62.	uKaur — 56. 11.
13.	tarhaba — 51. 6.	63.	tarnago — 67. 3.	13.	uKaph — 54. 10.	63.	udimab — 50. 5.
14.	tarmaïau — 74. 11.	64.	termaka — 65. 11.	14.	usbraz — 58. 4.	64.	uciail — 68. 4.
15.	thoïaün — 58. 4.	65.	terpher — 75. 3.	15.	uxphiel — 49. 4.	65.	üam — 45. 9.
16.	thuzrai — 61. 7.	66.	tirdiel — 71. 8.	16.	urdiel — 56. 11.	66.	uali — 75. 8.
17.	teievziel — 67. 4.	67.	tirmaiis — 69. 6.	17.	urmiel — 46. 10.	67.	üona — 41. 5.
18.	thaniel — 62. 8.	68.	torkam — 50. 6.	18.	uzdaz — 42. 6.	68.	uoim — 37. 10.
19.	taphtharati — 116. 48.	69.	torblaz — 57. 3.	19.	utrabar — 46. 10.	69.	umabal — 44. 8.
20.	thiriel — 63. 9.	70.	turbiam — 62. 8.	20.	utriumph — 50. 5.	70.	unoam — 43. 7.
21.	turbiel — 61. 7.	71.	truviel — 52. 8.	21.	utrabam — 41. 5.	71.	uriael — 46. 10.
22.	taxiar — 53. 8.	72.	tapazial — 63. 9.	22.	urabsaz — 46. 10.	72.	usaïem — 46. 10.
23.	talial — 46. 10.	73.	tepliaz — 55. 10.	23.	uribel — 62. 7.	73.	usaraph — 65. 11.
24.	taphta — 56. 11.	74.	tesapas — 83. 11.	24.	uKariel — 70. 7.	74.	ucrafaz — 79. 7.
25.	terphos — 70. 7.	75.	testimas — 82. 11.	25.	udiam — 52. 11.	75.	ufemas — 64. 10.
26.	timiel — 50. 5.	76.	tester — 78. 6.	26.	upiad — 58. 11.	76.	ufrem — 68. 5.
27.	tuvial — 52. 7.	77.	temisas — 76. 2.	27.	uquar — 66. 2.	77.	ufabias — 65. 11.
28.	tinerph — 68. 5.	78.	teor — 48. 2.	28.	ugon — 44. 8.	78.	wrom — 68. 4.
29.	tiKor — 41. 5.	79.	teba — 29. 3.	29.	uKaraz — 51. 6.	79.	udapaz — 66. 10.
30.	timbaiK — 57. 3.	80.	teglar — 61. 7.	30.	upriel — 50. 5.	80.	udreif — 89. 8.
31.	tizim — 49. 4.	81.	tegum — 60. 6.	31.	uKasim — 46. 10.	81.	abrauza — 41. 5.
32.	trakton — 51. 6.	82.	tegrim — 61. 7.	32.	udief — 50. 5.	82.	utiphiar — 68. 5.
33.	trephiaz — 58. 4.	83.	talaphaz — 57. 3.	33.	uram — 37. 10.	83.	urstant — 49. 4.
34.	trasmim — 57. 3.	84.	tieb — 29. 2.	34.	uramas — 66. 11.	84.	urmier — 52. 7.
35.	teciem — 57. 3.	85.	timar — 53. 8.	35.	urkus — 46. 10.	85.	urzuar — 46. 10.
36.	tabor — 29. 3.	86.	tibion — 64. 9.	36.	umeor — 51. 6.	86.	uabraK — 50. 5.
37.	tacmin — 22. 6.	87.	taliel — 46. 10.	37.	umin — 37. 10.	87.	unabaz — 34. 7.
38.	tasariel — 77. 7.	88.	talaza — 34. 7.	38.	ubamiar — 52. 7.	88.	uneamz — 51. 6.
39.	tirephur — 52. 7.	89.	talerph — 62. 8.	39.	ublaün — 64. 10.	89.	uphiaer — 55. 10.
40.	terbam — 76. 4.	90.	tophiem — 50. 5.	40.	urzaber — 45. 9.	90.	uKiart — 64. 9.
41.	terdin — 71. 9.	91.	tau — 40. 4.	41.	ugamer — 68. 5.	91.	uorodar — 86. 5.
42.	tauiar — 54. 9.	92.	taubrex — 89. 8.	42.	urpiel — 46. 10.	92.	uKimar — 55. 10.
43.	tapraK — 49. 4.	93.	tamabel — 46. 10.	43.	usabazar — 46. 10.	93.	urdaz — 40. 4.
44.	tamera — 54. 9.	94.	tanan — 47. 11.	44.	usaba — 27. 9.	94.	urkafaz — 41. 5.
45.	timphe — 50. 5.	95.	termor — 60. 6.	45.	ureal — 49. 4.	95.	uzarel — 29. 5.
46.	taremor — 65. 11.	96.	taphtara — 74. 11.	46.	urKiel — 46. 10.	96.	uzerbam — 81. 9.
47.	tiranar — 71. 8.	97.	tara — 38. 11.	47.	umbraz — 58. 4.	97.	ufrazar — 67. 4.
48.	thermoz — 58. 4.	98.	ticiel — 56. 11.	48.	ubbak — 52. 7.	98.	unieril — 52. 2.
49.	trieph — 55. 10.	99.	torbaz — 47. 11.	49.	uioph — 48. 3.	99.	ustapa — 42. 6.
50.	tamezar — 69. 5.	100.	tabae — 28. 10.	50.	uief — 39. 3.	100.	uzebehiki — 57. 10.

Transcription of 'The Registry of 2,400 Names'

#	V		#	Y		#	Z		#	Z	
	Vaül	43.7	51.	Vagla	35.8	1.	Zarel	28.10	51.	Ziblas	52.7
	Vaus	45.9	52.	Veba	43.7	2.	Zezbaho	57.3	52.	Zizim	34.7
	Vael	34.7	53.	Vara	24.6	3.	Zebul	52.7	53.	Zorphas	44.8
	Vriel	49.4	54.	Vakiaz	36.9	4.	Zariel	61.7	54.	Zordiel	46.10
	Valmun	52.7	55.	Vavu	45.9	5.	Zabaratti	54.9	55.	Zarkato	63.8
	Vraïel	48.3	56.	Vakaz	34.7	6.	Zaek	13.4	56.	Zarkaz	29.11
	Vava	44.8	57.	Vorka	42.6	7.	Zorrobabbel	49.4	57.	Zermer	47.11
	Varaia	50.5	58.	Valabin	49.4	8.	Zoroael	31.4	58.	Zermah	47.11
	Vahamain	58.4	59.	Valaim	47.11	9.	Zaruel	46.10	59.	Zapkim	31.4
	Vabsham	46.10	60.	Vottara	61.7	10.	Zorael	27.9	60.	Zadiem	25.7
	Vawa	46.10	61.	Vuriel	50.5	11.	Zarel	29.3	61.	Zuliel	29.11
	Vara	40.4	62.	Vulf	39.5	12.	Zaharin	42.6	62.	Zubel	54.7
	Vaïe	36.9	63.	Valf	39.3	13.	Zabamahir	27.10	63.	Zaka	13.4
	Virdaz	59.5	64.	Volf	51.6	14.	Zaglahin	30.3	64.	Zosbal	44.8
	Vaur	46.10	65.	Vilf	43.7	15.	Zirpharaï	63.9	65.	Zogo	26.8
	Vair	40.4	66.	Volf	29.3	16.	Zababahim	22.4	66.	Zarum	32.5
	Varama	63.8	67.	Vabam	27.10	17.	Zabaha	14.5	67.	Zaketoh	46.10
	Vaba	31.4	68.	Varpabaz	47.11	18.	Zabahaw	26.8	68.	Zadasim	21.3
	Veha	43.7	69.	Virbaz	61.7	19.	Zaraïae	36.8	69.	Zimchu	48.3
20.	Vaia	32.5	70.	Vagriel	61.7	20.	Zaroz	21.3	70.	Zimel	34.7
21.	Vagu	43.7	71.	Vorpiel	73.10	21.	Zarbaz	54.9	71.	Zozbam	45.9
22.	Voir	44.8	72.	Vazar	41.5	22.	Zergum	66.3	72.	Zima	20.2
23.	Votar	52.8	73.	Vram	29.3	23.	Zerbere	78.6	73.	Zabedon	23.5
24.	Vora	34.7	74.	Vria	36.3	24.	Zirphus	61.6	74.	Zelam	29.3
25.	Viha	27.10	75.	Vradaz	23.6	25.	Zurbam	27.10	75.	Zeliar	47.11
26.	Viona	43.7	76.	Vrou	21.4	26.	Zariaz	30.3	76.	Zezbo	54.9
27.	Vakiel	46.10	77.	Vrim	29.3	27.	Zakier	32.5	77.	Zadim	16.7
28.	Vana	36.9	78.	Vrakaz	29.3	28.	Zaphloz	54.7	78.	Zeplamaz	50.5
29.	Vraba	30.3	79.	Virpaz	37.3	29.	Zavar	41.5	79.	Zerkoz	46.10
30.	Valiel	48.3	80.	Varziel	50.5	30.	Zimsu	29.11	80.	Zoïe	16.7
31.	Vuar	41.5	81.	Vetrear	27.6	31.	Zierpaz	66.10	81.	Zarkiel	41.5
32.	Vurk	26.8	82.	Vutiar	54.9	32.	Zephaz	40.4	82.	Zabulon	29.3
33.	Varb	25.10	83.	Vargaez	57.3	33.	Zabalom	29.11	83.	Zabus	26.8
34.	Vanael	48.3	84.	Viaterf	25.5	34.	Zamar	32.5	84.	Zazor	16.7
35.	Valk	25.8	85.	Valebab	47.11	35.	Zuniel	29.11	85.	Zabeam	30.3
36.	Verbra	84.2	86.	Veldah	62.8	36.	Zurpial	30.3	86.	Zaglaim	28.10
37.	Vare	52.7	87.	Vemem	61.8	37.	Zorpiel	36.9	87.	Zaglotos	35.8
38.			88.	Vecierf	78.6	38.	Zaim	15.6	88.	Zaglum	33.6
39.	Vago	27.10	89.	Vedim	50.5	39.	Zabaz	6.	89.	Zeglair	46.10
40.	Vigaz	39.5	90.	Vebraf	63.11	40.	Zergon	52.8	90.	Zeneaz	29.3
41.	Vier	52.7	91.	Vekim	50.5	41.	Zerblas	77.7	91.	Zenam	41.5
42.	Vima	39.3	92.	Vakem	46.10	42.	Zablin	22.4	92.	Zenier	31.6
43.	Vako	27.10	93.	Vadimal	48.3	43.	Zapizo	33.6	93.	Zenakoz	41.5
44.	Vapraz	42.6	94.	Vardaroz	76.4	44.	Zaku	23.5	94.	Zerbemaz	63.9
45.	Vator	51.6	95.	Varki	49.4	45.	Zaki	14.5	95.	Zimaül	50.5
46.	Vuam	36.9	96.	Vostiak	58.4	46.	Zabeu	16.7	96.	Zeph	28.11
47.	Vorb	49.4	97.	Vidram	67.4	47.	Zeblim	40.4	97.	Zabaram	35.8
48.	Vork	41.5	98.	Vouara	50.5	48.	Zirmoz	34.7	98.	Zabeba	12.4
49.	Vivi	60.6	99.	Voak	40.4	49.	Zirmauz	34.9	99.	Zabieph	26.9
50.	Vapa	28.11	100.	Vabe	28.10	50.	Ziflas	44.8	100.	Zamki	19.10

Vérification des noms des Patr. Proph. et apôtres sur les alph. Caf. pour connoitre leurs vertus et puissances.

A			C			I					
1. adam	18.	9.	1. Cainam	31.	4.	1. iuri	28.	10.	46. iudi	44.	8.
2. arpasat	60.	6.	2. Cosam	33.	6.	2. iared	42.	6.	47. iedehon	31.	4.
3. abraham	41.	5.	3. Caïphe	37.	6.	3. isaac	24.	6.	48. iakin	27.	9.
4. aram	31.	4.	4. Cananeen	31.	6.	4. iacob	38.	11.	**K.**		
5. amram	32.	5.	5. Caïn	18.	9.	5. iudas	57.	3.	1. Kam	23.	6.
6. aminada	28.	10.	6. Caleb	26.	8.	6. iuda	29.	3.	**L.**		
7. addi	18.	9.	7. Core	32.	5.	7. iessé	44.	8.	1. Leviathan	80.	8.
8. amos	21.	3.	**D.**			8. ionas	36.	9.	2. Liviatan	82.	10.
9. aaron	25.	7.	1. David	45.	9.	9. iose	24.	7.	3. Lamech	41.	5.
10. abisué	40.	4.	2. Daniel	35.	8.	10. ioseph	63.	8.	4. Levi	48.	3.
11. amarias	59.	5.	3. Debora	28.	10.	11. iorim	32.	5.	5. Laban	27.	9.
12. achitob	42.	6.	4. demon	19.	10.	12. iesus	34.	7.	6. Labaham	36.	9.
13. achias	31.	4.	**E.**			13. ioanan	45.	7.	7. Lamaha	34.	7.
14. abiathar	61.	7.	1. Er	21.	0.	14. iean	28.	10.	8. Luc	40.	4.
15. achimas	35.	8.	2. Eli	15.	6.	15. ianna	26.	8.	9. Louis	44.	8.
16. azarias	48.	3.	3. Enos	21.	8.	16. ioïadas	45.	9.	10. Leon	30.	3.
17. assioram	64.	9.	4. Enoch	34.	7.	17. iosedech	47.	11.	11. Lion	20.	2.
18. abias	30.	3.	5. Eliazim	25.	3.	18. ioachim	31.	4.	**M.**		
19. achas	29.	11.	6. Eliezer	52.	7.	19. ioacim	30.	3.	1. malalael	49.	4.
20. amon	18.	9.	7. Eliazard	49.	4.	20. ioakin	32.	5.	2. mathusalem	77.	5.
21. abiud	40.	4.	8. Eliacim	30.	3.	21. ionathan	62.	8.	3. mathatas	83.	11.
22. azor	15.	6.	9. Eleazar	29.	3.	22. iadus	34.	7.	4. manna	29.	11.
23. achim	16.	7.	10. Ezechias	37.	10.	23. iason	35.	8.	5. melcha	41.	5.
24. ananel	44.	8.	11. Elioué	64.	7.	24. ionnathas	71.	8.	6. mathat	64.	10.
25. aristobule	94.	4.	12. Ezechiel	47.	11.	25. iosaphat	64.	10.	7. melchi	42.	6.
26. ananus	29.	2.	13. Esdras	27.	4.	26. ioram	32.	5.	8. mathatias	94.	4.
27. ananias	62.	7.	14. Erode	35.	8.	27. ioatham	60.	6.	9. mahat	41.	5.
28. abdias	31.	4.	15. Cressiel	62.	8.	28. iosias	49.	4.	10. mattathia	64.	10.
29. agée	13.	4.	**G.**			29. iecouias	55.	10.	11. manassés	75.	3.
30. andrea	32.	7.	1. Gabriel	47.	11.	30. ioazar	28.	8.	12. menelaus	69.	6.
31. abakuc	43.	7.	**H.**			31. ismael	29.	3.	13. mathan	57.	3.
32. amema	30.	3.	1. haï	19.	10.	32. iesu	21.	4.	14. mathias	68.	11.
33. abbel	16.	7.	2. hila	14.	5.	33. iosua	24.	6.	15. matten	64.	10.
34. adiozai	28.	10.	3. heber	22.	6.	34. ioabe	22.	4.	16. matuas	52.	8.
B.			4. hesrom	35.	8.	35. iehu	21.	4.	17. malakie	42.	7.
1. belba	24.	6.	5. her	15.	7.	36. iosué	35.	8.	18. malachi	36.	9.
2. belzebu	56.	10.	6. hellie	31.	4.	37. isaak	31.	4.	19. moze	34.	7.
3. boaz	17.	8.	7. heli ou jacob	22.	4.	38. iakob	38.	11.	20. micheas	52.	7.
4. baal	15.	6.	8. hiram	47.	11.	39. ioel	24.	7.	21. maare	46.	10.
5. baruc	15.	6.	9. hamos	29.	11.	40. iaque	47.	11.	22. mickée	25.	8.
6. balaam	28.	10.	10. hellisée	52.	7.	41. iake	26.	8.	23. mikael	31.	4.
7. balaam	27.	9.	11. helmadam	39.	3.	42. iude	40.	4.	24. Michel	40.	4.
8. barackie	57.	10.	12. hiram	33.	6.	43. iaphe	37.	10.	25. mesias	63.	9.
9. babilonne	53.	6.				44. isaïe	34.	7.	26. merian	56.	11.
10. bartelemi	64.	10.				45. ieremia	50.	8.			
11. betsakel	61.	6.									
12. biron	25.	7.									
13. beri	28.	10.									
14. belphagor	46.	10.									

Transcription of 'The Registry of 2,400 Names'

27. marie ... 44. 8.	2. Raab .... 21. 3.	**V.**	Les 28 maisons de la lune
28. mema ... 29. 11.	3. Rabomi ... 44. 8.	1. Vabim ... 37. 10	ou les diff. emplac. qu'il faut
29. meriam ... 55. 10.	4. Roboam ... 60. 6.	2. Vriel ... 49. 4.	obsérv. pour placer l'image
30. matias ... 62. 8.	5. Rana ... 32. 5.	3. Vaïa ... 43. 7.	de la lune dans les 28 cercles
N.	6. Rodias ... 67. 3.	4. Vava ... 46. 10.	d'op. des 28 jours, soit doublé
1. Noé ... 25. 7.	7. Rehu ... 47. 11.	**Z**	mois entier, soit dans les 4
2. nachor ... 34. 7.	8. Rafael ... 37. 10.	1. Zerzbahoth ... 82. 10.	op. de l'année qui sont chacune
3. nacor ... 33. 6.	9. Rabin ... 33. 6.	2. Zorobabel ... 45. 9.	de 7 jours; ce qui fait en tout
4. nakor ... 33. 6.	10. Rous ... 31. 4.	3. Zorobabbel ... 49. 4.	28. 2. equin. et 2 Solst.
5. naasson ... 25. 7.		4. Zorobbabel ... 47. 11.	
6. nathan ... 69. 5.	**S.**	5. Zoroael ... 31. 4.	1. alnath ... 47. 11.
7. neri ... 44. 8.	1. Seth ... 48. 3.	6. Zacarie ... 37. 10.	2. allothaim ... 50. 5.
8. neder ... 39. 2.	2. Sem ... 40. 4.	7. Zacarias ... 41. 5.	3. alchaonasone ... 80. 8.
9. nagé ... 24. 6.	3. Sarug ... 54. 9.	8. Zakarie ... 44. 8.	4. aldebaram ... 57. 3.
10. naum ... 43. 7.	4. Salomon ... 42. 6.	9. Zariel ... 61. 7.	5. alchataïa ... 58. 4.
11. nena ... 32. 5.	5. Simeon ... 62. 7.		6. alhauna ... 33. 6.
12. nahum ... 44. 8.	6. Salatiel ... 77. 7.	Mure ... 34. 7.	7. aldimiach ... 44. 8.
13. nehemias ... 61. 7.	7. Semeï ... 50. 8.	Mikael ... 31. 4.	8. alnaza ... 18. 9.
14. natan ... 47. 11.	8. Sadoc ... 46. 10.	ange du feu exterminateur	9. alchaam ... 41. 5.
15. ninive ... 60. 6.	9. Sareas ... 68. 5.	élémentaire.	10. algelioche ... 68. 4.
16. nebemie ... 47. 11.	10. Asxnou ... 73. 10.	aaron ... 25. 7.	11. arzobra ... 58. 4.
O.	11. Simon ... 37. 10.	gabriel ... 47. 11.	12. arzarpha ... 49. 4.
1. obed ... 33. 6.	12. Samarie ... 63. 9.	ange de l'eau	13. alhaire ... 48. 3.
2. ozi ... 29. 11.	13. Samaritene ... 92. 9.	iozué ... 36. 8.	14. achureth ... 67. 4.
3. ouias ... 38. 11.	14. Sabaha ... 31. 4.	rafael ... 37. 10.	15. agrapha ... 44. 8.
4. ozias ... 48. 3.	15. Sophonias ... 68. 3.	ou	16. azabene ... 26. 8.
5. ouest ... 62. 8.	16. Sophonia ... 58. 4.	raphael ... 54. 9.	17. alchil ... 28. 10.
6. osée ... 35. 8.	17. Sophonie ... 52. 7.	ange de la terre	18. alchas ... 42. 6.
7. ozée ... 35. 8.	18. Sedechias ... 49. 4.		19. allatha ... 47. 11.
8. oliab ... 24. 6.	19. Sedesias ... 81. 9.	Caleb ... 26. 8.	20. abuain ... 26. 8.
P.	20. Samouel ... 64. 10.	heï ... 17. 8.	21. abeda ... 10. 1.
1. Phaleg ... 45. 9.	21. Samuel ... 62. 9.	ange du sommeil	22. sadahe ... 27. 9.
2. Phares ... 68. 5.	22. Sephas ... 70. 7.	uru ... 28. 10.	23. sabadola ... 42. 6.
3. Phines ... 63. 8.	23. Saul ... 49. 4.	nuriel ... 46. 10.	24. Sadabath ... 58. 4.
4. Phideas ... 52. 7.	24. Satham ... 62. 9.	ange du feu spirituel	25. Sadalabra ... 55. 10.
5. Lus ... 23. 5.	25. Saeul ... 50. 5.	betsaleel ... 51. 6.	26. alpharec ... 59. 5.
6. Philipe ... 49. 4.	**T.**	Phanueli ... 69. 4.	27. alcharia ... 53. 8.
7. Phanuel ... 68. 5.	1. tharé ... 62. 8.	ange de la terreur	28. albotham ... 66. 3.
8. Saul ... 46. 10.	2. tite ... 66. 11.	oliab ... 24. 6.	onction
9. Pierre ... 55. 10.	3. tus ... 24. 6.	Karina ... 43. 7.	huile
10. L'hazer ... 56. 11.	4. tenaha ... 43. 7.	ange de la trompette	branche d'aloë, sa fleur.
11. Pharaon ... 58. 4.	5. tobie ... 51. 6.		branche de parfum sa fleur.
	6. thobie ... 64. 10.		branche fraiche
Q.	7. thir ... 42. 6.	Zariel ... 61. 7.	mirrhe sa fleur
R	8. thetrarque ... 91. 10.	Zakiab	branche de cinnamome, sa
1. Ragau ... 46. 10.	9. tau ... 40. 4.	ange de la mort	fleur odorifique.
	U.		branche d'akacias à odeur
	1. ur ... 24. 6.		sa fleur
			branche d'olivier fleur
			et fruit.

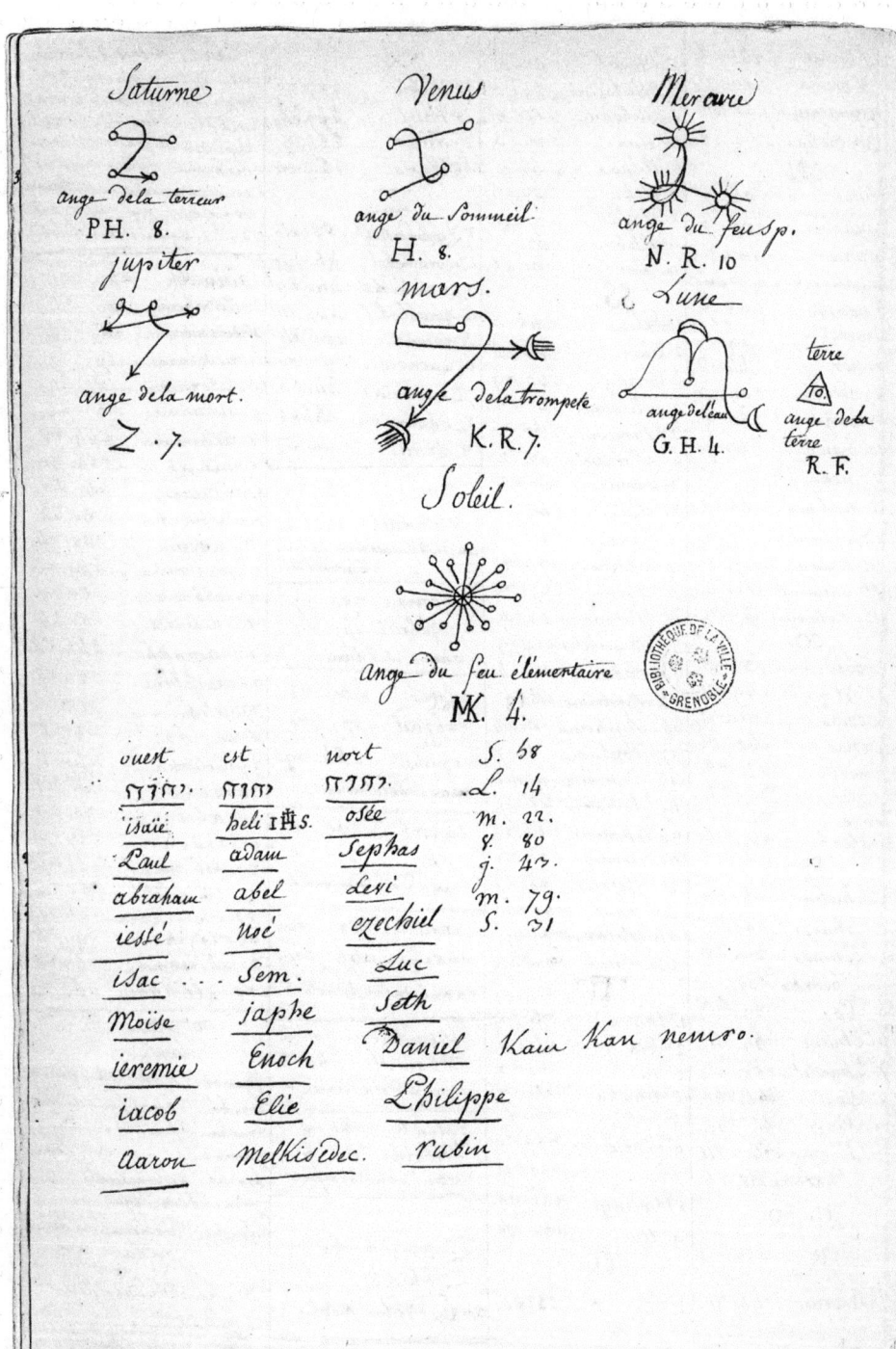

Transcription of 'The Registry of 2,400 Names'

Petit Registre

Phabah ——— 28.
Zaihab ...... 16 – 7.
gabhiel .-.— 01 – 4
Nafthabe .... 37.–10.
awala .... 37 – 10
vavraea ...... 55 – 10.
Nabha, ou rab-ha 28–10
Zutomka ——— 19 —10
reaf ——— 37. – 10.
poruta -- 28 – 10
Lioparaab ... 28 – 10.
phaca --- 28 – 10.
geadef --- 19. 10.
nakaba -- 28. –10.
Nursa ——— 28 –10.
rabol -- 37 – 10
Rafaël ——— 37 – 10
Zezbhahoth - 82. 10
Zäeg -- 10 – 10.
tetragrammenmathon 145 –10
Shamueli -71 — 8.

à vérifier

hananaï ——— 46 ..10
iaudaï -- 57. 3.
Bihel ——— 19 –10.
Schen ——— 43.– 8.

Transcription of:

T.4188 'Kabbalistic Names'

Transcription of 'The Registry of 2,400 Names'

	A.				A.		
1.	aaron	25.	7.	51.	abal	15.	6.
2.	aran	25.	6.	52.	agiael	24.	6.
3.	abigaïa	25.	7.	53.	ananael	14.	5.
4.	abnielli	37.	10.	54.	afanuel	52.	7.
5.	abara	22.	4.	55.	abariel	42.	6.
6.	araï	28.	10.	56.	abaïam	26.	8.
7.	amema	30.	3.	57.	abisaï	31.	4.
8.	abin	16.	7.	58.	agrathum	73.	10.
9.	achila	16.	7.	59.	abrathes	69.	6.
10.	anena	33.	6.	60.	abriak	39.	3.
11.	aglaï	23.	5.	61.	atariok	58.	4.
12.	agel	18.	9.	62.	aïabam	26.	8.
13.	amaïel	35.	8.	63.	avariel	61.	7.
14.	abia	12.	3.	64.	aglatim	48.	3.
15.	abahiel	26.	8.	65.	abelbab	33.	6.
16.	abaï	13.	4.	66.	aphareu	71.	8.
17.	abba		6.	67.	aham	22.	4.
18.	amabiel	36.	9.	68.	abematin	51.	6.
19.	asasiel	60.	6.	69.	adiabani	33.	6.
20.	anael	27.	9.	70.	adagum	36.	9.
21.	armathaer	75.	3.	71.	abramatha	65.	11.
22.	amoriak	40.	4.	72.	agranael	46.	10.
23.	abanati	47.	11.	73.	agnamel	50.	5.
24.	achiela	25.	7.	74.	agraïel	41.	5.
25.	athes	50.	5.	75.	adiozaï	28.	10.
26.	abra	20.	2.	76.	amiagrak	47.	11.
27.	adiaek	23.	5.	77.	agraphiel	57.	3.
28.	alim	19.	10.	78.	asaphriel	47.	11.
29.	aba		4.	79.	aryam	42.	6.
30.	abbel	16.	7.	80.	azaram	33.	6.
31.	aglaïa	24.	6.	81.	aniadim	34.	7.
32.	anenael	45.	9.	82.	aframoni	42.	6.
33.	abumati	62.	8.	83.	arkaïel	48.	3.
34.	asiaïof	54.	9.	84.	arphamon	47.	11.
35.	agiaé	17.	8.	85.	arkaul	57.	3.
36.	adoub	36.	9.	86.	adedaïon	27.	9.
37.	araïom	37.	10.	87.	adamon	23.	5.
38.	algaïa	28.	10.	88.	alphu	38.	11.
39.	azoaelo	28.	10.	89.	askuriel	64.	10.
40.	amiega	26.	8.	90.	atramaï	46.	10.
41.	afiedil	27.	9.	91.	atimor	51.	6.
42.	abaïlié	2.	6.	92.	alcowrun	60.	6.
43.	amieïé	32.	5.	93.	adornaïk	37.	10.
44.	abiori	3.	3.	94.	acrotainer	66.	3.
45.	azariel	41.	8.	95.	azmeradim	49.	4.
46.	aniel	31.	4.	96.	akiadvaraï	64.	10.
47.	abrama	33.	6.	97.	abranuatham	81.	9.
48.	algaïa	27.	9.	98.	azmadiek	35.	8.
49.	atagna	36.	9.	99.	atharkamaï	81.	9.
50.	ama	17.	8.	100.	arpagauſt	55.	10.

✠ 225

B.

1. bagnakin........35........8.
2. belbara..........42........6.
3. beraï.............29.......11.
4. bramaïel........53........8.
5. beroï.............29.......11.
6. belbazan........39........3.
7. bauriel...........31........4.
8. baraïel...........42........6.
9. betar.............39........3.
10. berua............24........6.
11. belbaïa..........34........7.
12. baïk..............14........5.
13. betsaléel........51........6.
14. belzebu.........55.......10.
15. belphagar......52........7.
16. buleïn............48........3.
17. bethabara......55.......10.
18. barau............41........5.
19. benaï............25........7.
20. baraberam.....52........7.
21. baïa.............13........4.
22. balam...........27........9.
23. balabam........36........9.
24. babal............17........8.
25. balzabac........22........4.
26. bernaïn.........39........3.
27. babbiel.........27........9.
28. ....
29. bethzebel......67........4.
30. biaoüm.........37.......10.
31. basaek..........33........6.
32. balel............28.......10.
33. bazaran.........43........7.
34. braphiel........56.......11.
35. bressamel......75........3.
36. brinziael.......60........6.
37. brozabahali....50...........
38. baïnamos......38.......11.
39. barbazara......67........3.
40. berdiarael.....70........7.
41. bahakin........29.......11.
42. bebaraï.........38.......11.
43. biratoï..........51........6.
44. burnaïam......53........8.
45. bomaha........28.......10.
46. benfaham.....45........9.
47. babaram.......36........9.
48. balamia........32........5.
49. baïma..........26........8.
50. bolaem........33........6.

B.

51. belzamaka.....39........3.
52. bataraïm.......54........9.
53. barabaze......43........7.
54. bernagol.......44........8.
55. binmiada......27........9.
56. bisraï...........32........5.
57. bartarem......61........7.
58. barnaïk........37.......10.
59. balbaïun......54........9.
60. biunam........13........7.
61. berzeroï.......61........7.
62. bianaï..........34........7.
63. bathik.........38.......11.
64. beruael........36........9.
65. barakïn........46.......10.
66. bededum.....38.......11.
67. beraman......46.......10.
68. biathok.......54........9.
69. baïnkaph.....45........9.
70. bethabaram...67........4.
71. brunzuael....58........4.
72. balphagum...58........4.
73. benican.......69........3.
74. baïamas......44........8.
75. baïntar.......42........6.
76. batraïm......39........3.
77. barzaïbal....51........6.
78. bamora......23........5.
79. blaham......34........7.
80. bathiel......48........3.
81. batuael......37.......10.
82. borbundi....78........6.
83. brammati...64.......10.
84. braïnka......38.......11.
85. briamatho..79........7.
86. bazaciel....27........9.
87. biratoni....52........7.
88. braïnton....48........3.
89. bremaïm...54........9.
90. braïam.....41........5.
91. baramati...64.......10.
92. biarmont...46.......10.
93. baïrmaï....37.......10.
94. batraïom...44........8.
95. barmaïoz...46.......10.
96. burklael...48........3.
97. balssabaton...55.......10.
98. bandiani...51........6.
99. biadkim...28.......10.
100. babad..................10.

Transcription of 'The Registry of 2,400 Names'

C.

1. casie............37.......10.
2. charaïel.........47.........4.
3. cobaïel..........50.........5.
4. cabzas ....35.........8.
5. chorbiel.........56.......11.
6. curaniel.........56.......11.
7. castiel...........47.......11.
8. cassiel...........46.......10.
9. cheduzi.........47.......10.
10. colbaz ....19.......10.
11. camïeï ....30.........3.
12. cheremiel ....63.........9.
13. charima.........42.........6.
14. caïmoïr ....35.........8.
15. cafien............28.......10.
16. casiael ....45.........9.
17. chorbiebaz......58.........4.
18. calzaba..........20.........2.
19. cazaram.........36.........9.
20. corphanas.......63.........9.
21. chermanin ......56.......11.
22. cabaron ....30.........3.
23. caphariel........66.........3.
24. curmaïn.........46.......10.
25. cordedamon.....55.......10.
26. carmanari ....68.........5.
27. cormaï..........35.........8.
28. ceremiel.........56.......11.
29. cememaram.....61.........7.
30. cimarmum .....56.......11.
31. cinaïm ....29.......11.
32. cimiek ....29.......11.
33. cimaka..........26.........8.
34. cimarmora .....46.......10.
35. cimakuz.........37.......10.
36. cikamiel ....41.........5.
37. capharnill.......67.........4.
38. capardaum .....81.........9.
39. calaram ....46.......10.
40. caphim ....33.........6.
41. capherma ....70.........7.
42. cribaïel ....57.........3.
43. crablaniel ....62.........8.
44. crekara..........56.......11.
45. cermoriak.......66.........3.
46. craphimi........52.........7.
47. crapatel ....76.........4.
48. crebiaman.......70.........7.
49. criblaïn ....60.........6.
50. credalo ....49.........4.

C.

51. cripaï ....44.........8.
52. crasaïel..........59.........5.
53. cristanaï ....63.........9.
54. crasmiel.........60.........6.
55. cresmaïul ....84.........3.
56. cebatiel ....53.........8.
57. craplasim ....72.........9.
58. crepundi ....72.........9.
59. cridaïn..........48.........3.
60. costail ....35.........8.
61. castamuel ....69.........6.
62. castamanaï ......61.........7.
63. capardiel........69.........6.
64. crabiel ....41.........5.
65. cazueli ....34.........7.
66. carazamiel ......49.........4.
67. crozamin........45.........9.
68. crusbamuel......87.........6.
69. crapiamin ......63.........9.
70. crirapael ....57.........3.
71. ciracuzim ......60.........3.
72. cepharnein ......58.........4.
73. cicim ....28.......10.
74. cecem...........20.........2.
75. carpini..........41.........5.
76. cardamor ....55.......10.
77. ceraphaïn ....58.........4.
78. cepharama ......57.........3.
79. ciciama ....47.......11.
80. carmaphal.......70.........7.
81. cazmema........44.........8.
82. cicimaha........38.......11.
83. cardiphas ....75.........3.
84. curphimas.......61.........7.
85. cordaïaz ....45.........9.
86. cermaz..........27.........9.
87. carmazim ......47.......11.
88. curmamiel .....56.......11.
89. curmiala ....44.........8.
90. cervael ....37.......10.
91. ceramiz ....33.........6.
92. celussim .... 4.........6.
93. celaïm ....27.........9.
94. celiak ....27.........9.
95. cebamaz ....25.........7.
96. cebim............22.........4.
97. cerbiam.........56.......11.
98. cediamas........46.......10.
99. ciraphis.........38.......11.
100. ....

D.

1. dabehan .... 29 .... 11.
2. dabriel .... 44 .... 8.
3. darkiel .... 44 .... 8.
4. damael .... 30 .... 3.
5. dianuel .... 55 .... 10.
6. dioï .... 22 .... 4.
7. demon .... 19 .... 10.
8. doriac .... 32 .... 5.
9. dabaïel .... 29 .... 11.
10. dazahor .... 26 .... 8.
11. dardier .... 60 .... 6.
12. din .... 15 .... 6.
13. dabu .... 26 .... 8.
14. dazaïn .... 21 .... 3.
15. daïanes .... 51 .... 6.
16. dabraïeli .... 48 .... 3.
17. dabas .... 26 .... 8.
18. daphara .... 47 .... 11.
19. dataïm .... 38 .... 11.
20. dardamin .... 58 .... 4.
21. darkaoz .... 46 .... 10.
22. darphaza .... 36 .... 9.
23. darmaïn .... 43 .... 7.
24. darazar .... 42 .... 6.
25. dazaba ....10.
26. dabeba .... 16 .... 7.
27. danaïel .... 40 .... 4.
28. damonim .... 31 .... 4.
29. daplataïm .... 59 .... 5.
30. darmakim .... 45 .... 9.
31. dalbazo .... 37 .... 10.
32. dalbiat .... 54 .... 9.
33. delphagor ...... 46 .... 10.
34. delphare .... 45 .... 9.
35. disphaïm .... 38 .... 11.
36. daïzarim .... 46 .... 10.
37. darephaus ...... 78 .... 6.
38. darkaphiel ..... 68 .... 5.
39. dindarphali ..... 69 .... 6.
40. diamos .... 34 .... 7.
41. dirai .... 29 .... 11.
42. dirmaz .... 27 .... 9.
43. dimaïel .... 36 .... 9.
44. dizuram .... 31 .... 4.
45. dibzaham .... 1 .... 5.
46. dilazaram ...... 46 .... 10.
47. dilermozam .... 56 .... 11.
48. difaul .... 5 .... 9.
49. dismahor .... 42 .... 6.
50. dirzmazim ..... 51 .... 6.

D.

51. diaphas .... 53 .... 8.
52. dalphegar ...... 54 .... 9.
53. dialphegor ..... 54 .... 9.
54. diablatoni ...... 56 .... 11.
55. darmemoz ..... 48 .... 3.
56. delbrakaï .... 60 .... 6.
57. desmaïael ...... 50 .... 5.
58. derphamiam ... 60 .... 6.
59. depharaïm ..... 57 .... 3.
60. debluzom ...... 45 .... 9.
61. demaraïn .... 47 .... 11.
62. dazalmun ...... 37 .... 10.
63. dermin .... 39 .... 3.
64. desphamam .... 58 .... 4.
65. demioas .... 54 .... 9.
66. deïm .... 15 .... 6.
67. diael .... 23 .... 5.
68. dormamez ..... 47 .... 11.
69. dorphiel .... 44 .... 8.
70. dermabaz ...... 30 .... 3.
71. donmahaz ...... 30 .... 3.
72. dormaïel .... 47 .... 11.
73. dokaphael ..... 57 .... 3.
74. doïolam .... 44 .... 6.
75. doramuz .... 34 .... 7.
76. dormiazim ..... 49 .... 4.
77. dorpaul .... 53 .... 8.
78. dormael .... 36 .... 9.
79. dorphtahar ..... 69 .... 6.
80. dorbuzar .... 73 .... 10.
81. dobaïam .... 51 .... 6.
82. doberzaphar ... 72 .... 9.
83. dobima .... 41 .... 5.
84. dobrazam ...... 59 .... 5.
85. dolphiel .... 46 .... 10.
86. dolferaï .... 50 .... 5.
87. donaïm .... 31 .... 4.
88. donaï .... 27 .... 9.
89. doniel .... 34 .... 7.
90. donarael .... 49 .... 4.
91. donorph .... 35 .... 8.
92. dabaraham ..... 47 .... 11.
93. dabelbaraus ... 59 .... 5.
94. dixzaz .... 14 .... 5.
95. delbabim .... 38 .... 11.
96. daïelim .... 33 .... 6.
97. deboram .... 40 .... 4.
98. deïazim .... 31 .... 4.
99. dakaraum ...... 63 .... 9.
100. diamha .... 28 .... 10.

Transcription of 'The Registry of 2,400 Names'

E.

1. eli . . . . 15. . . . . 6.
2. erua . . . . 23. . . . . 5.
3. eraïn. . . . . 37. . . . . 10.
4. elia . . . . 16. . . . . 7.
5. eliazak . . . . 28. . . . . 10.
6. enaïabam . . . . 40. . . . . 4.
7. eshamaïn. . . . . 58. . . . . 4.
8. eliael. . . . . 28. . . . . 10.
9. eïblik . . . . 33. . . . . 6.
10. elim . . . . 19. . . . . 10.
11. ebaïol. . . . . 29. . . . . 11.
12. efaraïn . . . . 40. . . . . 4.
13. estaïn . . . . 36. . . . . 9.
14. esbraïam . . . . 75. . . . . 3.
15. eraï . . . . 28. . . . . 10.
16. enoch. . . . . 34. . . . . 7.
17. eran . . . . 32. . . . . 5.
18. egaïum. . . . . 39. . . . . 3.
19. elechiel . . . . 42. . . . . 6.
20. elam. . . . . 25. . . . . 7.
21. emariel . . . . 52. . . . . 7.
22. ephratik. . . . . 67. . . . . 4.
23. ebiam. . . . . 30. . . . . 3.
24. emaraï . . . . 41. . . . . 5.
25. eblaïa . . . . 30. . . . . 3.
26. eraza. . . . . 21. . . . . 3.
27. eriepa. . . . . 44. . . . . 8.
28. ermazara . . . . 45. . . . . 9.
29. ermazin. . . . . 44. . . . . 8.
30. erbloï . . . . 54. . . . . 9.
31. erpata. . . . . 42. . . . . 6.
32. erzcaïn. . . . . 61. . . . . 7.
33. erbas . . . . 53. . . . . 8.
34. erbim . . . . 46. . . . . 10.
35. erbada . . . . 38. . . . . 11.
36. erbazar . . . . 54. . . . . 9.
37. erbumati . . . . 93. . . . . 3.
38. erzum . . . . 31. . . . . 4.
39. erphiel. . . . . 43. . . . . 7.
40. esꝑat. . . . . 43. . . . . 7.
41. ezmiel . . . . 33. . . . . 6.
42. ezmaïel . . . . 39. . . . . 3.
43. emmema . . . . 32. . . . . 5.
44. emmork . . . . 30. . . . . 3.
45. emaraual . . . . 47. . . . . 11.
46. emaraïk . . . . 43. . . . . 7.
47. enaïam. . . . . 37. . . . . 10.
48. ezphagor . . . . 42. . . . . 6.
49. elamaha. . . . . 35. . . . . 8.
50. esabaha . . . . 32. . . . . 5.

E.

51. esathaïm . . . . 65. . . . . 11.
52. emriam . . . . 41. . . . . 5.
53. embliak . . . . 48. . . . . 3.
54. etaïn. . . . . 35. . . . . 8.
55. etiaphim . . . . 61. . . . . 7.
56. etimmar . . . . 55. . . . . 10.
57. etsiamoz . . . . 47. . . . . 11.
58. enim. . . . . 23. . . . . 5.
59. enaphim . . . . 44. . . . . 8.
60. enoïm . . . . 26. . . . . 8.
61. enemrac . . . . 41. . . . . 5.
62. elka. . . . . 15. . . . . 6.
63. evaraï. . . . . 50. . . . . 5.
64. evoara . . . . 49. . . . . 4.
65. evionam . . . . 56. . . . . 11.
66. eviaphas . . . . 78. . . . . 6.
67. evim. . . . . 39. . . . . 3.
68. evormiaz. . . . . 46. . . . . 10.
69. evaïr. . . . . 49. . . . . 4.
70. edah . . . . 16. . . . . 7.
71. ediam. . . . . 26. . . . . 8.
72. ediemaz . . . . 28. . . . . 10.
73. edim. . . . . 17. . . . . 8.
74. ediaz . . . . 15. . . . . 6.
75. edimraz . . . . 25. . . . . 7.
76. edomuar . . . . 48. . . . . 3.
77. edomiak . . . . 36. . . . . 9.
78. edozel . . . . 44. . . . . 8.
79. edobram . . . . 60. . . . . 6.
80. edmierk. . . . . 51. . . . . 6.
81. edozaïm . . . . 33. . . . . 6.
82. edargon. . . . . 46. . . . . 10.
83. edophiel . . . . 42. . . . . 6.
84. edimmaz. . . . . 21. . . . . 3.
85. edunaï . . . . 42. . . . . 6.
86. ednemor . . . . 55. . . . . 10.
87. ednïma . . . . 41. . . . . 5.
88. ednem . . . . 48. . . . . 3.
89. eduï . . . . 36. . . . . 9.
90. edar . . . . 25. . . . . 7.
91. edabba. . . . . 13. . . . . 4.
92. edabara . . . . 29. . . . . 11.
93. etratoin . . . . 2. . . . . 7.
94. etaber. . . . . 40. . . . . 4.
95. etazim . . . . 40. . . . . 4.
96. etarphus . . . . 65. . . . . 11.
97. etianim . . . . 54. . . . . 9.
98. etaram . . . . 51. . . . . 6.
99. ezzamin. . . . . 29. . . . . 11.
100. ehib . . . . 19. . . . . 10.

	F.				F.		
1.	fanael	33	6.	51.	fadort	29	11.
2.	faniel	37	10.	52.	faglial	34	7.
3.	famiel	35	8.	53.	fermum	45	9.
4.	famieï	33	6.	54.	fephal	44	8.
5.	farmaes	50	5.	55.	ferphiel	46	10.
6.	fursiael	50	5.	56.	firdamot	55	10.
7.	fragne	42	6.	57.	fragamaz	47	5.
8.	faruel	51	6.	58.	flamaga	34	7.
9.	faraïa	35	8.	59.	flamzak	39	3.
10.	faïel	28	10.	60.	flerfaïm	60	6.
11.	favriaï	52	7.	61.	flarkam	51	6.
12.	farmon	35	8.	62.	flomar	37	10.
13.	falahaï	37	10.	63.	fekutar	45	9.
14.	formaïul	57	3.	64.	fumin	39	3.
15.	fiathahar	69	6.	65.	fuphial	49	4.
16.	farmagaï	48	3.	66.	fredanos	54	9.
17.	farmiel	46	10.	67.	fradamiarc	60	6.
18.	farmahor	50	5.	68.	fraïamin	50	5.
19.	farnaïel	51	6.	69.	faroï	34	7.
20.	fraïaïm	42	6.	70.	farmacha	41	5.
21.	furgaïab	49	4.	71.	fadirah	35	8.
22.	firmahum	56	11.	72.	famam	32	5.
23.	fusman	52	7.	73.	famira	33	6.
24.	fermaoz	43	7.	74.	fazer	39	3.
25.	farmaïel	52	7.	75.	faramieï	51	6.
26.	ferminael	49	4.	76.	fardaraph	80	8.
27.	firmaortha	48	3.	77.	feroar	43	7.
28.	fizamak	35	8.	78.	fesbraïam	78	6.
29.	fimiaz	20	2.	79.	felimar	40	4.
30.	fiuzak	27	9.	80.	ferabam	37	10.
31.	femphiel	42	6.	81.	fiuzek	45	9.
32.	famarik	48	3.	82.	fiark	36	9.
33.	femaraï	44	8.	83.	fiordaz	36	9.
34.	felliak	31	4.	84.	fresmaïa	63	9.
35.	fediam	29	11.	85.	freymaz	42	6.
36.	diamin	32	5.	86.	fismaïel	49	4.
37.	fragma	33	6.	87.	fraguiel	64	10.
38.	formidar	53	8.	88.	fazam	21	3.
39.	forphia	33	6.	89.	fragiel	41	5.
40.	fordimak	54	9.	90.	fizamo	27	9.
41.	forkiel	41	5.	91.	fordiel	51	6.
42.	forcatho	43	0.	92.	fomara	37	10.
43.	feluchim	38	11.	93.	festaïm	38	11.
44.	fanelli	41	5.	94.	fehamaz	27	9.
45.	faraha	34	7.	95.	frondia	41	5.
46.	faramos	45	9.	96.	fiphark	51	6.
47.	fardam	51	6.	97.	fehem	24	6.
48.	farkac	36	9.	98.	fehiar	32	5.
49.	farmam	42	6.	99.	fuhaï	44	8.
50.	fadamaz	26	8.	100.	fedbadem	28	10.

Transcription of 'The Registry of 2,400 Names'

	G.					G.			
1.	gamakin	38.	11.		51.	gaboïm	33.	6.
2.	gamiel	37.	10.		52.	gabarnum	50.	5.
3.	graphiel	56.	11.		53.	gabalim	29.	11.
4.	gabahou	28.	10.		54.	gabaniak	40.	4.
5.	gabuz	36.	9.		55.	gabiama	32.	5.
6.	gasmaran	65.	11.		56.	gablim	27.	9.
7.	gabbriel	49.	4.		57.	gadaphos	48.	3.
8.	gerina	38.	11.		58.	gristaphahor	83.	11.
9.	goames	50.	5.		59.	gremmaz	43.	7.
10.	gaha	17.	8.		60.	grabaïm	35.	8.
11.	grammema	50.	5.		61.	gradiabon	47.	11.
12.	gazabaïel	34.	7.		62.	giebaz	21.	3.
13.	grafaul	56.	11.		63.	gimnus	28.	10.
14.	gramabin	47.	11.		64.	gimaram	45.	9.
15.	gramathon	72.	9.		65.	giermin	43.	7.
16.	gradeban	43.	7.		66.	gordam	46.	10.
17.	gramaïel	53.	8.		67.	gabebim	30.	3.
18.	grazaïeli	45.	9.		68.	gabernoz	35.	8.
19.	grimar	49.	4.		69.	gaharam	47.	11.
20.	graphael	55.	10.		70.	geha	15.	6.
21.	gophtaï	47.	11.		71.	gihe	16.	7.
22.	geraïm	37.	10.		72.	gimel	29.	11.
23.	gimaos	34.	7.		73.	gouï	34.	7.
24.	guimakar	66.	3.		74.	gathel	50.	5.
25.	guimphas	68.	5.		75.	garziamé	61.	7.
26.	golga	25.	7.		76.	glaïa	23.	5.
27.	galgatar	62.	8.		77.	glaïa	22.	4.
28.	gladimar	45.	9.		78.	glerbaz	50.	5.
29.	glazieli	43.	7.		79.	gerpiam	46.	10.
30.	glermeïr	60.	6.		80.	gatronim	42.	6.
31.	glimphas	50.	5.		81.	gasgatha	71.	8.
32.	graphaul	73.	10.		82.	garmiem	48.	3.
33.	guma	31.	4.		83.	gadalorz	33.	6.
34.	gumael	45.	7.		84.	gagamaz	30.	3.
35.	gurphazi	52.	7.		85.	gagaïm	29.	11.
36.	guarpin	54.	9.		86.	gaguerat	78.	6.
37.	girgam	32.	5.		87.	gogiel	38.	11.
38.	gismaï	37.	10.		88.	gimiazam	33.	6.
39.	giphiel	39.	3.		89.	germebat	61.	7.
40.	gimazi	30.	3.		90.	gerias	51.	6.
41.	gripaham	56.	11.		91.	girumiel	48.	3.
42.	griphamiel	71.	8.		92.	girgaphim	61.	7.
43.	grodoni	51.	6.		93.	gliriel	45.	9.
44.	grismasam	76.	4.		94.	gezmoriak	49.	4.
45.	grimiar	53.	8.		95.	giuchuph	73.	10.
46.	griphix	53.	8.		96.	germaraz	49.	4.
47.	gabadom	29.	11.		97.	gueramon	68.	5.
48.	gabariel	49.	4.		98.	geurbaza	49.	4.
49.	gabarna	34.	7.		99.	gaïara	36.	9.
50.	gabem	22.	4.		100.	gadafel	28.	10.

H.

1.	heïrnuel	62	8.
2.	huht	33	6.
3.	helel	46	10.
4.	heli	22	4.
5.	hesmiael	50	5.
6.	habaïel	33	6.
7.	heel	21	3.
8.	helia	27	9.
9.	hodaïa	37	10.
10.	haniel	39	3.
11.	hoba	29	11.
12.	heloïn	34	7.
13.	hebef	22	4.
14.	hiaïn	25	7.
15.	hariael	48	3.
16.	beïbli	38	11.
17.	hasmadaï	49	4.
18.	haraman	53	8.
19.	haphan	53	8.
20.	heda	15	6.
21.	heïa	18	9.
22.	hagieli	34	7.
23.	hoblïn	53	8.
24.	hod	26	8.
25.	hagieli	31	4.
26.	haziel	36	9.
27.	huratapel	79	7.
28.	habamiah	37	10.
29.	habarin	43	7.
30.	harael	39	3.
31.	habad	16	7.
32.	haïr	27	9.
33.	hirmaz	27	9.
34.	horphim	36	9.
35.	herkaz	35	8.
36.	heifaz	40	4.
37.	hurph	36	9.
38.	haurim	46	10.
39.	herpazin	49	4.
40.	hédimerk	53	8.
41.	hephial	45	9.
42.	hepiatin	66	3.
43.	himdaraz	43	7.
44.	harmaoz	48	3.
45.	harmazar	52	7.
46.	hardifarz	69	6.
47.	haruïal	54	9.
48.	harmier	54	9.
49.	harphiari	66	3.
50.	harimik	45	9.

H.

51.	haliaz	25	7.
52.	hamaraz	41	5.
53.	haneramaz	59	5.
54.	halimaki	40	4.
55.	halobiaz	47	11.
56.	heziael	40	4.
57.	herlim	39	3.
58.	heprin	47	11.
59.	hepizaïn	46	10.
60.	haeparzar	60	6.
61.	hapiar	48	3.
62.	haprok	36	9.
63.	haplazel	56	11.
64.	haplimiel	52	7.
65.	hafart	36	9.
66.	heframnel	71	8.
67.	hefirmazor	48	3.
68.	hefadim	29	11.
69.	hafert	33	6.
70.	hafirim	41	5.
71.	hadidorc	55	10.
72.	hamafa	29	11.
73.	hannark	50	5.
74.	hagrial	48	3.
75.	hagumark	65	11.
76.	hagim	23	5.
77.	hagarim	47	11.
78.	hogramma	50	5.
79.	hagraton	55	10.
80.	hagretim	70	7.
81.	hagloïaz	33	6.
82.	heglim	27	9.
83.	hegnimor	52	7.
84.	hevaïm	43	7.
85.	hevaraz	49	4.
86.	huvael	36	9.
87.	huvael	4	6.
88.	hurvial	55	10.
89.	hurmiel	47	11.
90.	hurdamiel	68	5.
91.	huzueb	45	9.
92.	himphas	45	9.
93.	hormatin	61	7.
94.	hordophor	65	11.
95.	hachaphiel	56	11.
96.	hakimak	36	9.
97.	haclaphin	52	7.
98.	hagla	22	4.
99.	haelim	28	10.
100.			

Transcription of 'The Registry of 2,400 Names'

I.

1. ïereskaé .... 69 .... 6.
2. ïagiael .... 33 .... 6.
3. ïariel .... 48 .... 3.
4. ïorael .... 32 .... 5.
5. ïabaïm .... 26 .... 8.
6. inïadin .... 35 .... 8.
7. ïahanoda .... 46 .... 10.
8. ïaaïm .... 25 .... 7.
9. ïoanan .... 43 .... 7.
10. ïanoda .... 37 .... 10.
11. ïa .... 10.
12. ïudaï .... 48 .... 3.
13. ïoriep .... 44 .... 8.
14. ibhab .... 19 .... 10.
15. ïahe .... 22 .... 4.
16. ïabaham .... 34 .... 7.
17. ïaud .... 47 .... 11.
18. ïazel .... 36 .... 9.
19. iziael .... 37 .... 10.
20. izariel .... 49 .... 4.
21. ïaniel .... 40 .... 4.
22. ialdel .... 38 .... 11.
23. ïaliel .... 36 .... 9.
24. ïumael .... 43 .... 7.
25. ïabaïma .... 27 .... 9.
26. ïeremiel .... 64 .... 10.
27. ïadaï .... 24 .... 6.
28. ïakien .... 36 .... 9.
29. ïabamiah .... 38 .... 11.
30. ïadin .... 25 .... 7.
31. ïophiel .... 39 .... 3.
32. ïuva .... 24 .... 6.
33. in .... 14 .... 5.
34. ïaphé .... 37 .... 10.
35. idaumos .... 53 .... 8.
36. ïorep .... 43 .... 7.
37. ïosuaïm .... 37 .... 10.
38. ïoraki .... 32 .... 5.
39. ïumiel .... 46 .... 10.
40. ïabina .... 26 .... 8.
41. ïaphar .... 51 .... 6.
42. ibimaz .... 31 .... 4.
43. ïerabaz .... 32 .... 5.
44. ïamikar .... 46 .... 10.
45. ïazum .... 23 .... 5.
46. ïazabor .... 31 .... 4.
47. ïabahimik ...... 33 .... 6.
48. ïaxafel .... 29 .... 11.
49. ïacorboz .... 59 .... 5.
50. ïacophal .... 47 .... 11.

I.

51. ïesem .... 50 .... 5.
52. ïezaph .... 39 .... 3.
53. ïepharez .... 70 .... 7.
54. ïerim .... 40 .... 4.
55. ïerphim .... 44 .... 8.
56. ïardam .... 54 .... 9.
57. ïarmadin ...... 49 .... 4.
58. ïoabin .... 31 .... 4.
59. ïaphim .... 37 .... 3.
60. ïafaumor ...... 53 .... 8.
61. ïebimal .... 42 .... 6.
62. ïechal .... 35 .... 8.
63. ïeruïm .... 47 .... 11.
64. ïesbaor .... 64 .... 10.
65. ieſphas .... 59 .... 4.
66. ïerdimiaz ..... 57 .... 3.
67. iezbahar ...... 63 .... 9.
68. iozdanor ..... 55 .... 10.
69. iozcaph .... 60 .... 6.
70. iazkirim ...... 61 .... 7.
71. ïeazphiel ..... 46 .... 10.
72. ïendataz ..... 55 .... 10.
73. ïeïm .... 23 .... 5.
74. ïablina .... 31 .... 4.
75. ïablaza .... 25 .... 7.
76. iaflimak ...... 40 .... 4.
77. iaslinel .... 60 .... 6.
78. ïaraha .... 37 .... 10.
79. ïarbiel .... 63 .... 9.
80. ïerphimin ... 53 .... 8.
81. ïarkier .... 55 .... 10.
82. ïordiel .... 51 .... 6.
83. ïurman .... 52 .... 7.
84. irmata .... 45 .... 9.
85. irdaz .... 34 .... 7.
86. irkaviel .... 73 .... 10.
87. ivamel .... 50 .... 5.
88. iverphaz ..... 65 .... 11.
89. ivramun ..... 57 .... 3.
90. ivama .... 36 .... 9.
91. iviar .... 53 .... 8.
92. iviamum ..... 61 .... 7.
93. iriel .... 39 .... 3.
94. ivriel .... 48 .... 3.
95. ismat .... 46 .... 10.
96. isſphat .... 49 .... 4.
97. isdim .... 44 .... 8.
98. inuaï .... 26 .... 8.
99. ïopha .... 26 .... 8.
100. ïakide .... 28 .... 10.

K.

#	Name		
1.	kaïn	25.	7.
2.	kados	31.	4.
3.	kaphiel	48.	3.
4.	kawiam	48.	3.
5.	kasaïel	51.	6.
6.	kabeba	22.	4.
7.	kanema	43.	7.
8.	kabaher	39.	3.
9.	kabahoïr	44.	8.
10.	kabahot	35.	8.
11.	kaba	14.	5.
12.	kaaphon	44.	8.
13.	kaphamiel	65.	11.
14.	karaham	50.	5.
15.	kazhamaï	50.	5.
16.	kalvel	57.	3.
17.	kahel	30.	3.
18.	kerina	44.	8.
19.	kasaek	41.	5.
20.	kienan	40.	4.
21.	kedemel	43.	7.
22.	kinaeb	27.	9.
23.	kisiel	44.	8.
24.	kiphar	45.	9.
25.	kiriel	42.	6.
26.	kimazor	31.	4.
27.	kaphier	54.	9.
28.	kavidiel	60.	6.
29.	kermiel	51.	6.
30.	korziel	46.	10.
31.	karavial	75.	3.
32.	kardoïel	71.	8.
33.	karzim	47.	11.
34.	kurthiel	54.	9.
35.	kefal	30.	3.
36.	kezdiam	55.	10.
37.	kedimaz	33.	6.
38.	karmiam	51.	6.
39.	kiſtim	39.	3.
40.	kaïk	22.	
41.	kaez	17.	8.
42.	karuel	5.	20.
43.	karim	41.	5.
44.	kazamara	44.	8.
45.	karinel	58.	4.
46.	kaphanar	66.	3.
47.	kablim	31.	4.
48.	kahabar	40.	4.
49.	kakor	30.	3.
50.	karmor	41.	5.

K.

#	Name		
51.	karia	38.	11.
52.	kazarba	47.	11.
53.	kadamel	43.	7.
54.	kiaz	14.	5.
55.	keïazim	41.	5.
56.	karabaza	47.	11.
57.	karph	39.	3.
58.	kophim	31.	4.
59.	kribiel	55.	10.
60.	krabahot	43.	7.
61.	kiſthom	46.	10.
62.	kieſphot	56.	11.
63.	kierphaz	43.	7.
64.	kierphim	47.	11.
65.	kierbaz	65.	11.
66.	kiork	30.	3.
67.	keïmaz	27.	9.
68.	kerbabaz	55.	10.
69.	kerial	50.	5.
70.	kerbin	50.	5.
71.	kabrozar	52.	7.
72.	kadedum	45.	9.
73.	kinsk	32.	5.
74.	keph	35.	8.
75.	kaleph	48.	3.
76.	karphuam	65.	11.
77.	kieku	34.	7.
78.	kindar	45.	9.
79.	kophial	39.	3.
80.	kaza	13.	4.
81.	kormaï	35.	8.
82.	kordida	46.	10.
83.	korieli	43.	7.
84.	kaïrmorti	56.	11.
85.	kelphizim	57.	3.
86.	kalbaz	35.	8.
87.	kriaph	51.	6.
88.	kephaz	37.	10.
89.	kïerpin	45.	9.
90.	kim	16.	7.
91.	kïum	33.	6.
92.	kabrel	49.	4.
93.	kadrïeli	53.	8.
94.	kazimari	57.	3.
95.	karhaï	48.	3.
96.	deardim	58.	4.
97.	keſtokok	53.	8.
98.	kerful	66.	3.
99.	kerfuzim	52.	7.
100.	kanenac	46.	10.

Transcription of 'The Registry of 2,400 Names'

L.

#	Name		
1.	labefg	22	4.
2.	lamaha	34	7.
3.	labaïa	25	7.
4.	leel	27	9.
5.	larhama	53	8.
6.	labetka	54	9.
7.	lamatieu	69	6.
8.	labsaïa	42	6.
9.	labath	46	10.
10.	laphaïu	57	3.
11.	lamaz	26	8.
12.	larim	42	6.
13.	laraïe	44	8.
14.	larphaï	50	5.
15.	larphau	61	7.
16.	lavaïa	44	8.
17.	laviel	58	4.
18.	lazim	31	4.
19.	labahor	34	7.
20.	labum	42	6.
21.	lamek	38	11.
22.	labaton	42	6.
23.	liephim	44	8.
24.	limph	30	3.
25.	lamak	35	8.
26.	labim	26	8.
27.	lophim	31	4.
28.	larfazel	68	5.
29.	lerraph	57	3.
30.	laratiel	72	9.
31.	larzael	43	7.
32.	laphiel	49	4.
33.	labiam	35	8.
34.	lerraz	38	11.
35.	limphiel	44	8.
36.	limeos	41	5.
37.	larpiel	51	6.
38.	ladiam	35	8.
39.	ladamoz	33	6.
40.	labaïr	33	6.
41.	laham	33	6.
42.	liabaz	19	10.
43.	lierzim	51	6.
44.	liah	23	5.
45.	limel	33	6.
46.	linsiel	47	11.
47.	liaphos	50	5.
48.	ligtau	55	20.
49.	loïmaz	27	9.
50.	lhauk	47	11.
51.	l'herua	37	10.
52.	libiemat	63	9.
53.	lizimak	44	8.
54.	lermiok	52	7.
55.	labark	40	4.
56.	lakordi	51	6.
57.	lerramum	64	10.
58.	lerphi	44	8.
59.	lierbau	69	6.
60.	lazarab	34	7.
61.	leazar	38	11.
62.	l'iepin	42	6.
63.	lakviel	59	5.
64.	laïeli	39	3.
65.	lavim	50	5.
66.	liviatam	73	10.
67.	leviazar	68	5.
68.	levimaz	54	9.
69.	leduit	60	6.
70.	labieuf	58	4.
71.	larziek	55	10.
72.	larkiel	51	6.
73.	lazarzac	36	9.
74.	lamin	3	6.
75.	labaï	24	6.
76.	labaïel	36	9.
77.	labaham	36	9.
78.	lafieli	37	10.
79.	lafamiel	47	11.
80.	lem	26	8.
81.	lemia	31	4.
82.	lezim	37	10.
83.	letiaba	48	3.
84.	lambia	44	8.
85.	lama	25	7.
86.	liufiel	43	7.
87.	liephaz	40	4.
88.	liems	34	7.
89.	limezar	45	9.
90.	limpiel	41	5.
91.	lezphar	53	8.
92.	lekaz	26	8.
93.	lekaham	46	10.
94.	lerbas	66	3.
95.	lizarom	40	4.
96.	learma	43	7.
97.	lorfauel	75	3.
98.	ladabar	37	10.
99.	liemin	36	9.
100.	lahife	28	10.

M.

#	Name		
1.	marmarath	86.	5.
2.	markiel	52.	7.
3.	maumor	49.	4.
4.	mozé	34.	7.
5.	maakin	31.	4.
6.	mor	19.	10.
7.	mater	60.	6.
8.	macha	23.	5.
9.	machatam	55.	10.
10.	meliuel	43.	7.
11.	mïchan	43.	7.
12.	maguth	48.	3.
13.	miael	29.	11.
14.	mikael	31.	4.
15.	mihah	27.	9.
16.	maraï	40.	4.
17.	malcha	40.	4.
18.	mael	25.	7.
19.	mema	29.	11.
20.	moriac	32.	5.
21.	misraïn	43.	7.
22.	misrael	41.	5.
23.	maketo	50.	5.
24.	masasoï	61.	7.
25.	memaïaï	48.	3.
26.	mutuïeg	54.	9.
27.	matomik	47.	1.
28.	mauriel	58.	4.
29.	miliel	34.	7.
30.	mataï	42.	6.
31.	mitraton	58.	4.
32.	makael	36.	9.
33.	mirma	32.	5.
34.	miriak	45.	9.
35.	meram	46.	10.
36.	mazero	49.	4.
37.	matera	61.	7.
38.	matha	45.	9.
39.	maturam	63.	9.
40.	marsaïel	54.	9.
41.	mortiphaz	50.	5.
42.	mormier	47.	11.
43.	merkam	54.	9.
44.	mimiar	42.	6.
45.	mizraham	45.	9.
46.	miselel	61.	7.
47.	mibiath	64.	10.
48.	morhpiel	44.	8.
49.	miam	29.	11.
50.	mizor	30.	3.

M.

#	Name		
51.	macraph	55.	10.
52.	markimaz	46.	10.
53.	markien	54.	9.
54.	marzamon	49.	4.
55.	minphau	53.	8.
56.	minifooz	43.	7.
57.	mertazer	69.	6.
58.	memahar	55.	10.
59.	milifin	35.	8.
60.	milifas	54.	9.
61.	morotas	48.	3.
62.	marfiel	58.	4.
63.	maraï	40.	4.
64.	maphor	47.	11.
65.	mebar	42.	6.
66.	maba	16.	7.
67.	mablaïm	39.	3.
68.	matazab	37.	10.
69.	matohar	63.	9.
70.	malazor	39.	3.
71.	magum	43.	7.
72.	magiel	35.	8.
73.	magafor	42.	6.
74.	megeriel	60.	6.
75.	megim	30.	3.
76.	megum	46.	10.
77.	mehel	35.	8.
78.	mahala	34.	7.
79.	miatroh	50.	5.
80.	mim	20.	2.
81.	maem	26.	8.
82.	marchiel	65.	11.
83.	marmaon	53.	8.
84.	maratief	68.	5.
85.	maziel	40.	4.
86.	mafima	28.	10.
87.	mazim	32.	5.
88.			
89.	murdiel	57.	3.
90.	murgim	43.	7.
91.	murkad	38.	11.
92.	mudina	50.	5.
93.	mubim	52.	7.
94.	mabiadin	39.	3.
95.	mazmara	44.	8.
96.	mazaur	39.	3.
97.	mazaba	18.	9.
98.	maduel	57.	3.
99.	madiam	36.	9.
100.	maketoeh	64.	10.

Transcription of 'The Registry of 2,400 Names'

N.

1. nuriel .... 46 .... 10.
2. neran .... 49 .... 4.
3. nena .... 32 .... 5.
4. neramah .... 57 .... 3.
5. neraïn .... 50 .... 5.
6. noriab .... 31 .... 4.
7. neaketo .... 60 .... 6.
8. nazaïel .... 37 .... 10.
9. nehema .... 47 .... 11.
10. naha .... 23 .... 5.
11. noé .... 25 .... 7.
12. neum .... 47 .... 11.
13. nehemias .... 61 .... 7.
14. naïn .... 28 .... 10.
15. nermas .... 60 .... 6.
16. nermin .... 50 .... 5.
17. nerdabas .... 71 .... 8.
18. nerphim .... 52 .... 7.
19. nerdaï .... 59 .... 5.
20. nemro .... 40 .... 4.
21. nermias .... 64 .... 10.
22. nebin .... 39 .... 3.
23. naïmaka .... 39 .... 3.
24. norphiel .... 44 .... 8.
25. narriel .... 54 .... 9.
26. napus .... 38 .... 11.
27. ninphas .... 53 .... 8.
28. nadamas .... 50 .... 5.
29. nerph .... 46 .... 10.
30. nibim .... 34 .... 7.
31. niaphim .... 48 .... 3.
32. neikaz .... 31 .... 4.
33. noïmor .... 32 .... 5.
34. nabazar .... 36 .... 9.
35. nadimiel .... 44 .... 8.
36. nordinaph ..... 68 .... 5.
37. nuphaï .... 45 .... 9.
38. nauph .... 48 .... 3.
39. namar .... 44 .... 8.
40. nazieli .... 44 .... 8.
41. nerdedum ..... 79 .... 7.
42. nasal .... 44 .... 8.
43. nagor .... 33 .... 6.
44. nagimaz .... 30 .... 3.
45. nariaz .... 42 .... 6.
46. ninphuz .... 48 .... 6.
47. nierbaza .... 55 .... 10.
48. niarscok .... 71 .... 8.
49. nimaï .... 32 .... 5.
50. nefizar .... 47 .... 11.

N.

51. nefkaz .... 30 .... 3.
52. nakir .... 35 .... 8.
53. nablaï .... 36 .... 9.
54. ....
55. namier .... 48 .... 3.
56. namikal .... 44 .... 8.
57. naniam .... 45 .... 9.
58. napiel .... 48 .... 3.
59. nathiel .... 59 .... 5.
60. natiaph .... 71 .... 8.
61. nazidin .... 46 .... 10.
62. nadara .... 37 .... 10.
63. nezial .... 49 .... 4.
64. nimazer .... 55 .... 10.
65. nia .... 19 .... 10.
66. niapazar .... 45 .... 9.
67. nordaïaz .... 45 .... 9.
68. nosterph .... 61 .... 7.
69. naba .... 17 .... 8.
70. niopier .... 51 .... 6.
71. nifari .... 49 .... 4.
72. nelfiaz .... 41 .... 5.
73. neleïl .... 44 .... 8.
74. nediel .... 42 .... 6.
75. nacabos .... 38 .... 11.
76. necam .... 38 .... 11.
77. nekim .... 34 .... 7.
78. necorim .... 54 .... 9.
79. neormin .... 51 .... 6.
80. neodial .... 61 .... 7.
81. norizim .... 47 .... 11.
82. noviat .... 56 .... 11.
83. novrier .... 55 .... 10.
84. novrizao .... 56 .... 11.
85. navior .... 58 .... 4.
86. nivimaz .... 50 .... 5.
87. niveron .... 67 .... 4.
88. neron .... 41 .... 5.
89. naphor .... 57 .... 3.
90. nerzari .... 63 .... 9.
91. nisauru .... 46 .... 10.
92. nadermoz ..... 44 .... 8.
93. nobem .... 40 .... 4.
94. nargiel .... 57 .... 3.
95. nerphial .... 60 .... 6.
96. nardin .... 56 .... 11.
97. nargael .... 55 .... 10.
98. nargol .... 57 .... 9.
99. naïgla .... 32 .... 5.
100. nada .... 17 .... 10.

O.

#	name	col2	col3
1.	orza	20.	2.
2.	orsaliel.	47.	11.
3.	orka	27.	9.
4.	opiel.	35.	8.
5.	odin	36.	9.
6.	ofal.	35.	8.
7.	osmaï.	36.	9.
8.	ormada	30.	3.
9.	orcan	47.	11.
10.	orphia	32.	5.
11.	orphieli	62.	8.
12.	ormar.	42.	6.
13.	odiam	44.	8.
14.	obiada	41.	5.
15.	odaba.	29.	11.
16.	odem	35.	8.
17.	oeau	45.	9.
18.	odazazar	47.	11.
19.	omim.	25.	7.
20.	omiar.	39.	3.
21.	ophïeïl.	39.	3.
22.	ofiel	39.	3.
23.	ocamos	47.	11.
24.	oliaba.	25.	7.
25.	orapiel.	53.	8.
26.	orphaz.	31.	4.
27.	oniel.	33.	6.
28.	onuel.	47.	11.
29.	oparaz	36.	9.
30.	obliak	51.	6.
31.	orkiel.	40.	4.
32.	ozial.	41.	5.
33.	osamaz	34.	7.
34.	oramiel	49.	4.
35.	obima	40.	4.
36.	ochem	44.	8.
37.	okathon	60.	6.
38.	ochimias.	61.	7.
39.	omarem.	56.	11.
40.	omael.	30.	3.
41.	odarzel	69.	6.
42.	oïam.	33.	6.
43.	oviel.	47.	11.
44.	omariel	56.	11.
45.	omiraz.	32.	5.
46.	obialim	54.	9.
47.	ocraphum.	87.	6.
48.	otraphim.	53.	8.
49.	otamazar.	53.	8.
50.	oquierk	60.	6.

O.

#	name	col2	col3
51.	olaman	45.	9.
52.	oliam	34.	7.
53.	oliphaz	38.	11.
54.	olial	33.	6.
55.	orkok.	36.	9.
56.	obrassam.	77.	5/7.
57.	ocak	37.	10.
58.	omarab	38.	11.
59.	ovrim.	40.	4.
60.	oviamas.	67.	4.
61.	overmos	66.	3.
62.	oquiak.	45.	9.
63.	oquin.	39.	3.
64.	oquimaz	40.	4.
65.	ofarmaz.	49.	4.
66.	osalim	38.	11.
67.	omifas	44.	8.
68.	oror	26.	8.
69.	opheum.	53.	8.
70.	odiam	44.	4/8.
71.	ocliem	51.	6.
72.	oclierf	68.	50.
73.	omamiel	46.	10.
74.	orkam	39.	3.
75.	opatiel.	59.	5.
76.	opel	34.	7.
77.	opreum	57.	3.
78.	oprim.	32.	5.
79.	okiel.	33.	6.
80.	ozamel.	43.	7.
81.	ouriel.	46.	10.
82.	opharum.	55.	10.
83.			
84.	opleum	53.	8.
85.	obigaï.	48.	3.
86.	obliar.	58.	4.
87.	olaphiem.	57.	3.
88.	olimphur	54.	9.
89.	olarkiel	58.	4.
90.	onariem.	56.	11.
91.	oneman.	47.	11.
92.	oparpiel.	56.	11.
93.	ogliam.	43.	7.
94.	ogum	45.	9.
95.	ortatiel.	64.	10.
96.	ogla	28.	10.
97.	oglazim	47.	11.
98.	ogargaza	54.	9.
99.	oelim	38.	11.
100.	oïeg	28.	10.

Transcription of 'The Registry of 2,400 Names'

P.

1. priel............39........3.
2. piezel...........53........8.
3. piriel...........52........7.
4. puzim..........40........4.
5. parsiel..........57........3.
6. pazmiel.........44........8.
7. pazarim.........48........3.
8. parbazar........69........6.
9. permerf.........78........6.
10. perdim..........63........9.
11. permaz.........47.......11.
12. pollior..........44........8.
13. poliamas........56.......11.
14. perpazar........62........8.
15. proviaz.........45........9.
16. perbiam.........76........4.
17. pakaph.........50........5.
18. parkarath.......91.......10.
19. pisimas.........65.......11.
20. piuth...........48........3.
21. pimandra.......65.......11.
22. pielzal..........47.......11.
23. porkatol........61........7.
24. parsaba.........93........3.
25. pikim...........30........3.
26. pissim..........48........3.
27. pafath..........54........9.
28. peruel..........60........6.
29. parial...........54........9.
30. padaïn..........35........8.
31. paraet..........54........9.
32. panam..........42........6.
33. perman.........59........5.
34. perzi............54........9.
35. pebokas.........67........4.
36. pedabos.........49........4.
37. pidum..........54........9.
38. pizimo..........44........8.
39. pirma...........38.......11.
40. pirdom.........59........5.
41. piar.............40........4.
42. pervazo.........55.......10.
43. pelh............37.......10.
44. païlh............32........5.
45. pindar..........55.......10.
46. piuzem.........61........7.
47. pephaz..........47.......11.
48. pedari..........55.......10.
49. pekol...........41........5.
50. pelph..........46.......10.

P.

51. pimia...........31........4.
52. pizelph.........61........7.
53. pordas..........54........9.
54. prafaz...........27........9.
55. prisem..........59........5.
56. prunzel.........56.......11.
57. prakaz..........31........4.
58. pladiel..........43........7.
59. plaïm...........34........7.
60. pluzari..........58........4.
61. pripham........55.......10.
62. preziel..........58........4.
63. prefras..........64.......10.
64. prakazi.........45........9.
65. prekim..........43........7.
66. prakaïm.........43........7.
67. prophaz.........34........7.
68. preblum........64.......10.
69. prokaliz.........43........7.
70. praul...........49........4.
71. paul............46.......10.
72. pauel...........59........5.
73. purkin..........40........4.
74. pauk............47.......11.
75. prapak.........47.......11.
76. pigraph.........60........6.
77. pieg............30........3.
78. païgu...........42........6.
79. pagla...........29.......11.
80. pagrazim........54........9.
81. poguel..........62........8.
82. polgiel..........41........5.
83. pegreph.........72........9.
84. pegim..........36........9.
85. pebok..........48........3.
86. padataz.........42........6.
87. pataphel........70........7.
88. pitim...........48........3.
89. piatar...........60........6.
90. peïvim..........61........7.
91. pavaz...........39........3.
92. pitariz..........61........7.
93. pateïram........77........7.
94. plimaz..........29.......11.
95. perphazer......83.......11.
96. paramo.........49........4.
97. pazabel.........31........4.
98. pezerph.........69........6.
99. pethzebu.......95........5.
100. paba............19.......10.

✠ 239

	Q.				Q.		
1.	quaba	25	7.	51.	qrediel	51	6.
2.	quael	44	8.	52.	qravarel	78	6.
3.	querbaz	85	4.	53.	qrakin	36	9.
4.	quophi	40	4.	54.	qrazara	39	3.
5.	quibazar	61	7.	55.	qradramos	58	4.
6.	quliers	54	9.	56.	qriuzer	64	10.
7.	qauzarba	73	10.	57.	qrimtazar	59	5.
8.	qarbier	76	4.	58.	qrapher	59	5.
9.	quirbem	70	7.	59.	qirmaz	41	5.
10.	quiriat	71	8.	60.	qaeïr	36	9.
11.	qarziel	61	7.	61.	qlazam	37	10.
12.	querbim	78	6.	62.	qlaum	52	7.
13.	quamazar	54	9.	63.	qlaph	46	10.
14.	quorka	41	5.	64.	qlandrier	87	6.
15.	quorkin	47	11.	65.	qlapas	57	3.
16.	quazer	54	9.	66.	qazaïm	32	5.
17.	qubiel	60	6.	67.	qadaï	31	4.
18.	quaciel	44	8.	68.	qemnel	68	5.
19.	quamiel	50	5.	69.	qasfas	67	4.
20.	quvriel	49	4.	70.	qadumel	62	8.
21.	qorssiel	49	4.	71.	qarkaz	44	8.
22.	qundiam	58	4.	72.	qarkaï	37	10.
23.	qimkaz	33	6.	73.	qaravael	69	6.
24.	quebrak	68	5.	74.	qariaïm	57	3.
25.	quephiel	70	7.	75.	qiadamon	47	11.
26.	querful	87	6.	76.	qizfrim	67	4.
27.	qaba	20	2.	77.	qiarz	43	7.
28.	quabaraz	44	8.	78.	qrembas	69	6.
29.	qarak	45	9.	79.	qranthas	70	7.
30.	quaskork	66	3.	80.	qeradas	65	11.
31.	qermaz	49	4.	81.	qastiel	60	6.
32.	querzer	82	10.	82.	quarciel	73	10.
33.	qasamar	66	3.	83.	qadamaz	36	9.
34.	qaidaz	34	7.	84.	qerphum	74	11.
35.	quebaum	71	8.	85.	qalatier	77	7.
36.	quemar	63	9.	86.	qulmaïr	52	7.
37.	qulizeb	57	3.	87.	quelzim	63	9.
38.	quapiel	66	11.	88.	qanemaz	49	4.
39.	quekal	55	10.	89.	qublar	68	5.
40.	queteph	86	5.	90.	qambak	51	6.
41.	quaph	45	9.	91.	qaorziel	62	8.
42.	quetak	63	9.	92.	qaztaraf	62	8.
43.	qutron	32	5.	93.	qobiazam	55	10.
44.	quekom	51	6.	94.	qabliem	45	9.
45.	qalak	39	3.	95.	quaber	41	5.
46.	qarief	50	5.	96.	quaphexaz	64	10.
47.	qerkiel	63	9.	97.	qelkar	55	10.
48.	qurkaniel	64	10.	98.	qelbus	67	10.
49.	qurasin	68	5.	99.	qaïmer	51	6.
50.	qrefiar	55	10.	100.	qabeï	28	10.

Transcription of 'The Registry of 2,400 Names'

	R.		
1.	rahaba	30	3.
2.	raab	21	3.
3.	raphiel	55	10.
4.	rachiel	41	5.
5.	rakié	35	8.
6.	raphael	54	9.
7.	renua	48	3.
8.	rabaïa	31	4.
9.	rabazar	40	4.
10.	rieph	50	5.
11.	radas	41	5.
12.	rem	38	11.
13.	rabas	39	3.
14.	rams	37	10.
15.	remara	57	3.
16.	raphim	47	11.
17.	ratamar	68	5.
18.	reziel	57	3.
19.	raviel	64	10.
20.	raplaz	40	4.
21.	ramiar	52	7.
22.	rakiel	42	6.
23.	rakot	39	3.
24.	radamaz	37	10.
25.	rimphoth	67	4.
26.	remati	69	6.
27.	romor	31	4.
28.	reskiel	67	4.
29.	riblas	63	9.
30.	ruzum	34	7.
31.	rus	24	6.
32.	raneam	53	8.
33.	rabataz	42	6.
34.	rephalon	67	4.
35.	refimar	58	4.
36.	rimdar	57	3.
37.	rakorum	50	5.
38.	rezam	44	8.
39.	rapimas	64	10.
40.	ratagum	68	5.
41.	ragraton	64	10.
42.	rama	31	4.
43.	regoblam	77	7.
44.	regual	59	5.
45.	raquer	68	5.
46.	radimoz	36	9.
47.	rafulun	67	4.
48.	requel	70	7.
49.	rosquiel	58	4.
50.	ramazer	63	9.
51.	riam	39	3.
52.	reïmak	50	5.
53.	renaum	69	5.
54.	rakozor	41	11.
55.	radagor	42	6.
56.	reïplier	68	5.
57.	reïm	39	3.
58.	raïm	31	4.
59.	raka	29	11.
60.	rimpher	59	5.
61.	rimplas	58	4.
62.	remder	62	8.
63.	rioph	42	6.
64.	rimphalaz	56	11.
65.	radam	35	8.
66.	rimtam	51	6.
67.	repim	52	7.
68.	relim	44	8.
69.	ralarnos	59	5.
70.	ralerk	57	3.
71.	ramieph	58	4.
72.	renmial	56	11.
73.	rukiam	47	11.
74.	ruziart	57	3.
75.	rucïdim	62	8.
76.	rubelar	65	11.
77.	ruchiem	60	6.
78.	raskas	64	10.
79.	ravael	52	7.
80.	raviem	65	11.
81.	rauph	52	7.
82.	rivar	57	3.
83.	rivopar	67	4.
84.	rizzium	63	9.
85.	rescieli	82	10.
86.	rekamel	64	10.
87.	rekemun	67	4.
88.	raïo	33	6.
89.	reïmviel	74	11.
90.	rodamiel	61	7.
91.	raphlaz	47	11.
92.	rabadaz	27	9.
93.	raglaï	40	4.
94.	ragamar	56	11.
95.	rorkar	51	6.
96.	rophuel	67	4.
97.	rokaphial	64	10.
98.	roboar	65	11.
99.	raphlas	64	10.
100.	rabeh	28	10.

S.

#	name	a	b
1.	sabaha	31	4.
2.	samuel	63	9.
3.	sephas	70	7.
4.	soratha	60	6.
5.	sisim	52	7.
6.	sahen	40	4.
7.	satel	60	6.
8.	serphiel	83	11.
9.	sagum	49	4.
10.	samael	44	8.
11.	samel	46	10.
12.	sehenhakim	72	9.
13.	sachiel	42	4.
14.	sabamaï	44	8.
15.	saramahau	79	7.
16.	sarabin	52	7.
17.	sariaïn	60	6.
18.	subarmaïr	83	11.
19.	saba	22	4.
20.	saïel	40	4.
21.	samiek	46	10.
22.	samabeï	46	7.
23.	sautanaeli	71	8.
24.	suceïn	52	7.
25.	saraha	46	10.
26.	serphiaz	60	6.
27.	serthia	63	9.
28.	serki	55	10.
29.	serpier	73	10.
30.	sophlaz	39	3.
31.	sorkaph	59	5.
32.	sotimas	63	9.
33.	sopliar	51	6.
34.	sokuel	62	8.
35.	sorbas	62	8.
36.	sormiel	49	4.
37.	sordiael	60	6.
38.	sordinel	68	5.
39.	sorkos	45	9.
40.	sogomas	61	7.
41.	soloïf	41	5.
42.	solle	36	9.
43.	salper	59	5.
44.	sadamar	54	9.
45.	sodome	56	11.
46.	soko	33	6.
47.	simmiel	50	5.
48.	siphel	54	9.
49.	seraphim	76	4.
50.	saregato	78	6.
51.	seïrph	57	3.
52.	sem	40	4.
53.	sablak	42	6.
54.	sabiau	50	5.
55.	sabraïm	51	6.
56.	selseph	80	8.
57.	sacritas	76	4.
58.	sratas	59	5.
59.	sariepel	79	7.
60.	sarph	47	11.
61.	segal	47	11.
62.	seblar	64	10.
63.	sebiam	57	3.
64.	selaras	76	4.
65.	sarphazal	61	7.
66.	sirus	44	8.
67.	sabdeba	31	4.
68.	sedim	44	8.
69.	sedarph	63	9.
70.	sedre	61	7.
71.	seremiel	82	10.
72.	saul	49	4.
73.	surkiaz	37	10.
74.	surviam	56	11.
75.	soltias	66	3.
76.	sol	27	9.
77.	soviadaraz	69	6.
78.	savidas	78	6.
79.	satiel	61	7.
80.	setimador	82	10.
81.	setimador	62	8.
82.	setraf	57	3.
83.	semîtra	59	5.
84.	setraton	78	6.
85.	sethiaz	63	9.
86.	sagigar	50	5.
87.	sagaz	28	10.
88.	saciel	41	5.
89.	soclial	59	5.
90.	socraphas	93	3.
91.	sasavar	77	7.
92.	sukapa	49	4.
93.	sukamadi	56	11.
94.	surathiel	71	8.
95.	sþriam	47	11.
96.	smarko	56	11.
97.	sdeforazar	69	6.
98.	saparam	65	11.
99.	sobdabar	60	6.
100.	sabefa	28	10.

Transcription of 'The Registry of 2,400 Names'

T.

1.	thamael	57	3.
2.	tanié	43	7.
3.	telnobech	72	9.
4.	tetra	53	8.
5.	tubiel	60	6.
6.	tauaha	43	7.
7.	tetramah	74	11.
8.	thahon	49	4.
9.	thou	40	4.
10.	tubiela	61	7.
11.	turiel	46	10.
12.	tharapha	74	11.
13.	tarmaïau	51	6.
14.	tarhaba	74	11.
15.	thoïaïm	58	4.
16.	thuzraï	61	7.
17.	teïaziel	67	4.
18.	thaniel	62	8.
19.	taphtharati	116	484.
20.	thiriel	63	9.
21.	turbiel	61	7.
22.	taziar	53	8.
23.	talial	46	10.
24.	taphta	56	11.
25.	terphas	70	7.
26.	timiel	50	5.
27.	tinial	52	7.
28.	tinerph	68	5.
29.	tikor	41	5.
30.	timbaïk	57	3.
31.	tizim	49	4.
32.	trakton	51	6.
33.	trephiaz	58	4.
34.	trasmim	57	3.
35.	teciem	57	3.
36.	tabor	39	3.
37.	tacmin	42	6.
38.	tasariel	77	7.
39.	turphur	52	7.
40.	terbam	46	4.
41.	terdin	42	9.
42.	tamiar	54	9.
43.	taprak	49	4.
44.	tamera	54	9.
45.	timphe	50	5.
46.	taremor	65	11.
47.	tiranar	71	8.
48.	tiermoz	58	4.
49.	trieph	55	10.
50.	tamezar	59	5.

T.

51.	taſtha	53	8.
52.	trabliam	51	6.
53.	trepieh	62	8.
54.	trimphos	59	5.
55.	trigiſt	49	4.
56.	trakiel	47	11.
57.	trephiel	60	6.
58.	tugram	59	5.
59.	torphim	46	10.
60.	tamazor	47	11.
61.	triakar	60	6.
62.	terzebul	99	9.
63.	tarnago	57	3.
64.	termaka	65	11.
65.	terpher	75	3.
66.	tirdiel	7	8.
67.	tirmaüs	69	6.
68.	torkam	50	5.
69.	torblaz	57	3.
70.	turbiam	62	8.
71.	truviel	53	8.
72.	tapazial	63	9.
73.	tepliaz	55	10.
74.	tesapas	83	11.
75.	tessimas	83	11.
76.	teſter	78	6.
77.	temisas	75	3.
78.	teor	48	3.
79.	teha	39	3.
80.	teglar	61	7.
81.	tegum	60	6.
82.	tegrim	61	7.
83.	talaphaz	57	3.
84.	tieb	39	3.
85.	timar	53	8.
86.	tibion	54	9.
87.	taliel	46	10.
88.	talaza	4	7.
89.	talerph	62	8.
90.	tophiem	50	5.
91.	tau	40	4.
92.	taubrez	89	8.
93.	tamabel	46	10.
94.	tanau	47	11.
95.	termor	60	6.
96.	taphtara	74	11.
97.	tara	38	11.
98.	ticiel	56	11.
99.	torbaz	47	11.
100.	tabaé	28	10.

	U.					U.		
1.	uru	28.	10.		51.	urclaz	50.	5.
2.	ustaek	37.	10.		52.	urgabel	49.	4.
3.	urataek	56.	11.		53.	udamar	68.	5.
4.	uraïel	46.	10.		54.	uglaï	49.	4.
5.	urmeïz	44.	8.		55.	usizim	52.	7.
6.	uael	33.	6.		56.			
7.	urmaz	32.	5.		57.	uquim	46.	10.
8.	urfim	44.	8.		58.	uquaras	67.	4.
9.	urkam	45.	9.		59.	uraz	26.	8.
10.	udaz	39.	3.		60.	utapiel	57.	3.
11.	ubazar	59.	5.		61.	uziab	38.	11.
12.	ukaphiel	69.	6.		62.	ukaur	55.	11.
13.	ukaph	55.	10.		63.	udimab	50.	5.
14.	usoraz	58.	4.		64.	uciaïl	58.	4.
15.	urphiel	49.	4.		65.	uïam	45.	9.
16.	urdiel	56.	11.		66.	uali	35.	8.
17.	urmiel	46.	10.		67.	uïona	41.	5.
18.	uzdaz	42.	6.		68.	uoïm	37.	10.
19.	utrabar	46.	10.		69.	umabal	44.	8.
20.	utrimph	50.	5.		70.	unoam	43.	7.
21.	utrabam	41.	5.		71.	uniael	46.	10.
22.	urabsaz	46.	10.		72.	usaïem	46.	10.
23.	uribel	52.	7.		73.	usaraph	65.	11.
24.	ukariel	70.	7.		74.	ucrafaz	79.	7.
25.	udiam	56.	11.		75.	ufemas	64.	10.
26.	upiad	38.	11.		76.	ufrem	68.	5.
27.	uguar	66.	3.		77.	ufabias	65.	11.
28.	ugon	44.	8.		78.	udrom	58.	4.
29.	ukaraz	51.	6.		79.	udapaz	55.	10.
30.	upriel	50.	5.		80.	udrerf	89.	8.
31.	ukafim	46.	10.		81.	utrauza	41.	5.
32.	udief	50.	5.		82.	utiphiar	68.	5.
33.	uram	37.	10.		83.	urstant	49.	4.
34.	uramas	56.	11.		84.	urmier	52.	7.
35.	urkus	46.	10.		85.	urzuar	46.	10.
36.	umeor	51.	6.		86.	uabrak	50.	5.
37.	umim	37.	10.		87.	umabaz	34.	7.
38.	uhamiaz	52.	7.		88.	uneamz	51.	6.
39.	ublaïn	64.	10.		89.	uphiaer	55.	10.
40.	urzaber	45.	9.		90.	ukiart	54.	9.
41.	ugamer	68.	5.		91.	ucrodar	86.	5.
42.	urpiel	46.	10.		92.	ukimar	55.	10.
43.	usabazar	46.	10.		93.	urdaz	40.	4.
44.	usabazar	27.	9.		94.	urkafaz	41.	5.
45.	ureal	49.	4.		95.	uzarel	59.	5.
46.	urkiel	46.	10.		96.	uzerbam	81.	9.
47.	umbraz	58.	4.		97.	ufrazar	67.	4.
48.	ubbak	52.	7.		98.	unieril	63.	9.
49.	uioph	48.	3.		99.	ustapa	42.	6.
50.	uïef	39.	3.		100.	uabehiki	37.	10.

Transcription of 'The Registry of 2,400 Names'

V.

1. vaïel . . . . 43 . . . . 7.
2. vaus . . . . 45 . . . . 9.
3. vael . . . . 34 . . . . 7.
4. vriel . . . . 49 . . . . 4.
5. valmum . . . . 52 . . . . 7.
6. vraïel . . . . 48 . . . . 3.
7. vava . . . . 44 . . . . 8.
8. varaïa . . . . 50 . . . . 5.
9. vahamaïn . . . . 58 . . . . 4.
10. vabaham . . . . 46 . . . . . . 10.
11. vawa . . . . 46 . . . . . . 10.
12. vara . . . . 40 . . . . 4.
13. vaïe . . . . 36 . . . . 9.
14. virdaz . . . . 59 . . . . 5.
15. vaur . . . . 46 . . . . . . 10.
16. vaïr . . . . 40 . . . . 4.
17. varama . . . . 53 . . . . 8.
18. vahamaïn . . . . 31 . . . . 4.
19. veha . . . . 43 . . . . 7.
20. vaïa . . . . 32 . . . . 5.
21. vagu . . . . 43 . . . . 7.
22. voïr . . . . 44 . . . . 8.
23. votar . . . . 53 . . . . 8.
24. vora . . . . 34 . . . . 7.
25. viha . . . . 37 . . . . . . 10.
26. viona . . . . 43 . . . . 7.
27. vakiel . . . . 46 . . . . . . 10.
28. vana . . . . 36 . . . . 9.
29. vraba . . . . 30 . . . . 3.
30. valiel . . . . 48 . . . . 3.
31. vuar . . . . 41 . . . . 5.
32. vurk . . . . 35 . . . . 8.
33. varb . . . . 55 . . . . . . 10.
34. vanael . . . . 48 . . . . 3.
35. valk . . . . 35 . . . . 8.
36. verbra . . . . 84 . . . . 3.
37. vare . . . . 52 . . . . 7.
38. . . . .
39. vago . . . . 37 . . . . . . 10.
40. vigaz . . . . 39 . . . . 3.
41. vier . . . . 52 . . . . 7.
42. vima . . . . 39 . . . . 3.
43. vako . . . . 37 . . . . . . 10.
44. vapraz . . . . 42 . . . . 6.
45. vator . . . . 51 . . . . 6.
46. vuam . . . . 36 . . . . 9.
47. vorb . . . . 49 . . . . 4.
48. vork . . . . 41 . . . . 5.
49. vivi . . . . 60 . . . . 6.
50. vapa . . . . 38 . . . . . . 11.

V.

51. vagla . . . . 35 . . . . 8.
52. veba . . . . 43 . . . . 7.
53. vaza . . . . 24 . . . . 6.
54. vakiaz . . . . 36 . . . . 9.
55. vavu . . . . 45 . . . . 9.
56. vakaz . . . . 34 . . . . 7.
57. vorka . . . . 42 . . . . 6.
58. valabin . . . . 49 . . . . 4.
59. valaïm . . . . 47 . . . . . . 11.
60. voltara . . . . 61 . . . . 7.
61. vuziel . . . . 50 . . . . 5.
62. vulf . . . . 39 . . . . 3.
63. valf . . . . 39 . . . . 3.
64. velf . . . . 51 . . . . 6.
65. vilf . . . . 43 . . . . 7.
66. volf . . . . 39 . . . . 3.
67. vabam . . . . 37 . . . . . . 10.
68. varpabaz . . . . 47 . . . . . . 11.
69. virbaz . . . . 61 . . . . 7.
70. vagriel . . . . 61 . . . . 7.
71. verpiel . . . . 73 . . . . . . 10.
72. vazar . . . . 41 . . . . 5.
73. vram . . . . 39 . . . . 3.
74. vria . . . . 36 . . . . 3.
75. vradaz . . . . 33 . . . . 6.
76. vrou . . . . 31 . . . . 4.
77. vrim . . . . 39 . . . . 3.
78. vrakaz . . . . 39 . . . . 3.
79. vierpaz . . . . 57 . . . . 3.
80. vazziel . . . . 50 . . . . 5.
81. vetrear . . . . 87 . . . . 6.
82. vatiar . . . . 54 . . . . 9.
83. vargaez . . . . 57 . . . . 3.
84. viaterf . . . . 95 . . . . 5.
85. valebab . . . . 47 . . . . . . 11.
86. veldah . . . . 62 . . . . 8.
87. vemem . . . . 62 . . . . 8.
88. vecierf . . . . 78 . . . . 6.
89. vedim . . . . 50 . . . . 5.
90. vebraf . . . . 65 . . . . . . 11.
91. vekim . . . . 50 . . . . 5.
92. vakem . . . . 46 . . . . . . 10.
93. vadinal . . . . 48 . . . . 3.
94. vardaroz . . . . 76 . . . . 4.
95. varki . . . . 49 . . . . 4.
96. voſtiak . . . . 58 . . . . 4.
97. vidram . . . . 67 . . . . 4.
98. vouara . . . . 50 . . . . 5.
99. voak . . . . 40 . . . . 4.
100. vabe . . . . 28 . . . . . . 10.

✠ 245

Z.

#	name	a	b
1.	zazel	28	10
2.	zezbaho	57	3
3.	zebul	52	7
4.	zariel	61	7
5.	zabarath	54	9
6.	zaek	13	4
7.	zorrobabbel	49	4
8.	zoroael	31	4
9.	zaruel	46	10
10.	zorael	27	9
11.	zarel	39	3
12.	zaharin	42	6
13.	zabamahir	37	10
14.	zaglahin	30	3
15.	zirpharaï	63	9
16.	zababahim	22	4
17.	zabaha	14	5
18.	zabaham	26	8
19.	zaraïae	35	8
20.	zaraz	21	3
21.	zarbaz	54	9
22.	zergum	66	3
23.	zerbere	78	6
24.	zirphas	51	6
25.	zurbam	37	10
26.	zariaz	30	3
27.	zakier	32	5
28.	zaphloz	34	7
29.	zavar	41	5
30.	zimsu	29	11
31.	zierpar	55	10
32.	zephaz	40	4
33.	zabalam	29	11
34.	zamar	32	5
35.	zumiel	29	11
36.	zurpial	30	3
37.	zorpiel	36	9
38.	zaïm	15	6
39.	zabaz		6
40.	zergon	53	8
41.	zerblas	77	7
42.	zablin	22	4
43.	zapipo	33	6
44.	zaku	23	5
45.	zaki	14	5
46.	zabem	16	7
47.	zeblim	40	4
48.	zirmoz	34	7
49.	zirmauz	34	9
50.	ziflas	44	8
51.	ziblas	52	7
52.	zizim	334	7
53.	zorphas	44	8
54.	zordiel	46	10
55.	zarkato	53	8
56.	zarkaz	29	11
57.	zermez	47	11
58.	zermah	47	11
59.	zaphim	31	4
60.	zadiem	25	7
61.	zuliel	29	11
62.	zubel	34	7
63.	zaka	13	4
64.	zosbal	44	8
65.	zogo	26	8
66.	zarum	32	5
67.	zaketoh	46	10
68.	zadafim	21	3
69.	zimchu	48	3
70.	zimel	34	7
71.	zozbam	45	9
72.	zima	20	2
73.	zabedon	23	5
74.	zelam	39	3
75.	zeliar	47	11
76.	zezbo	54	9
77.	zadim	16	7
78.	zaplamaz	50	5
79.	zerkoz	46	10
80.	zaïe	16	7
81.	zarkiel	41	5
82.	zabulon	39	3
83.	zabus	26	8
84.	zazor	16	7
85.	zaboam	30	3
86.	zaglaïm	28	10
87.	zaglotos	35	8
88.	zaglum	33	6
89.	zeglaïr	46	10
90.	zeneaz	39	3
91.	zenam	41	5
92.	zenier	51	6
93.	zenakaz	41	5
94.	zerbenaz	63	9
95.	zimaül	50	5
96.	zeph	38	11
97.	zabaram	35	8
98.	zabeba	13	4
99.	zabieph	36	9
100.	zamki	19	10

Transcription of 'The Registry of 2,400 Names'

Verification of the names of the Patriarchs, Prophets and Apostles on the Cabalistic Alphabet, to know their virtues and powers.

A.

1. adam . . . . 18 . . . . 9.
2. arapasat . . . . 60 . . . . 6.
3. abraham . . . . 41 . . . . 5.
4. aram . . . . 31 . . . . 4.
5. amram . . . . 32 . . . . 5.
6. aminada . . . . 28 . . . . 10.
7. addi . . . . 18 . . . . 9.
8. amos . . . . 21 . . . . 3.
9. aaron . . . . 25 . . . . 7.
10. abisué . . . . 40 . . . . 4.
11. amarias . . . . 59 . . . . 5.
12. achitob . . . . 42 . . . . 6.
13. achias . . . . 31 . . . . 4.
14. abiathar . . . . 61 . . . . 7.
15. achimas . . . . 35 . . . . 8.
16. azarias . . . . 48 . . . . 3.
17. assioram . . . . 54 . . . . 9.
18. abias . . . . 30 . . . . 3.
19. achas . . . . 29 . . . . . . 11.
20. amon . . . . 18 . . . . 9.
21. abiud . . . . 40 . . . . 4.
22. azor . . . . 15 . . . . 6.
23. achimas . . . . 16 . . . . 7.
24. ananel . . . . 44 . . . . 8.
25. aristobule . . . . 94 . . . . 4.
26. ananus . . . . 39 . . . . 3.
27. ananias . . . . 52 . . . . 7.
28. abdias . . . . 31 . . . . 4.
29. agée . . . . 13 . . . . 4.
30. andrea . . . . 52 . . . . 7.
31. abakuc . . . . 43 . . . . 7.
32. amema . . . . 30 . . . . 3.
33. abbel . . . . 16 . . . . 7.
34. adiozuï . . . . 28 . . . . 10.

B.

1. belbu . . . . 24 . . . . 6.
2. belzebu . . . . 55 . . . . 10.
3. boaz . . . . 17 . . . . 8.
4. baal . . . . 15 . . . . 6.
5. baruc . . . . 15 . . . . 6.
6. balaam . . . . 28 . . . . 10.
7. balam . . . . 27 . . . . 9.
8. barachie . . . . 37 . . . . 10.
9. babilonne . . . . 33 . . . . 6.
10. bartelemi . . . . 64 . . . . 10.
11. betsaleel . . . . 51 . . . . 6.
12. biron . . . . 25 . . . . 7.
13. beri . . . . 28 . . . . 10.
14. belphagor . . . . 46 . . . . 10.

C.

1. caïnam . . . . 31 . . . . 4.
2. cosam . . . . 33 . . . . 6.
3. cahiphe . . . . 37 . . . . 6.
4. canancen . . . . 51 . . . . 6.
5. caïn . . . . 18 . . . . 9.
6. caleb . . . . 26 . . . . 8.
7. core . . . . 32 . . . . 5.

D.

1. david . . . . 45 . . . . 9.
2. daniel . . . . 35 . . . . 8.
3. debora . . . . 28 . . . . 10.
4. demon . . . . 19 . . . . 10.

E.

1. est . . . . 21 . . . . 3.
2. eli . . . . 15 . . . . 6.
3. enos . . . . 21 . . . . 3.
4. enoch . . . . 34 . . . . 7.
5. eliazim . . . . 35 . . . . 8.
6. eliezer . . . . 52 . . . . 7.
7. eliazard . . . . 49 . . . . 4.
8. eliacim . . . . 30 . . . . 3.
9. clczar . . . . 39 . . . . 3.
10. ezechiaz . . . . 37 . . . . 10.
11. elionée . . . . 34 . . . . 7.
12. ezechial . . . . 47 . . . . 11.
13. esdras . . . . 67 . . . . 4.
14. erode . . . . 35 . . . . 8.
15. ezessiel . . . . 62 . . . . 8.

G.

1. gabriel . . . . 47 . . . . 11.

H.

1. haï . . . . 19 . . . . 10.
2. hila . . . . 14 . . . . 5.
3. heber . . . . 33 . . . . 6.
4. hesrou . . . . 35 . . . . 8.
5. her . . . . 25 . . . . 7.
6. helliée . . . . 31 . . . . 4.
7. heli ou jacob . . . . 22 . . . . 4.
8. hircan . . . . 47 . . . . 11.
9. hamos . . . . 29 . . . . 11.
10. hellissée . . . . 52 . . . . 7.
11. helmadam . . . . 39 . . . . 3.
12. hiram . . . . 33 . . . . 6.

	I.		
1.	inri	28.	10.
2.	ïared	42.	6.
3.	isaac	24.	6.
4.	ïacob	38.	11.
5.	iudas	57.	3.
6.	iuda	39.	3.
7.	iessé	44.	8.
8.	iomas	36.	9.
9.	iose	34.	7.
10.	ioseph	53.	8.
11.	iorim	32.	5.
12.	iesus	34.	7.
13.	ïoanan	43.	7.
14.	ieau	28.	10.
15.	iama	26.	8.
16.	ïoïdas	45.	9.
17.	iosedech	47.	11.
18.	ioachim	31.	4.
19.	ioacim	30.	3.
20.	ioakin	32.	5.
21.	ionathan	62.	8.
22.	iadus	34.	7.
23.	iason	35.	8.
24.	iomathas	71.	8.
25.	iosaphat	64.	10.
26.	ioram	32.	5.
27.	ioatham	60.	6.
28.	iosias	49.	4.
29.	ieconias	55.	10.
30.	ioazar	35.	8.
31.	ismael	39.	3.
32.	iesu	31.	4.
33.	iosua	24.	6.
34.	ioabe	22.	4.
35.	iehu	31.	4.
36.	iosué	35.	8.
37.	isaak	31.	4.
38.	iakob	38.	11.
39.	iocel	34.	7.
40.	iaque	47.	11.
41.	iake	26.	8.
42.	iude	40.	4.
43.	iaphé	37.	10.
44.	isaïe	34.	7.
45.	ieremia	53.	8.
46.	ïudi	44.	8.
47.	iedehou	31.	4.
48.	iakin	27.	9.

	K.		
1.	kam	23.	5.

	L.		
1.	leviathan	80.	8.
2.	liviatan	82.	10.
3.	lamech	41.	5.
4.	levi	48.	3.
5.	labam	27.	9.
6.	labaham	36.	9.
7.	lamaha	34.	7.
8.	luc	40.	4.
9.	louis	44.	8.
10.	leon	30.	3.
11.	lion	20.	2.

	M.		
1.	malalael	49.	4.
2.	mathusalem	77.	5.
3.	mathatas	83.	11.
4.	mama	29.	11.
5.	melcha	41.	5.
6.	mathat	64.	10.
7.	melchi	42.	6.
8.	mathatias	94.	4.
9.	mahat	41.	5.
10.	mathehia	64.	10.
11.	manassés	75.	3.
12.	menelaus	69.	6.
13.	mathan	57.	3.
14.	mathias	65.	11.
15.	matieu	64.	10.
16.	matuas	53.	8.
17.	malakïe	43.	7.
18.	malachi	36.	9.
19.	mozé	34.	7.
20.	micheas	52.	7.
21.	maarc	46.	10.
22.	michée	35.	8.
23.	mikael	31.	1.
24.	michel	40.	4.
25.	mesias	53.	9.
26.	merian	56.	11.
27.	marie	44.	8.
28.	mema	29.	11.
29.	meriam	55.	10.
30.	matias	62.	8.

Transcription of 'The Registry of 2,400 Names'

N.
1. noé . . . . 25 . . . . 7.
2. nachor . . . . 34 . . . . 7.
3. nacor . . . . 33 . . . . 6.
4. nakor . . . . 33 . . . . 6.
5. naasson . . . . 25 . . . . 7.
6. nathan . . . . 57 . . . . 5.
7. neri . . . . 44 . . . . 8.
8. neder . . . . 39 . . . . 3.
9. nagé . . . . 24 . . . . 6.
10. naum . . . . 43 . . . . 7.
11. nena . . . . 32 . . . . 5.
12. nahum . . . . 44 . . . . 8.
13. nehemias . . . . 61 . . . . 7.
14. natan . . . . 47 . . . . 11.
15. ninnive . . . . 60 . . . . 6.
16. nehemie . . . . 47 . . . . 11.

O.
1. obed . . . . 33 . . . . 6.
2. ozi . . . . 29 . . . . 11.
3. onias . . . . 38 . . . . 11.
4. ozias . . . . 48 . . . . 3.
5. ouest . . . . 53 . . . . 8.
6. osée . . . . 35 . . . . 8.
7. ozée . . . . 35 . . . . 8.
8. oliab . . . . 24 . . . . 6.

P.
1. phaleg . . . . 45 . . . . 9.
2. phares . . . . 68 . . . . 5.
3. phines . . . . 53 . . . . 8.
4. phideas . . . . 52 . . . . 7.
5. pus . . . . 23 . . . . 5.
6. philipe . . . . 49 . . . . 4.
7. phanuel . . . . 68 . . . . 5.
8. paul . . . . 46 . . . . 10.
9. pierre . . . . 55 . . . . 10.
10. phazer . . . . 56 . . . . 11.
11. pharaon . . . . 58 . . . . 4.

Q. 0
R.
1. ragau . . . . 46 . . . . 10.
2. raab . . . . 21 . . . . 3.
3. rabonni . . . . 44 . . . . 8.
4. roboam . . . . 60 . . . . 6.
5. rana . . . . 32 . . . . 5.
6. rodias . . . . 57 . . . . 3.
7. rehû . . . . 47 . . . . 11.
8. rafael . . . . 37 . . . . 10.
9. rabin . . . . 33 . . . . 6.
10. rous . . . . 31 . . . . 4.

S.
1. seth . . . . 48 . . . . 3.
2. sem . . . . 40 . . . . 4.
3. sarug . . . . 54 . . . . 9.
4. salomon . . . . 42 . . . . 6.
5. simeon . . . . 52 . . . . 7.
6. salatiel . . . . 77 . . . . 7.
7. semeï . . . . 53 . . . . 8.
8. sadoc . . . . 46 . . . . 10.
9. sareas . . . . 68 . . . . 5.
10. sisznon . . . . 73 . . . . 10.
11. simon . . . . 37 . . . . 10.
12. samarie . . . . 63 . . . . 9.
13. samaritene . . . . . . 92 . . . . 9.
14. sabaha . . . . 31 . . . . 4.
15. sophonias . . . . 66 . . . . 3.
16. sophonia . . . . 58 . . . . 4.
17. sophonie . . . . 52 . . . . 7.
18. sedechiaz . . . . 49 . . . . 4.
19. sedessias . . . . 81 . . . . 9.
20. samouel . . . . 64 . . . . 10.
21. samuel . . . . 63 . . . . 9.
22. sephas . . . . 70 . . . . 7.
23. saul . . . . 49 . . . . 4.
24. satham . . . . 63 . . . . 9.
25. saeul . . . . 50 . . . . 5.

T.
1. tharé . . . . 62 . . . . 8.
2. tite . . . . 56 . . . . 11.
3. tus . . . . 24 . . . . 6.
4. tenaha . . . . 43 . . . . 7.
5. tobié . . . . 51 . . . . 6.
6. thobié . . . . 64 . . . . 10.
7. thir . . . . 42 . . . . 6.
8. thetraque . . . . 91 . . . . 10.
9. tau . . . . 40 . . . . 4.

U.
1. ur . . . . 24 . . . . 6.

V.
1. vabim . . . . 37 . . . . 10.
2. wriel . . . . 49 . . . . 4.
3. vaüa . . . . 43 . . . . 7.
4. wava . . . . 46 . . . . 10.

Z.

1.	zezbhahoth	82	10.
2.	zorobabel	45	90.
3.	zorrobabbel	49	4.
4.	zorobbabel	47	11.
5.	zoroael	31	4.
6.	zacarie	37	10.
7.	zacarias	41	5.
8.	zakarie	44	8.
9.	zariel	61	7.

moze .... 34 .... 7.
mikael .... 31 .... 4.
angel of elemental exterminating fire.

aaron .... 25 .... 7.
gabriel .... 47 .... 11.
angel of water.

iozué .... 35 .... 8.
rafael .... 37 .... 10.
or
raphael .... 54 .... 9.
angel of earth.

caleb .... 26 .... 8.
heï .... 17 .... 8.
angel of sleep.

uru .... 28 .... 10.
huriel .... 46 .... 10.
angel of spiritual fire.

betsaleel .... 51 .... 10.
phamieli .... 58 .... 10.
angel of terror.

oliab .... 24 .... 6.
karina .... 43 .... 4.
angel of the trumpet.

zariel .... 61 .... 7.
zahïab ....
angel of death.

The 28 houses of the moon or the different locations that must be observed to place the image of the moon in the 28 circles, opposite the 28 days, in either of the 4 operations of the year which are 7 days; which all together make 28, 2 equinoxes, and 2 solstices.

1.	alnath	47	11.
2.	allothaïm	50	5.
3.	alchaomasone	80	8.
4.	aldebaram	57	3.
5.	alchataïa	58	4.
6.	alhama	33	6.
7.	aldimiach	44	8.
8.	alnaza	18	9.
9.	alchaam	41	5.
10.	algelioche	58	4.
11.	arzobra	58	4.
12.	arzarpha	79	4.
13.	alhaïre	78	3.
14.	achureth	67	4.
15.	agrapha	44	8.
16.	azabene	26	8.
17.	alchil	28	10.
18.	alchas	42	6.
19.	allatha	47	11.
20.	abnaïa	26	8.
21.	abeda	10	1.
22.	sadahe	27	9.
23.	sabadola	42	6.
24.	sadabath	58	4.
25.	sadalabra	55	10.
26.	apharec	59	5.
27.	alcharia	53	8.
28.	albotham	66	3.

anointing oil.
aloe branch, its flower.
branch of perfume, its flower.
sliced branch of myrrh, its flower.
branch of cinnamon, its fragrant flower.
branch of fragrant acacias,
its flower.
olive branch flower
and fruit.

T.4188.1 Fonds Prunelle de Lière
'The Registry of 2,400 Names'

T.4188.1 Fonds Prunelle de Lière 'The Registry of 2,400 Names'

caracteres. A.

A 1		A 14.		A 27.		A 40.	
	hebreux.				caldéen.		
2.		15.		28.		41.	
3.		16.		29.		42.	
4.		17.		30.		43.	ismaëlite
5.		18.		31.		44.	
6.		19.		32.	tartare	45.	
7.		20.		33.		46.	
8.		21.		34.		47.	
9.		22.		35.	siriaque	48.	
10.		23.		36.		49.	
11.	phenicien	24.		37.		50.	
12.		25.		38.		51.	noachite
13.		26.		39.		52.	

T.4188.1 Fonds Prunelle de Lière 'The Registry of 2,400 Names'

Caracteres. A.

A.		A.		A.		A.	
53.		66.		79.		92.	
54.		67.	2rabe	80.		93.	Samarie.
55.		68.		81.		94.	
56.		69.		82.		95.	
57.		70.		83.		96.	
58.		71.		84.		97.	
59.	Iaponite	72.		85.	egiptien.	98.	
60.		73.		86.		99.	
61.		74.		87.		100.	
62.		75.	Grec.	88.			caractère de Saturne.
63.		76.		89.			
64.		77.		90.			
65.		78.		91.			

✠ 255

hieroglyphes. A

A	3	A		A		A	
1.	hebr.	14.		27.	Caldéen	40.	
2.		15.		28.		41.	
3.		16.		29.		42.	
4.		17.		30.		43.	ismaël
5.		18.		31.		44.	
6.		19.	Castane	32.		45.	
7.		20.		33.		46.	
8.		21.		34.		47.	
9.		22.		35.	siriaque	48.	
10.		23.		36.		49.	
11.	phenicien	24.		37.		50.	
12.		25.		38.		51.	noachite
13.		26.		39.		52.	

T.4188.1 Fonds Prunelle de Lière 'The Registry of 2,400 Names'

hieroglyphes A

A 53.		A 66.		A 79.		A 92.	
54.		67.	arabe.	80.		93.	Samarie
55.		68.		81.		94.	
56.		69.		82.		95.	
57.		70.		83.	Égipte.	96.	
58.		71.		84.		97.	
59.	japonite.	72.		85.		98.	
60.		73.		86.		99.	
61.		74.		87.		100.	
62.		75.	grec	88.			car. de mercure.
63.		76.		89.			
64.		77.		90.			
65.		78.		91.			

5. Caractères B.

B 1.	hebraïque	B. 14.		B 27.		B. 40.	
2.		15.		28.		41.	siriaque
3.		16.		29.		42.	
4.		17.		30.		43.	
5.		18.		31.	Caldéen	44.	
6.		19.		32.		45.	
7.		20.		33.		46.	
8.		21.	tartare	34.		47.	
9.		22.		35.		48.	
10.		23.		36.		49.	
11.	phénicien	24.		37.		50.	
12.		25.		38.		51.	ismaëlite
13.		26.		39.		52.	

T.4188.1 Fonds Prunelle de Lière 'The Registry of 2,400 Names'

Caractères. B.   6.

B 53.	B 66.	B 79.	B 92.
B 54.	B 67.	80.	93.
55.	68.	81. Egipte.	94.
56.	69.	82.	95.
57.	70.	83.	96.
58.	71. japonite.	84.	97.
59.	72.	85.	98.
60.	73.	86.	99.
61. noechite.	74.	87.	100.
62.	75.	88.	Car. de Saturne.
63.	76.	89.	
64.	77.	90.	
65.	78.	91. arabe	

hieroglyphes B.

B.		B.		B.		B.	
1.	*hebraïque*	14.		27.		40.	
2.		15.		28.		41.	*Siriaque.*
3.		16.		29.		42.	
4.		17.		30.		43.	
5.		18.		31.	*Caldéen*	44.	
6.		19.		32.		45.	
7.		20.		33.		46.	
8.		21.	*tartare.*	34.		47.	
9.		22.		35.		48.	
10.		23.		36.		49.	
11.	*Phenicien.*	24.		37.		50.	
12.		25.		38.		51.	*ismaelite*
13.		26.		39.		52.	

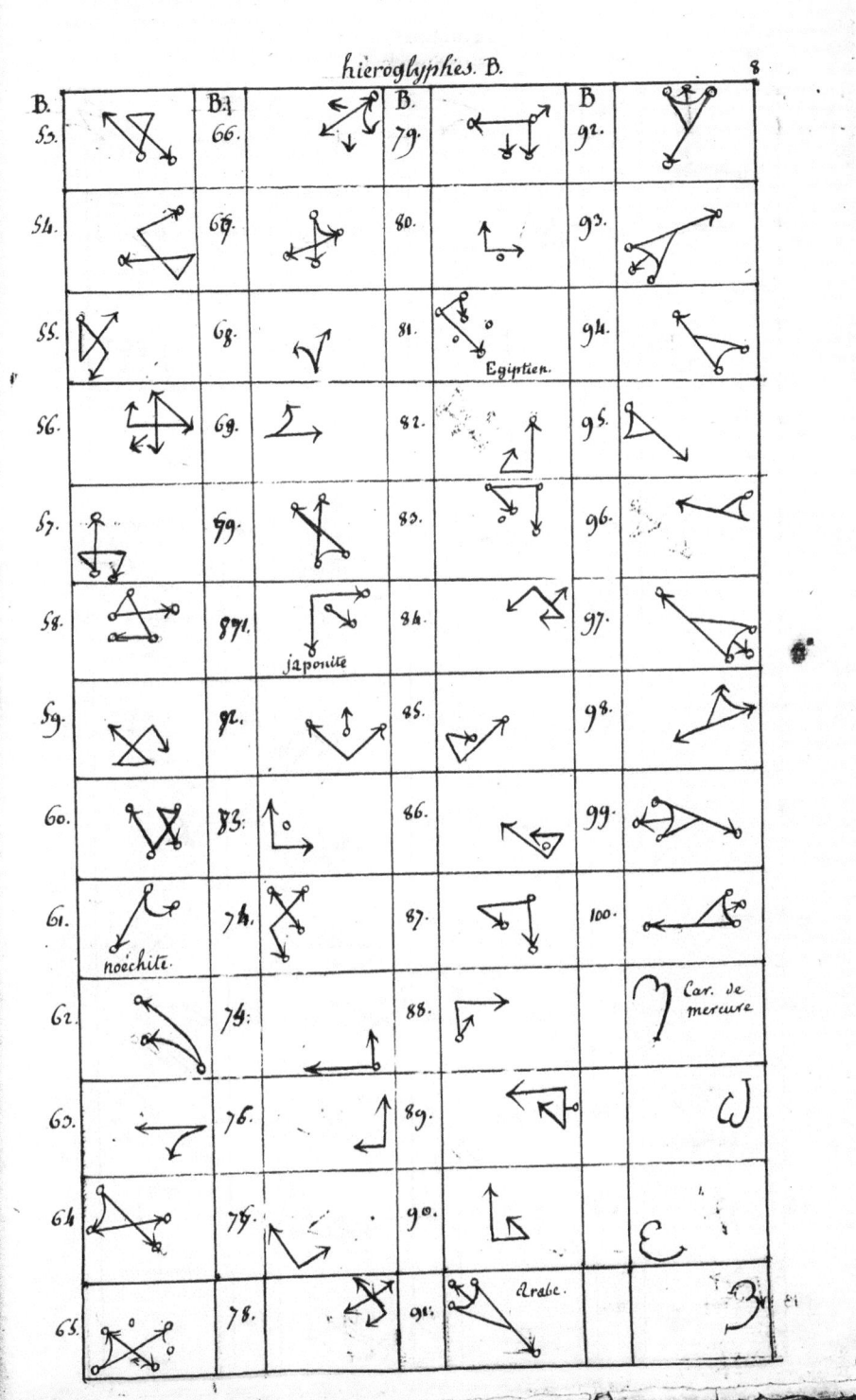

Caractères C. hiéroglyphes

C.		C.		C.		C.	
1.	hebraïque	14.		27.		40.	
2.		15.		28.		41.	Siriaque
3.		16.		29.		42.	
4.		17.		30.		43.	
5.		18.		31.	Caldéen	44.	
6.		19.		32.		45.	
7.		20.		33.		46.	
8.		21.	tartare	34.		47.	
9.		22.		35.		48.	
10.		23.		36.		49.	
11.	phénicien	24.		37.		50.	
12.		25.		38.		51.	ismaëlite
13.		26.		39.		52.	

T.4188.1 Fonds Prunelle de Lière 'The Registry of 2,400 Names'

Caractères C.

C.		C.		C.		C.	
53.		66.		79.		92.	
54.		67.		80.		93.	
55.		68.		81. Egiptien.		94.	
56.		69.		82.		95.	
57.		70.		83.		96.	
58.		71. japonite.		84.		97.	
59.		72.		85.		98.	
60.		73.		86.		99.	
61. noéchite.		74.		87.		100.	
62.		75.		88.			Caractère de Saturne
63.		76.		89.			
64.		77.		90.			
65.		78.		91. arabe			

✠ 263

hieroglyphes C

C.		C.		C.		C.	
1.	hebreux	14.		27.		40.	
2.		15.		28.		41.	Siriaque
3.		16.		29.		42.	
4.		17.		30.		43.	
5.		18.		31.	Caldéen	44.	
6.		19.		32.		45.	
7.		20.		33.		46.	
8.		21.	Tartare	34.		47.	
9.		22.		35.		48.	
10.		23.		36.		49.	
11.	phénicien	24.		37.		50.	
12.		25.		38.		51.	ismaëlite
13.		26.		39		52.	

T.4188.1 Fonds Prunelle de Lière 'The Registry of 2,400 Names'

hieroglyphes C.   12.

C. 53.		C. 66.		C. 79.		C. 92.	
54.		67.		80.		93.	
55.		68.		81.	Egipte.	94.	
56.		69.		82.		95.	
57.		70.		83.		96.	
58.		71.	japonii.	84.		97.	
59.		72.		85.		98.	
60.		73.		86.		99.	
61.	noechite	74.		87.		100.	
62.		75.		88.			car. de mercure.
63.		76.		89.			
64.		77.		90.			
65.		78.		91.	arabe		

✣ 265

The Green Book of the Élus Coëns

13.							
D. 1.	hebreux	D. 14.		D. 27.		D. 40.	
2.		15.		28.		41.	Grec.
3.		16.		29.		42.	
4.		17.		30.		43.	
5.		18.		31.	Siriaque	44.	
6.		19.		32.		45.	
7.		20.		33.		46.	
8.		21.	Caldéen.	34.		47.	
9.		22.		35.		48.	
10.		23.		36.		49.	
11.	tartare	24.		37.		50.	
12.		25.		38.		51.	Samaritain
13.		26.		39.		52.	

T.4188.1 Fonds Prunelle de Lière 'The Registry of 2,400 Names'

Caractères. D.   14.

D		D		D		D	
53.		66.		79.		92.	
54.		67.		80.		93.	
55.		68.		81. ismaélite		94.	
56.		69.		82.		95.	
57.		70.		83.		96.	
58.		71. Egipte		84.		97.	
59.		72.		85.		98.	
60.		73.		86.		99.	
61. arabe		74.		87.		100.	
62.		75.		88.			Caractère de Saturne.
63.		76.		89.			
64.		77.		90.			
65.		78.		91. indien			

✠ 267

hieroglyphes

D		D		D		D	
1.	*hebreux*	14.		27.		40.	
2.		15.		28.		41.	*Grec.*
3.		16.		29.		42.	
4.		17.		30.		43.	
5.		18.		31.	*Siriaque*	44.	
6.		19.		32.		45.	
7.		20.		33.		46.	
8.		21.	*Caldéen*	34.		47.	
9.		22.		35.		48.	
10.		23.		36.		49.	
11.	*tartare*	24.		37.		50.	
12.		25.		38.		51.	*Samaritain*
13.		26.		39.		52.	

T.4188.1 Fonds Prunelle de Lière 'The Registry of 2,400 Names'

hyeroglyphes D. 16.

D 53.	D 66.	D 79.	D 92.
54.	67.	80.	93.
55.	68.	81. ismaélite.	94.
56.	69.	82.	95.
57.	70.	83.	96.
58.	71. Egipte.	84.	97.
59.	72.	85.	98.
60.	73.	86.	99.
61. arabe.	74.	87.	100.
62.	75.	88.	Car. de mercure.
63.	76.	89.	
64.	77.	90.	
65.	78.	91. indien	

The Green Book of the Élus Coëns

Caractères. E.

#		#		#		#	
E. 1.	(beniamin)	E. 14.		E. 27.		E. 40.	
2.		15.		28.		41.	(Gad)
3.		16.		29.		42.	
4.		17.		30.		43.	
5.		18.		31.	(Ruben)	44.	
6.		19.		32.		45.	
7.		20.		33.		46.	
8.		21.	(lévitique)	34.		47.	
9.		22.		35.		48.	
10.		23.		36.		49.	
11.	(judaïque)	24.		37.		50.	
12.		25.		38.		51.	(Ephraïm)
13.		26.		39.		52.	

T.4188.1 Fonds Prunelle de Lière 'The Registry of 2,400 Names'

Caractères E.   18.

E. 53.		E. 66.		E. 79.		E. 92.	
54.		67.		80.		93.	
55.		68.		81. Zabulon.		94.	
56.		69.		82.		95.	
57.		70.		83.		96.	
58.		71. Dan.		84.		97.	
59.		72.		85.		98.	
60.		73.		86.		99.	
61. Siméon.		74.		87.		100.	
62.		75.		88.		Caractère de Saturne	
63.		76.		89.			
64.		77.		90.			
65.		78.		91. Asser.			

The Green Book of the Élus Coëns

E. 1.	Beniamin	E. 14.		E. 27.		E. 40.	
2.		15.		28.		41.	Gad.
3.		16.		29.		42.	
4.		17.		30.		43.	
5.		18.		31.	Ruben	44.	
6.		19.		32.		45.	
7.		20.		33.		46.	
8.		21.	Levi	34.		47.	
9.		22.		35.		48.	
10.		23.		36.		49.	
11.	Iuda	24.		37.		50.	
12.		25.		38.		51.	Ephraim
13.		26.		39.		52.	

T.4188.1 Fonds Prunelle de Lière 'The Registry of 2,400 Names'

hieroglyphes E · 20.

E 53.		E 66.		E 79.		E 92.	
54.		67.		80.		93.	
55.		68.		81. Zabulon.		94.	
56.		69.		82.		95.	
57.		70.		83.		96.	
58.		71. Dan.		84.		97.	
59.		72.		85.		98.	
60.		73.		86.		99.	
61. Simon.		74.		87.		100.	
62.		75.		88.			Car. de mercure.
63.		76.		89.			
64.		77.		90.			
65.		78.		91. asser			

✠ 273

Caracteres F.

F		F		F		F	
1.	iapon.	14.		27.		40.	
2.		15.		28.		41.	Egipte.
3.		16.		29.		42.	
4.		17.		30.		43.	
5.		18.		31.	tartare	44.	
6.		19.		32.		45.	
7.		20.		33.		46.	
8.		21.	turc et Barbar	34.		47.	
9.		22.		35.		48.	
10.		23.		36.		49.	
11.	Cananéen au midi	24.		37.		50.	
12.		25.		38.		51.	Kaïn au midy.
13.		26.		39.		52.	

Caracteres F

F. 53.		F. 66.		F. 79.	F. 92.
54.		67.		80.	93.
55.		68.		81. assirien	94.
56.		69.		82.	95.
57.		70.		83.	96.
58.		71.	amalecite	84.	97.
59.		72.		85.	98.
60.		73.		86.	99.
61. Grec.		74.		87.	100.
62.		75.		88.	Car. de Saturne.
63.		76.		89.	
64.		77.		90.	
65.		78.		91. madianite	

hieroglyphes F.

F.		F.		F.		F.	
1.	japon.	14.		27.		40.	
2.		15.		28.		41.	Egipte.
3.		16.		29.		42.	
4.		17.		30.		43.	
5.		18.		31.	Tartare	44.	
6.		19.		32.		45.	
7.		20.		33.		46.	
8.		21.	turc et barbare.	34.		47.	
9.		22.		35.		48.	
10.		23.		36.		49.	
11.	Cananéen.	24.		37.		50.	
12.		25.		38.		51.	Kaïn
13.		26.		39.		52.	

T.4188.1 Fonds Prunelle de Lière 'The Registry of 2,400 Names'

hieroglyphes F.

F. 53.		F. 66.		F. 79.	F. 92.
54.		67.		80.	93.
55.		68.		81. assirien.	94.
56.		69.		82.	95.
57.		70.		83.	96.
58.		71. amalécite		84.	97.
59.		72.		85.	98.
60.		73.		86.	99.
61. Grec.		74.		87.	100.
62.		75.		88.	Caractère de mart.
63.		76.		89.	
64.		77.		90.	
65.		78.		91. medianite.	

25.   Caractères G.

G.		G.		G.		G.	
1.	jébuséen.	14.		27.		40.	
2.		15.		28.		41.	iaphite
3.		16.		29.		42.	
4.		17.		30.		43.	
5.		18.		31.	joseph.	44.	
6.		19.		32.		45.	
7.		20.		33.		46.	
8.		21.	Cananéen.	34.		47.	
9.		22.		35.		48.	
10.		23.		36.		49.	
11.	Sidonite.	24.		37.		50.	
12.		25.		38.		51.	Sem
13.		26.		39.		52.	

T.4188.1 Fonds Prunelle de Lière 'The Registry of 2,400 Names'

Caractères G.

G. 58.	G. 66.	G. 79.	G. 92.
54.	67.	80.	93.
55.	68.	81. libanite.	94.
56.	69.	82.	95.
57.	70.	83.	96.
58.	71. Egipta.	84.	97.
59.	72.	85.	98.
60.	73.	86.	99.
61.	74.	87.	100.
62.	75.	88.	Car. de venus.
63.	76.	89.	
64.	77.	90.	
65.	78.	91. gabaonite.	

hiéroglyphes G.

#		G		G		G	
G 1	jébuséen	14.		27.		4a	
2		15.		28.		41.	japhite.
3		16.		29.		42.	
4		17.		30.		43.	
5		18.		31.	joseph.	44.	
6		19.		32.		45.	
7		20.		33.		46.	
8		21.	Cananéen.	34.		47.	
9		22.		35.		48.	
10		23.		36.		49.	
11	Sidonite.	24.		37.		50.	
12		25.		38.		51.	Sem.
13		26		39.		52.	

T.4188.1 Fonds Prunelle de Lière 'The Registry of 2,400 Names'

hieroglyphee G.   28.

G. 53.		G. 66.		G. 79.		G. 92.	
54.		67.		80.		93.	
55.		68.		81. *libanite.*		94.	
56.		69.		82.		95.	
57.		70.		83.		96.	
58.		71. *egipte*		84.		97.	
59.		72.		85.		98.	
60.		73.		86.		99.	
61. *tirien.*		74.		87.		100	
62.		75.		88.			*Car. de mars.*
63.		76.		89.			
64.		77.		90.			
65.		78.		91. *Gabaonite.*			

Caractères H.

H.	29.	H. 14.		H. 27.		H. 40.	
1.	Nemro.	14.		27.		40.	
2.		15.		28.		41.	David
3.		16.		29.		42.	
4.		17.		30.		43.	
5.		18.		31.	mosaïque	44.	
6.		19.		32.		45.	
7.		20.		33.		46.	
8.		21.	jacobite	34.		47.	
9.		22.		35.		48.	
10.		23.		36.		49.	
11.	amorréen.	24.		37.		50.	
12.		25.		38.		51.	Esau.
13.		26.		39.		52.	

T.4188.1 Fonds Prunelle de Lière 'The Registry of 2,400 Names'

Caracteres **H**.

H 53	H 66.	79.	H	H 92.	
54.	67.		80.	93.	
55.	68.		81. harkien.	94.	
56.	69.		82.	95.	
57.	70.		83.	96.	
58.	71. Egipte.		84.	97.	
59.	72.		85.	98.	
60.	73.		86.	99.	
61. hetien	74		87.	100.	
62.	75.		88.		Car. de Venus
63.	76.		89.		
64.	77.		90.		
65.	78.		91. Seth.		

hieroglyphes

H 1.		H 14.		H 27.		H 40.	
	nemro.						
2.		15.		28.		41.	David.
3.		16.		29.		42.	
4.		17.		30.		43.	
5.		18.		31. mosaïque.		44.	
6.		19.		32.		45.	
7.		20.		33.		46.	
8.		21. iacobite.		34.		47.	
9.		22.		35.		48.	
10.		23.		36.		49.	
11. amorréen.		24.		37.		50.	
12.		25.		38.		51. Esau.	
13.		26.		39.		52.	

hieroglyphes H 32.

H 53.	H 66.	H 79.		H 92.	
54.	67.	80.		93.	
55.	68.	81. harkien.		94.	
56.	69.	82.		95.	
57.	70.	83.		96.	
58.	71. Egipte.	84.		97.	
59.	72.	85.		98.	
60.	73.	86.		99.	
61. hétien	74.	87.		100.	
62.	75.	88.			Car. de Mars.
63.	76.	89.			
64.	77.	90.			
65.	78.	91. Seth.			

Caractères I.

#		#		#		#	
1.	⟨symbol⟩ Galiléen.	14.	⟨symbol⟩	27.	⟨symbol⟩ Iduméen.	40.	⟨symbol⟩
2.	⟨symbol⟩	15.	⟨symbol⟩	28.	⟨symbol⟩	41.	⟨symbol⟩
3.	⟨symbol⟩	16.	⟨symbol⟩	29.	⟨symbol⟩	42.	⟨symbol⟩
4.	⟨symbol⟩	17.	⟨symbol⟩	30.	⟨symbol⟩	43.	⟨symbol⟩
5.	⟨symbol⟩	18.	⟨symbol⟩	31.	⟨symbol⟩	44.	⟨symbol⟩
6.	⟨symbol⟩	19.	⟨symbol⟩	32.	⟨symbol⟩	45.	⟨symbol⟩
7.	⟨symbol⟩	20.	⟨symbol⟩	33.	⟨symbol⟩	46.	⟨symbol⟩
8.	⟨symbol⟩	21.	⟨symbol⟩ nazaréen.	34.	⟨symbol⟩	47.	⟨symbol⟩ orientaux.
9.	⟨symbol⟩	22.	⟨symbol⟩	35.	⟨symbol⟩	48.	⟨symbol⟩
10.	⟨symbol⟩	23.	⟨symbol⟩	36.	⟨symbol⟩	49.	⟨symbol⟩
11.	⟨symbol⟩ Sichem.	24.	⟨symbol⟩	37.	⟨symbol⟩ iosué.	50.	⟨symbol⟩
12.	⟨symbol⟩	25.	⟨symbol⟩	38.	⟨symbol⟩	51.	⟨symbol⟩
13.	⟨symbol⟩	26.	⟨symbol⟩	39.	⟨symbol⟩	52.	⟨symbol⟩

T.4188.1 Fonds Prunelle de Lière 'The Registry of 2,400 Names'

Caracterce I. —34.

i. 53.		i. 66.		i. 79.		i. 92.	
54.		67.	i'abite.	80.		93.	
55.		68.		81.		94.	
56.		69.		82.		95.	
57.	Salomon.	70.		83.		94.	
58.		71.		84.		95.	renvoi à la Suite Des nazareens
59.		72.		85.		96.	
60.		73.		86.		97.	
61.		74.		87.		98.	
62.		75.		88.		99.	caractère de Venus.
63.		76.		89.			
64.		77.	Egipte.	90.			
65.		78.		91.			

hieroglyphes 1.

35

1.	[Galiléen]	14.		27.		40.	
2.		15.		28.		41.	[iosué]
3.		16.		29.		42.	
4.		17.		30.		43.	
5.		18.		31.	[iduméen]	44.	
6.		19.		32.		45.	
7.		20.		33.		46.	
8.		21.	[nazaréen]	34.		47.	
9.		22.		35.		48.	
10.		23.		36.		49.	
11.	[Sichem]	24.		37.		50.	
12.		25.		38.		51.	[orientaux]
13.		26.		39.		52.	

hieroglyphes I. 36

I 53.		I 66.		I 79.		I 92.	
54.		67.		80.		93.	
55.		68.		81. Egipte		94.	
56.		69.		82.		95.	
57.		70.		83.		96.	
58.		71. iabite.		84.		97.	
59.		72.		85.		98.	
60.		73.		86.		99.	
61. Salomon.		74.		87.		100	
62.		75.		88.			Car. de Mars
63.		76.		89.			
64.		77.		90.			
65.		78.		91. phi listins.			

37. Caractères K.

I. K		K. 14		K. 27		K. 40	
	Dagon						
2.		15.		28.		41.	Abiamite.
3.		16.		29.		42.	
4.		17.		30.		43.	
5.		18.		31.	iuiph	44.	
6.		19.		32.		45.	
7.		20.		33.		46.	
8.		21.	Roboam.	34.		47.	
9.		22.		35.		48.	
10.		23.		36.		49.	
11.	Saül	24.		37.		50.	
12.		25.		38.		51.	Zorobabel.
13.		26.		39.		52.	

Caractères K 38.

K 53.	K 65.	K 78.	K 91.	
54.	66.	79.	92.	
55.	67.	80. ℵ ieau.	93.	
56.	68.	81. ℵ	94.	
57.	69.	82. ℵ	95.	
58.	70. Enoch.	83. ℵ	96.	
59.	71.	84.	97.	
59.	72.	85.	98.	
60. Abraham.	73.	86.	99.	
61.	74.	87.	100. Car. de Venus.	
62.	75.	88. ℵ	B	
63.	76.	89.	B	
64.	77.	90. Egipte.	B	

The Green Book of the Élus Coëns

hieroglyphes K.

39

K.1. Dagon	K.14.	K.27.	K.40.
2.	15.	28.	41. Abiamite.
3.	16.	29.	42.
4.	17.	30.	43.
5.	18.	31. inipsh	44.
6.	19.	32.	45.
7.	20.	33.	46.
8.	21. Roboam.	34.	47.
9.	22.	35.	48.
10.	23.	36.	49.
11. Saul.	24.	37.	50.
12.	25.	38.	51. Zorobabel.
13.	26.	39.	52.

T.4188.1 Fonds Prunelle de Lière 'The Registry of 2,400 Names'

hieroglyphes K.

40.

K.		K.		K.		K.			
53.		66.		79.		92.			
54.		67.		80.		93.			
55.		68.		81. iean.		94.			
56.		69.		82.		95.			
57.		70.		83.		96.			
58.		71.	Enoch	84.		97.			
59.		72.		85.		98.			
60.		73.		86.		99.			
61.	Abraham.	74.		87.		100.			
62.		75.		88.			Car. de mars.		
63.		76.		89.					
64.		77.		90.					
65.		78.		91. Egipte					

The Green Book of the Élus Coëns

41.   Caracteres L

L 1. Babilonien.	L 14.	L 27.	L 40.	
2.	15.	28.	41. payen	
3.	16.	29.	42.	
4.	17.	30.	43.	
5.	18.	31. jeriko.	44.	
6.	19.	32.	45.	
7.	20.	33.	46.	
8.	21. Iob	34.	47.	
9.	22.	35.	48.	
10.	23.	36.	49.	
11. iosaphat.	24.	37.	50.	
12.	25.	38.	51. Sarasin.	
13.	26.	39.	52.	

T.4188.1 Fonds Prunelle de Lière 'The Registry of 2,400 Names'

Caractères L.

L.		L.		L.		L.		
53.		66.		79.		92.		
54.		67.		80.		93.		
55.		68.		81. Egipte.		94.		
56.		69.		82.		95.		
57.		70.		83.		96.		
58.		71. des Medes		84.		97.		
59.		72.		85.		98.		
60.		73.		86.		99.		
61. iudith		74.		87.		100.		
62.		75.		88.			Car. de jupiter.	
63.		76.		89.				
64.		77.		90.				
65.		78.		91. Betulien				

hieroglyphes L.

L.		L.		L.		L.	
1	Babilonien	14.		27.		40.	
2.		15.		28.		41.	payen.
3.		16.		29.		42.	
4.		17.		30.		43.	
5.		18.		31.	ieriko	44.	
6.		19.		32.		45.	
7.		20.		33.		46.	
8.		21.	iob	34.		47.	
9.		22.		35.		48.	
10.		23.		36.		49.	
11.	iosaphat	24.		37.		50.	
12.		25.		38.		51.	Sarasin
13.		26.		39.		52.	

T.4188.1 Fonds Prunelle de Lière 'The Registry of 2,400 Names'

hiéroglyphes L

L. 53		L. 66.		L. 79.		L. 92.	
54.		67.		80.		93.	
55.		68.		81. egipte.		94.	
56.		69.		82.		95.	
57.		70.		83.		96.	
58.		71. dac medel.		84.		97.	
59.		72.		85.		98.	
60.		73.		86.		99.	
61. iudith		74.		87.		100.	
62.		75.		88.			Car. de mars.
63.		76.		89.			
64.		77.		90.			
65.		78.		91. Bétulien.			

✠ 297

Caractères M.

M.		M.		M.		M.	
1.	isaachem	14.		27.		40.	
2.		15.		28.		41.	niniviens
3.		16.		29.		42.	
4.		17.		30.		43.	
5.		18.		31.	izakar	44.	
6.		19.		32.		45.	
7.		20.		33.		46.	
8.		21.	nephtali	34.		47.	
9.		22.		35.		48.	
10.		23.		36.		49.	
11.	Manassés	24.		37.		50.	
12.		25.		38.		51.	egipt. et méridiens
13.		26.		39.		52.	

Caractères M.

M. 53.	M. 66.	M. 79.	M. 92.	
54.	67.	80.	93.	
55.	68.	81. Debora.	94.	
56.	69.	82.	95.	
57.	70.	83.	96.	
58.	71. Samuel	84.	97.	
59.	72.	85.	98.	
60.	73.	86.	99.	
61. Sauvage nord-ouest.	74.	87.	100.	
62.	75.	88.		Car. de jupiter.
63.	76.	89.		
64.	77.	90.		
65.	78.	91. Elie.		

hyeroglyphes M

M 1. isaachem	M 14.	M 27.	M 40.
2.	15.	28.	41. niniviens.
3.	16.	29.	42.
4.	17.	30.	43.
5.	18.	31. izeKar.	44.
6.	19.	32.	45.
7.	20.	33.	46.
8.	21. nephtali.	34.	47.
9.	22.	35.	48.
10.	23.	36.	49.
11. Manassés.	24.	37.	51.
12.	25.	38.	52. Egip⁵ et méridiens
13.	26.	39.	53.

T.4188.1 Fonds Prunelle de Lière 'The Registry of 2,400 Names'

hieroglyphes. M

M. 63.	M. 66.	79.	M.	M. 92.	
64.	67.	80.		93.	
65.	68.	81. Debora.		94.	
66.	69.	82.		95.	
67.	70.	83.		96.	
68.	71. Samuel	84.		97.	
69.	72.	85.		98.	
60.	73.	86.		99.	
61. Sauvage. nordouest	74.	87.		100.	
62.	75.	88.			Cer. de la dune.
63.	76.	89.			
64.	77.	90.			
65.	78.	91.			

✠ 301

Caractères N.

N.		N.		N.		N.	
1	Elisée	14.		27.		40.	
2.		15.		28.		41.	Prophete Balaam.
3.		16.		29.		42.	
4.		17.		30.		43.	
5.		18.		31.	egiptiens avec Aaron.	44.	
6.		19.		32.		45.	
7.		20.		33.		46.	
8.		21.	Reine de Seba au midi. israeli.	34.		47.	
9.		22.		35.		48.	
10.		23.		36.		49.	
11.	Datan et Abiron	24.		37.		50.	
12.		25.		38.		51.	Paul ou Saül
13.		26.		39.		52.	

T.4188.1 Fonds Prunelle de Lière 'The Registry of 2,400 Names'

Caractères N.

N.		N.		N.		N.	
53.		66.		79.		92.	
54.		67.		80.		93.	
55.		68.		81. Daniel.		94.	
56.		69.		82.		95.	
57.		70.		83.		96.	
58.		71. meKebte.		84.		97.	
59.		72.		85.		98.	
60.		73.		86.		99.	
61. olimpien.		74.		87.		100.	
62.		75.		88.		Cer. de jupiter.	
63.		76.		89.			
64.		77.		90.			
65.		78.		91. ioué.			

hieroglyphes N

N°		N°		N°		N°	
1.	*Elisée*	14.		27.		40.	
2.		15.		28.		41.	*prophete Balaam*
3.		16.		29.		42.	
4.		17.		30.		43.	
5.		18.		31.	*Egipt.s avec Aaron*	44.	
6.		19.		32.		45.	
7.		20.		33.		46.	
8.		21.	*Reine de Seba au midi Uvaeli*	34.		47.	
9.		22.		35.		48.	
10.		23.		36.		49.	
11.	*Datan et Abiron*	24.		37.		50.	
12.		25.		38.		51.	*paul ou Saül*
13.		26.		39.		52.	

T.4188.1 Fonds Prunelle de Lière 'The Registry of 2,400 Names'

hieroglyphes. N.

N.		N.		N.		N.	
53.		66.		79.		92.	
54.		67.		80.		93.	
55.		68.		81.	proph: Daniel.	94.	
56.		69.		82.		95.	
57.		70.		83.		96.	
58.		71.	Makabée.	84.		97.	
59.		72.		85.		98.	
60.		73.		86.		99.	
61.	olimpiens	74.		87.		100.	
62.		75.		88.			Car. de la lune
63.		76.		89.			
64.		77.		90.			
65.		78.		91.	iosué.		

✝ 305

The Green Book of the Élus Coëns

Caractères O.

O		O		O		O	
1. osée	—	14.		27.		40.	
2.		15.		28.		41. jeremie	N
3.		16.		29.		42.	N
4.		17.		30.		43.	N
5.		18.		31. habakuc		44.	N
6.		19.		32.		45.	N
7.		20.		33.		46.	
8.		21. Belzebu		34.		47.	
9.		22.		35.		48.	
10.		23.		36.		49.	
11. Zakarie		24.		37.		50.	
12.		25.		38.		51. Adam	Ⓐ
13.		26.		39.		52.	Ⓥ

Caractères O.

O.		O.		O.		O.	
53.		66.		79.		92.	
54.		67.		80.		93.	
55.		68.		81. Esdras.		94.	
56.		69.		82.		95.	
57.		70.		83.		96.	
58.		71. Amos		84.		97.	
59.		72.		85.		98.	
60.		73.		86.		99.	
61. ionathan.		74.		87.		100.	
62.		75.		88.			Car. de jupiter.
63.		76.		89.			
64.		77.		90.			
65.		78.		91. Egip³ ioseph et Heber			

hieroglyphes O.

O.		O.		O.		O.	
1.	ozée.	14.		27.		40.	
2.		15.		28.		41.	ieremie.
3.		16.		29.		42.	
4.		17.		30.		43.	
5.		18.		31.	habakuc.	44.	
6.		19.		32.		45.	
7.		20.		33.		46.	
8.		21.	Belzebu.	34.		47.	
9.		22.		35.		48.	
10.		23.		36.		49.	
11.	Zakarie.	24.		37.		50.	
12.		25.		38.		51.	adam.
13.		26.		39.		52.	

T.4188.1 Fonds Prunelle de Lière 'The Registry of 2,400 Names'

hieroglyphes O.

Caractères P.

#		#		#		#	
P.1	Taré et nakor	P.14		P.27		P.40	
2		15		28		41	Sédéciar
3		16		29		42	
4		17		30		43	
5		18		31	aaron	44	
6		19		32		45	
7		20		33		46	
8		21	uru. Caleb	34		47	
9		22		35		48	
10		23		36		49	
11	Olial et Betsalel	24		37		50	
12		25		38		51	nehemie
13		26		39		52	

Caractères P.

P. 53.		P. 66.		P. 79.		P. 92.	
54.		67.		80.		93.	
55.		68.		81. Dagonite		94.	
56.		69.		82.		95.	
57.		70.		83.		96.	
58.		71.		84. Bagnakin		97.	
59.		72.		85.		98.	
60.		73.		86.		99.	
61. Salomon Roboam.		74.		87.		100.	
62.		75.		88.		Car. de jupiter.	
63.		76.		89.			
64.		77.		90.			
65.		78.		91. phaxamos en Egipte			

hieroglyphes P.

P		P		P		P	
1	Taré et Nakor.	14.		27.		40.	
2		15.		28.		41.	Sedecias
3		16.		29.		42.	
4		17.		30.		43.	
5		18.		31.	aaron.	44.	
6		19.		32.		45.	
7		20.		33.		46.	
8		21.	uru Caleb.	34.		47.	
9		22.		35.		48.	
10		23.		36.		49.	
11	Oliab et Betsaleel	24.		37.		50.	
12		25.		38.		51.	nehemie
13		26.		39.		52.	

hieroglyphes P.

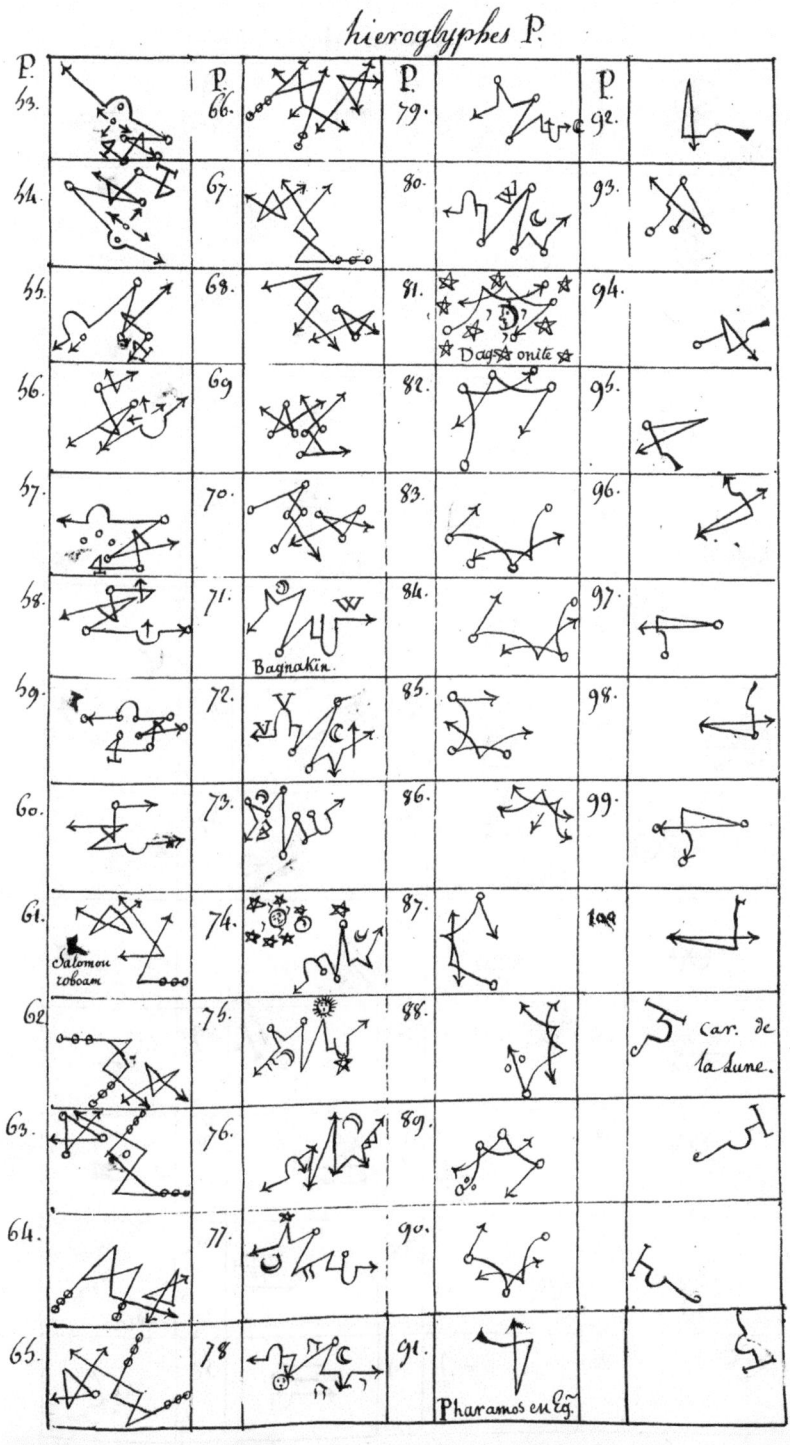

Caractères q.

q.		q.		q.		q.	
1.	d'Asie	14.		27.		40.	
2.		15.		28.		41.	Ananias
3.		16.		29.		42.	
4.		17.		30.		43.	
5.		18.		31.	Enos	44.	
6.		19.		32.		45.	
7.		20.		33.		46.	
8.		21.	Eleazar	34.		47.	
9.		22.		35.		48.	
10.		23.		36.		49.	
11.	henoch	24.		37.		50.	
12.		25.		38.		51.	abias
13.		26.		39.		52.	

T.4188.1 Fonds Prunelle de Lière 'The Registry of 2,400 Names'

Caractères q

q.		q.		q.		q.	
q.53.		q.66.		q.79.		q.92.	
54.		67.		80.		93.	
55.		68.		81. Daniel		94.	
56.		69.		82.		95.	
57.		70.		83.		96.	
58.		71. Esdras		84.		97.	
59.		72.		85.		98.	
60.		73.		86.		99.	
61. Mathusalem		74.		87.		100.	
62.		75.		88.			Car. de Jupiter
63.		76.		89.			
64.		77.		90.			
65.		78.		91. Moré Egipta			

THE GREEN BOOK OF THE ÉLUS COËNS

hieroglyphes. q.

q.		q.		q.		q.	
1.	d'asie.	14.		27.		40.	
2.		15.		28.		41.	Ananias.
3.		16.		29.		42.	
4.		17.		30.		43.	
5.		18.		31.	Enos 3.	44.	
6.		19.		32.	4.	45.	
7.		20.		33.	3.	46.	
8.		21. eleazar	34.		3	47.	
9.		22.		35.	4.	48.	
10.		23.		36.	5.	49.	
11. henoch.		24.		37.	6.	50.	
12.		25.		38.	2.	51.	Abias
13.		26.		39.	7.	52.	

T.4188.1 Fonds Prunelle de Lière 'The Registry of 2,400 Names'

hieroglyphes q.

q.		q.		q.		q.	
53.	✶	66.		79.		92.	
54.		67.		80.		93.	
55.		68.		81. Daniel.		94.	
56.		69.		82.		95.	
57.		70.		83.		96.	
58.		71. Esdras.		84.		97.	
59.		72.		85.		98.	
60.		73.		86.		99.	
61. mathusalem		74.		87.		100.	
62.		75.		88.			Car. de la Lune.
63.		76.		89.			
64.		77.		90.			
65.		78.		91. mozé.			

✝ 317

The Green Book of the Élus Coëns

Caracteres R.

R.		R.		R.		R.	
1.	Nathan.	14.		27.		40.	
2.		15.		28.		41.	Iacob.
3.		16.		29.		42.	
4.		17.		30.		43.	
5.		18.		31.	Phaleg	44.	
6.		19.		31.		45.	
7.		20.		33.		46.	
8.		21.	Zorobel.	34.		47.	
9.		22.		35.		48.	
10.		23.		36.		49.	
11.	Dathan et abiron	24.		37.		50.	
12.		25.		38.		51.	Ionas
13.		26.		39.		52.	

T.4188.1 Fonds Prunelle de Lière 'The Registry of 2,400 Names'

Caractères R.

R. 53		R. 66		R. 79		R. 92	
54		67		80		93	
55		68		81	agar et ismael en Égip.	94	
56		69		82		95	
57		70		83		96	
58		71	Abel	84		97	
59		72		85		98	
60		73		86		99	
61	Labahan	74		87		100	
62		75		88			Car. de jupiter
63		76		89			
64		77		90			
65		78		91	Baal		

✠ 319

THE GREEN BOOK OF THE ÉLUS COËNS

hieroglyphes R.

R.		R.		R.		R.	
1.	Nathan.	14.		27.		40.	
2.		15.		28.		41.	iacob.
3.		16.		29.		42.	
4.		17.		30.		43.	
5.		18.		31.	phaleg.	44.	
6.		19.		32.		45.	
7.		20.		33.		46.	
8.		21.	Zorobel	34.		47.	
9.		22.		35.		48.	
10.		23.		36.		49.	
11.	Dathan et abiron	24.		37.		50.	
12.		25.		38.		51.	ionas.
13.		26.		39.		52.	

hieroglyphes. R.

R. 53.		R. 66.		R. 79.		R. 92.	
54.		67.		80.		93.	
55.		68.		81. *Agar et ismael en Egypte*		94.	
56.		69.		82.		95.	
57.		70.		83.		96.	
58.		71. *Abel.*		84.		97.	
59.		72.		85.		98.	
60.		73.		86.		99.	
61. *Labeham.*		74.		87.		100.	
62.		75.		88.			car. du Soleil.
63.		76.		89.			
64.		77.		90.			
65.		78.		91. *Baal.*			

Caractères S.

S.		S.		S.		S.	
1.	aggée	14.		27.		40.	
2.		15.		28.		41.	lamech
3.		16.		29.		42.	
4.		17.		30.		43.	
5.		18.		31.	merian	44.	
6.		19.		32.		45.	
7.		20.		33.		46.	
8.		21.	Leon Pape	34.		47.	
9.		22.		35.		48.	
10.		23.		36.		49.	
11.	iosias	24.		37.		50.	
12.		25.		38.		51.	St Louis
13.		26.		39.		52.	

T.4188.1 Fonds Prunelle de Lière 'The Registry of 2,400 Names'

Caracteres S.

S. 53	S. 66	S. 79	S. 92
54	67	80	93
55	68	81 Debora	94
56	69	82	95
57	70	83	96
58	71 godefroy	84	97
59	72	85	98
60	73	86	99
61 Egiptien	74	87	100
62	75	88	Car. de Mercure
63	76	89	
64	77	90	
65	78	91 Boas	

hieroglyphes S

S.		S.		S.		S.	
1.	aggée	14.		27.		40.	
2.		15.		28.		41.	damech
3.		16.		29.		42.	
4.		17.		30.		43.	
5.		18.		31.	merian	44.	
6.		19.		32.		45.	
7.		20.		33.		46.	
8.		21.	Leon Pape.	34.		47.	
9.		22.		35.		48.	
10.		23.		36.		49.	
11.	iosias	24.		37.		50.	
12.		25.		38.		51.	St. louis.
13.		26.		39.		52.	

T.4188.1 Fonds Prunelle de Lière 'The Registry of 2,400 Names'

hieroglyphes. S.

S. 53.		S. 66.		S. 79.		S. 92.	
54.		67.		80.		93.	
55.		68.		81. Debora.		94.	
56.		69.		82.		95.	
57.		70.		83.		96.	
58.		71. Godefroy.		84.		97.	
59.		72.		85.		98.	
60.		73.		86.		99.	
61. Egiptien.		74.		87.		100.	
62.		75.		88.			Car. du Soleil.
63.		76.		89.			
64.		77.		90.			
65.		78.		91. Boar.			

37

Caractères T.

T.		T.		T.		T.	
1.	Paul.	14.		27.		40.	
2.		15.		28.		41.	assioram.
3.		16.		29.		42.	
4.		17.		30.		43.	
5.		18.		31.	azar.	44.	
6.		19.		32.		45.	
7.		20.		33.		46.	
8.		21.	Andrea.	34.		47.	
9.		22.		35.		48.	
10.		23.		36.		49.	
11.	Sephas.	24.		37.		50.	
12.		25.		38.		51.	amarias.
13.		26.		39.		52.	

T.4188.1 Fonds Prunelle de Lière 'The Registry of 2,400 Names'

Caracteres T.

T. 53.		T. 66.		T. 79.		T. 92.	
54.		67.		80.		93.	
55.		68.		81. op. romaine		94.	
56.		69.		82.		95.	
57.		70.		83.		96.	
58.		71. misrael.		84.		97.	
59.		72.		85.		98.	
60.		73.		86.		99.	
61. iessé.		74.		87.		100.	
62.		75.		88.			Car. de jupiter.
63.		76.		89.			
64.		77.		90.			
65.		78.		91. st. luc.			

hieroglyphes T.

T.		T.		T.		T.	
1.	Paul.	14.		27.		40.	
2.		15.		28.		41.	assioram.
3.		16.		29.		42.	
4.		17.		30.		43.	
5.		18.		31.	azor.	44.	
6.		19.		32.		45.	
7.		20.		33.		46.	
8.		21.	Andrea.	34.		47.	
9.		22.		35.		48.	
10.		23.		36.		49.	
11.	Sephas.	24.		37.		50.	
12.		25.		38.		51.	amarias
13.		26.		39.		52.	

T.4188.1 Fonds Prunelle de Lière 'The Registry of 2,400 Names'

hieroglyphen T.

T.		T.		T.		T.	
53.		66.		79.		92.	
54.		67.		80.		93.	
55.		68.		81. op. romaine.		94.	
56.		69.		82.		95.	
57.		70.		83.		96.	
58.		71. misrael en egipte		84.		97.	
59.		72.		85.		98.	
60.		73.		86.		99.	
61. iessé		74.		87.		100.	
62.		75.		88.			Car. du Soleil.
63.		76.		89.			
64.		77.		90.			
65.		78.		91. s. Luc.			

Caractères U.

U.		U.		U.		U.	
1.	St auguſtin	14.		27.		40.	
2.		15.		28.		41.	Levi.
3.		16.		29.		42.	
4.		17.		30.		43.	
5.		18.		31.	Belba.	44.	
6.		19.		32.		45.	
7.		20.		33.		46.	
8.		21.	iſaie	34.		47.	
9.		22.		35.		48.	
10.		23.		36.		49.	
11.	Ezechiel.	24.		37.		50.	
12.		25.		38.		51.	Mathias.
13.		26.		39.		52.	

T.4188.1 Fonds Prunelle de Lière 'The Registry of 2,400 Names'

Caracteres U.

U. 53.		U. 66.		U. 79.		U. 92.	
54.		67.		80.		93.	
55.		68.		81. op. de Beroï		94.	
56.		69.		82.		95.	
57.		70.		83.		96.	
58.		71. heli.		84.		97.	
59.		72.		85.		98.	
60.		73.		86.		99.	
61. Gabaniak et Noechita		74.		87.		100.	
62.		75.		88.			Car. de Mercure
63.		76.		89.			
64.		77.		90.			
65.		78.		91. Pitonitien			

The Green Book of the Élus Coëns

hieroglyphes U.

U.		U.		U.		U.	
1.	St Augustin	14.		27.		40.	
2.		15.		28.		41.	Levi.
3.		16.		29.		42.	
4.		17.		30.		43.	
5.		18.		31.	Belba.	44.	
6.		19.		32.		45.	
7.		20.		33.		46.	
8.		21.	Isaïe.	34.		47.	
9.		22.		35.		48.	
10.		23.		36.		49.	
11.	Ezechiel.	24.		37.		50.	
12.		25.		38.		51.	Mathias
13.		26.		39.		52.	

T.4188.1 Fonds Prunelle de Lière 'The Registry of 2,400 Names'

hieroglyphes U

U.		U.		U.		U.	
53.		66.		79.		92.	
54.		67.		80.		93.	
55.		68.		81. cap. de Beroi		94.	
56.		69.		82.		95.	
57.		70.		83.		96.	
58.		71. heli.		84.		97.	
59.		72.		85.		98.	
60.		73.		86.		99.	
61. gabaniak et nocchite		74.		87.		100.	
62.		75.		88.			Car. du Soleil.
63.		76.		89.			
64.		77.		90.			
65.		78.		91. pitonitieu			

✠ 333

Caractères V.

V.		V.		V.		V.	
1	Gédeon.	14.		27.		40.	
2.		15.		28.		41.	iudas.
3.		16.		29.		42.	
4.		17.		30.		43.	
5.		18.		31.	Rabboni.	44.	
6.		19.		32.		45.	
7.		20.		33.		46.	
8.		21.	iosué iesu.	34.		47.	
9.		22.		35.		48.	
10.		23.		36.		49.	
11.	ioel	24.		37.		50.	
12.		25.		38.		51.	op. dej brui mapp
13.		26.		39.		52.	

T.4188.1 Fonds Prunelle de Lière 'The Registry of 2,400 Names'

Caractères V.

V.		V.		V.		V.	
53.		66.		79.		92.	
54.		67.		80.		93.	
55.		68.		81. *Elisée.*		94.	
56.		69.		82.		95.	
57.		70.		83.		96.	
58.		71. *Caleb.*		84.		97.	
59.		72.		85.		98.	
60.		73.		86.		99.	
61. *Wumos achas*		74.		87.		100.	
62.		75.		88.			*Car. de mercure.*
63.		76.		89.			
64.		77.		90.			
65.		78.		91. *Chiram.*			

The Green Book of the Élus Coëns

hieroglyphes V.

V.		V.		V.		V.	
1	Gedeon.	14.		27.		40.	
2.		15.		28.		41.	iudas
3.		16.		29.		42.	
4.		17.		30.		43.	
5.		18.		31.	Rabboni	44.	
6.		19.		32.		45.	
7.		20.		33.		46.	
8.		21.	iosué iesu.	34.		47.	
9.		22.		35.		48.	
10.		23.		36.		49.	
11.	ioel	24.		37.		50.	
12.		25.		38.		51.	op. des 3 magi.
13.		26.		39.		52.	

T.4188.1 Fonds Prunelle de Lière 'The Registry of 2,400 Names'

hieroglyphes V.

V.		V.		V.		V.	
53		66.		79		92.	
54.		67.		80.		93.	
55.		68.		81. Elisée.		94.	
56.		69.		82.		95.	
57.		70.		83.		96.	
58		71. Caleb.		84.		97.	
59.		72.		85.		98.	
60.		73.		86.		99.	
61. idumos achas		74.		87.		100	
62.		75.		88.			Car. du Soleil
63.		76.		89.			IE
64		77.		90			IE
65.		78.		91. chiram			IE

Caractères Z.

N.		N.		Z.		Z.	
1	Gedeon.	14.		27.		40.	
2.		15.		28.		41.	Elisée.
3.		16.		29.		42.	
4.		17.		30.		43.	
5.		18.		31.	Egipte.	44.	
6.		19.		32.		45.	
7.		20.		33.		46.	
8.		21.	op. du Demon.	34.		47.	
9.		22.		35.		48.	
10.		23.		36.		49.	
11.	Beruch.	24.		37.		50.	
12.		25.		38.		51.	op. de Leviathan
13.		26.		39		52.	

T.4188.1 Fonds Prunelle de Lière 'The Registry of 2,400 Names'

Caractères Z

Z.		Z.		Z.		Z.	
53.		66.		79.		92.	
54.		67.		80.		93.	
55.		68.		81. Daniel.		94.	
56.		69.		82.		95.	
57.		70.		83.		96.	
58.		71. Paul.		84.		97.	
59.		72.		85.		98.	
60.		73.		86.		99.	
61. Melchisedec. a.d.		74.		87.		100.	
62.		75.		88.			Car. de Mercure
63.		76.		89.			
64.		77.		90.			
65.		78.		91. Isaac.			

hiéroglyphes
~~caractères~~. Z

Z.		Z.		Z.		Z.	
1.	Gédeon.	14.		27.		40.	
2.		15.		28.		41.	Elisée
3.		16.		29.		42.	
4.		17.		30.		43.	
5.		18.		31.	Egipte	44.	
6.		19.		32.		45.	
7.		20.		33.		46.	
8.		21.	op. du Demon.	34.		47.	
9.		22.		35.		48.	
10.		23.		36.		49.	
11.	Baruch.	24.		37.		50.	
12.		25.		38.		51.	Leviathan.
13.		26.		39.		52.	

T.4188.1 Fonds Prunelle de Lière 'The Registry of 2,400 Names'

hiéroglyphes 2.

№		№		№		№	
53.		66		79		92.	
54.		67		80		93	
55.		68.		81.		94	
					Daniel.		
56.		69		82.		95.	
57.		70.		83.		96.	
58.		71.		84.		97.	
			Paul.				
59		72.		85.		98.	
60		73.				99	
61.		74.				100	
	Melchisedech.						
62.		75					Car. du Soleil
63.		76.					
64.		77.					
65.		78.			isaac.		

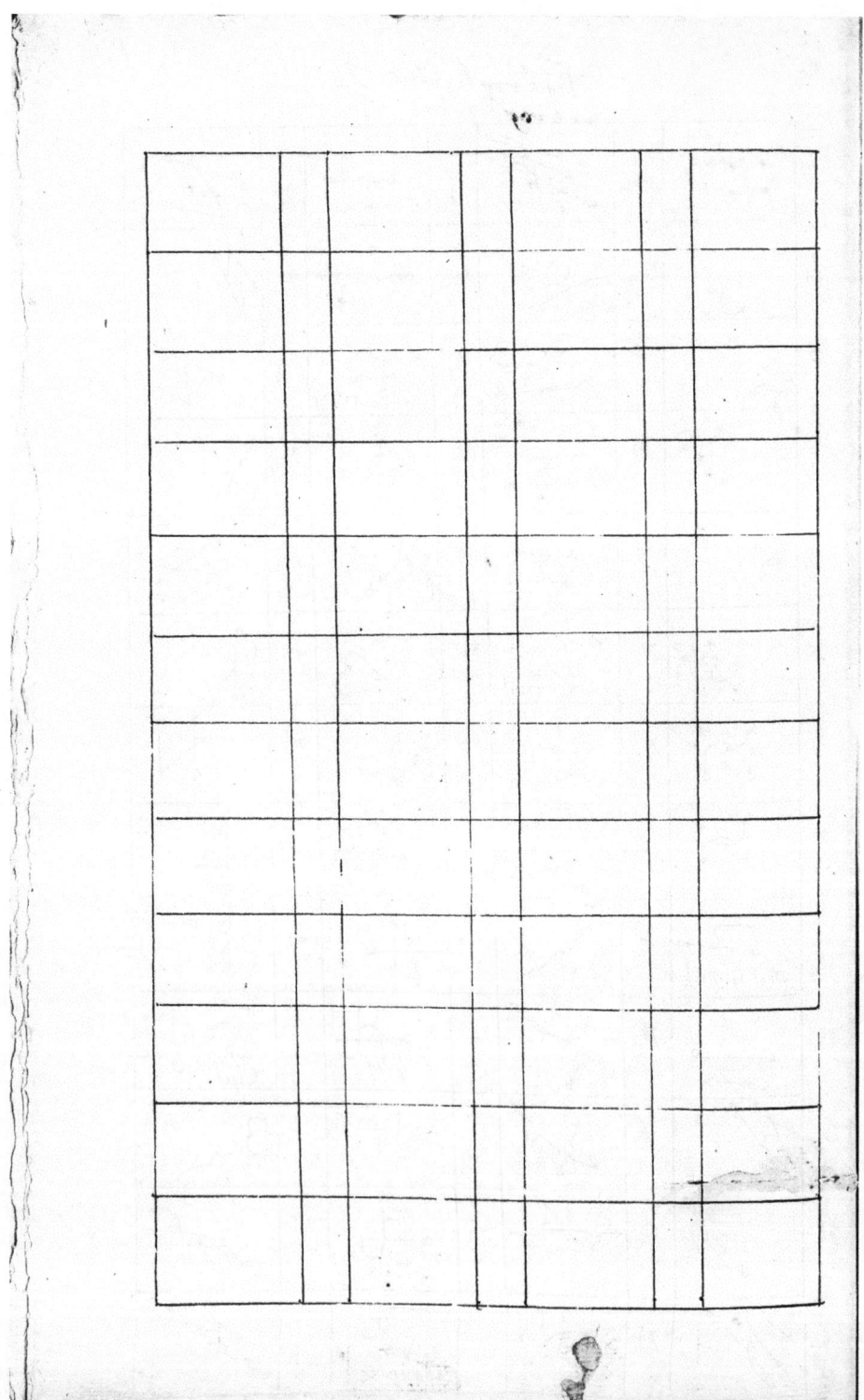

T.4188.1 Fonds Prunelle de Lière 'The Registry of 2,400 Names'

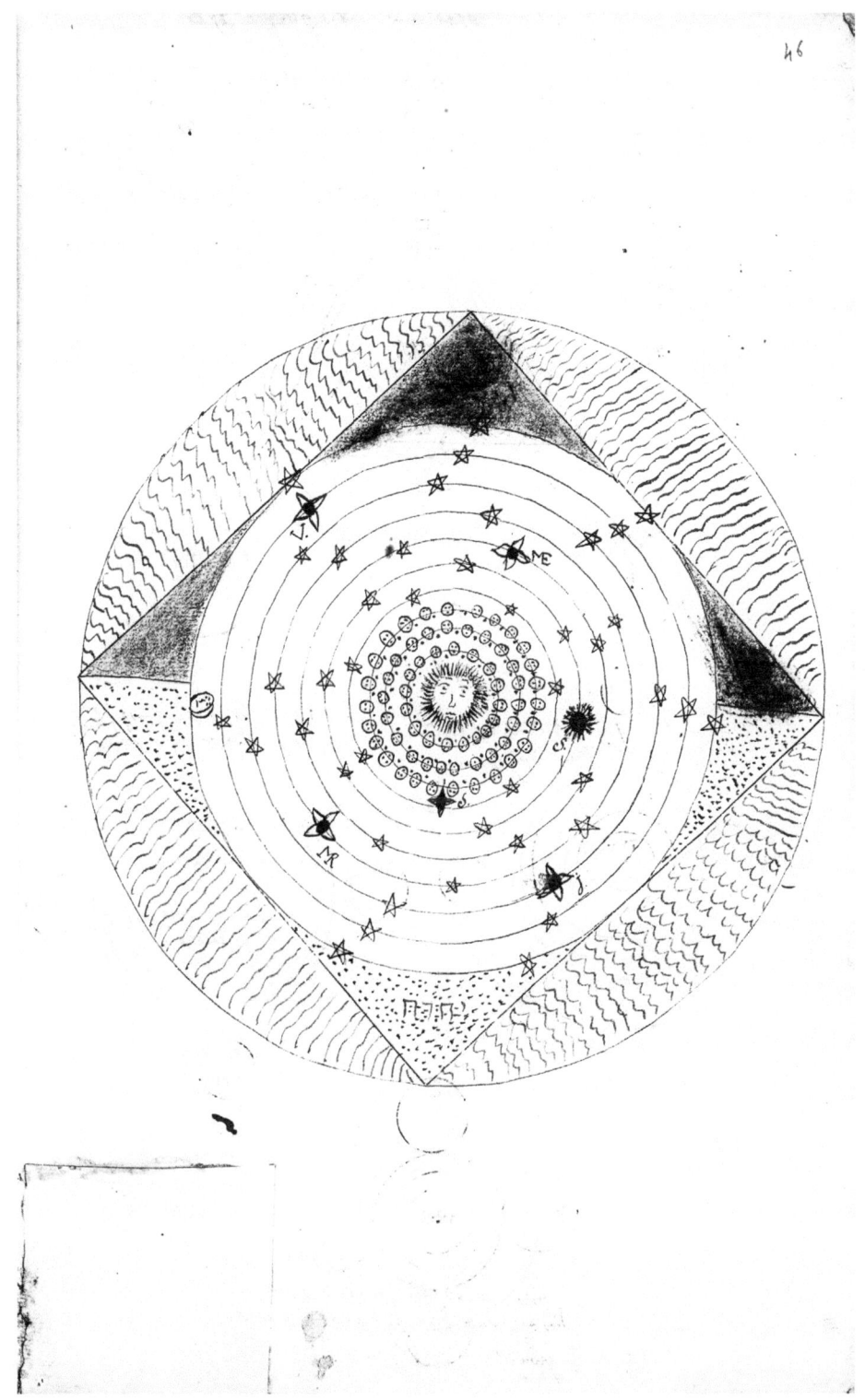

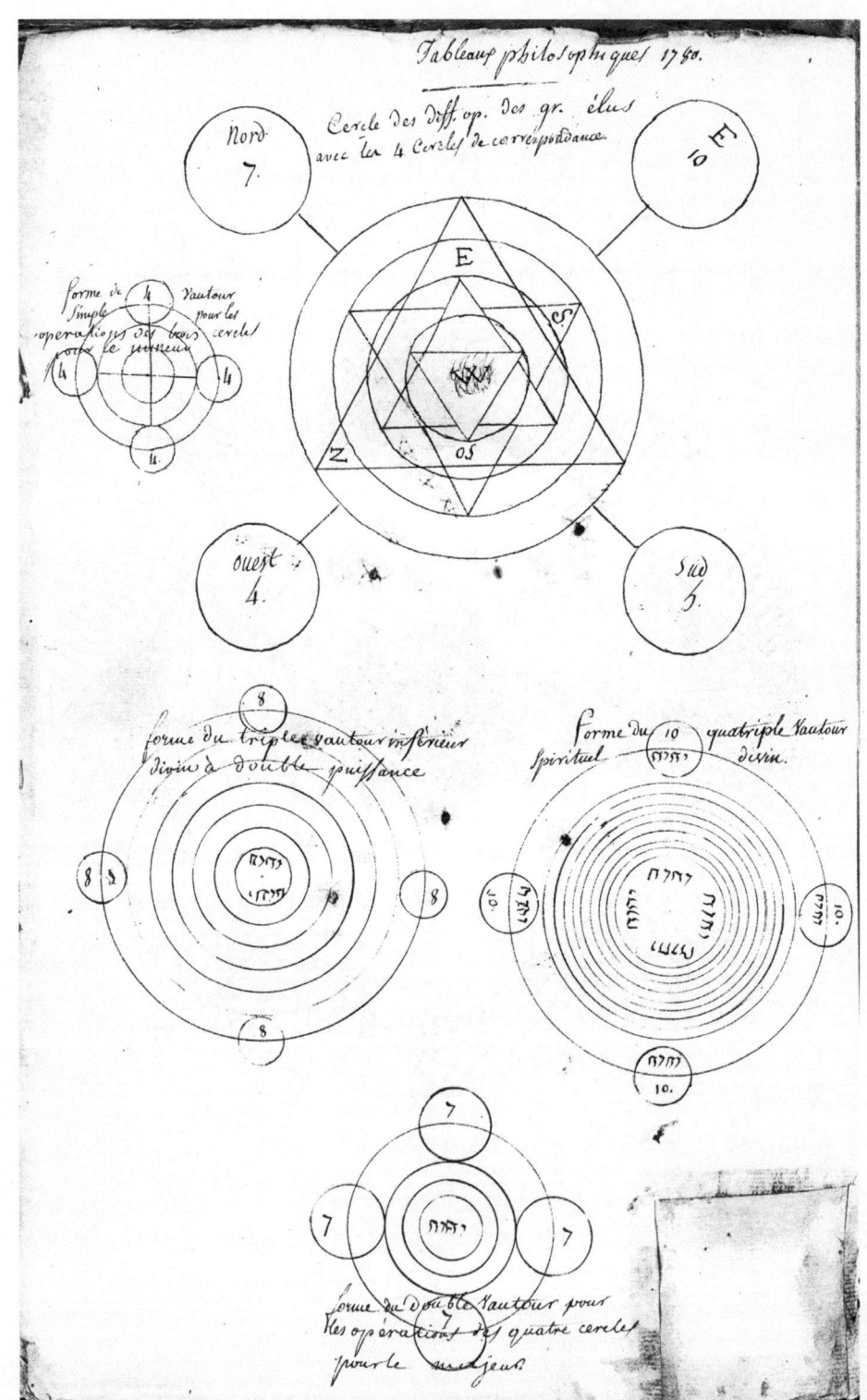

T.4188.1 Fonds Prunelle de Lière 'The Registry of 2,400 Names'

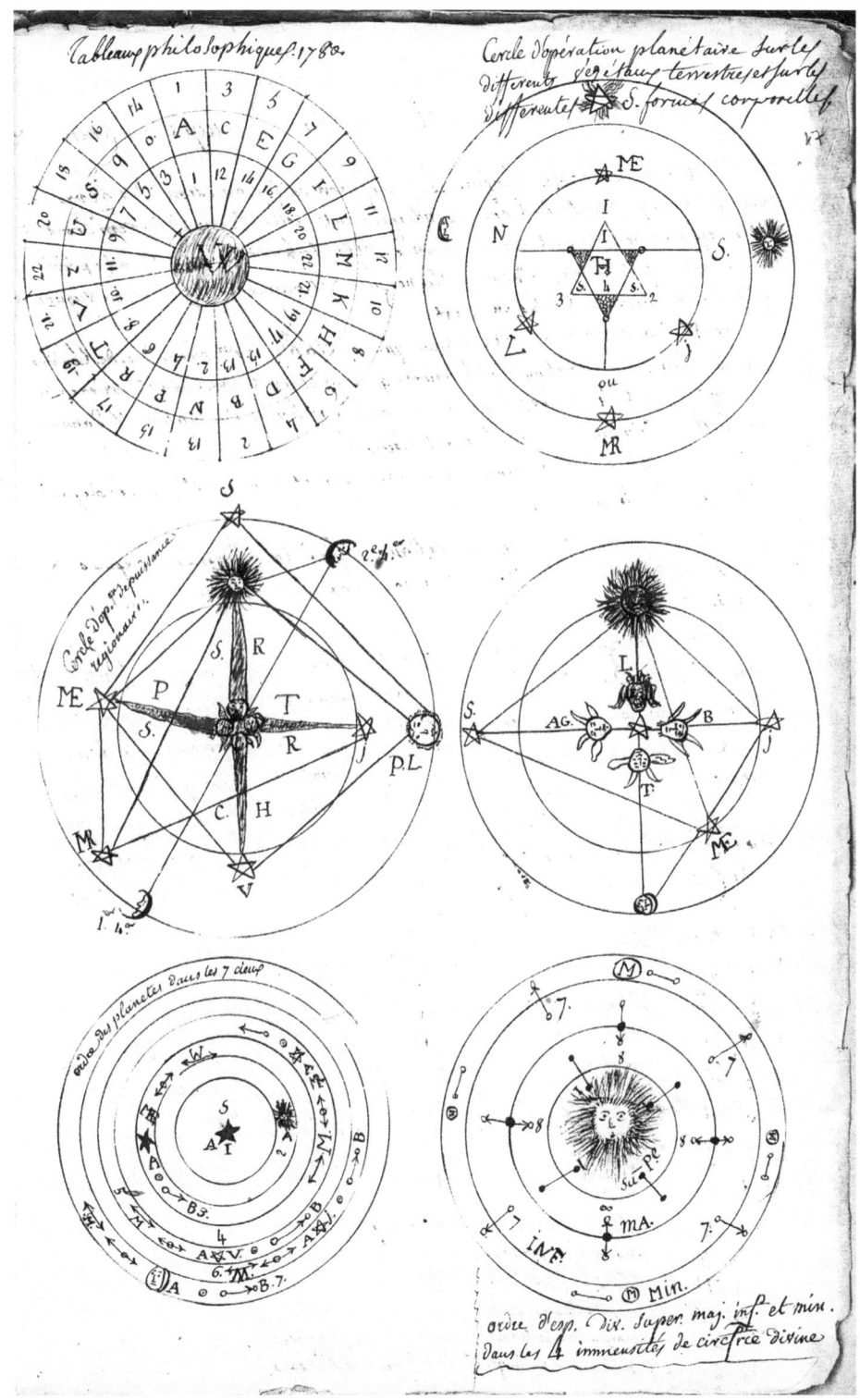

Instruction sur la Bougie du Centre. 1774

On nomme cette Cérémonie purfcaon ou Circoncision des Lèvres. Les 3 ppaux chefs de l'ord. pratiqueront cette Cérm. et la rem[p]ront telle qu'elle leur avait été enseignée. Elle Subsistait avant la captivité, mais elle fut alors perdue, elle ne fut retrouvée et remise en vigueur qu'à la renais. des Vertus en 2448.

Le 1er des 3 chefs est Abraham qui a établi le 1er mémoire de l'ordre par la Règle, la pratique et l'heure qu'il prescrivit pour la 1ère prière du jour qui durait 4 heures depuis 6 jusqu'à 10 heures du matin. Il donnait tout le Reste du jour à son travail temp[ore]l.

Le 2d Chef est Isaac qui pratiqua et fixa la 2e prière depuis Midi jusqu'à 4 heures.

Le 3e est Jacob qui pratiqua et fixa la 3e prière depuis 8 heures du Soir jusqu'à Minuit et consacra le reste de la nuit au Repos temp[orel].

Nous purifions nos lèvres à la flamme de la Boug. du Centre, afin que notre Bouche Soit pure pour prononcer le mot qui y est tracé, com[me] les patriarches chefs de l'ordre purifioient leurs Car. Alph. romains pour Servir de Com[me]n[t]. à celui qui opère pour apprendre à connoître par les d[i]ff. répétitions, les Chefs qu'il voudra Se procurer pour le Bien de son Ame, ainsi que les Car. seront produits Naturel[le]m[en]t par la force de l'op. ou et par la ferme parole et l'intention de Celui qui opère.

A. 1 יהוה, Dieu
B. 2 homme Divin
C. 3 forme corporelle
D. 4 ame ou homme divin
E. 5 loi et prévarication
F. 6 intellect Spir.l et op.on
G. 7 esp. bon et Comp.
H. 8 esp. Sup.r Divin
I. 9 nature de forme corporelle
K. 10 grace divine
L. 11 vertu contre la confusion
M. 12 op. de l'homme Dieu terrestre
N. 13 fruit d'op. spirituelle
O. 14 merite de peine
P. 15 avantage, production heureuse
Q. 16 recompense spirituelle
R. 17 béatitude, Succès d'opération Spir. divine
S. 18 adversité, persécution et abandon Spir. divin et perils
T. 19 Satisfaction d'hom-Dieu
U. 20 tentation peché
V. 21 prévarication, alliance d'esp. pervers
Z. 22 fatigue et inquietude d'ame et d'esp.

T.4188.1 Fonds Prunelle de Lière 'The Registry of 2,400 Names'

T.4188.8 THE DE LIÈRE SERPENT DRAWINGS

3   4188 (VII)

Ce cahier est fort enigmatique
bien qu'il soit évidemment une
illustration des doctrines et des divers
enseignements et méthodes de Dom
Martines de Pasqually.

Faut-il y voir un cahier de
dessins de l'Agent Inconnu ?
qui sont ainsi désignés sur le catalogue
que Willermoz dressa :
(" – Feuilles de tableaux préliminaires
    « figures informes – 6 avril 1785
) " – Exposition de l'œuvre universelle
    en écrit et en figures – id –
Lyon (Ms. 5477. p. 2)
(Il faudrait dans ce cas supposer
  que quelqu'un, St Martin (?) les
  aurait sans doute retouchés car il
  sont bizarres plutôt qu'informes…)

T.4188.8 The de Lière Serpent Drawings

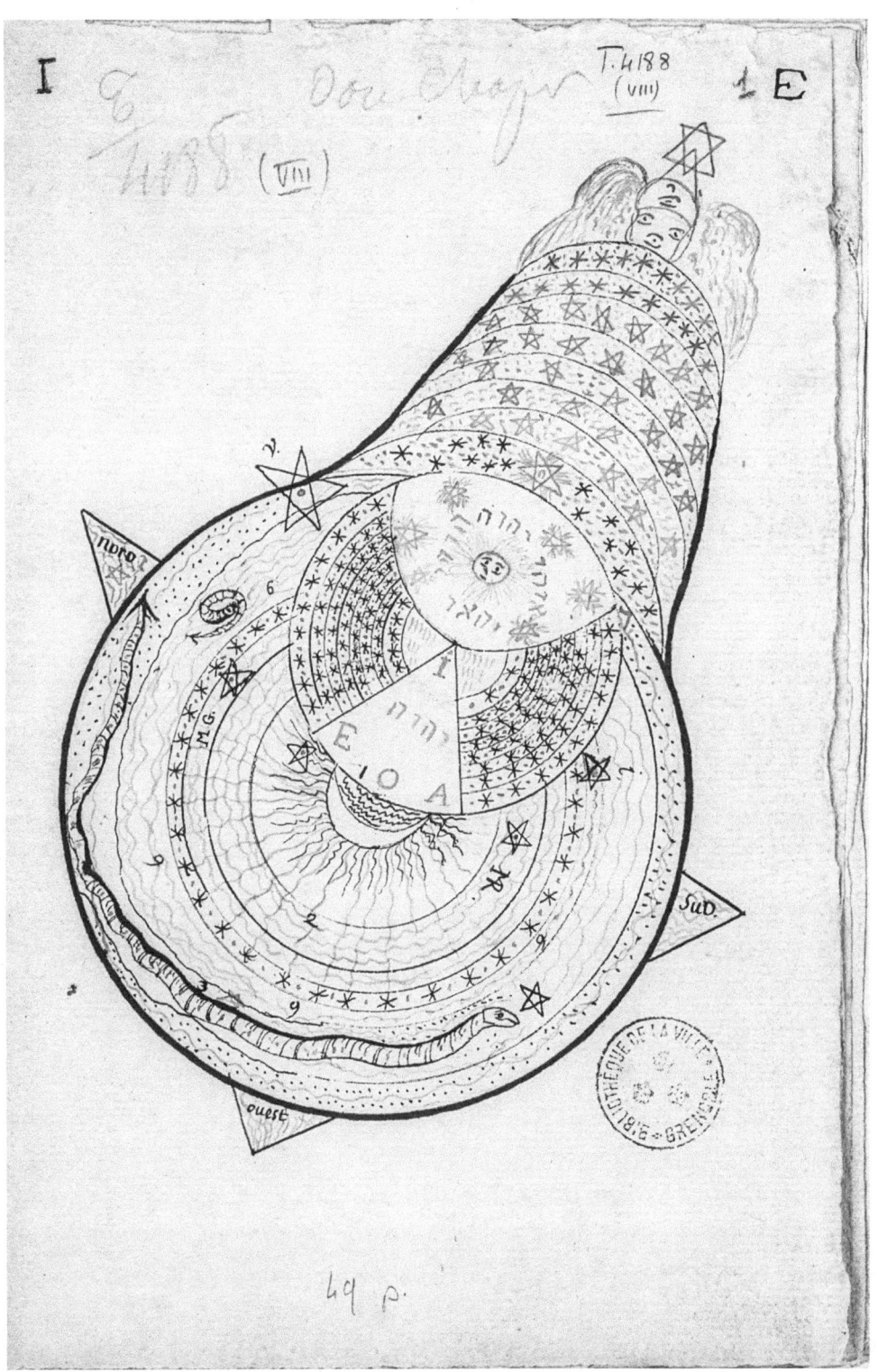

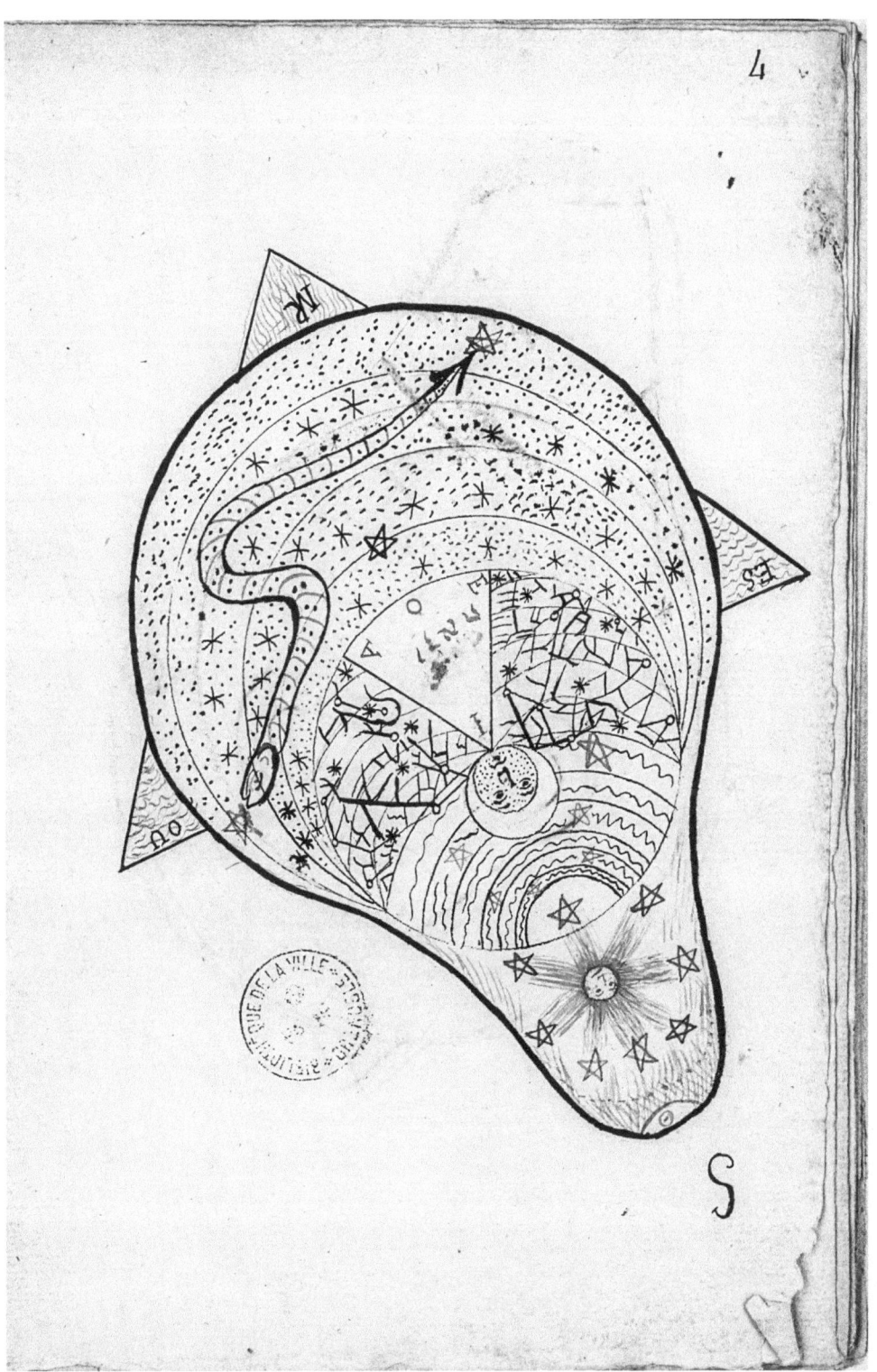

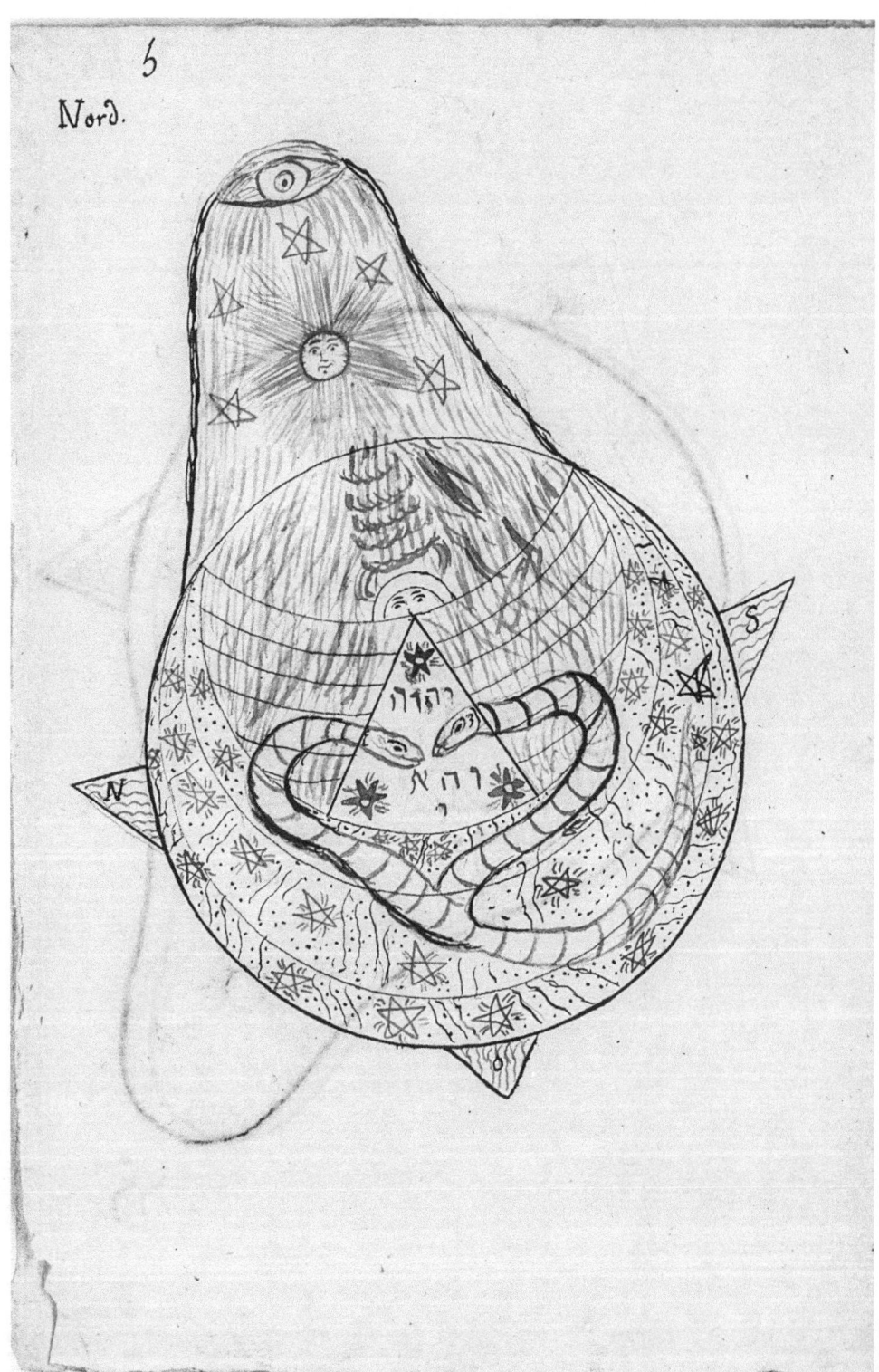

6

7.

T.4188.8 The de Lière Serpent Drawings

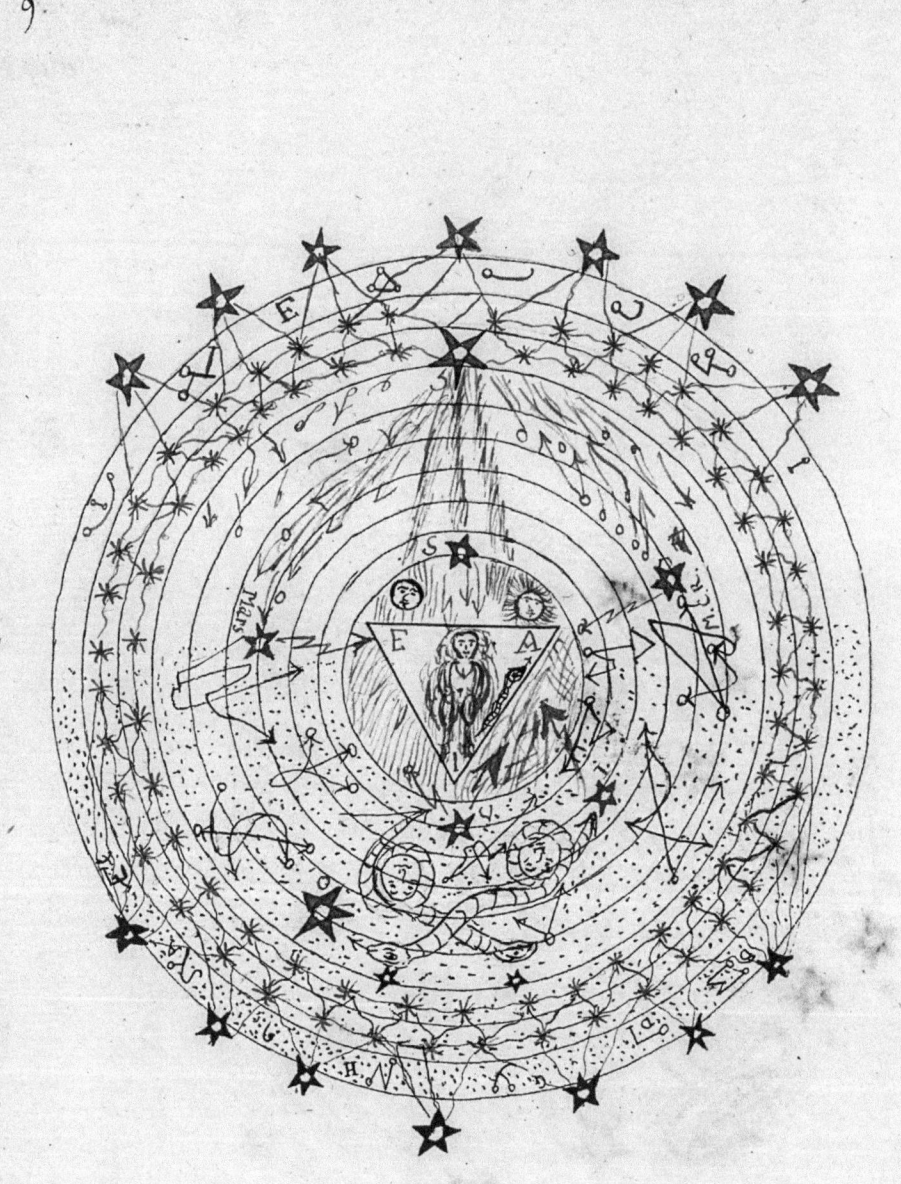

10

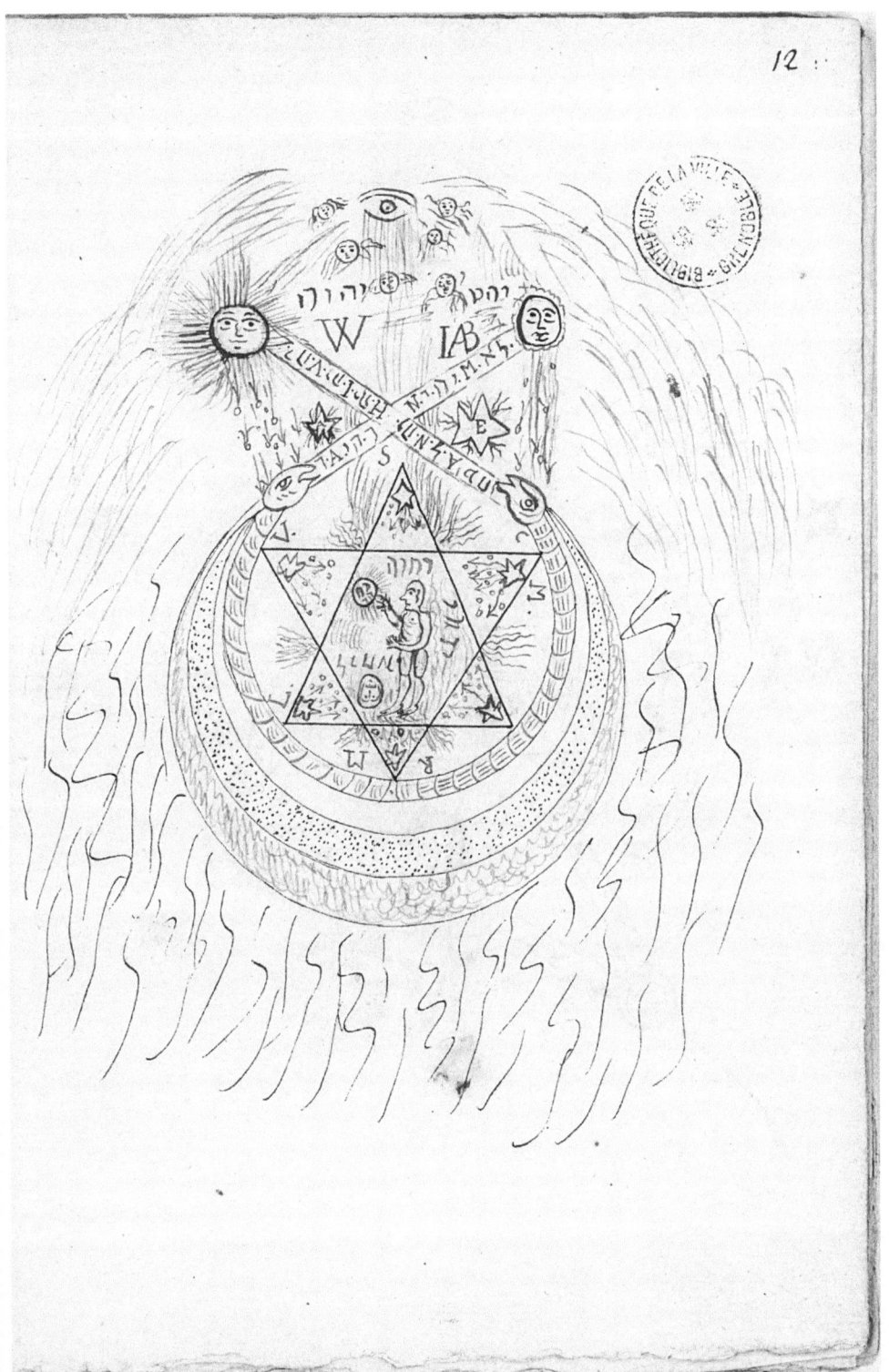

The Green Book of the Élus Coëns

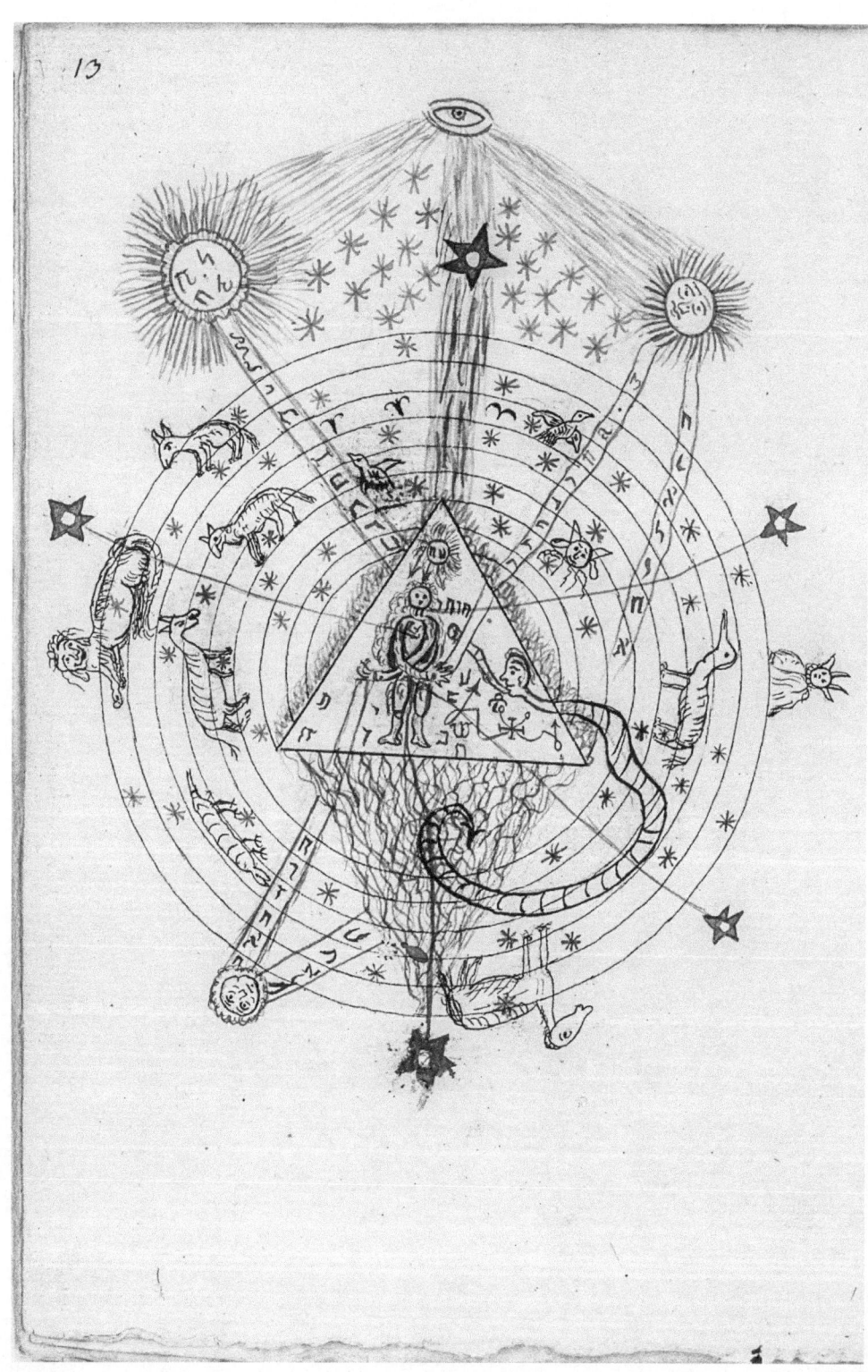

14

15.

T.4188.8 The de Lière Serpent Drawings

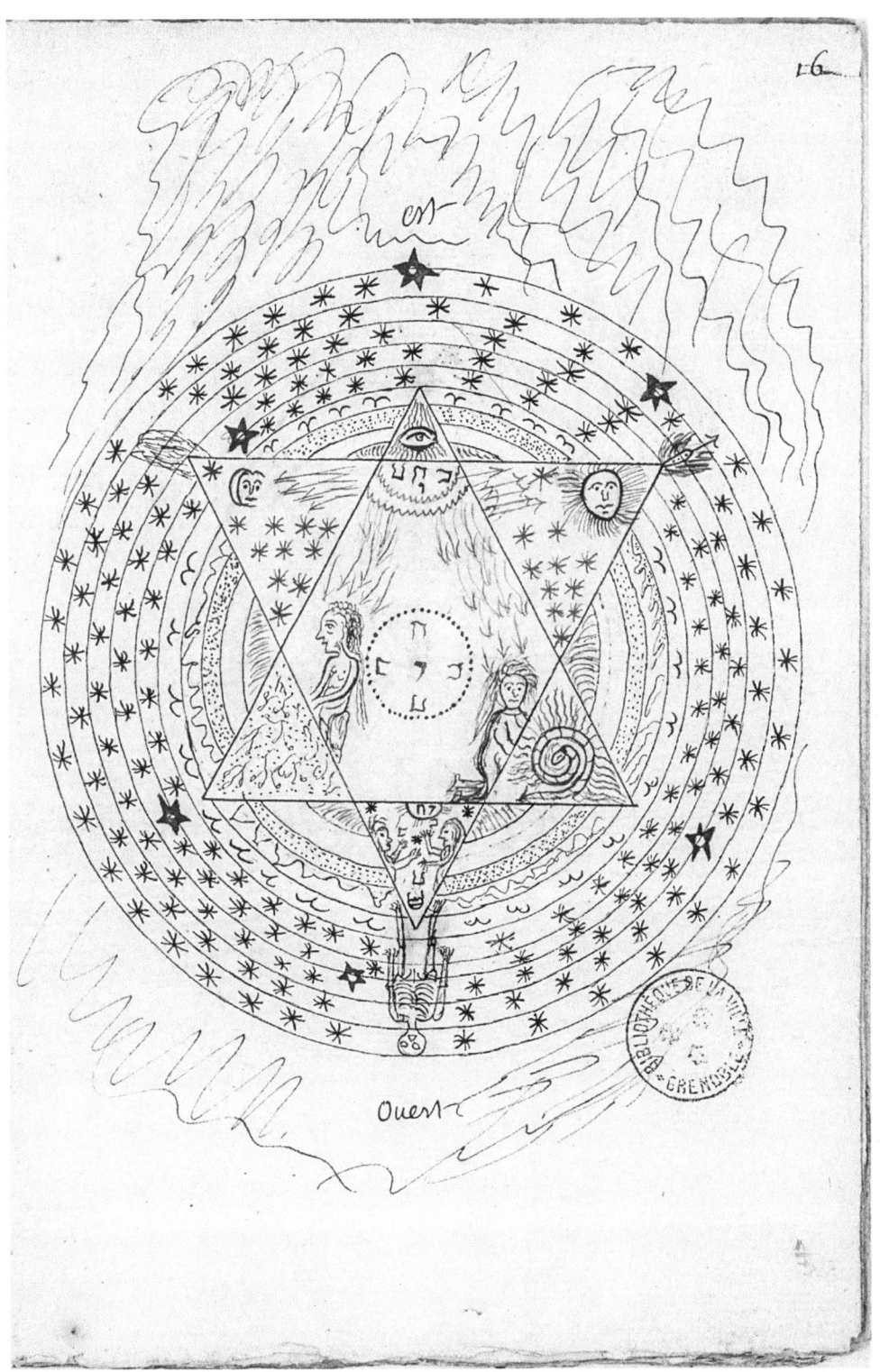

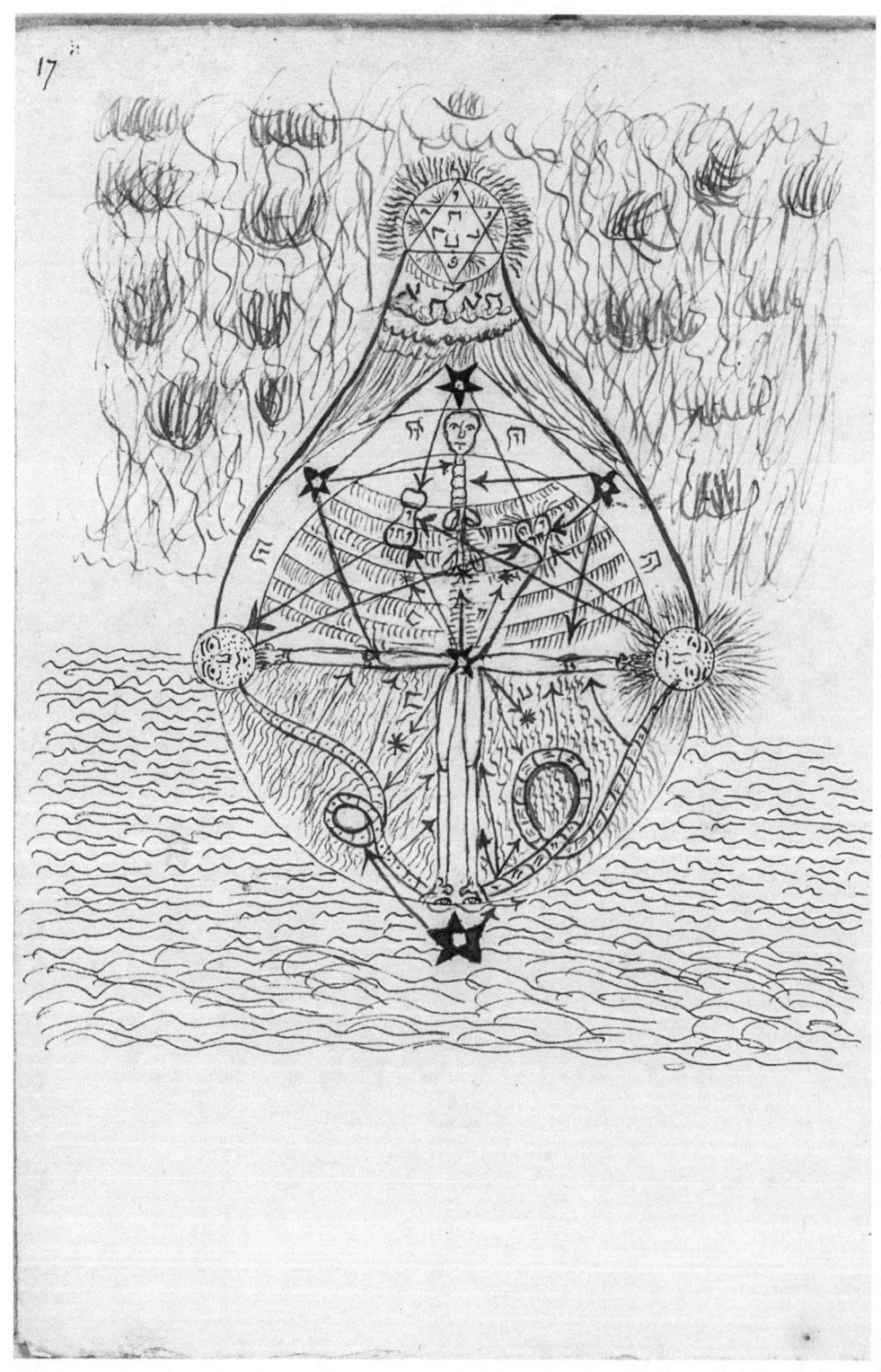

18

19.

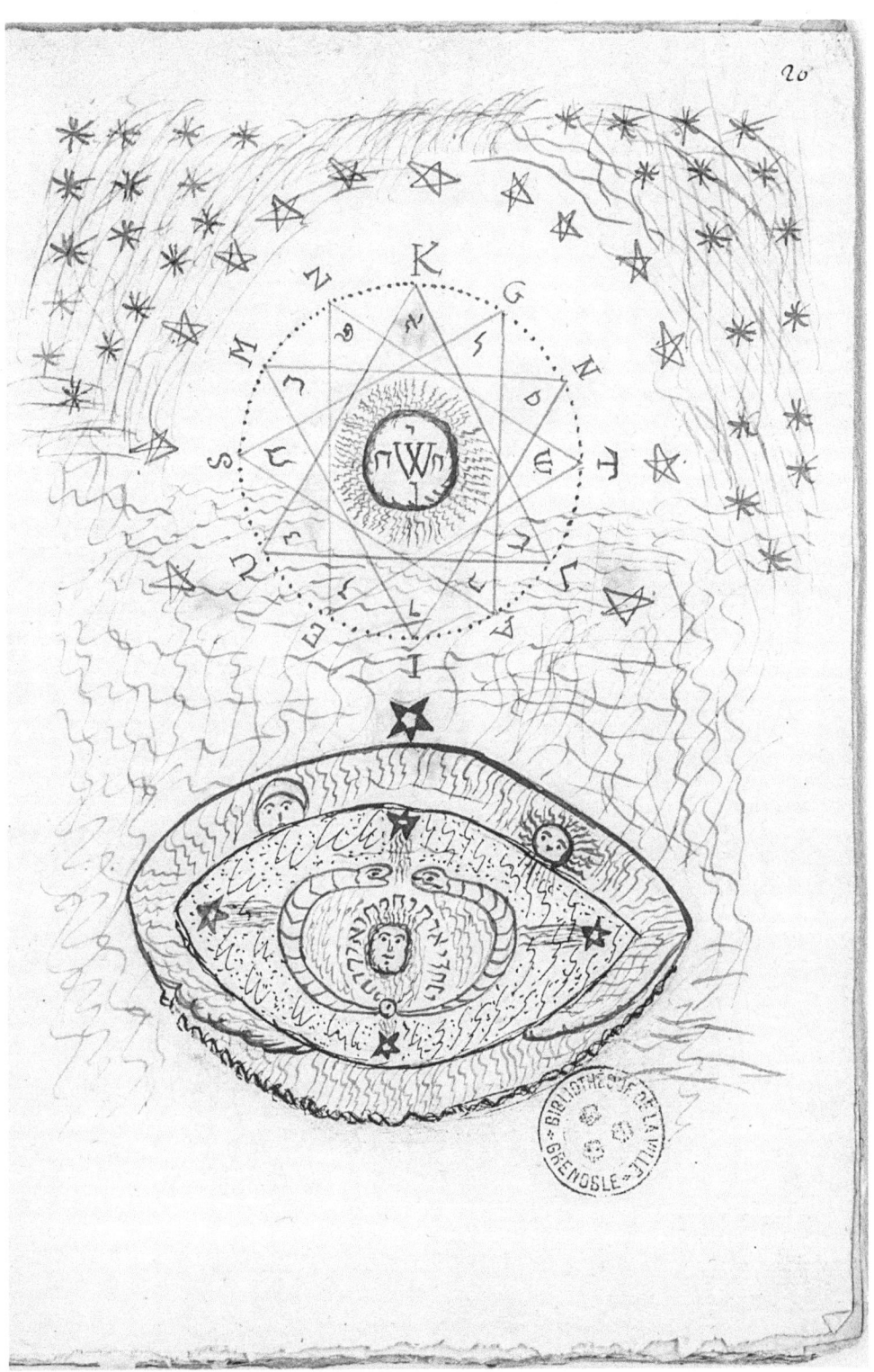

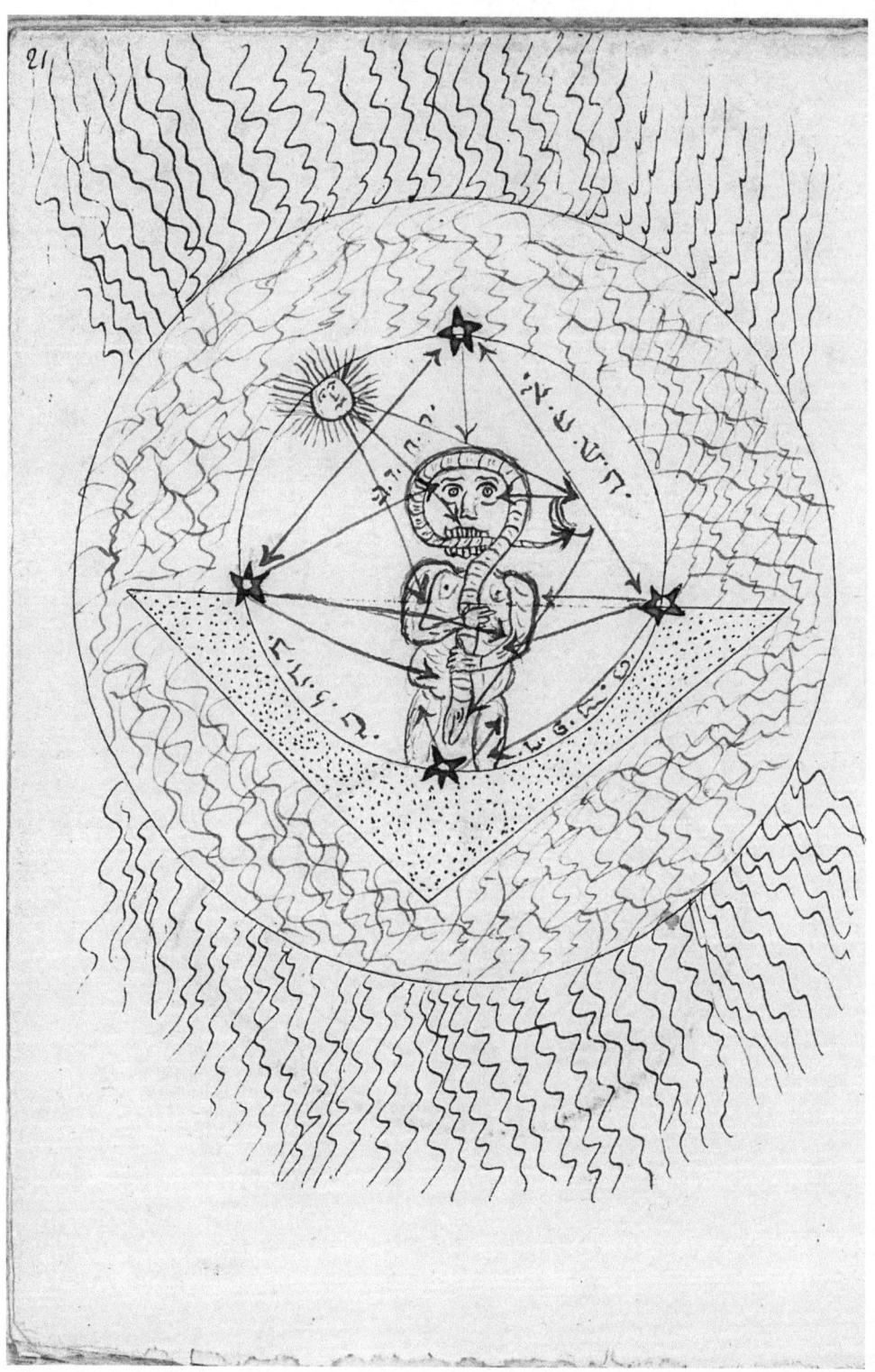

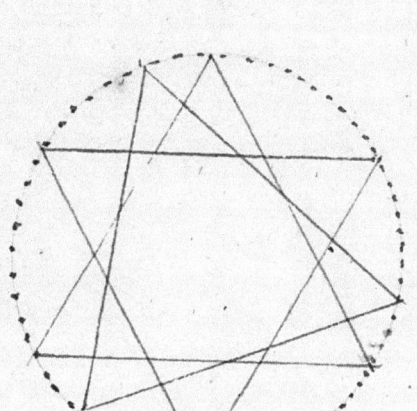

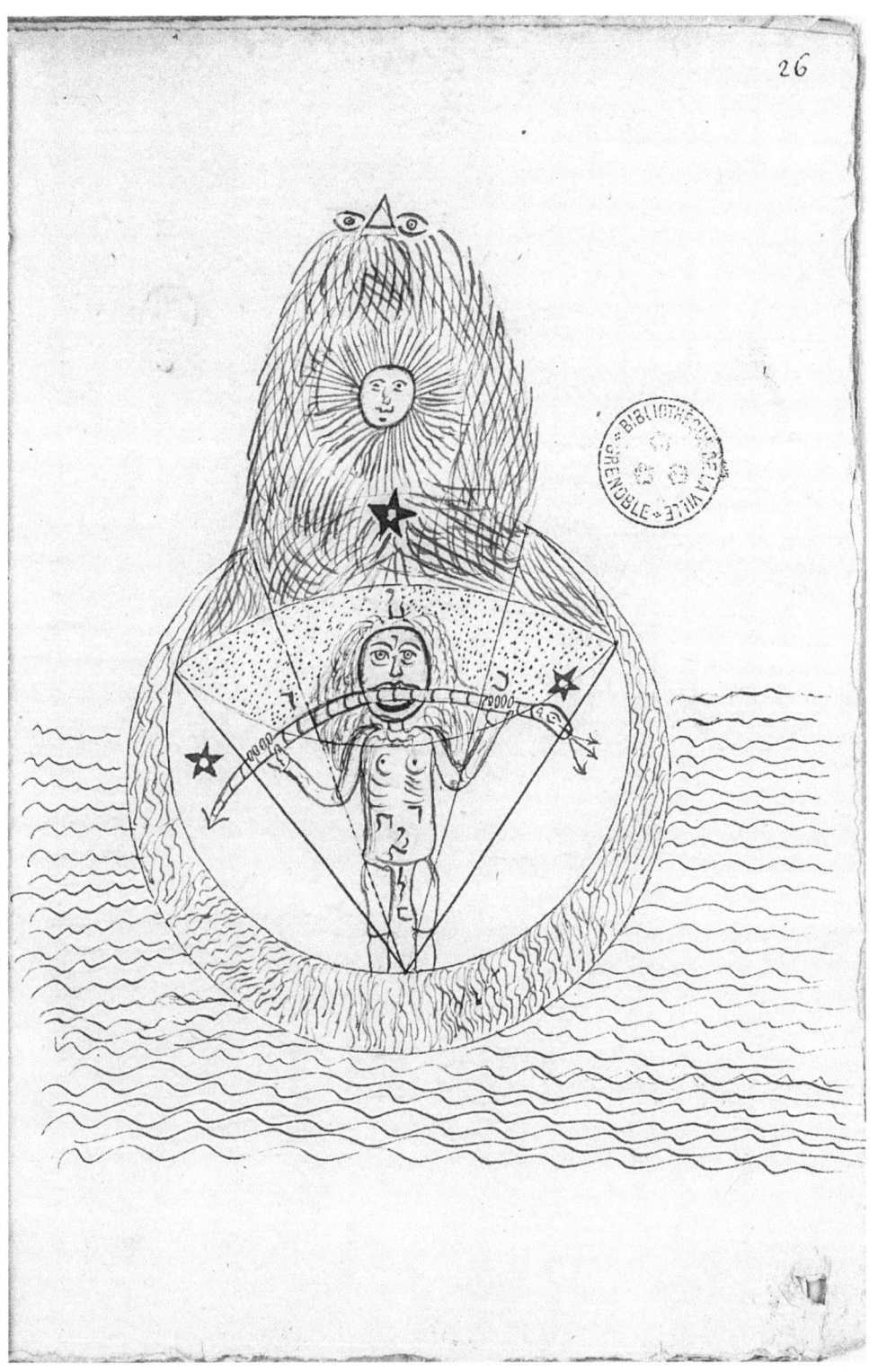

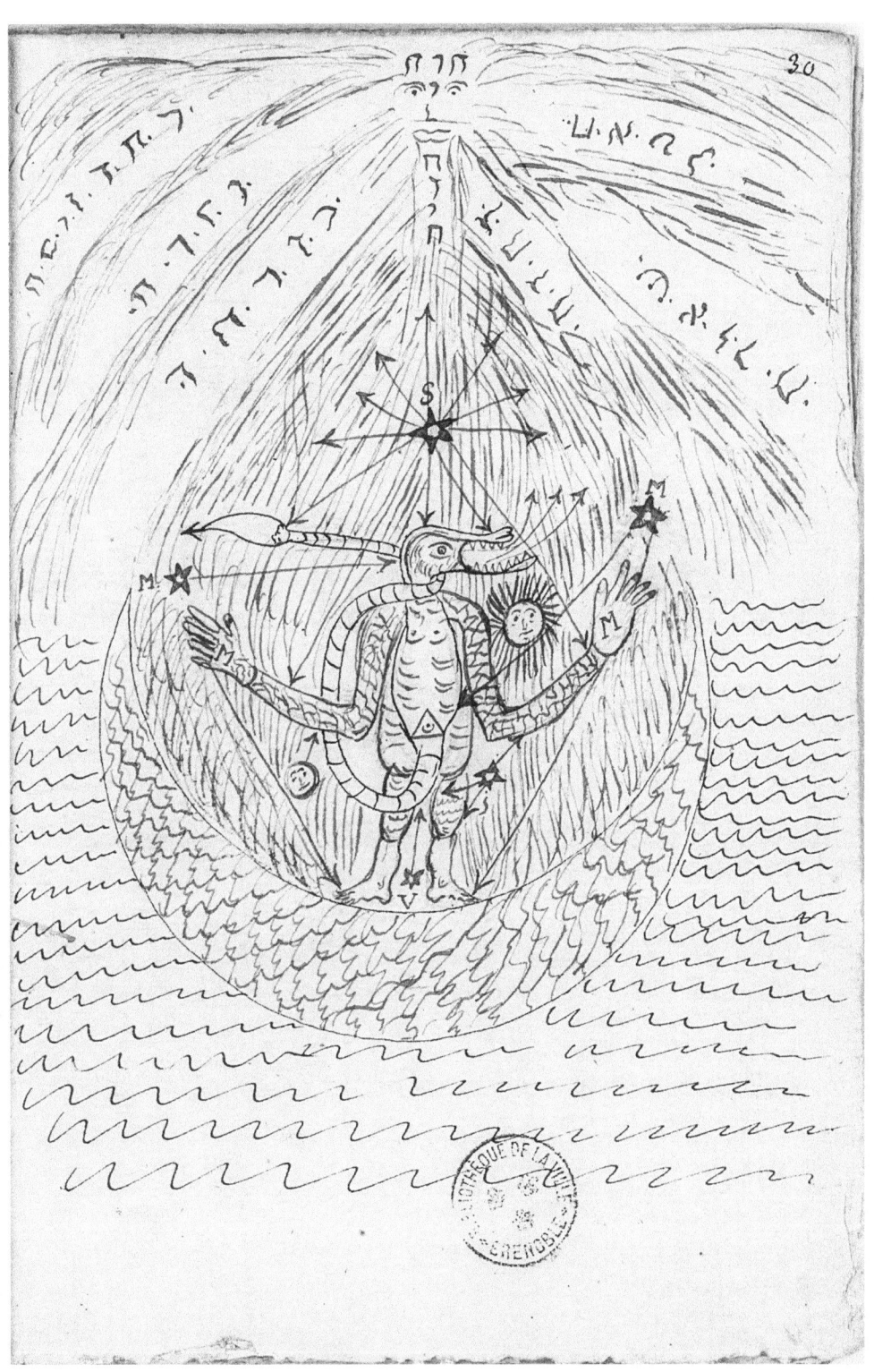

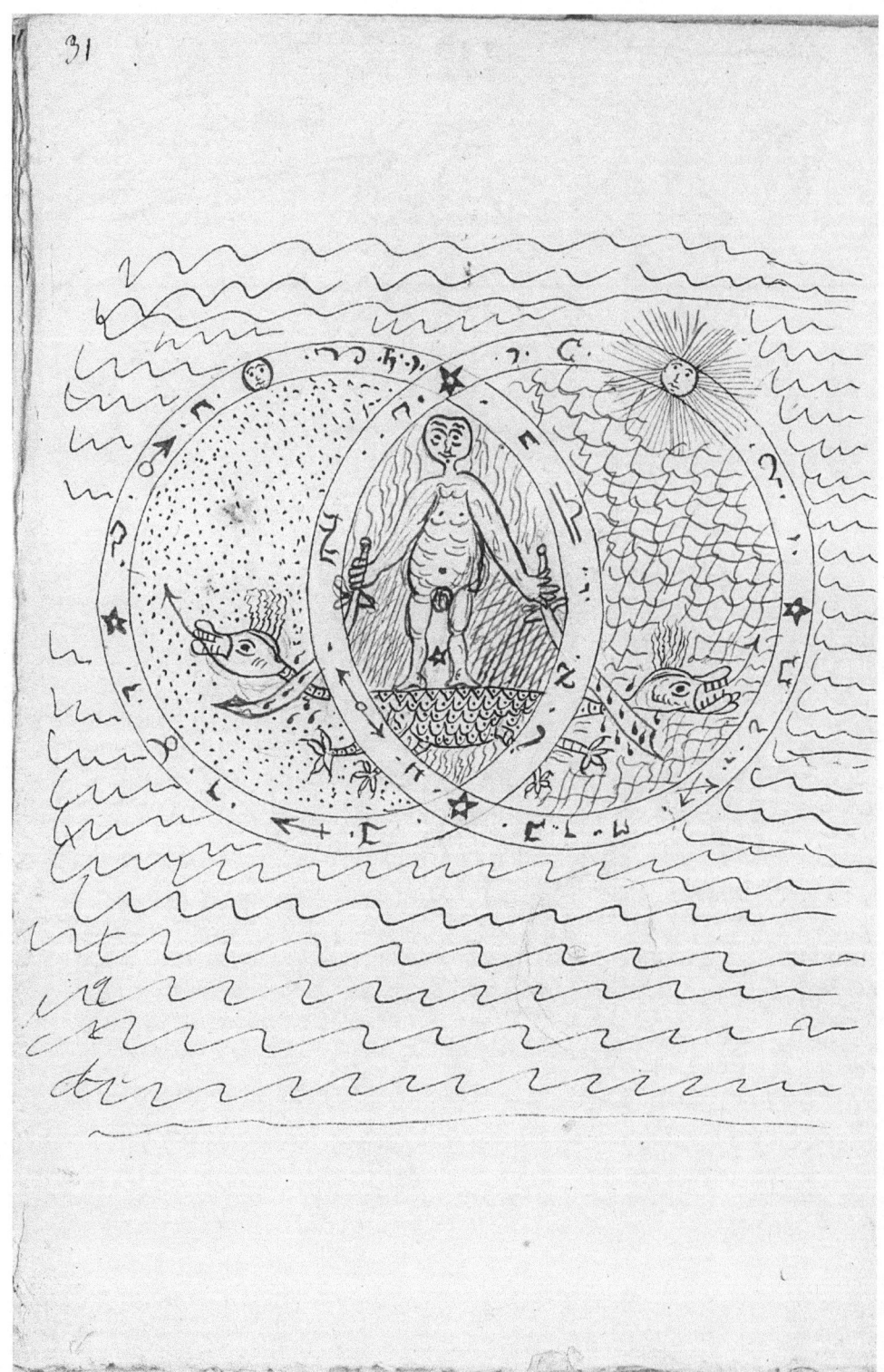

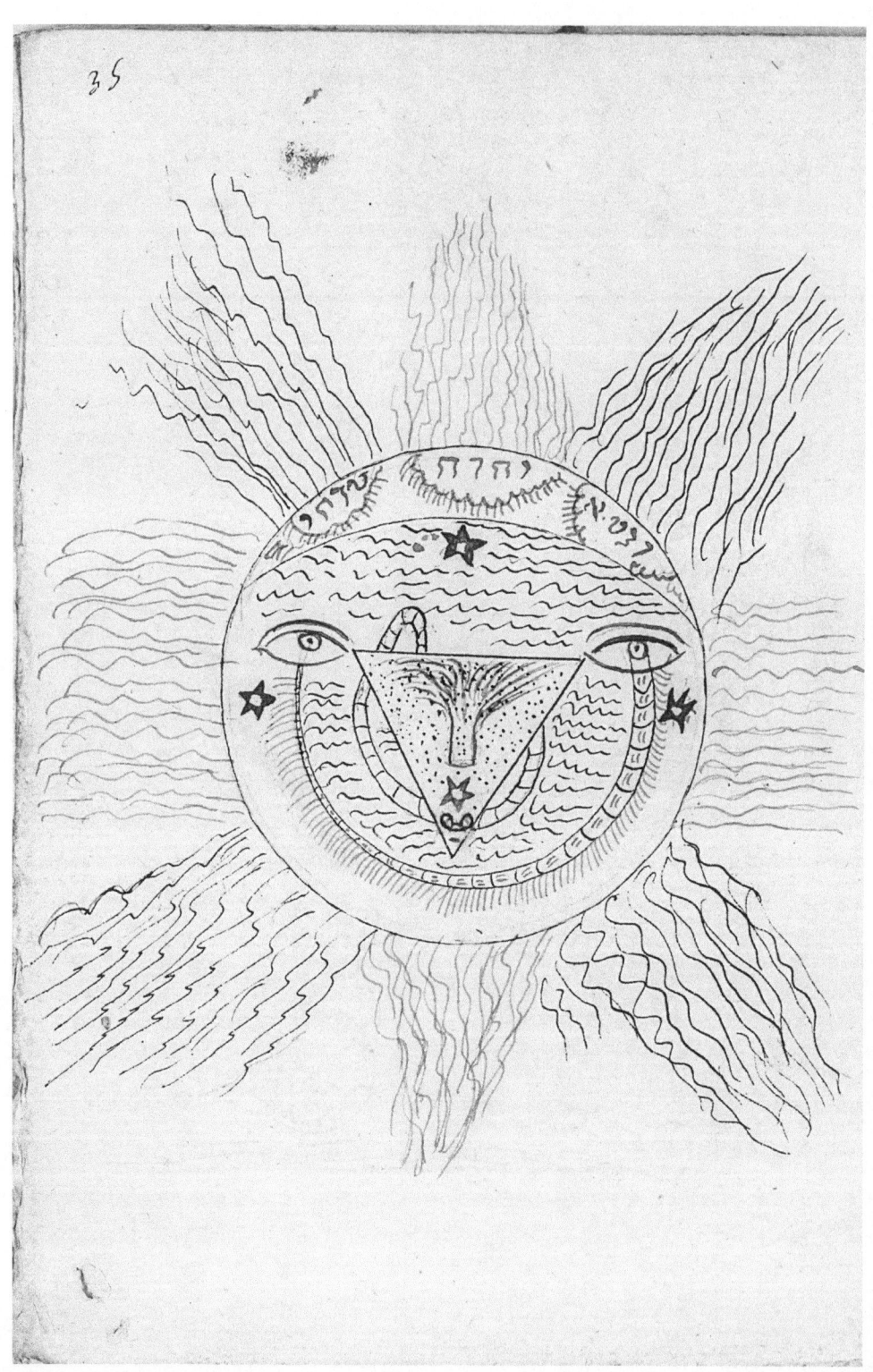

37

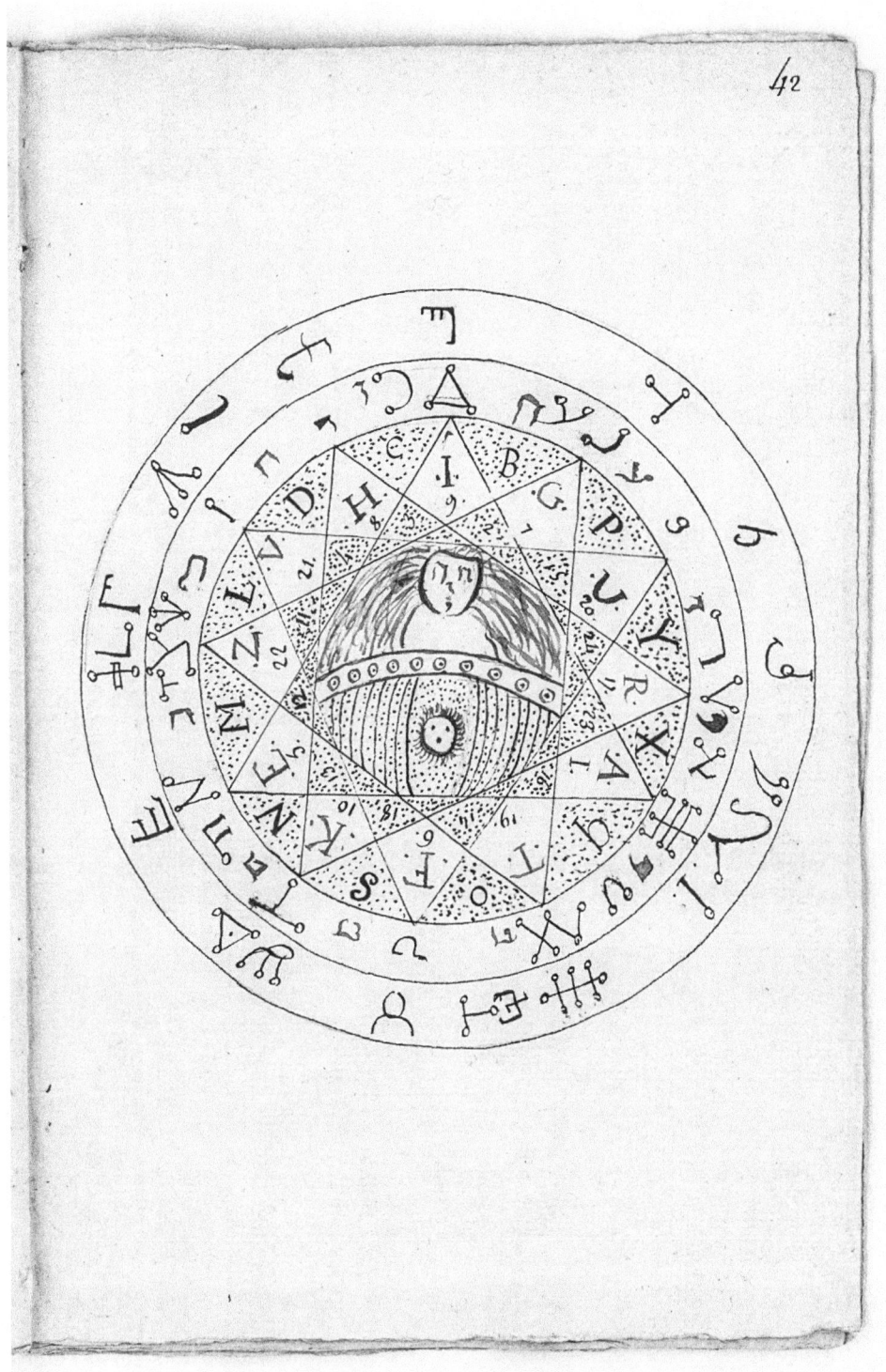

ECHELLE des nombres formant la figure terrestre dans toute sa forme corporelle tant en latitude qu'en courbe. Cette échelle sert encore pour observer la longitude de la surface terrestre au centre celeste. L'échelle de Longitude est celle de l'ouest à l'est, et celle de latitude est du nord au sud.

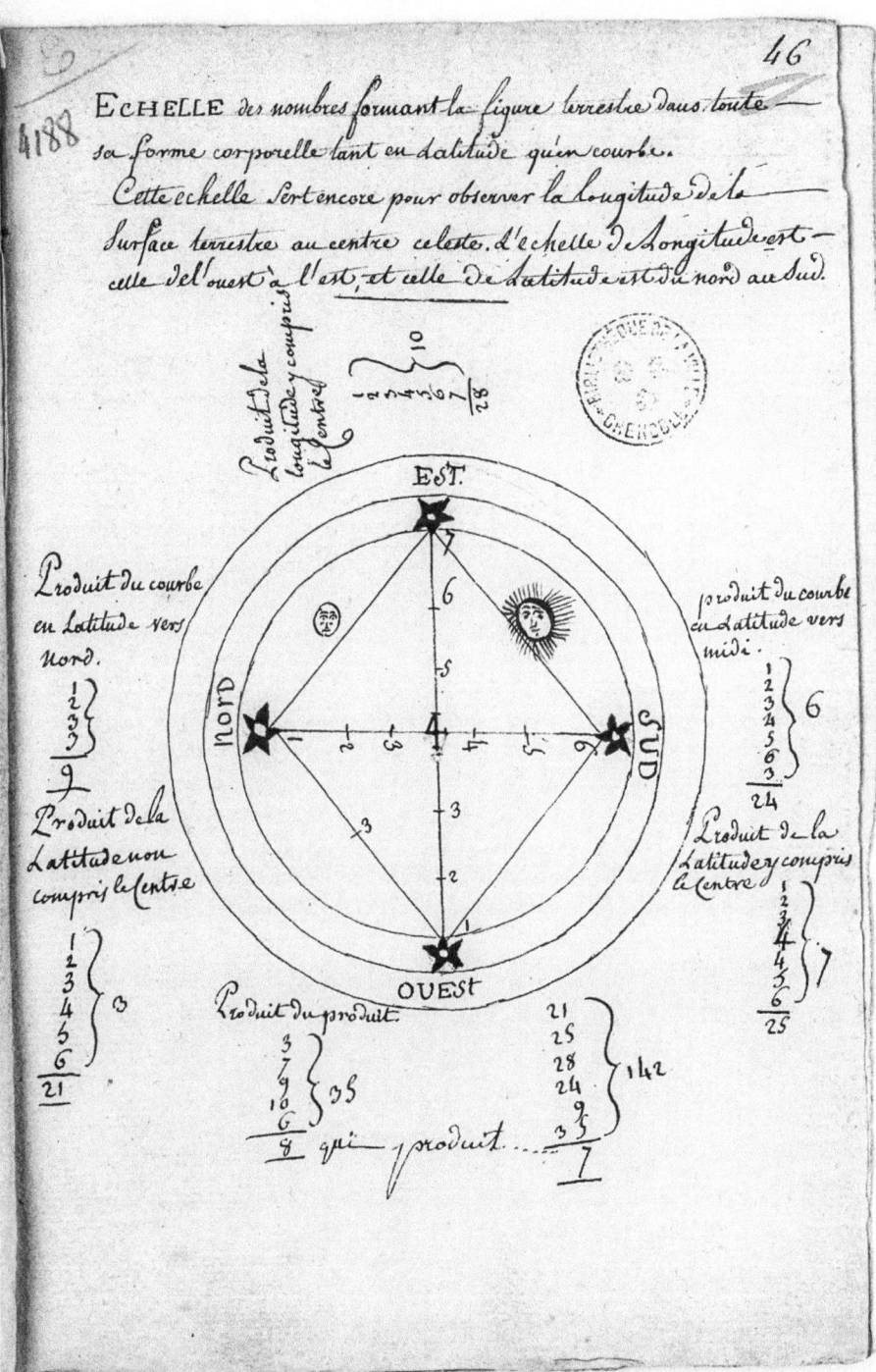

Appendix:
Catechisms of Coëns

APPENDIX.
CATECHISMS OF COCOA.

Appendix

Catechism of the Philosophers
Élus Coëns of the Universe (1770)

Q. Are you an Apprentice Coën?
A. Yes, M[ost] R[espectable] M[aster] I am.

Q. How were you received?
A. By the order of the R[espectable] M[aster] and that of the Temple.

Q. In what condition were you received an Apprentice Coën?
A. I was neither naked nor clothed, my body placed at the centre of six circles, forming a long square and four squares.

Q. What did you see when you were in that position during your stay in the circles?
A. I did not see or hear anything that the human mind could understand.

Q. Why was that?
A. Because my body was deprived of the use of all its senses.

Q. What do you see after your body had received the use of its senses?
A. I saw first a vast light, and I heard a terrible noise, and I drew near three great columns, one of the Wind to the North, the other of Cloud to the South and the other of Fire to the East.

Q. Did you notice the hieroglyphics that were written on it?
A. Yes, M[ost] R[espectable] M[aster].

Q. What do these hieroglyphs represent on these three columns?
A. The hieroglyph on the Northern column represents to us the wisdom that the true Coëns must have in order to enjoy the rights and privileges that the Order offers them at every moment of their life.

Q. What are these rights and privileges?
A. The knowledge of the three parts that make up the human body, its existence, and our Master.

Q. What does the hieroglyph represent on the South column?
A. That no man can attain the perfect knowledge which the Order offers to every zealous Brother without himself developing the mysteries which are designated by this hieroglyph.

Q. How can he discover something so hidden?
A. By working tirelessly for the general good of the Order, he will thereby acquire the benevolence of the chiefs who work with him to ensure he enjoys the rights and the fruits that he alone must draw from his labours.

Q. What does the hieroglyph represent on the Eastern column?
A. The powerful instruments that the G[reat] A[rchitect] employed for the construction of his Universal Temporal Temple.

Q. What shape does this vast Temple have?
A. It has a triangular shape from North to South and extended to the East.

Q. How deep is it?
A. From the surface to the centre.

Q. How tall is it?
A. Numberless cubits.

Q. Who covers it?
A. A heavenly canopy dotted with stars.

Q. What shape does this Temple have?
A. A long square.

Q. What is its length?
A. 300 cubits.

Q. What is its width?
A. 200 cubits.

Q. How tall is it?
A. 600 cubits.

Q. How deep is it?
A. 70 cubits.

Appendix

Q. How much of it do you divide?
A. In 3, in 5 and in 7.

Q. What does the 1st division by 3 represent to you?
A. The three chief leaders of the creation of the Universal Temple who were represented to us by the three chief leaders who built the Temple of the Lord on the Holy Mountain Moria of Jerusalem.

Q. How do you name them?
A. Solomon, Chiram[1] and Hiram.

Q. What do the three chiefs of the construction of the so-called Temple of Solomon represent to you, and how were they figured in the Temple?
A. Solomon is represented by the column of the North, Hiram King of Tire by that of the South, and Chiram by that of the East.

Q. How do you name these three columns?
A. Iu, Din, Ya.

Q. What do these three words represent?
A. Iu was the hieroglyphic word which was placed on the column of the North and which designated wisdom; Din, which was placed on the column of the South, designated the strength of his crime; and Ya was on that of the East, it designated the beauty of the construction of the Temple of the Lord.

Q. What are the different numbers that were attached to these columns?
A. On that of the North 3, on that of the South 5 and that of the East, 7.

Q. What do the three numbers 3, 5, 7 represent?
A. The number 3 represents the three different ways that the G[reat] A[rchitect] was employed in the construction of the first Universal Temple. The number 5 represents its ruin; and the number 7 his reconciliation.

Q. How many temples are there, in what places and for whom were they raised?
A. There are 7 kinds. The first is in the East for the G[reat] A[architect of the] U[niverse] by *Hely* and *Adam*. The 2nd by *Kain* towards the South, the 3rd by *Enoch* to the North, the 4th by *Noah* on the waters, the 5th by *Abraham* between East and West, the 6th by *Moses* in the promised land, and the 7th by *Solomon* in *Jerusalem*.

---

1 Hiram Abiff. French phonetical Hebrew spelling.

Q. How many kinds of philosophies are in use today in the world?
A. Of 5 kinds: to know the symbolic, the theoretical, the practical, the composite and the apocryphal.

Q. What does symbolic philosophy teach?
A. To get closer to the mysterious knowledge that the G[reat] A[rchitect] employed in the construction of the Universal Temple which He Himself built by His own Eternal Word.

Q. What does the theoretical teach?
A. It demonstrates the symbols that are analogous to the mysteries that the G[reat] A[rchitect] employed in the construction of His Temple. It is only by the theoretical that we can manage to use more particularly the attributes which are in use in the Order and which are the reward of the works of the ff [brethren].

Q. What does the practical teach?
A. It teaches building on both spiritual and material bases.

Q. What does the composite teach?
A. It teaches us the different orders that have been in the various nations of the whole World, their prevarication, their remission and their expulsion by order of the G[reat] A[rchitect].

Q. What does the apocryphal teach?
A. Nothing that can be analogous to true philosophy.

Q. Why do they use a square, a compass, a perpendicular, a level, and others instruments belonging to the Order?
A. Because the apocryphal philosophers could not obtain from us the true mysterious ceremonies which the Order contains and teach, which has caused many persons to attribute to themselves some of our instruments and assembling themselves in their own right arrogating the title of workmen of Solomon's Temple.

APPENDIX

Q. What are their words and what do they mean in the order of construction of Solomon's Temple?

A. The word *Jakin Tubalkain*[2] designates a column which was near the so-called Temple where the Apprentice assembled to receive their pay, it was placed towards the North. There was another which served the Fellows for the same purpose; it was placed towards the South and was named *Booz* and *Schiboleth*[3]. The word they call being that of the Master is *Mak-Benac* and *Giblin*.[4] The word of Elu[5] is the one they give to those they claim to have avenged the death of Chiram, it is *Nekum* or *Nekam*[6]. Those of the Scots[7] are *Neder Berry* and *Salmon*[8]; those of the Knights of the East are *Judah Benjamin* and *Zerubbabel;* the password: *freedom,* one answers: *revenge;* the secret word of Elu is *Moabon;* password: *Abiram.* The murderers are Hiram and Hoben, and the password is *helcam;* other Scottish words are *Jakin Schiboleth, Moabon, Gabon, Mahakin;* Prince of Jerusalem, the word is *Ador* Knight of the Sun, the word is *Stibion*[9] for the pass; the knight is the oldest rank, the words are: *Shem,* the other says: *Ham,* and the other: *Japheth.* Sovereign Commander of the Temple their word is *inry*[10], the password is Salomon. The Sovereign of Rose-Croix, his word is *inry* and the one who passes is *Emmanuel.* Prince of the Black Eagle, the word is *messias,* the word that passes is *och.* The Illustrious English Provost Judge of Solomon, the word is *tile.* Whoever passes *zinchu,*[11] the Perfect Master, the word is *Jeva Moabum.* The password is *Sabalon.*[12]

---

2 French Moderns spelling of Jachin and Tubal Cain. Note that the Moderns version of the word and password of an Entered Apprentice are inverted from the Antients word and Password of an Entered Apprentice. This was the original word and password, and was inverted by the Antients as a means of distinction between their members and the rival Moderns Grand Lodge.
3 French Moderns spelling of Boaz and Schiboleth. Note that the Moderns version of the word and password of a Fellow Craft are inverted from the Antients word and Password of a Fellow Craft. This was the original word and password, and was inverted by the Antients as a means of distinction between their members and the rival Moderns Grand Lodge.
4 French Moderns spelling of the Master Word and Password. Note that these are the Moderns version of the word and password of a Master Mason, and these were changed by the Antients as a means of distinction between their members and the rival Moderns Grand Lodge. Corruption of Mac-Benac and Giblim.
5 Elect of the Nine.
6 French word for the Elect of the Nine degree.
7 Perfect Elect Master.
8 Corruption of Berith, Neder, Selemouth, from the 14° Perfect Elect Master.
9 Corruption of Stibium.
10 I.N.R.I. Latin. Iesus Nazarenus Rex Iudaeorum. Jesus of Nazareth, King of the Jews.
11 Corruption of Tito and Xinchu, from the degree of Intimate Secretary.
12 Corruption of Moabon and Gabalon, from the degree of Perfect Master.

Q. What do you understand in all these apocryphal words?
A. I understand that apocryphal philosophers having no knowledge of the true philosophy have collected with great care and put into use all these words to support their society by the mysterious air they give to it. But this resource proves their ignorance of things that are contained in the Order of Philosophers Élus Coëns.

Q. How many signs do you have in the philosophy of Élus Coëns?
A. There are six.

Q. Make them. (He makes them)
Q. How much currency do you have in the Order?
A. Four. Blue, black, white and red.

Q. What is the blue colour?
A. The first colour that the man saw when he had his eyes drawn by order of the G[reat] A[rchitect].

Q. What does white represent?
A. The state of poverty and candour in which the G[reat] A[rchitect] created the first Man.

Q. What is red?
A. The radiant star of fire that made itself felt when he was in the presence of the Master.

Q. What is black?
A. The darkness of the place from which the body of the First Man emerged by permission of the Master.

Q. What is the state of the Philosopher Elu Coën?
A. To be free, virtuous and free from all vice, equal to Kings and a friend of princes and the poor when spiritually clothed with the character of Elu Coën.

Q. What must a true Coën follow?
A. Three things, namely; piety, temperance and charity towards all brethren.

Q. What should he flee?
A. Three things. Slander, gossip and intemperance.

Q. How do apprentices of our Order travel?
A. From West to East.

Appendix

Q. Why that?
A. To seek the light.

Q. Did you find the light you were looking for?
A. No, R[espectable] M[aster], I found it only a long time after my first research.

Q. When did you find it, and how did you get it?
A. By my constancy, my zeal and my perseverance in all the circumstances of the Order.

Q. From whom did you receive this light?
A. From the goodness of the R[espectable] M[aster] d'Orient who recognised in me the qualities required to reach the sublime knowledge of the Order.

Q. What are the qualities required in a layman to be received Elu Coën?
A. He must be affable, of good life and manners, sociable to all kinds of people, sober, discreet, devoid of all dishonest vice, virtuous, and that there has never been any stain of infamy in his family. Either in his direct line or in the lateral.

Q. In how many classes do you divide the Order of Élus Coëns?
A. In six classes, as the G[reat] A[rchitect] employed six days in the construction of the Universal Temple, so the Order of the Elect Coëns is divided into six different parts to acquire the different mysterious sciences which are contained in these six classes.

Q. What are the different attributes of our Order?
A. Every square, level, compass, perpendicular that are designated by the four principal signs of the symbolic Philosophy.

Q. How do you name them?
A. The guttural, pectoral, manual and pedal.

Q. Do you have jewels in the Temple?
A. Yes, very much R[espectable] M[aster].

Q. What are they?
A. Every square, every single, double, triple and quadruple triangle, and all circumferences in all directions.

Q. How long do you serve your Master?
A. From Monday morning until Saturday evening.

Q. With what do you serve him?
A. With chalk, terrine and charcoal.

Q. What do these three emblems represent to you?
A. The three earthly, temporal and spiritual divisions.

Q. What are the Masters of our Order working on?
A. On the rough stone.

Q. What do Apprentices work on?
A. On the cubic point stone.

Q. What are the Fellows working on?
A. To erect buildings on their bases and make them perfect in their construction.

Q. Why do the ff [brethren] Élus Coëns use words in the temple as well as outside the temple to recognise themselves?
A. Chiram agreed with all the workers who were working on the construction of the Temple in Jerusalem that they would use different words to distinguish those who were employed in this construction, as well as for those subject to the general call that was made three times every day, either to put them to work, or to take their reflection in the forecourt, or to admit them to prayer and give thanks to the Lord for works they had done during the day.

Q. Did these words have no other purpose than to distinguish the different nations employed in the work of the Temple?
A. They were still used to allow the entry of various Masters, Apprentices and Fellows in their different classes; as well as to leave it, that is to say that the password was used for the entry and the word of order was deposited to the chief of the West. Afterwards, they rose in silence. This word only came after the evening prayer. This is why the Élus Coëns make their prayers to the G[reat] A[rchitect] before opening and closing their Temple and after they deposit the word of Order which is recorded in the corners of their temple to the chief in the West.

Q. How many kinds of nations were employed in the construction and service of the Temple?
A. Of five kinds, namely the Jews, the Syriacs, the Sidonites, the Gabaonites and the Lebanites.

Q. What were the different jobs of these five kinds of nations?
A. The Jews placed stone upon stone to raise the walls of the Temple according to the plan that had been given to them by the Master. The Sidonites came out and went down with the stones of the quarries. The Syriacs transported them to the gates of

the Temple, the Gabaonites served to carry water and other clean and necessary utensils for the construction and the need of the workers. The Lebanese worked on the interior ornaments of the Temple and conveyed them to the river's edge, and part of the Sidonites and Syriacs carried them from there to the porch of the Temple, set them up and placed them in the Temple.

Q. What is the sign of the Master? (He gives it)

Q. How were you when you received [the grade of] Master?

A. I was in the middle of an inverted triangle, my body forming five different positions, poorly dressed, rope at the collar, barefoot, and in this way I contracted my obligation.

Q. What do these different positions represent, as well as the poor [state of] dress that you were in?

A. The first position of the body placed in a triangle represents that which Adam held before the G[reat] A[rchitect] when he commanded him mastery over the whole terrestrial surface. The others represent his prevarication, his reconciliation made by the three different penalties that he was obliged to endure in order to regain favour with the Eternal.

Q. What are the three different penalties that Adam was forced to suffer?

A. That of the body, that of the soul and that of the spirit.

Q. How did you imagine them?

A. Namely in the way that the three different tortures that are felt by the newly received brother in our Order, which are by fire, water and earth.

Q. In what parts of the Earth are they figured and how are they designated?

A. They are depicted on the West, North and South. That of the West represents that of the spirit; that of the South, represents that of the soul, and that of the North that of the body.

Q. What do all these things represent to us?

A. The punishment inflicted on the brother towards the West represents the submissive spirit. That which is inflicted towards the South, that of the soul at the moment of the prevarication; and that to the North represents the dissolution of the three different parts or materials that make up the body of the Man.

Q. What are these three different parts and what is the number contained in each of them in particular?

A. These three parts are that of bone, fluid and flesh. They are all three contained together but they are substantiated separately even though they are one and the same body. The number contained in each of them is three. So 3 times 3 is 9.

Q. What does the number of 3 times 3 tell you?

A. It indicates that the three different materials that make up the body are composed each of the other two, which is represented to us by the three elements that could not exist without the help of the others. That's why they wear the same number of 3 x 3, so that the parts that make up the body are together with the three elements twice nine.

Q. Why do these two different numbers carry the odd number rather than the even?

A. Because these two different numbers existed one without the other as it says in Genesis, God takes out the body of the Woman from that of the Man, just as the G[reat] A[rchitect] took out the elements of the Earth and divided them each into their content so that the elements and the Earth still have the number of 2 times 9.

Q. Why do you admit only three elements?

A. Because the air is not really one and emanates completely from the others without which there is no more than the body without its soul.

Q. What is the use of the air?

A. The air taken as an element is more material than the others and it is on it that the stars and the planets print the force of their action to communicate it to solid bodies.

Q. How many temporal Temples are built on the whole Earth's surface?

A. Seven.

Q. How many columns were supported?

A. Each on seven columns.

Q. Name these seven different Temples.

A. That of Adam, Enoch, Melchizedek, Moses, Solomon, Zerubbabel, and that of Christ, which is presently in existence.

Q. What are the seven columns on which these different Temples were supported?

A. They represent to us the seven main leaders who traced in their different classes the different plans for the workers who were employed with good will in the construction of the Temple of the Lord.

Q. What do you mean by the different plans that the chiefs traced in the different classes?

A. I mean the different sciences that each of them possessed and taught to those who were worthy of achieving it.

Q. How was the different knowledge identified in the Temple and how did it come down to us?

A. It was designated in the very construction of Solomon's Temple which was built in seven years, and also by its dedication in this seventh year; it was [represented] in the Temple by seven different stars placed in seven different places. This knowledge, which contains all the sciences previously scattered in the Universe, has been transmitted to us only by the great care that the chiefs took when they passed it on to students worthy of possessing it, with the most rigorous defences of communicating them to the perverse laymen, and that's how it came to us.

Q. Why did the Temple of Solomon take seven years to build, and why did the dedication take place in the seventh year?

A. The G[reat] A[rchitect] allowed that it may be known to the workers of this construction that there was a big difference between His work and that of Men; He did not want, as He had said by His own Law, that man would use the seventh day at labour.

Q. What instruments were used for the construction of Solomon's Temple?

A. None.

Q. What does the construction of the Temple without the help of tools composed of metals and different instruments represent?

A. It designates the construction of the body of Man that the G[reat] A[rchitect] created by His own Word, and His ornaments designate to us the three precepts which the Eternal put in His heart at the moment of Creation in order that He may learn to use and make use of all created things.

Q. Do you know the Temple of Solomon?

A. Yes, very much R[espectable] M[aster].

Q. Where was it built?
A. On the mountain of Moria.

Q. Give me a dissertation of the things that were used for this construction.
A. 1°) There were stones of different qualities, measures and proportions.

> 2°) The different materials that were found in the earth on which the Temple was built.
> 3°) The location and the real name of the mountain where it was built.
> 4°) The names of the different nations employed in this construction and their quantity.
> 5°) The expenditure and the measurement of the wages which were given to the workmen.
> 6°) The houses that were built on the walls of the Temple.
> 7°) The doors of the Temple.
> 8°) Vases, vessels and vessels of brass.
> 9°) The ministers of holiness.
> 10°) The sanctity of service at the Shrine of the Priests.

Q. The mountain on which the temple of Jerusalem was built, was it hollow or full?
A. It was hollow.

Q. How did one realise that this mountain was hollow?
A. It was when Solomon ordered the foundations of the Temple; the workmen who worked there could no longer penetrate further, warning the Wardens who had verified the fact, and reported it to Solomon, who then ordered that the place should no longer be touched, and reserved it to be the Inner Sanctum of the Temple; he set back the foundations 100 cubits and the workers who were employed to make the new trenches found seven Arches that circled the place destined to be the Inner Sanctum.

Q. Who opened the Arches?
A. Solomon himself, alone.

Q. Which Arch opened first?
A. The one towards the West.

Q. Which one did he open second?
A. The one on the North side.

Appendix

Q. Which one did he open the third?
A. That of the East.

Q. What was the fourth?
A. The one which was at the entrance of the vault.

Q. Which one did he open fifth?
A. The one on the South side.

Q. What did he find in the Archway facing the West?
A. He found different materials and precious stones; he was instructed in their different qualities and the use he could make of them for the interior decoration of the Temple.

Q. What did he find in the Northward one?
A. He found iron, cast iron, tin, coral, gold, and silver.

Q. What did he find in the East?
A. Quantities of hieroglyphic characters by which he learned that the Temple of the G[reat] A[rchitect], directed and built by Men, was not on common ground, since it did not take its origin from the earth below, but that it was a virgin land descended on purpose or transported for the construction of the Temple.

Q. What did he find in the central Arch?
A. He found nothing material, but he learned more particularly the mysteries that the G[reat] A[rchitect] offered to the eyes of the nations for the construction of the Temple of Jerusalem built without the help of tools made of metals. He learned more about the strength and power that his wisdom had hitherto acquired for him both over nations and created things, only to perpetuate itself in all the knowledge that the G[reat] A[rchitect] had communicated to him; animal, spiritual, divine, terrestrial and material.

Q. What did he find in the fifth?
A. An infinite number of hieroglyphs that he could neither read nor number, he learned by this that he was stripped of his power and his universal sciences, of which the G[reat] A[rchitect] had told him in his state of wisdom. He was then only a mere mortal and even guiltier than the rest.

Q. Why was the fifth Arch so fatal to Solomon?
A. Because the G[reat] A[rchitect] had forbidden him to open it before the time marked under penalty of making his posterity wander among the nations, the opening of this Arch was destined for the one who was to manifest his glory in the centre of the Universe.

Q. Why did Solomon not open the 6th and 7th Arches?
A. Because these two Arches being the figure and the resemblance of the G[reat] A[rchitect] they could only be opened by Him, since it is He who gave beginning to all things, it belongs only to Him to give them.

Q. Who are these 7 Arches represented by?
A. By the seven days that the G[reat] A[rchitect] put in the construction of the lodge and its universal Temple, by the seven planets that each have a particular virtue, and by the seven seven-branched candlesticks as well as by the seven seals of which is spoken of in the Talmud or in the Apocalypse which is the truth of Scripture.

Q. What does the vault and the earth on which the Temple was built represent to us?
A. It represents to us the place from which the body of the First Man came out, and the virgin land represents to us the separation of the material and the spiritual, it represents where Adam was placed on the Earth when the G[reat] A[rchitect] said to him: *Look to this mountain, it is above all meaning, it bears three names and these names multiply to infinity.*

Q. What are these three names?
A. Mor Ya Iu[13], who announce to us the origin of the body of the First Man, as well as the precepts, the law, and the prophets. That is why the G[reat] A[rchitect] said to him: *This mountain was holy and held by me before Creation since it is on her that you were created; respect it all like your mother, since she is holy. Whenever you raise your eyes upwards, so when you lower them on this Earth, or fix them on the plants it produces, you will praise and sanctify the living God who created you;* then He made know to him the different instruments used for the construction of the Universal Temple.

Q. How did he know them?
A. From the different positions he made to his body, he showed him that his body was the emblem of the various instruments he had used for the construction of the entire Universe.

---

[13] French phonetical pronunciation of Moriah.

Appendix

Q. How many numbers do you divide?
A. In 3, 5, 6 and 7.

Q. What does the first division mean by three?
A. It represents the time of the creation of Adam which was at the third hour of the evening. It is why we give Apprentice the number 3.

Q. What does the second represent by 5?
A. The hour of the creation of Eve and the moment of the prevarication of Adam.

Q. What does division represent by 6?
A. The expulsion of the First Man from the presence of the G[reat] A[rchitect] for revealing the mysteries that had been entrusted to him.

Q. What is the fourth represented by 7?
A. The reconciliation of the First Man, after having suffered 7 times 7 the deserved penalties by the G[reat] A[rchitect] that finally allows him to climb the famous staircase no longer straight as formerly but spiralled.

Q. In what part of the Earth did these things happen?
A. In the Holy Land of Mount Moria.

Q. By whom were these things transmitted to us?
A. By our first Masters.

Q. Where are they represented?
A. In the Temple of the Lord built by Chiram under the orders of Solomon.

Q. What were these figures and where were they placed?
A. The first number 3 was placed in the North, and were represented in his division by a simple circumference, a triangle, and a perpendicular which are the emblem of the immense knowledge that the First Man possessed before his prevarication.

Q. Where was the second division by 5 and who told us?
A. It was placed at the South and was represented by two circumferences in which there was a triangle, a square, and a compass; emblems of the prevarication of the First Man when he wanted to build temples without order from G[reat] A[rchitect], and wanted to use his Holy Name in vain; which had been further represented by the division which took place and lasted six weeks among the temple workers in the fifth year of its construction.

Q. Where was the third division by six and who told us?

A. Between South and North. It was represented by six half circumferences which allude to the six stations which the First Man was forced to go in the West to get his perfect reconciliation with the G[reat] A[rchitect]. It was again represented at the construction of the Temple by supervisors and Master drivers who, when they had badly placed the workers or badly executed the orders or plans drawn by the Master would go up on the six half circles, holding the right hand squared on the heart, and thus designated their fault and their repentance.

Q. Where was the fourth by 7 and who indicated it?

A. To the East. It was represented to us by 7 circumferences in which there was a quadruple triangle, seven stars and a column, which is the emblem of the perfect reconciliation of all men with the G[reat] A[rchitect] of the U[niverse]. What was again represented to us during the construction by the reconciliation of the workers, and by the felicity they had recovered from their leader.

Q. In how many parts was the Temple Centre divided; that which the apocryphal name the Middle Chamber?

A. In five horizontal parts represented by a receptacle in its centre.

Q. What does this division and its centre represent for us?

A. It represents to us that the works made by the hands of men, as well as their divisions, have little stability. The centre represents to us the general reconciliation of the four nations with the G[reat] A[rchitect], which has been figured to us by the death of our Respectable Master whom the apocryphal people call Chiram.

Q. What do the different steps taken in our Temple of Élus Coëns represent for us?

A. The various ceremonies are the same of those that are performed in all spiritual temples, and whose remembrance we do for all our brethren by repeating them before all. The different words and different positions represent the various Holocausts that were offered to the Lord in the Temple, either for thanksgiving, for atonement, or for prosperity or exclusion. The different steps represent the different places where the different sacrifices were made, and where the different temples were raised.

Q. How many spiritual and temporal temples have there been?

A. Five. That of Enoch, Moses, Solomon, Zerubbabel and the Messiah.

Appendix

Q. What do these five temples represent to us?

A. The five times that unfortunate arrivals have come to all Men because of their transgression by permission of G[reat] A[rchitect].

Q. What are these troublesome times?

A. The first announced by Enoch is the plague that the G[reat] A[rchitect] of U[niverse] sent to hit the land and confuse the two nations that had transgressed against the laws and submerged them in water. These two nations were represented by two columns which Set and Enos.[14] had constructed, one of which was of earth situated towards the South and the other of stone situated towards the North; that of earth was destroyed by water, and that of stone subsisted.

Q. What do these two columns mean, one carried away and the other subsistent?

A. The column swept away marks the destruction of the wicked, and the one that has resisted represents the society and the justness of the rest of the people that the G[reat] A[rchitect] retained by his own Word for the regeneration of the Men that exist today.

Q. What does the Temple of Moses represent to us?

A. He predicted the destruction of idolaters and their idols. These people prided themselves on ignoring a vengeful and remunerating God, and to live even more freely, they had banished from their homes all that related to the true divinity, the destruction of the Egyptian people by the Waters during the passage announced their own by the Iron.

Q. What did Solomon predict?

A. He predicted the great confusion that the Hebrews would find themselves one day, their captivity and their servitude, which was represented by the great divorce that began among them in the sixth year of the construction of the Temple. He also predicted the complete destruction of the Temple and the city of Jerusalem, which was announced by the destruction of the two beautiful cities of Sodom and Gomorrah which were reduced to ashes not being able to escape the scourge of God.

---

14   Genesis 4:26, KJV. And to Seth, to him also there was born a son; and he called his name Enos: then began men to call upon the name of the Lord.

Q. What did Zerubbabel predict?
A. He predicted the fate of the different nations who were opposed to the construction of his universal Temple, in which all the nations of the world had to come together to make a general reconciliation with the G[reat] A[rchitect], which had been figured by the alliance of Cyrus with the Hebrews when he granted them freedom.

Q. What does the Messiah predict?
A. The Messiah predicted all the epochs and tribulations of the whole World, past, present and future, being itself the first and last spiritual Temple represented to us by the Old and the New Testament that we have adopted to be our guide and support every day of our present and future life, as confirmed by the present example that we have before our eyes.

Q. What did Cyrus announce to the Hebrews, as well as the opponents against the construction of the temple of Zerubbabel?
A. The covenant of Cyrus represents a reminder of the Gentiles to God; its opponents represent the adultery that the Hebrews committed against the orders of the G[reat] A[rchitect] whose punishment will exist until the end of the centuries, they will no longer have access to the general reconciliation at the end of the rebirth of the World.

Appendix

Catechism of Master Coëns

Q. Are you a Master Coën?
A. Yes, M[ost] R[espectable] M[aster], I am.

Q. How will I know you?
A. By the different circumstances of my reception in the spiritual circles, by the different oppositions and the different combats I experienced and exercised for my admission.

Q. Have you won?
A. I am received.

Q. In what parts of the world have you fought?
A. In the 4 celestial regions and the 3 terrestrial.

Q. What did you observe in these different combats?
A. The different virtues, faculties, properties and powers that are innate in each of its inhabitants.

Q. What is the first combat you made?
A. That of the Southern region.

Q. That is the second?
A. One of the Western region.

Q. What is the third?
A. That of the Northern one.

Q. What is the fourth?
A. That of the Eastern.

Q. What is the nature of the combat in the Southern part?
A. To repel the intelligence of this region, to defeat its leaders, to cancel their power by the superiority of mine.

Q. What of the West?
A. To dispel the intelligence of this first region, and to deliver by the power of my word, the minor slaves who had fallen prey to these regionaries.

Q. What is the North?
A. To fight my own will and to submit it to the doubly strong spirit in all its perfection of purity.

Q. What of the East?
A. To bind and destroy any kind of spiritual being who was trying to operate in this region under the appearance of a virtue of divine power, whereas it should be recognised only as spiritual, material or demonic.

Q. Why does the general terrestrial body have only three regions and the celestial four?
A. Because it is only the theatre and the receptacle of atonement; the celestial is that of reconciliation.

Q. How do you distinguish the three terrestrial regions?
A. From the general terrestrial body to the sensitive circle: from there to the visual circle known as the solar circle.

Q. How do you distinguish the four celestial regions?
A. From the divinity to the circle of double divine power, from there to the super-celestial circle to the Saturnine circle known as the rational.

Q. How do you distinguish the universal general temporal body from the celestial divine spirit?
A. The superiority of one over the other can only be distinguished by their form, action, and operation.

Q. What is the form of the celestial divine?
A. Four perfect circumferences in proportion, in virtues, in action, and in operation, which is clearly explained by thought, action, operation, and contemplation, which teaches us the true quatriple divine essence.

Q. Why did we teach you that the divine immensity was only four circles?
A. For us to be a perfect guarantor of the various particular and personal operations that each spiritual being must perform in the presence of the divinity and that of all his spiritual brothers.

Q. What are we learning to know about these four circles forming the divine immensity?

A. That there are only four kinds of spiritual beings, who must perform divine worship, as they are called by divine wisdom. The *denary* spirit 10, the spirit of dual *octonary* power 8, the major *septenary* spirit 7 and minor *quaternary* spirit 4.

Q. So there are only four classes of spirits?

A. No M[ost] R[espectable] M[aster] there cannot be others without degrading the power and sanctity of the divine spiritual power, and that proves that it cannot be otherwise, there are only four celestial regions.

Q. What is the form of the terrestrial and universal temporal general body?

A. It is triangular, but both numbers by their mixed temporal, spiritual ternary are likely to be counted by their *septenary* and Saturnine intimacy and their own *nonary* number which is the chief number of deformity and annihilation; the act of listening to corporeal forms.

Q. Will the same thing happen to the four circumferences which form the divine immensity as to the general terrestrial and universal corporeal form?

A. No, M[ost] R[espectable] M[aster].

Q. Why so?

A. Because the form of the divine immensity is purely spiritual and not subject to time, because there is in it no substance of matter or revolution, instead all the metamorphoses being material composites capable of revolution both corporeal and spiritual.

Q. Do you then give superiority to the divine immensity over that of the universal?

A. Yes, M[ost] R[espectable] M[aster], and it cannot be doubted by the circular form of this same immensity which is innumerable and indivisible in all respects, being of the faculty of spirit to write its circumference without material limits, which cannot be given to the faculty of temporal material bodies.

Q. What are the Master Coëns working on?

A. To the perfect knowledge of temporal, spiritual power and divine spiritual power.

Q. What difference is there between these two powers?

A. Spiritual temporal power is passive because it is limited by the delay of time, and that divine spiritual power having never had time cannot be susceptible to change; this is the superiority of the divine power over the temporal power.

Q. How many kinds of spiritual classes do you admit in the temporal Universe?
A. Three kinds: the class of *ternary* spirits, that of the *septenary* spirits and the material *nonary* spirits.

Q. What is the virtue of each of these spirits in their classes?
A. The virtue of the *ternary* spirits consists in presiding over the matter which constitutes the different corporeal forms contained in this Universe, that of the *septenary* spirits consists in presiding over the law of universal time and that of the *nonary* spirits is to contravene against the various operations of these *ternary* and *septenary* spirits as well as against the action and the operation of the different bodily and spiritual beings which are likely to operate in this Universe for the greater glory of the Eternal and the justice of its inhabitants.

Q. In what part of the Universe can Master Coëns obtain the perfect knowledge of the universal spiritual temporal power?
A. In striving to know their bodily and spiritual origin perfectly, they will safely know the powerful virtues contained in the seven different planetary bodies, from which they will learn to distinguish precisely how much greater is the virtue which is enclosed in their particular body than that which is even contained in the whole Universe.

Q. How will you convince me of the truth in what you say?
A. By the Creation or formation of this Universe which is the principle of the time of subjection, which serves to restrain the formidable power contained in the particular body which surrounds it, and which is put into privation by the universal veil which covers it; this is a sufficient proof of the superiority of the particular power over all those contained in the Universe.

Q. What is this power so formidable that you say is locked up so rigidly?
A. It is, Most Respectable Potent Master, that which the Creator had put innate in the first Man-God of the Earth. If he had not prevaricated, there would have been no particular body of matter for him, and the Universe would not have served him such a terrible veil, having not been formed for him in the first principle.

Q. What are the Master Coëns taking care of?
A. The interpretation and explanation of the different meanings and spiritual faculties that are given to humanity under symbols, emblems and allegories.

Appendix

Q. If Master Coëns are concerned with the explanation of spiritual and temporal symbols, emblems and allegories, I will ask you then what are the beginning of the first Man-God on Earth in this Universe?

A. To be the true mediator and reconciler of the first prevaricating beings towards the Creator.

Q. How could he have done such a great privilege on beings who were superior to him in their primal emanation?

A. By the superior and powerful act of his operations which had delivered these first beings from their privation by effecting their reconciliation.

Q. Did this first Man-God perform these great wonders?

A. No, M[ost] R[espectable] M[aster].

Q. Who is to blame?

A. His own will, by which Man, instead of using only the great glory and divine justice and strong power that the Creator put in him, used it only for his own glory and satisfaction, to the detriment of those who were spectators of his mission, which made this first being [fall into] deprivation.

Q. What does the prevarication and reconciliation of the first Man-God of the Earth refer to?

A. His prevarication alludes to that of perverse spirits, and his reconciliation to that of every spiritual being after their spiritual atonement.

Q. What does the massacre made on Abel by his brother Cain refer to?

A. This murder is referring to the one that the perverse spirits have committed on the First Man's spiritual person to rob him and ultimately destroy the faculty of his divine power, as Cain operated on his brother Abel's person for the same object.

Q. What advantages did this First Man receive from the murder committed on the person of his son Abel?

A. Two kinds of advantages; the first to cooperate in the purification of one's corporeal form and then to one's spiritual reconciliation, the second to cooperate in the sanctification of the product of its material operation for which it was susceptible of temporal legitimacy as to the form and spiritual as to the minor.

Q. What shall I know here of the certainty of all these things?

A. By the incorporation of Christ as a Man-God of the Earth in a material body, by his temporal advent among the men of the Earth, by his works and temporal spiritual operations and by the one he performed as a Divine Man after having stripped himself of the old body, or after his resurrection.

Q. Why did he do that among men?

A. To physically demonstrate to us the first power of the first man, and that which is still in his power since his reconciliation.

Q. What does the death of this Divine Man tell us?

A. It confirms to us that the right Abel was given by the demonic intelligence of Man, and makes clear to us the necessity of the pain of the material forms for their purification and the punishment of the minor to effect his reintegration.

Q. What more did the death of Abel predict to the first man?

A. It predicted not only the faculty of reconciliation of the First Man and his work but also that of all his future seed that was manifested and confirmed by the death of the Man-God and the Divine of this Universe.

Q. What are the different places where these two beings were immolated?

A. The place of the world where Abel was immolated refers to the fixed abode of the bodies of the wicked denominated by the Eternal South of the Universe where Cain was relegated, and the place of the world where Christ died and resurrected alludes to the glorious home of the righteous since there was his divine spiritual election.

Q. What is the meaning of the advent of M[ost] P[otent] M[aster] Enoch among the posterity of the M[ost] P[otent] M[aster] Seth?

A. This event was prophesied amongst people of the past, present and future; the past through the intimate connection that Enoch had with his nation to whom he taught the means of operating the divine worship, the present by the fruit which he drew from all his spiritual operations in favour of this posterity, and the future by his escape from the bosom of the corruption which arose in that nation.

Appendix

Q. What does the escape of the M[ost] P[otent] M[aster] from the bosom of this posterity refer to?

A. The tremendous corruption that will occur among all the nations of the Universe towards the end of Time when the righteous will be withdrawn to be spiritual witnesses of the manifestation of the Glory of the Lord in their favour, and of his justice against the prevaricators, as the Divine Man has confirmed to us, removing from him in the centre of his receptacle a righteous man, and leaving the other wandering and a spiritual wanderer against whom divine justice must be operated.

Q. What is the meaning of the construction of the ark of Noah and its posterity so enclosed with the various animals?

A. I am still ignorant of all these symbolic and emblematic things, not being able to penetrate them until after my limited age.

Q. How old are you Master Coën?

A. Since 2 years, 3, 4, 5, 6 and 7 years.

Q. What are the various numbers that fix our age as Master Coëns?

A. The number 2 explains the confusion where were the principles of matter in their state of indifference. The number 3 the consistency of its form, the number 4 the action, the number 6 the contraction, and the number 7 its junction with the spirit.

Q. Do not these same numbers explain to us something more?

A. Yes, M[ost] R[espectable] M[aster], the number 2 is given to the demonic intelligence, the number 3 to spirt of the Earth, the number 4 in the minor spirit, the number 5 to the demonic spirit, the number 6 to the elemental spirit and the number 7 to the power of the major spirit that operates and operates in favour of the minors who claim it.

Q. What do Master Coëns work on most often?

A. On the rough stone, on the cubic point and on the tracing board.

Q. Explain to me these different allegories.

A. The work that the Master Coëns does on the rough stone represents the work he has to do on the imperfection and impurity of his corporal form in order to prepare and dispose his form to receive the sacred character that must be printed on it to in order achieve perfection in his operations and invocations.

Q. What does the work on cubic point stone refer to?
A. This work alludes to the different Planetary bodies emblematically represented by a five-pointed star that used to acquire a perfect knowledge of the power of the major and lesser spirits who preside in these bodies, and that Master Coëns put it into practice and action during their operations.

Q. What is the work on the tracing board?
A. To whom do the Grand Master Coëns or Grand Architects make in the centre of their circumferences on which they trace the fruit from their figurative operations emblematically by a tracing board.

Q. Do you know what kind of work on the tracing board?
A. No, M[ost] R[espectable] M[aster], but I know the tracing board because I saw it work.

Q. How many temples are there in the Universe?
A. Three kinds: the general, the particular and the universal.

Q. What are they represented by?
A. By the sensible circle, the visual and the rational circle.

Q. Do you know the work that is done in each of these temples?
A. I do not know it yet, not being devoted to such operations.

Q. By whom are we still figured?
A. By the first spiritual temple that the M[ost] P[otent] M[aster] Enoch built among the seed of Seth, by which Moses built in Israel and that of Solomon in Jerusalem.

Q. Do you know the need for the construction of these three temples?
A. Yes, M[ost] R[espectable] M[aster], Enoch directly explains to us the divine worship, Moses the ceremonial and Solomon the material temporal spiritual worship.

Q. What are the different materials that the various leaders used for the construction of these buildings?
A. Those which M[ost] P[otent] M[aster] Enoch used were purely spiritual; those of Moses were spiritual temporal figured by the incorruptible wood of which was built his temple and by the purity of the matter which surrounded it, those which were used for the construction of Solomon's temple are the different stones, the different woods and the different metals that have been worked by different nations to serve as ornaments to this building.

Appendix

Q. I do not see anything spiritual in the different materials that have been used in this construction.

A. No, M[ost] R[espectable] M[aster], there is nothing spiritual except the order Solomon received from the G[reat] A[rchitect of the] U[niverse] for the construction of this building, and the spiritual workers who carved the stones in the different quarries from which ordinary men took out and down to be transported to their destination.

Q. Explain the different stones, wood and various metals Solomon used in this construction?

A. The various nations who rose up to bring about the destruction of Solomon's Temple occasioned by the prevarications. What has this to do with me is the existence of the first two that I named.

Q. Why has this temple not been rebuilt?

A. Because it degenerated into a Temple of matter and did not stay as stone to stone, which will happen to the Temples whether particular, general or universal when they cease to be preserved in purity and holiness.

Q. Know you if we have tried rebuilding the temple?

A. No, M[ost] R[espectable] M[aster], I do not know, on the contrary, I know as sure Zerubbabel, Darius and Insrtapa wanted to undertake this reconstruction. However, as soon as they ransacked the earth to draw the appropriate stones to the building, countless flaming fires devoured and dangerously marked the workmen who searched it.

Q. Explain these flames of fire coming out of the earth to devour the workmen labouring on it?

A. They teach us physically and authentically that Solomon's workmen have no manner of carving stones in the quarries that were used to build his temple.

Q. Why did not the beautiful building rebuild itself?

A. Because this temple was only the emblematic and allegorical symbolic figure of the general and particular universal one, it is destroyed as the material temple, which will happen to the temporal temples.

Q. The construction of this temple and its destruction must be a well-considered type or figure and very striking for the instruction of members of the Order, and for ordinary men of the earth?

A. Yes, M[ost] R[espectable] M[aster] it is a figure who served the humans of that time and still serves those of today to know the manifestation of glory and divine righteousness, bodily and spiritual origin and the spiritual faculty that man has in his power to communicate himself to the Lord and all that depends on it.

Q. What are you referring to when you discuss the construction of Solomon's Temple without tools made of metals, as well as the unknown workers who carved the stones in the quarries with fairness and proportion to be employed in this construction?

A. This construction without tools made of metals really refers to the construction of the first particular material temple, or to the bodily construction of the first man in which he lives, which was built by the spirit without the aid of physical operations. The unknown workmen who have proportionately and accurately prepared the stones employed are certainly alluding to the different spirits which the Lord has consecrated in virtue and power to bring forth from them an essence of apparent matter, and which presides over it to make it susceptible to serve as a form to be subjected to the use of temporal action.

Q. In how many parts was the Temple of Solomon divided?

A. In three parts: the porch for the preparation, the Temple for the elect and the sanctuary for the Grand Architects or Grand Master Coëns.

Q. Since the Temple of Solomon is an exact repetition of our particular temple, no doubt the division is equal to it?

A. M[ost] R[espectable] M[aster] Yes, my particular temple is also divided into three parts, namely the lower from the lower belt marked by a red scarf designating the Porch; the second, that of the breast cut by a green-colored belt of water marking the particular temple, the third is the head encircled around the head of a blue ribbon which designates the sanctuary.

Q. You do not speak of the Holy of Holies?

A. No, M[ost] R[espectable] M[aster], because the Holy of Holies was not confused with those three classes which were only used for the preparation and the ceremonial of divine worship, while the Holy of Holies was only used for the operation and the communication of the divine spirit with the minor spirit.

Appendix

Q. The Holy of Holies is therefore not at home?

A. No, M[ost] R[espectable] M[aster], it cannot be fixed in my particular temple.

Q. And where is it fixed?

A. It is permanent in all parts of the universe; I will know how to bring it nearer to me, as Solomon had brought it closer to his temple, I shall be able to operate and communicate to it.

Q. Do you know the various ornaments that have been used as interior decoration in the Temple of Solomon and the relationship between these ornaments and those decorating our particular temple, as well as their symbolic temporal and spiritual figures?

A. I know some but ignores the other, not having the required age yet.

Q. What are the two columns in the temple of Solomon referring to, and their equal proportion?

A. The column that was set toward the north alludes to the degradation of the first body of glory of the first fallen man of the earth, who became subject of a body of matter after his prevarication, which made him mysterious apprentice in this lower world until perfect reconciliation.

Q. What is the reference to the one at the south?

A. At the provocation of his iniquitous operation.

Q. These two columns do not they tell us anything more?

A. They teach us to know perfectly the origin of the two species of minor beings, that of their different forms, and that of their different temporal virtues and spiritual powers.

Q. How did Solomon distinguish the superiority of one of these columns?

A. He put a solar figure on the north and a lunar figure on the south.

Q. What are these two figures referring to?

A. The solar figure teaches us to know the superiority of the action of the celestial body represented by that of the body of man, and the lunar figure the inferiority of the general terrestrial body represented by that of the woman. That is why we put different names and different words on each of these two columns, and the profane man cannot interpret them.

Q. What was the temple of Solomon built on?
A. On three powerful columns that have been explained allegorically: strength, wisdom and beauty.

Q. To whom do you give strength?
A. To the thought figured by that of Abraham.

Q. To whom do you give wisdom?
A. To the action represented by that of Isaac.

Q. To whom do you give beauty?
A. The operation of the spirit represented by the one Jacob did when he fought against the spirit. These three things were represented to us by the strong thought of Solomon, by the great wisdom of Hiram his great architect in charge of the operation of the construction of the temple.

Q. What were the most precious ornaments of the temple of Solomon?
A. The simple equilateral triangle, the double and the triple triangle, the candlestick with 7 branches, the 4 large vats, the ark and its tabernacle.

Q. What is the equilateral triangle?
A. The true image of the first form that matter would take according to what was conceived in the imagination of the Creator.

Q. Why has the equilateral triangle been considered among the ancients with such respect, and is it still among us?
A. Because it is the true receptacle of the whole universe, on which all action, contraction, reaction are made by the beings superior to him.

Q. What is the great truth of this triangle so that it is looked upon with such consideration?
A. Because it contains within itself the three coeternal numbers which served to co-operate formation, creation, universal formation and the powerful faculty of every spiritual being.

Q. What does the double equilateral triangle allude to in the universal circle?
A. The intimate bond of the double triangle is truly that of the heavenly body with the terrestrial general body, immediately attached to the correspondence of all the bodies in the universe.

Appendix

Q. What does the triple triangle refer to?
A. At the close liaison of the three regional chiefs, though unequal in their temporal operations.

Q. What are the other ornaments alluding to?
A. I cannot explain them because they have not yet been revealed to me.

Q. How do you make the creation numbers of the form of the simple, the double and the triple triangle?
A. Three for the single, six for the double, and nine for the triple triangle.

Q. What are these different numbers referring to?
A. The imperfection of the action of the material form when it is deprived of its perfect spiritual connection.

Q. What is the quality of Master Coën?
A. That of journeyman serving in the circles of the operations of the Grand Master Coëns.

Q. How long are they companions?
A. Days, weeks, months and whole years according to their faculties, virtues and powers which the Order can communicate to them of its own free will.

Q. Where will we find the reception of the Grand Master Coëns in the Order?
A. In the great book of life from page 3, 6, 7 to the beginning of the one of 8.

Q. What are the distinctive marks of the Master Coëns?
A. The red band from left to right.

Q. What are the signs and words of recognition?
A. (He gives them)

Q. At what time do you open the doors of the sanctuary of the Order?
A. First after the sunset.

Q. What time do you close?
A. At the very last hour of the day they were opened.

Q. Why do Coën Apprentices and Fellows not have a general education in the Order?
A. Because they are considered the perfect receptacles of the order on which the Grand Masters operate to make them susceptible to retaining the impression of the power of their operation.

Appendix

Grand Masters also called Grand Architects

Q. Are you a Grand Master Coën?

A. Yes, M[ost] R[espectable] M[aster], I am, and glory to be, until the separation of my soul from my body.

Q. How were you received Grand Master Coën?

A. In the centre where the holy light reigns, assisted by four heavenly regional chiefs represented by four great supervisors who were each placed in the centre of the four circles in correspondence of the particular temple.

Q. How old were you when were received a Grand Master Coën?

A. At the age of 60, assigned to the care that I consecrated in atonement for my ordination.

Q. How were you ordained and by whom was this care done?

A. By the thought and knowledge of the Lord, and by the power of his word, and the intention of his deputies.

Q. Of what use were the four regional chiefs in the favour of your reception?

A. To dispel and dispel by their spirituality any species of imperfect being that could have defiled me.

Q. What are the Grand Master Coëns occupied with?

A. The purification of the senses of matter to make them susceptible to participate in the various operations celebrated.

Q. What is the work of the Grand Master Coën?

A. To build new tabernacles and to rebuild the ancients on the example of the old masters to prepare them and make them suitable to receive at house the words of the powers that govern and operate the different operations to be created.

Q. How many kinds of tabernacles are there in the great universal temple?

A. Four, there cannot be more.

Q. Name them.

A. Two materials represented by the particular body of the man and the woman, the third one that Moses built spiritually, the fourth one that is spiritual temporal called the Sun that the G[rand] A[rchitect] of the U[niverse] destined to contain within all the names and sacred words of temporal and spiritual creation distinguished by his wisdom, the torch of life for this temporal place.

Q. What does the ark mean that Moses had built to deposit the tabernacle that had been built temporally?

A. This Ark is nothing more than a repetition of the one Adam built and in which there were only material tabernacles to witness the righteousness that was exerted on the children of men for the covenant they had made with the daughters of Cain.

Q. What does the Ark of Noah allude to?

A. She prophesied the one that Moses had built to bring Israel out of the righteousness of the demons and to subject him to the conduct and justice of the Lord, which is represented to us by the various animals that were put in the Ark and confirmed by the different nations that the Ark of Moses saved from the wrath of the Creator, that can be considered by the brute animals to refer to idolaters, and by reasonable animals to the children of God.

Q. What does the name of Noah mean?

A. Saved from the waters.

Q. And that of Moses?

A. From the waters.

Q. What is the tabernacle that Moses put in the centre of the Ark?

A. The Ark being the true figure of the terrestrial general body, for the same reason the tabernacle is that which designates the particular place where the Creator communicated with the first creature without being confused with the earth.

Q. By whom is this confirmed?

A. By Moses, when he entered the tabernacle to communicate himself to the Lord, receive orders and manifest them for the greater glory of the deity.

Appendix

Q. Why did Moses always stand before the tabernacle when he spoke to Israel?

A. As the tabernacle was the place consecrated to be the depository of all divine, spiritual, temporal, and corporeal powers and powers, he stood thus to receive all the intelligences to make Israel retain an impression of what he wished to communicate to him by order of the Lord.

Q. How many doors were there in this tabernacle?

A. Four which allude to the fourfold divine essence, to the four powers given to man and the four heavenly regional powers.

Q. Which ones do the Grand Master Coëns have the right to strike and open?

A. They have the right to strike all four, but they have the power to open the north one and close the south one.

Q. Why do Grand Master Coëns not have the power to open all four to the example of Moses who opened them when he wanted?

A. Because Grand Master Coëns of our Order are still only temporal beings, and they will have such power when they will become the example of first spiritual wise men.

Q. Since the tabernacle of Moses is a figure of the material world, in which part do we find the figure of the said four doors?

A. Because the Grand Master Coëns of our Order are still only temporal beings, and they will not be able to have such power until they have become like the first sages of spiritual men.

Q. Since the tabernacle of Moses is a figure of the material world, in what part will we find the figure of the four aforesaid doors?

A. At the head like the most elevated part of our archélique body and the thought, designating the east gate, the power of the understanding given to the ear designating the north gate, the contemplation given to the view designating the gate of the south, and the word designating the west gate given to the power of the operation.

Q. What are these four doors alluding to?

A. They allude to the four principal chiefs operating the universe, represented by the four large vats at the four corners of Solomon's Tempe.

Q. What are these four large vats still referring to?

A. To the four high temporal priests who performed the divine worship in humans and figured by the four evangelists who carried the various spiritual operations to the four parts of the world.

Q. What are the four chief leaders operating in the universe?
A. Ely under Adam, Enoch under the seed of Seth, Melchizedek under the posterity of Abraham, and Christ in favour of all created beings.

Q. What are the four high priests who performed the divine worship in humans?
A. Soliman among the Ishmaelites, Rharamoz among the Egyptians, Aaron among the Israelites and Paul among the Christians.

Q. What is the seven-pointed candelabrum referring to?
A. To the seven heavenly powers, to the seven spiritual gifts, and to the seven operations that the Lord displayed for the creation of this universe, which was represented by the seven-branched candelabrum that was put into the temple of Solomon and perpetuated until to us by the one who subsisted among the Romans.

Q. What is the power of the Grand Master Coëns?
A. To paint and trace all the emblems of the order when it is ordered to offer the perfumes, to consecrate his fellow to the circle of the Grand Master Coëns and to apply their powerful word to the four heavenly regions, and the three earthly and carefully watch over the ceremonial of temporal spiritual operations.

Q. What is the qualification of the Grand Master Coën?
A. Leader of the holy arch and guardian of the doors of the tabernacle.

Q. How long do the Grand Master Coëns serve their powerful master?
A. 6 days for the two equinoxes, 12 for the two solstices, 14 days for the perfect operation of the two equinoxes, 14 days for the two solstices, after 7 years for their perfect reconciliation.

6 + 12 + 14 + 14 + 7 = 53 = 8

Q. What is the faculty of the Grand Master Coëns?
A. To operate their virtue and power on Wednesday and Saturday of each week, every month of the year and in all the perilous circumstances where the case requires, to operate their work and impose their hands at right angles on all things that are convenient to their operations.

Q. What are the circumstances of the reception of a Grand Master Coëns?
A. They are given if the grandmaster requires it.

Appendix

Q. At what time do you open the doors of the universal tabernacle?
A. Although the time, the days, the months and the year are limited, they are opened in all the perilous circumstances of this life of tears.

Q. What is the sign of the Grand Master Coën?
A. It is given if it is ordered. 3, 4, 6, 7, 8, and 10 for the perfect master.

Q. What are the names and powerful words that consecrate the Grand Master of our order?
A. To those whom the Creator gave to Moses, his great Master Coën, to make them reversible and to consecrate his fellow man to divine spiritual operations.

Q. What are the broken tables of Moses alluding to, those which he brought down to the Israelites?
A. I do not know, I stay in the power of whoever is before me.

Appendix

Grand Elect of Zerubabble also called Knights of the East

Q. Are you under the election of Zerubbabel?

A. Yes, M[ost] R[espectable] M[aster], and the intimate alliance of Assyria with the unfortunate rest of Israel is not unknown to me.

Q. How are you making this alliance and what does it refer to?

A. This alliance consists of the liberty which Assyria gave to the tribes of Israel, after the expiration of their captivity, which again alludes to that which Jehovah will do with every creature created after the expiration of time and their perfect reconciliation.

Q. By whom are these things represented to us?

A. By the agreement that Zerubbabel made with Cyrus and the fruits of their operations, which determined the king to give all sorts of help to the tribes of Israel to whom he had just given liberty, in spite of all those who opposed it.

Q. And by whom are they confirmed to us?

A. By the Christ of whom Zerubbabel is a type and who by his operations is a type of all redemption; the opponents of Assyria against the freedom of Israel are a type of iniquitous operations when they opposed those of the Redeemer.

Q. How many tribes were in captivity in Babylon?

A. Judah, Benjamin, and part of the Levites.

Q. Are you from any of these tribes?

A. No, M[ost] R[espectable] M[aster] I am one of those who have always enjoyed freedom.

Q. How do you name it?

A. Ephraim, the last of the Hebrews and the first of the elect.

Q. How did you penetrate and conceive the powerful convention that Zerubbabel had contracted with Cyrus to set Israel free, since you were not captive?

A. By the intimate relation and intimate connection of all the spiritual and temporal operations of Zerubbabel with ours, which means nothing escapes our correspondences.

Q. At what age was Zerubbabel subjected to captivity?
A. From the age of 7 until 70 accustomed to complete the captivity.

Q. How old were you when you were elected Great Zerubbabel of Israel, and what is your temporal age?
A. My age is 70 and the age of my spiritual election is 7 years.

Q. What do you think about the 7 x 7 years you enjoy in this world?
A. To the doubly powerful spirit reigning in this low world represented by the double septenary character represented by the perfect age of Zerubbabel and by his spiritual reign.

Q. What is the duty of your election?
A. To fight my material passions to make them spiritual, to defeat the enemies of truth and those of freedom, following the example of Zerubbabel who fought and conquered.

Q. Where did this wise and peaceful Zerubbabel fight and defeat?
A. At the crossing of the formidable bridge of the river called Starbuzarnaï which means passage of confusion and the counting of this name represents it to us as I explain it.

Q. Count the name of the river.
A. Star 1; bu 2; zar 3; na 4; 5.

Q. What are the different operations that Zerubbabel did for Israel during his captivity?
A. 7 particular and 70 annual, the annual ones consisted in reminding the slaves of their first crime to their just punishment, their atonement and their perfect reconciliation and the seven particular warned those same slaves of their future freedom, of the different eras that had occurred in the past to Israel, those present and all those that must occur to them in the future.

Q. Where did Zerubbabel manifest the most 7 particular operations?
A. At the break of the six arches which formed the bridge of the said river, and letting the seventh survive without having damaged it.

Q. Why did Zerubbabel break the so-called arches, which are the instruments he used for this operation?
A. I do not know since the deliverers had no knowledge of them.

Appendix

Q. Why this?

A. Because their material temple was not yet rebuilt and they had not yet offered a burnt offering to the Creator.

Q. How is it possible that Zerubbabel has destroyed such a beautiful bridge without the aid of tools containing metals, what is this operation alluding to and the seventh arch which he has left in all his perfection?

A. This event reminds us of the Temple of Solomon, which was likewise constructed without tools made of metals; Solomon had at his disposal unknown workmen who cut the stones in the quarries. Why should we not find that Zerubbabel had in his power those of material destruction?

Q. You do not speak to us of the type of the seventh arch?

A. The seventh arch left in all its perfection alludes to the perfect existence of the mind: that nothing in the entire universe exists and subsists only through it, and that all the form beings in this universe are not only apparent beings who must be as quickly dispelled as they were conceived in the imagination of the mind whose neglected arch is the image of perfect existence.

Q. Did you work on rebuilding Solomon's Temple?

A. No, M[ost] R[espectable] M[aster].

Q. Why so?

A. By the force of the opponents against this rebuilding, prophesied by the multitude of those who opposed our passage of the river and our freedom.

Q. What do all these things explain?

A. That the rebuilding of this temple was only the figure of our material temple which the spirit was to rebuild, that it was not the power of man to make such a rebuilding.

Q. What is your name?

A. Israel.

Q. Where did you get the name of Israel that you are wearing instead of Heber's, since you are a child of Heber?

A. The name of Israel comes from the iniquitous operation that Jacob did in fighting against the spirit, having succumbed in this operation, he was marked on the left leg and his name of Jacob was changed to that of Israel which means strong against God, having sinned against the spirit.

Q. What does this change of personal name represent?
A. This change of name prophesied the change of the divine law which Jehovah would bring out of the Hebrews to transmit to the enemies of Israel where it still resides.

Q. By whom was this event predicted?
A. By Moses when he broke the first tables of divine law which he had received from the Creator in favour of the Hebrews.

Q. The Hebrews therefore received no divine law by Moses?
A. No, M[ost] R[espectable] M[aster] they received one from him, but it was not quite like the first he had given them.

Q. How do you distinguish that this law given by Moses to Hebrews is not the same as the first?
A. Because the thought and the hand of man had not been exercised in the first as it was done in the second.

Q. What does this event explain to us?
A. That Israel would remain under the purely ceremonial law without being able to perform the divine worship, the true law being out of their hands.

Q. What is the veil that Moses put on his face when he gave the second law to Israel?
A. This veil alludes to the veil that the mind takes when it wants to give itself to communicate corporeally to the one who invokes it.

Q. Does not the veil make another allusion?
A. Yes, M[ost] R[espectable] M[aster] this veil confirms the veiled law that Israel received from Moses by his lack of confidence in the power of the Lord and their leader.

Q. What do the wandering Hebrews explain to us and the law that has been taken away from them?
A. The wandering Hebrews are a type of the error of the first converts, and the delighted law is that of what will happen in all men who will be caught off guard from the worship of divinity and who will be spiritual wanderers as well as Israel in the temporal.

Q. What is the power number of Zerubbabel's elect?
A. 3, 7 and 8, which allude to the spiritual power of the earth, to the temporal spiritual power, and to that of the double divine spiritual power.

Appendix

Q. What is the kind of operations of Zerubbabel's elected officials?
A. Water, earth and fire.

Q. At what time do they open their jobs?
A. Every 7th month on the 7th day of the first quarter of the moon which is from the 7th day of the first quarter of the March moon to the 7th day of the first quarter of the October moon, when Israel received the second law and came out of the cities of Egypt.

Q. By whom have you been consecrated Elect of Zerubbabel?
A. By the Double Power and by that of Zoroal and Zoroael, his two spiritual associates.

Q. Explain to us the names of these three characters who have devoted you to this august dignity.
A. Zerubbabel says enemy of confusion, Zoroal enemy of matter and Zoroael protector of minors as friend of wisdom.

Q. What is your rank?
A. Friend of God, protector of virtue and teacher of truth.

Colophon

✠

Translated by Stewart Clelland,
18°, H.R.D.M. of K.L.W.N.G, IV°

Developmental and Copy Editing by Josef Wäges,
32°, B∴F∴, F∴G∴C∴R∴

Layout, Design, and Consulting by W.B. Steve Adams,
32° K.C.C.H., F∴G∴C∴R∴

✠

EsotericEditions.com

✠

Typeset in Garamond Premier Pro and Apple Symbols.
Produced using Adobe InDesign, Illustrator, and Photoshop.
Text edited in Microsoft Word and Scrivener.

Stewart Clelland, Knight of Swords
Original painting by Bro. Ivan D. Ivanov, Bulgaria

Josef Wäges, Knight of Cups
Original painting by Bro. Ivan D. Ivanov, Bulgaria

Steve Adams, Knight of Wands
Original painting by Bro. Ivan D. Ivanov, Bulgaria

WS - #0018 - 130125 - C0 - 229/152/24 - CC - 9780853185994 - Gloss Lamination